Highland Minister

The Life and Poems of
Rev. Angus MacKinnon, Aultbea

D1610906

Canadian Cataloguing in Publication
Data

MacKinnon, Angus,
    Highland Minister: the life and poems
of Rev. Angus MacKinnon, Aultbea

Text in English and Gaelic
ISBN 0- 9698337-5-X

    1. MacKinnon, Angus. 2. Free Church of
Scotland--Clergy--Biography. 3. Clergy--Scotland--
Biography.
I. Title.

BX9225.M255539A3 1997 285',234'092 C97-900494-2

Highland Minister

The Life and Poems of
Rev. Angus MacKinnon, Aultbea

A Biography
by his son
Angus Matheson MacKinnon

THE
CATALONE
PRESS

Front cover: Castle Moil, the ruined stronghold of the MacKinnons, at
Kyleakin, Isle of Skye.   Photo by R.F. Garnett

Printed in Canada by City Printers, Sydney, N.S. Canada
Cover design: Harve Grant

Published by:

 The Catalone Press,
P.O. Box 1878,
Sydney, N.S.
Canada

Reverend Angus MacKinnon
Preacher, Pastor and Poet

Scotland

The Isle of Skye

Eilean a' Cheo
(The Misty Isle)

Aultbea

PARISH OF LOCHEWSIDE

SLAGGAN

MELLON UDRIGIL

ACHGARVE

MELLON CHARLES

IDRIGIL

COVE

ORMSCAIG

BUALNALUIB

LAIDE

CULCONICH   BADFEARN

TISHNAFILINE

AIRD

AULTBEA

ISLE EWE

FIREMORE

INVERASDALE

BRBA

NAAST

TOURNAIG

BOOR

INVEREWE

NORTH WEST

NOT SHOWN
LITTLE
LOCHBROOM
AND
KINLOCHEWE
MISSIONS.

POOLEWE

CIRCA 1942

LOCHMAREE

CONTENTS

List of Poems
(With English Translations)

Acknowledgements

I am indebted to the following in Scotland, for their willingness to help, largely through correspondence, while the book was being written in Canada.

My cousin, Mary-Ann MacKinnon MacKenzie, Galtrigil and Donald MacKenzie, Galtrigil; my sister, Ina Lamont, Inverness; my sister, Rachel Gollan, and Rev Alasdair Gollan, Lochcarron; William S. Anderson, Curator, Free Church College, Edinburgh; Han MacLeod, Aultbea; Isobel MacAulay, Glasgow; Danny Grant, Session Clerk Aultbea; Roddie MacDonald elder, Aultbea; Rev Alasdair Ferguson, minister of Locheweside; Kenneth Cameron, Glasgow; Rev R. MacKenzie, Glenelg, Clerk of Free Church Presbytery of Lochcarron; Professor Hugh Cartwright, Free Church College Edinburgh.

Rev. George Thompson, Edinburgh.

Special thanks to Mary my wife who helped me in so many ways to discharge this long-standing debt to my father's memory.

A.M.K

12

Dedicated to all faithful parish ministers of the Gospel

Chapter 1

Roots

Reverend Angus MacKinnon was born into this world on a cold winter's night in January, 1885, on the Isle of Skye on the west coast of Scotland. He was the eighth and youngest child of John Angus and Rachel MacKinnon, nee MacPherson. His birthplace was the small coastal settlement of Galtrigil, a stone's throw from Shiadair. Both these hamlets of crofters were part of Borreraig. This cluster of coastal villages comprises part of the original Glendale, the name immortalised in history, literature and song, and chosen for numerous settlements in North America, and wherever Highlanders migrated, to make their second home. Galtrigil, the outermost village on the promontory, was the birthplace of Donald Macleod who, after Culloden, guided Prince Charlie across the Minch to Lewis

Young Angus was the pet of the family. He had three older sisters, Annie, Katie and Maggie, and four older brothers, John, Peter, Ewen and Donald. These were born over the previous twenty years, and brought up in the grim aftermath of the mid-19th century potato famine. They lived through the noble struggle for basic human dignity, personified in the members of the Land League. Angus came into this world, when the scars of social struggle and economic hardship had scarcely healed. It is as if he got the tail end of a storm, a cruel economic, social and political storm, that led the majority of the populous glen to leave their rugged habitat for the city, or to take ship for a new life, especially in Canada and America. Childhood for him meant some relief from the tension of day-to-day deprivation compared to that endured by his older siblings. Yet by any standards his childhood life was simple and spartan, with little or no concession to the comforts of living that are taken for granted in a reasonably affluent society. There was always the haunting shadow of the struggle for survival and the latter could not be dissociated from childhood even for the youngest member of the MacKinnon family.

We mention here some factors of history and geneology, the basic raw materials in the environment of which this future herald of the Gospel, was a product. Since the subjugation of the Highlanders after the last abortive assertion of the royal house of Stewart in the '45 Jacobite Rising, there was an uneasy peace throughout the Scottish Highlands with the 'powers that be' in London and its servile lackeys in Edinburgh. Feudal oppression in land tenure, as well as ethnic and cultural suppression were legally justified as tools to deprive the Highlanders of their historic identity and their social clan system. Public policy meant the replacement of people with sheep, in the shameful Clearances. A somewhat restricted Press ensured that the general public in Britain were not given the facts of economic deprivation and social injustice that might embarrass the 'establishment' and question its legitimacy. Popular philosophy lent itself to a laissez-faire insensitivity to the secular and spiritual needs of the common people. Looking at the background to the three Jacobite Risings of the late 17th and 18th century, it is easy to see the people's disenchantment with the pragmatic Protestantism, that had first been superficially grafted onto the class system of Feudal secularism in England, a parochial insular church concept that narrowed the Christian world vision to something almost quaint if not ridiculous. State and Church were identified as one, with Czarist conviction that 'he who resists the State, resists God.' You could say that the State, while stripping the monarch of his or her divinity, dressed itself in the same suit. Such changes were fuel for revolt, and they rationalised the restless longing to give a second chance to the Stuarts. Large numbers of Protestants as well as Catholics came out in support of the Prince in the '45. There is possibly some substance in the assumption that Rome, having failed to recapture rebel Protestant England in the abortive 1588 Armada invasion, was now trying another thrust, using the last remnants of the Scottish Roman Catholic adherents, coupled with the many Protestants disillusioned with the Westminster government and dull German Geordies now ruling the incongruous marriage of disparate states of Scotland and England. In short, having failed to get in at the front door of ecclesiastically wayward Britain, they now attempted to gain entrance at the back door, resuscitating the claim of the autocratic Stuarts who were handicapped with their fatal doctrine of 'the Divine Right of Kings.'

Apart from such political theorising there was the down-to-earth reality for the majority of people struggling for ordinary human fairness. This disillusionment with constipated government would make any citizen consider almost any alternative. Failure on the part of the 'powers that be' in facing the basic issues of land tenure, economics and social adjustment, and in dealing with them as the reasonable responsibilities of informed government, resulted in a sentimental haze being cast like a smoke screen over the Highland scene.

By default, the Protestant Church was not blameless in the widespread support given to the Jacobite cause. Inertia, lassitude, indifference left the Highland people of Scotland especially, without the complete Bible in their own language until the end of the 18th century (1802). It is hard to accept, but the Indians of Maine in North America had the Bible translated into their own tongue, by Rev John Eliot, a hundred and fifty years before the present Gaelic Bible was available for the Gaelic-speaking population of Scotland. It was not the established endowed Presbyterian National Church which took the initiative in this. The wonderful work was due to the thrust of the lay society called the Society for Propagating Christian Knowledge. This voluntary body did more for the Gaelic world, its education and spiritual good, in ten years than the National Established Church of Scotland since the days of John Knox and Andrew Melville, in the latter half of the 16th century. It is difficult to omit the word 'suppression' in the neglect of the Highlands in this respect. The first initiative for a Bible in the language of the ordinary Highland people came from Ireland. The Bible was translated into Gaelic, albeit with a strong leaven of Irish Gaelic in the language used. The Hebrew Old Testament was translated into Gaelic by Dr William Bedel, Provost of Trinity College,

Dublin, and the Greek New Testament by Dr. William Donald. These were published in one volume in 1690.

The Gaelic-speaking Highlands were now on a par with the English-speaking world. The Gaelic Bible was waiting to be used. Here was the dynamic spiritual weapon that could change this warlike people of the mountains and glens, and integrate them into a sophisticated Christian society.

The other requirement was literacy, achievable by implementing the goal of the Reformers, John Knox and Andrew Melville, namely a school in every parish. But this was not to be.

This Bible was not made available to Gaelic speakers. It would appear that the Protestant Churches, Presbyterian and Episcopal, did not see fit to give it to their adherents. At the same time a limited number printed by the Anglicans could be found in Roman Catholic homes both in Scotland and Nova Scotia, where at least one first edition in very good condition can be found to this day.[1]

It would appear that the whole Celtic Church, Roman and Reformed had the potential for Bible reading. But the Gaelic Bible, provided by the Anglican Church in Ireland, was withheld from the Gaelic-speaking Highlands of Scotland, whether through cost or through inertia. That is a stain on the church history of Scotland. In the greater part of the Highlands, nominally Reformed, the absence of the Bible for use in church and home, the Lamp of life for the human journey, as the common language, explains much of the lack of spiritual knowledge, and the residual element of plain wildness, which lingered on into the mid-eighteenth century in the Highlands, and the irrational support given to the 'lost' House of Stuart, and the Roman Church's dream of a United Britain again

1. See appendix

reinstated in the world family and flying the colours of the Papal flag. History would yet prove that the Britain that withstood overt military invasion, was more likely to lose its hard won historic identity, through internal apostacy and deriliction of religious responsibility. In Speyside, large numbers of men followed Prince Charlie. These were adherents of the national reformed church. Many women likewise were ardent supporters of the Jacobite Cause. One thinks of Rev Peter Grant, the Gaelic Hymn writer, and his two aunts, who were at the same time loyal Presbyterians. No Highlander can compute his debt to the S.P.C.K. for their work. The New Testament was published in standard Gaelic as we know it, in 1767, and the whole Bible along with the Psalms in metre and Paraphrases, in 1802. The direct result can be seen in the dynamic spiritual and intellectual thrust of the 19th century in the ecclessiastical life of the Highlands and Islands.

After the '45, the romanticism of the Celtic culture tickled the fancy of the rich and the powerful. The clan chiefs with notable exceptions were shown 'the treasures of Egypt' and abandoned their people, in their afflictions, usurping the land rights of the latter in personified ownership. The chiefs were feted and fawned over in the social circles of the idle rich in Edinburgh and London. There was a quiet and clandestine legitimization of their title to the historic lands. Once the collective ownership of the clan to their historic lands was achieved by the current chiefs, the way was open for the ethnic clearances which followed.

How gullible and naive the Celtic chiefs were, as they capitulated to the cynical psyche of Rome's successor, the British Empire! How plausible and profitable the selling out of their people appeared to be! Blinded by temptation, disarmed by flattery, it is not so much that they sold out their heritage, but that they let it go. For many the 'mess of pottage' was satisfying and sweet for only a season, but long-term would lead to their humiliation. For a while the ballrooms of Edinburgh and London echoed to the tamed Highland music, now disarmed of its vigour. Likewise the scions of great clans, were also tamed and now shackled by the gloved claws of conformist society. The rich idle ladies fingered the tartan-coloured attire of these Highland chiefs who were encouraged or co-erced to dress up like peacocks as the latest wonder of shallow, exploitive society.

In contrast, the people of the glens and mountains were suppressed in newly-forged legal chains in a deliberate attempt to sap their ethnic and cultural vigour. Observers took note of the clothing of the people—the same without a change for night as well as day—barely enough to keep the shivering body and soul together, as families clung together against the damp and cold of an indifferent climate. In spite of thousands of men recruited to the armies of the Empire, the population increased, especially in coastal regions and that included Skye and specifically, Glendale. The increase, due in part to the sudden and short-lived prosperity of the kelp industry, brought a social and economic crisis. In this, people lived close to subsistence level, with little margin between death and survival. Sub-division of crofts was often fourfold. The land simply could not support this quadrupled population. When access to mined deposits of phosphates made the rich natural seaweed harvest of the coasts obsolete, there was a real crisis. The solution was clear; export the people to the colonies. This apparently rational policy masked the real reason-- clear the land of people and landowners can then grow rich on sheep.

All this is fully documented in Highland history in successive Statistical Records, as a rule compiled by local ministers. The peak crises were graphically dramatised in such emotional writings as those of Rev Dr. Norman MacLeod's Gaelic journal *An Gaidheal*, the moving account of the Highland Diaspora. Later in recent years, the Scots- Canadian, Arthur Prebble, in his book on the Highland Clearances, catalogued the batches of evicted thousands as whole families were parcelled off in steerage or deck cargo for passage across the oceans. Still today at the beginning of the third millennium, after Christ's birth, an uneasy peace rests on the 'mist-covered mountains', where the Clearances have more than a hint of the notorious contemporary 20th century designation of 'ethnic clearances' as witnessed and so cynically accepted, in Bosnia in Europe and in Burundi in Africa.

History reveals a curious picture as its sequences succeed one another like a film over the course of time. Close to the year 2000 A.D., an exile returns to Scotland and notes a changed overall picture. Of course there is still a basic residual native population in many places. But in some places, take for example Shieldaig or Ullapool in Wester Ross, or Glendale, in Skye where Reverend Angus MacKinnon was born and brought up, the ethnic substitution is almost complete. Only a few Gaelic speaking people, mostly in the twilight of their years live in the croft houses. Incomers with different cultural and linguistic affinities are more numerous. Further there is almost an insidious trend of deliberate economics in the seeming ease with which grants are given to incomers. At the same time native people born and brought up, who spent their lives in the cities, are penalised with burdensome taxes, when they seek to retain, maintain and improve the traditional crofthouses of their childhood. You could well be across the Atlantic in a pluralist settlement of different people. In both cases, the native population identified with the land are depleted in numbers. Their language is scarcely heard and used much less in home and community. There is indeed a kind of renaissance in that Gaelic music and culture is given time on the radio and television. But in spite of media exposure, the long-term signs of change are there. English has to a large extent become the language of worship in the church. The old school in Borreraig, once full of a hundred children is now a private residence. The big school in Glendale is marked for closure. As you pause outside the school playground, there are only a dozen children enjoying a respite from the classroom. And in place of the laughter and teasing of one another in the Gaelic language, the recreation of the children is all in English.

There is also another fact that is hard to separate from the evolution of the events of past history, where landowners with some notable exceptions were, if not active, at least passive in the expulsion process of their own people. Many of the great houses of the clans are reduced to nominal social and economic status. It is true that some chiefs brought improvement. One thinks of Atholl's tree experiments of cross-pollination, which has produced the famous Scottish larch. But for the most part the contribution of landowner/ chief was negative and at times patronising. The Fyrish Monument, seen above Evanton on top of a hill, a useless mock colonade of stones, represents the pathetic attempt to provide some work for the people, by Munro of Foulis. The Duke of Sutherland also provided relief work, employing scores of men to build a pyramid to his own memory, again on top of a hill, so that posterity would be reminded of his good works.

The fact is that little real effort was made before the end of the 18th century, to bring religious education to the Gaelic population. The key to freedom is literacy, as literacy is the key to dynamic evangelical spiritual enlightenment. The long shadow of social injustice in the grim ethnic Diaspora called the *Fuadach*, the Highland Clearances, stigmatises Scottish history and rests as a guilty indictment on those in positions of power. But also, the prejudice against the Highlands, its language and its people undoubtedly retarded and suppressed the ability of the Scottish Gael to make his maximum contribution to the Scottish nation. As late as at the General Assembly in 1900, the religious life in the Highlands was referred to as 'varnished barbarism.' Such language in the context of church and national debate, leaves deep wounds, even though they be excused as spontaneous epithets resorted to in the heat of controversy.

We know deep within us that truth has many sides, and we all are to some extent the victims of prejudice. We are subjective, and also like everyone else we understand only in part. Further, our most seasoned perspectives are not without some form of egotistical bias, or influence of our programmed upbringing, ethnically and educationally. If this is a reasoned hypothetical problem, there is a pragmatic solution by judging results. This is 'perceived truth'. And who can deny its validity! If you looked for parallels in the 20th century, you could take China's attempt to eradicate Tibetan nationalism, religion and culture, or Russia's grim suppression of the Chechens. Some would see a parallel in the smouldering ongoing erosion of the Kurd identity with their ancient Highland habitat sandwiched in between the triumvirate of Turkey, Iran and Iraq. A similar case could include the Celtic Basque people in their struggle to assert their identity in the French/Spanish border provinces. And it is hard to exclude North America's historic suppression of the native Indian. Just think of it. Canada's *nouveau regime* of Anglophiles bought the whole of Toronto land area (known in the commercial world as the Golden Triangle), from the Indians for the princely sum of ten English shillings—about a half dollar. That transaction is more than superficial 'perceived truth,' whether people like it or not. And though legal, must qualify as a historic swindle. But the English would never concede this, any more than Spain would acknowledge its 16th century trade with the Inca Empire of Peru was robbery. No wonder moral monitors and self-appointed political policemen carry little weight, for many of the winners in history have won over the backs of the helpless. This is not to give a *carte blanche* approval to every small ethnic or cultural entity that asserts autonomy. But at the same time it is impossible to see the doings of history, without the smear of shame lingering like a cancerous moral aberration on succeeding generations.

The MacKinnons

My father, like every Highlander, was consciously linked to his ancestry, in the broader sense, and specifically signified by his clan name, his *sloinneadh,* his people. Thus he belonged to the clan or simply the children of Fingon, historically part of the family of Saint Columba, and the kings of Ireland. The clan can be traced in unbroken line back to Fergus II (A.D.502). Certainly, evidence identifies their royal links with Alpin, king of the Picts, who was slain in 837 A.D. near Dundee. This accounts for their slogan 'Cuimhnich bas Alpin' which came to mean, 'Fight in honour of your Alpin Blood.' They are identified as active and powerful in helping Robert Bruce free Scotland from slavery at Bannockburn. The MacKinnons were a warlike clan, expressing their loyalty in deeds. Ecclesiastically the known history is connected to the Columban church in Ireland and in Scotland. A well-preserved Celtic Stone in Iona, the headquarters of the Celtic Church in Scotland, records the bishopric of one, Lachlann and also his son, John MacKinnon in the 15th century. In some manuscripts the original Iona was spelt 'Y'.

In the Monumental Records of the island, we find Y to be the prevailing name...Crux Lachlanni MacFiongone et ejus filii Iohannis Abbatis de Hy, facta AD 1489.....Fingonnus Prior de Y; Hic jacet Ioann es MacHingone Abbas de Y. qui obut AD 1500...

'MacKinnon' phonetically means 'beloved son.' But philology points to the name simply, the 'son of Fingon', who was the great grandson of King Alpin. As a civil social entity, the clan were dispossessed of their lands in Mull by the MacLeans. These were known as the dark MacKinnons, almost Iberian in appearance. Subsequent to this, their history is identified with Strath on the eastern seaboard of the island, where their stronghold, Castle Moil or Dun-Akin now stands, as a ruined monument to their days of clan influence and affluence. It should be mentioned that the MacKinnons also had land in Arran and Scalpay, Harris. Large numbers of MacKinnons from the Moidart area as well as Mull, Skye,

Scalpay, the Uists and Harris, emigrated to Canada and the United States. The fortunes of the MacKinnons had waned, especially after the third and last Jacobite Rising, in 1745 in which the clan in the person of their aged chief, gave unequivocal, if misplaced loyalty to the Stuarts.

My father's people lived within the jurisdiction of the MacLeods with their headquarters at Dunvegan. His people had Norse blood in their veins, and in some ways contrasted to the historical mainstream of the clan. To this day, this identity of ancestry, strengthened by intermarriage with MacLeods, carries with it full rights within the privileged parameters still extant, associated with the MacLeods of Dunvegan. This was the 'Siol Thormoid', the Norman MacLeods, who came out to advantage, in the historic fighting and feuding for precedence, against their brethren in their own clan, chiefly the more northerly placed 'Siol Torcuill,' the Torquil MacLeods of Lewis, and with other clans. It is clear that the MacKinnon chief and his clan came to ruin because of their alignment with the Jacobite Cause, a misfortune painfully signified by the derelict castle at Kyleakin. Other chiefs stayed with the Hanoverian regime. The pause for sober second thoughts, realistically could dictate their destiny and obviate ruin with imprisonment and even hanging for treason, by the contemporary government. Some clans came out on the side of the Stuart Cause, against the will of their chief. This was the case in Speyside among the Grants, Stewarts and MacPhersons and others of Atholl. They joined Prince Charles' army, going south to Edinburgh, while their chief, the Duke, sat tight in his castle, a cowed prisoner of common sense or political expediency, depending upon one's perspective. The government found in the Duke of Cumberland an early version of a Nazi commander, in the vindictive merciless cruelty which turned the Highlands into a place of desolation and mourning, when he 'cleaned up' the Highlands after the defeat of Culloden.

Though reduced in clan status and impoverished by the fortunes of history, there is an integrity exhibited by the MacKinnons unequalled among the other Highland clans, as a selfless virtue, which makes all who are identified with the clan feel proud of their history and their heritage. How else can 20th century MacKinnons feel, even those across the ocean in the New World, when they read of historic Bannockburn, Scotland's victory over the English, and there beside the Scottish king Robert the Bruce, is the MacKinnon chief with his clan, armed with targe and claymore, with the MacInneses, a sept of their clan and their official clan bowmen.

Hear the commentary by the poet, Sir Walter Scott, describing the prelude to the battle of Bannockburn.

> Each warrior to his weapon sprung,
> And targe upon his shoulder flung
> Impatient for the fight.
> **MacKinnon's** chief, in warlike grey,
> Had charge to master their array,
> And guide their barks to Brodick Bay.

Anyone familiar with the sequel of the Highland Clearances is bound to consider that the lot of the exiled people in North America could reasonably be called a blessing in disguise. It is true that no one can measure the pain of estrangement, the pathos of separation, the deprivation of the

sensory joy of a Highlander waking up to a new morning
and raising his eyes to the ancients mountains of his homeland.
But it is not unjustified to use the terms emancipation,
freedom, release from tyranny, from oppression, from poverty
and even nature's shroud of cold damp, the prevailing
characteristic of the Scottish Highland climate, when speaking
of the great exodus. A returning exile at the time I write still
takes weeks to recover from the chill damp cold, experienced
during a month's visit to ancient Alba.

Rev Angus's father belonged to the North arm of Loch
Dunvegan, namely Waternish, like Glendale also MacLeod
country. He courted Rachel MacPherson from Glendale, won
her hand in marriage and crossed over to make his home in
Galtrigil, Glendale and raise his family there. His wife Rachel
was a woman of very strong character and Christian devotion.
It is true that women generally in the Celtic world—the Celts
populated most of Europe until the Roman era—were
considered equal with men, and accorded precedence if gifts
and endowments merited it. A Roman commentator gives a
journalistic description of Boudicca, the queen of the Celtic
tribe of the Iceni in south-eastern Britain in the first century:

> She was huge of frame, terrifying in aspect, and
> with a harsh voice. A great mass of bright red hair fell
> to her knees: she wore a great twisted golden torc,
> and a tunic of many colours, over which was a thick
> mantle, fastened by a brooch. Now she grasped a spear,
> to strike fear into all who watched her.

Of course the Celtic warrior queen of the Iceni was
unique, like the giant William Wallace, the Scots patriot, more
than a thousand years later. The women in the Highlands were
vivacious and often strikingly beautiful. One thing is certain

that they were not easily tamed. In the Isle of Skye, particularly, history suggests that they claimed a high degree of feminine assertiveness. There is a parallel with one place near at hand, namely the Shetland Islands. Here specifically in the islands of Out-Skerries there is a matriarchal society where the women act in a dominant role. There is a reason for this. The men have been traditionally away from home at the fishing. It followed that running the home, the croft and the community was therefore the responsibility of the women. If not, nothing at all would be done. The other parallel is found in Thailand, another matriarchal society. Here traditionally a women illustrated her dominance in relation to marriage. Instead of a man having several wives as in the Arab world, where women were traditionally subordinate to the male in the secular and the religious sphere, a wife had several husbands simultaneously.

In the ecclesiastical and secular life of the community, traditionally men discharged their natural responsibilities as leaders in war and peace. But distinction of function should not be construed as a denial of equality between the sexes. Further, Scripture historically and rationally follows natural aptitude. Man is the fulcrum of collective society. The perceived precedence given to him in the Christian teaching, carries with it full responsibility not only for himself but for his family or group of families. Common sense teaches that a man is nothing without a woman. And a woman's influence and contribution can be such that it is the decisive factor for good in both the religious and the secular context.

During the struggles of the Land League in the 1850's onward until the crisis in 1885, women showed their assertiveness. The leading agitator for justice was the Gaelic poetess, Mary MacPherson, whom I refer to elsewhere. In the struggle against the para-military police forces sent to suppress the 'revolt', women were in the front line of resistance with the men. In Dunvegan, a ship full of Glasgow policemen had to turn away from the quay, before a continuous volley of rocks thrown at them from a militant and fearless crowd of women. When the 'military' sought to capture the men leaders at the battle of the Braes, it is said that 'the women fought like Amazons,' with a tigerish ferocity.

That indomitable spirit still is there in Skye, and is manifest especially in the formative influence upon children, and also in the hour of crisis for family or community. Indeed in spite of repressive conventions both secular and ecclesiastical, it is clear that in most situations women are the driving force and men take second place, when basic decisions are made. Both Flora MacDonald and Dame Flora Macleod, spent time in North America and are household names in all cultural circles in modern Canada and the United States. As unique and noted women of their day, they gave Skye women a kind of precedence where assertive parity with men was affirmed in spite of perceived repressive action by church and state.

It was to my grandfather's advantage that he married a woman from Glendale, Rachel MacPherson, related to the above-mentioned poetess, Mary MacPherson. Rachel, in a quieter less demonstrative way in the context of home and family, was also a powerful individual. It was her drive that led the family, in common humble economic circumstances with the rest of the community, to have a new, relatively modern home erected, mason-built and comprising finished timbers and metal roof, bought and delivered from Glasgow.

therefore stood out as the first 'white house' in contrast to the 'black houses' in the community.

But the greatest privilege which my father treasured was the incomparable blessing of being weaned, nurtured and shaped by a profoundly spiritual and devout mother. The boy became a man, with the seed of noble aspiration already sown. In Providence and in time, this would germinate in the fruitful soil of his young life, spiritually and intellectually, making him a useful and loyal servant of God in his day and generation.

Chapter 2

Bardic Tradition

There was *bardachd,* poetry, in my father's blood. His mother was closely related to three noted Skye bards, Donald MacLeod (*Domh'll nan Oran*), and his son Neil Macleod, best known to the general public, as the bard of Skye; the third was Mary MacPherson. These poets expressed the antithesis of their oppressed people to the thesis of accepted policy by the 'powers that be,' which issued in the dark evils of legalised oppression. Their graphic poetry filled the gap of public expression, in a day when there was no mouthpiece of a local newspaper. The sublime language which clothed their thinking made an indelible impression upon their generation. As secular literature it continues to be a legacy of matchless human expression, a treasure opened to the reader through the key of its own incomparable Celtic linguistic identity

Poetry was the expression of aspiration, and social comment on the immediate happenings of every day events. At the same time poetry was the medium of Celtic linguistic identity with history and the uniqueness of the Highlander and his habitat. Thus children memorised their ancestral bardachd or poetry, and spent evenings singing the songs of their people, gathered together in their homes, by the light of the peat fire, and the rushlight of seabird oil. Sadness and nostalgia, so deeply felt by thousands of people forced to leave their beloved Glendale, and the Isle of Skye are carved in Highland memory in poems like *'Cumha Eilein a' Cheo'* (Lament for the Misty Island) and *'Anns a Ghleann 'san robh mi og'*. (In the Glen where I was young) by Neil MacLeod. There is no doubt that the Island of Skye, with its scenic beauty and tranquil pastoral setting is simply without rival. The two poets, father and son, in spite of the evils endured at the hands of oppressive or thoughtless landowners and authorities, were very conscious of this beauty and composed poems to express it, as did that other member of the bardic trio, Mary MacPherson, *Mairi Mhor nan Oran.* More than any other, she also helped by her satirical verse to marshall a spirit of practical advocacy of legislative change. Hear her condemnation of the insipid and impotent clergy who were puppets of their patrons, or, more charitably, the victims of a system that suppressed the right of the church to spiritual freedom.

> Tha luchd teagaisg cho beag churaim
> Faicinn caradh mo luchd duthcha
> 'S iad cho balbh air anns a chupaid
> 'S ged bu bruidean bha 'g an eisdeachd

Translation:

> The preachers have so little care
> Seeing the ill-treatment of my Isle's folk
> And so silent about it in the pulpit
> As if brute beast were listening to them.

Mary MacPherson holds a unique place in the context of Skye. She touches its people especially as a bard of nature. Thus my cousin MaryAnn's husband, Donald MacKenzie, also from Shiadar, quoted to me his favourite verse from one of her poems;

> Sealladh na bu bhreagha
> Riamh cha'n fhaca sul,
> Spreidh a muigh 'gam feurachd,
> Air maduinn Cheitinn chiuin.

> 'N uiseag air a sgiath,
> Seinn gun fhiamh a ciuil,
> 'San ceo mu cheann Beinn Sianathaig
> Is an sliabh fo dhruichd.'

Translation:

> A view more beautiful
> The eye has never seen,
> The cattle out grazing,
> On a tranquil May morning.

> The lark on its wing,
> Sings its song without fear,
> And mist shrouds Ben Shianag,
> Its slopes soaked in dew.

Young Angus, my father had that bardic gift in himself. When a little boy, he heard his mother remonstrating with the older brothers for being reluctant to go for a creel of peats— the family peat bank being some considerable distance up the hill. He took the big creel on his back and left the house.

He was back very soon with an *ultach,* an armful of peats, in the bottom of the creel. He had gone to a neighbour's peat stack near at hand, but he being only a little boy, could carry only a little fuel, rather than a full creel expected of his older brothers. His mother understood his action, but his older brothers and sisters kept ribbing him for 'stealing' the peats from another's stack. Little Angus stood with bowed head, then replied,

> *Suil gu deas, agus suil gu tuath,*
> *Lamh a buireadh anns a chruach,*
> *'Smath tha fios aig an Ti tha shuas,*
> *'Gum bheil i cruach mo nabuidh.*

Translation:

> A look to south, and a look to north,
> The tempted hand within the stack,
> The One above, He knows full well,
> That it's my neighbour's peatstack.

It appeared natural for the little boy to frame his thoughts in verse.

My father was exposed to both the secular or social aspects of poetry and also the spiritual. All his life, the secular and the spiritual lingered with him in such a way that they were an essential part of him. When he was growing up, his kinsman Neil Macleod was already acknowledged as the bard of Skye. Often in later life my father would lapse into reverie at the fireside with his family and come out with Gaelic verse. 'Who composed that poem?' his children would ask. 'Who else', was his answer, 'but my cousin Neil Macleod, in *Anns a Ghleann 'san robh mi og'*. For him the poem encapsulated the preciousness of his upbringing in Glendale, in the riches and integrated closeness of community, bound by ties of cultural and economic history and so powerfully animated by the Gaelic language.

Here is an excerpt that captures the lost and precious past.

Ann an dubhlachd gharbh a'geamhradh
Cha b'e ann bu ghainn' ar spors;
Greis air sugradh, greis air dannsa,
Greis air canntarachd is ceol;
Biodh gach seanair aosmhor, liath,
'G innseadh sgialachdan gun gho,
Mu gach gasgeach fearail, greannmhor,
Bh'anns a ghleann 'n uair bha iad og.

Translation:

In the dark wild winter
There was time for diversion,
Time for sporting, time for dancing,
Time for music by mouth and instruments;
Hoary old grandfathers,
Relating faultless tales,
About the many manly heroes,
Who were in the Glen when they were young.

But no sentiment of romantic love nor ethnic ties to land and history, could adequately fulfil the yearning for spiritual aspiration. Is that not true of every human being! Is it not true that when the spiritual chords of redemptive forging love are struck in evangelical language, like music, the elective power of heaven, that excludes no human being, awakens the longings of the soul! Thus my father was drawn to the classic spiritual poems of Dugald Buchannan, and the less profound but evangelical poems of Peter Grant, and also those of the Apostle of the North, Dr. MacDonald of Ferintosh.

This was the household religious cultural literature of the Gaelic world, and the food for the soul, similar to the works of Robert Burns in Lowland Scotland in the area of the secular. My father's gift of memory and love for the spiritual, made the poems of the great Christian bards his travelling companions until the end of his life journey.

Chapter 3

Social Environment

I n order to understand my father's life, it is necessary to mention some of the background events, taking place prior to, and during the years of his upbringing. These include the social and civil issues that affected the common people. A taste of economic prosperity and the increasing pace of social change in the radical movements accompanying the grim development of England's 'dark Satanic mills' as portrayed in William Blake's wistful longing for the Christian New Jerusalem, brought a new and almost urgent militancy to Scotland and even to the long-suffering Highlands. This became a vocal and effective means of shaking up the establishment and righting at least some inequities.

The movement mentioned earlier, known as the Land League was the focus of this collective democratic agitation. This grew in the latter half of the 19th century. Its greatest hour was in its struggles with the authorities in the Island of Skye. Glendale was not behind in this, and their local leaders were fined and some incarcerated in the dungeon of the Castle at Dunvegan and in the Calton Jail in Edinburgh. I listened to my old uncle's account as history, still freshly minted from his childhood, came before his mind. I saw the pain cross his face as he tried to put the thoughts behind him But I would not let him.

'You owe it to me, Uncle Donald,' I said. 'Tell me as you knew it. Tell me what happened.'

The picture of the wrongs of yesterday inflicted on my people where my father was born and brought up, brings a mixture of anger and sadness whenever I dwell upon it.

It was like this. Following the 1745 Jacobite Rising, the ancient *run-rig* agriculture of alternating cultivation of strips of land held in collective ownership with its economic limitations was replaced by the tenure of individual crofts. With the new system, the relation of landowner to people was broken. In its place, the pattern of feudal land tenure and the servile relation that this implied, was introduced. This led to many injustices. The landowner now exacted feudal days of labour for his own land, so much so that the crofter or tenant had less and less time to eke out a living for himself. The landowner grew richer, the common people poorer. The chiefs/ landowners were divorced from the people; their henchmen, the factors, did their dirty work. The land service now given to the tacksman by the tenants was in effect a new feudalism, the import of a discredited relic from Norman England, a concomitant of the infamous class system that stigmatises the secular and ecclesiastical fabric of England to this day, with its apex in the monarchy and cripples Christian community from fulfilling just aspiration. The 'powers that be' saw this tool as an effective means of taming the Celts once and for all, and bringing the wild Highlander to heel.

As my old uncle opened the door to the past, I followed him as a person would, who enters the vaults of his ancestors. The key events of formative history rose in graphic clarity before my mind. People, my father's people, his *sloinneadh* now in their graves, rose up animated and vocal in the struggle for human dignity and justice before a repressive and alien Anglicised culture, language and government. The climax of the struggle was precipitated by the paranoid sheriff of Inverness-shire calling for a para-military force to be sent from Glasgow to suppress the 'rising' in Skye. This honourable civil revolt against glaring injustice was led by veterans who fought and were wounded in the Crimean War.

Picture these men, if you will, dignified, aged men, the elders of their community and of their church, being treated as common criminals, and thrown into the dungeon prison of the castle of the MacLeods at Dunvegan. Just you think of it, men who less than thirty years before, fought in the Crimean War for their country, now back in their Highland homes, humiliated like this. Several had wounds. More than one had a mutilated limb. One had lost an eye, in a cordite explosion. These noble citizens now were treated like common scum. Their shameful treatment at the hands of the Authorities is an indelible stain upon the very fabric of the local Scottish puppet authorities. Jacobite *phobia* should have long died out. To claim it was still there ready to set the Highland heather on fire, was a superstitious myth that did not merit a place in mature and informed thinking. Just think of the incongruity of a Royal Navy battleship anchored off the shore at Glendale, with her big guns trained on the pitiful thatched roofs of the crofters' humble homes! Picture the pinnaces ferrying marines ashore to raise the British flag and suppress the threatened revolt. What ridiculous and mindless decisions brought an *ironclad* of the Royal Navy to train its guns on the beautiful landscape of the crofting community of Glendale!

Shame is the synonym for the action of the Authorities in their treatment of the people and especially these veteran soldiers who had fought for their queen, country and the British Empire. It is impossible to omit the glaring contrast with the treatment of Cromwell's Parliamentary soldiers when they came to the age for retirement in the 17th century. What of those also in the subjugation and 'civilizing' of the Highlands after the last Jacobite risings! This was effected by using considerable numbers of troops, mainly English, ethnically selected from the south of Britain, free from any trace of Celtic rebellious propensities. The English government or the government in England, repeated the Roman strategy of placing a string of forts along the line of the Highland Fault for the military occupation of the Highlands, chiefly Fort William, Fort Augustus, Inverness and Fort George. It is interesting to note that these soldiers, mostly English, instead of regarding the land they occupied as alien and its people as hostile, took a liking to the Highlands in which they served. The soldiers of the 'occupation' obviously liked the people, the 'barbarous Celtic savage' whom they had been hired to subdue. They did not want to go back to England. Rather they made their choice. They would spent their life after service, in the Highlands which they had come to subdue.

But the point that is significant as a norm of comparison is this, that on retirement, these soldiers settled in the Highlands, comfortably cushioned by pension and privilege. Evidence of this is the fact that they were able to finance a good education for their children, many of the latter making an outstanding contribution to the professions. One thinks of the name Porteus. A soldier's son of that name became minister at Delny, Easter Ross. He was a highly esteemed servant of Christ and his church. In contrast, treatment of the Land League radicals, many of them honourable ex-soldiers, was quite different. The whole sordid story is recorded in history books. For light on my father's background, enough to say that he was related through his mother to the leader, John MacPherson, who is remembered as the 'Glendale Martyr.' In Glendale you can see an enclosure, with a commemorative stone which marks the place of confrontation between the people and soldiers.

The stone reads,

TO COMMEMORATE
THE ACHIEVEMENTS OF
THE GLENDALE LAND LEAGUERS
1882 - 1886
LOCUS WHERE 600 CROFTERS CHALLENGED
THE GOVERNMENT FORCES
IMPRISONED
JOHN MACPHERSON, GLENDALE MARTYR
REV. D MACCALLUM, DONALD MACLEOD
JOHN MORRISON

My father was born shortly after the land controversy reached a crisis of confrontation in 1883. His birth therefore and his young life coincided with the appointment in 1885 of a Commission and the passing of the Crofters' Holding Act a year later. With it, tyranny and oppression by landowners was countered by a measure of enlightened justice. In practice,

some rents were reduced to a third. With the diligent advocacy
of influential friends of the Highlands, like Professor Blackie
in Edinburgh, and the interest of a sympathetic Press, a more
humane attitude accompanied a responsible interest on the
part of the government, national and local, in the lives of the
people. In this new setting, crofters began to emerge from a
primal level of subsistence. In degrees, they would come to
own newly built white-washed two-storey homes. Seasonal
employment in the south or at the fishing, would enable them
to achieve a tolerably viable living. Primo-geniture, however,
meant that the migration of most of the large families would
now accelerate.

Chapter 4

Episodes from Early Life

W hen my father was about six years old, a new house was built not far away from the 'black house' the thatch-roofed house in Galtrigil. The roofless thick stone walls and chimney stack and fireplace in the gable of the old home can still be seen. The new home was built on the other side of the small prominence, called *Meall a Chlachair*, the hill of the mason. This sturdy white-washed croft house, still in the MacKinnon family, is now fully modernised and can be seen today, well kept and occupied throughout the year as a holiday home.

The new MacKinnon house lies snugly in the lee of the hill, giving it protection from the predominantly westerly winds coming in from the Minch. This wind quadruples in velocity as it bounces off the craggy headland, and the uplift sweeps across the exposed coastal hamlets. Beyond the house, the land slopes down to the edge of the outer extremity of Loch Dunvegan, dropping vertically over forty foot cliffs to the incoming seas. The successive waves throw themselves at the rocks, in a perpetual snarling gesture of frustration. The shape of the sculptured coast-line is proof of their relentless fury. Mounds of undulating ground record the crofting agriculture with the *cas chrom*, the man operated foot plough. These *feannags* (lazyboys) are built-up strips of land by which the shallow depth of the land is increased for the crops of barley, oats and potatoes, the staple crops upon which the people depended for their livelihood from the land.

The young swimmer

My father had a penchant for swimming. Self-taught, he found it hard to keep out of the water. And remember, the sea for him was not a tame gentle inland pool. Rather, it lay below the cliffs at the foot of the croft, a growling frightening mass of breaking waves, plucking at the rocks. In the summer in which the new family home was built, he was already a fearless swimmer although he was only six years of age. But more, his siblings used to look on, as he would make a running dive, flinging his body out over the forty foot high cliffs to the sea below. No one else in the family could do this, nor even wanted to try. His confidence in the power of his body and in his self-taught swimming skills was unique to himself. Four instances illustrate this over a period from boyhood to adolescence.

Bringing home a dinner

One day he heard his mother praying that God would provide her with some food as she had nothing in the house with which to feed the family. Little Angus looked out and saw the sheepskin buoys of fishing nets in the middle of Loch

Dunvegan. He swam out to the nets and returned with enough for a meal for everyone that evening.

Too young

When the new house was being built, with all the masonry completed at a cost of five pounds sterling, all the other building materials of wood and roofing and windows were ordered from Glasgow. My old uncle Donald, recalling the events of his childhood, told me of that day when the MacBrayne steamer, the *Dunara Castle* paused on her trip in to the harbour at Dunvegan, and anchored off Galtrigil and Shiadar.

It was a calm summer morning. There was great excitement as this was a calendar event in their lives. The six family small zulu-type fishing boats, called *sgoths,* each about twenty feet in length and eight feet beam were enlisted to ferry the building materials ashore from the steamer. Three boats were loaded and the other three acted as tugs to tow the burdened boats to land. The older boys got aboard the s*goths,* keeping out of the way at the bow. Little Angus was considered too young and he was left with tears in his eyes, standing with wistful longing on the shore. When the boats were out at the steamer, a crew member on the *Dunara Castle* called attention to a movement, presumably a seal some distance away. To the amazement of all it turned and came to the boats. Of course this was no seal, but little Angus. He had run some distance along the shore, swam out, and then turned to get to the steamer, before anyone realised it. I felt a great pride filling my whole being as Uncle Donald spoke of my father, streaking like a fish, straight to their own family boat. There was no scold from father as he lifted his youngest son from the water, all dripping wet. There was a shouted order from the captain, Dugald MacNab from Tarbert, Kintyre, on the bridge of the *Dunara Castle*. Little Angus was taken aboard, dried and admired by crew and passengers—in those days people made vacation trips on the MacBrayne steamers. Now the little boy, from Shiadar was the hero of the day. He was taken to the open bridge and presented to the captain.

What a proud man little Angus was that day! He was only six years old, but he felt like a king, and was treated like one for his persistence and his prowess as a swimmer.

The 'Anointing'

This focus on the youngest of the family was seen remarkably in a spiritual context, according to my uncle Donald, about the same time. The occasion was a visit to the home in Shiadar from the minister, Mr MacColl. While the minister was visiting the family, the minister's driver had left the gig to find a discreet place a little distance away for nature's needs. No one noticed the absence in the house of the youngest of the family. Little Angus had slipped outside, saw the empty gig, and climbed aboard, taking up the reins of the horse in his two hands. The driver spotted him, ran back, ejected the little boy unceremoniously, at the same time giving him a strong verbal scolding. Just leaving the home, the aged minister intercepted the little boy, now crestfallen and humiliated. Young Angus was now submissively waiting for the second blow, a final spirit-breaking ecclesiastical rebuke. The old minister reached him, and put his hand under the chin of the child, lifting it up and looking into the young face. Then, he turned the boy round, still holding him with his left hand on the shoulder, and his right hand laid over the little

boy's black-haired head. He spoke to the driver saying,
'Leig leis a'leanabh so agus na bi ris. Tha lan-chinnt'
agam gu 'm bi e fhathasd, na mhinisdear tarbhach agus
ainmeil air son an Tighearna, 'na latha 'sna ghinealach.'
(Leave this boy alone and do not scold him. I am convinced
that he will yet be a profitable and noted minister for the Lord,
in his day and generation)

It is hard not to see the parallel in Scripture, when Samuel
the prophet came to Bethlehem to anoint a son of Jesse to be
a future king. Let Scripture speak in the incomparable
language of the Authorised English translation of the Hebrew.

Again Jesse made seven of his sons to pass
before Samuel. And Samuel said unto Jesse,
The Lord hath not chosen these.

And Samuel said unto Jesse, Are here all
thy children? And he said, There remaineth yet
the youngest, and behold he keepeth sheep. And
Samuel said unto Jesse, Send and fetch him:
for we will not sit down till he come hither.

And he sent, and brought him in. Now he
was ruddy, and withal of a beautiful countenance, and goodly to look to. And the Lord said,
Arise, anoint him: for this is he.

Then Samuel took the horn of oil, and
anointed him in the midst of his brethren: and
the Spirit of the Lord came upon David from
that day forward.   (1Samuel 16:10-13)

Many years later, my father spoke of the two ministers of
his childhood, Mr. MacColl and Mr. MacRae. I used to look

into my father's face when he recounted stories from the past. As he spoke of them, I used to wonder and wish that I had known them. For there was a wistful look of reverent and loving recollection in my father's face and his voice evinced a subtle change of gentleness, as he relived again the precious memories, especially of that day. That was a landmark day which he never forgot, a day when the scolding of condemnation for the spirited ploy of a little boy, was changed into the powerful reception of God's benediction as a 'child of promise', by the prophetic action of his sanctified childhood minister.

The original skateboard

I mentioned that my father regularly dived forty feet from the cliff-top to the sea below. This was a daring act which no other would think of doing. It meant that he had to run down to the cliff edge at speed, to throw himself outwards in a running dive. If he failed to get the distance, he would be killed on the jagged merciless rocks at the base of the cliff. My father told me about this incident himself as he recalled his childhood days in Glendale. Only a person who had experienced it could give a picture in graphic detail as he did. My uncle Donald corroborated this and gave the perspective of the onlookers.

It was about two years after the new house was built, which made little Angus eight years old. On this particular day my father ran down the slope of the croft and dived over the cliff into the sea. His brothers Ewen and Donald followed to the edge of the cliff, scanning the waters below, to see where he would surface. But there was no sign of him. They feared the worst, namely that he had hit the rocky bottom. Anguish and frustration gripped them as they could do nothing to help. Time passed and their hearts failed them as hope for their young brother's life faded.

Then they lifted their eyes to something a considerable distance from the shore. There was little Angus, lying on the water, and moving along at a great speed. They could hardly believe their eyes. His legs were still and his arms were not in motion.

They called to him, 'Aonghas, Aonghas'. My uncle Donald told me then what transpired. My father turned at an angle like a motorcyclist on land, or a surfer on a modern surfboard, or aqua-scooter. Then little Angus waved to his amazed brothers. Now to go back to my father's first-hand account to me fifty years later. When he dived, his hands hit the shoulders of an ocean skate, about six feet long. (We caught one of these in the net in my own young days.) As the alarmed giant flat-fish moved forward on the bottom, almost automatically my father's hands closed on the front sides of the head of the huge fish. The skate accelerated. My father's action caused the skate's back to arch down and the head to come up. The result was that he found himself soon on the surface, a unique experience of thrills never before recorded. The spectacular surf-ride on the skate's back ended as the rider waved to his brothers and the skate freed himself, and plunged down into its home waters of the deep.

The swimming prize

The last illustration of Angus's skills in the water relates to his developed ability to swim under water for a protracted period. He spent many times roaming and exploring the sea-bottom. His brothers became accustomed to this, but that day when he hitched a ride on the skate would never be forgotten. He was under water for a considerable time, before his hold on the skate eventually caused the fish to reach the surface, a good way out from the watching brothers on the cliff-top.

In the last story, the three youngest brothers, now in their teens, Ewen, Donald and Angus found themselves in Portobello, near Scotland's capital city of Edinburgh. I reiterate here the account given by my uncle Donald, as accurately as I can. It was a summer day and the town annual gala brought thousands of people to share in the events and competitions of this already popular holiday resort and its desirable sandy beaches. The older brothers persuaded Angus to enter a swimming competition at the big open air pool. The swimmers lined up, the starter's whistle blew and they were off like horses on a race track. The swimmers could be seen through the surface of the water and the crowd roared encouragement, without any competitor having a clear lead. As they swam, the line became broken as some lagged behind. Then a silent hush came over the crowd. My uncle Donald told the story. His young brother, the Highland youth from Glendale, who had never swam in a municipal pool before, only the cold clear waters of the Minch, the lad who had before now no opportunity to test his skills against those of any other swimmer, brought that hush to the onlookers. In an explosive acceleration, my father shot forward in a dynamic thrust that left the rest behind him. As he reached the finishing line, he rose up and turned round. 'Yes', said uncle Donald, 'he waved to the crowd, turning round to each side.' It seemed that he enjoyed every minute of it. And the crowd in Portobello responded. With some of the other competitors still in the water, the hushed silence gave way to a spontaneous roar of acknowledgment. For here was clearly a natural champion.

There is little doubt that the performance of the Highland youth that day in Portobello indicated that he had the calibre that could draw recognition in national and international circles in the less class structured social order of a hundred years later. Can you not envisage how a potential champion would have been identified with the increased emphasis on sport of a later day! But then the new world interplay of sport made possible through easier communication and travel, was just 'finding its feet' as it were in the revival of the Greek Olympic Games. But there was no sequel of scout recognition for this obviously talented winner.

The fact is that my father's healthy life-style, his love of swimming, the taxing demands of manual labour on crofts without horses to carry burdens or pull ploughs, gave him a developed physique, which was particularly powerful as he grew to manhood. In 1914, when he was medically examined as a recruit for the army, the shape of his legs became the focus of special interest. His leg muscles were so developed that the front protruded outward so that the shinbone could not be felt. The leg muscles curved outward and forward similar to the calf muscles at the back. He told how, as young boys, they thought nothing of carrying heavy burdens. Uncle Donald recalled how he and my father carried a boll of meal home from the mill in Dunvegan, some eight miles away, both boys barefoot and the road little more than a cart track.

My uncle Donald has given these anecdotes which show something of the life style of my father's boyhood and the physical demands which made him strong and sinewy. A strong physical constitution would stand him in good stead, in shaping him for the great 'calling' that was his destiny to fulfil.

Chapter 5

A Glimpse of Hardship

It is difficult for people in our relatively prosperous day, to realise the privations which were standard as part of everyday life, in the years between the mid 1840's with the Potato Famine until the economic betterment brought on by the fishing boom and revised legislation introduced at the turn of the 19th century. As a rule, the climate was relatively mild, even in winter, on the west coast of Scotland. Just think of it, palm trees grew well. I think of estates like Sir William MacKinnon's in Clachan, Kintyre, or that of Sir Osgood MacKenzie where the Inverewe gardens in Wester Ross are a spectacular stopping place for tourists.

But there were the exceptions. In the winter of 1895 when my father was ten years old, there was a spectacular freeze-up. In that winter, early photographs show the harbours frozen over, all round the coasts of Britain, with fishing boats, and coasters stuck fast in the ice. As I write, it is hard to avoid the observation that just this winter of 1995-96, there were reports of temperatures dropping down to minus 25 degrees centigrade. One effect was that the pipes of water systems in thousands of dwellings in both Scotland and England became a victim of the frost, and parts of the U.K. were turned into a plumber's paradise of work opportunity. Truly it is said in the old proverb, 'It's an ill wind that does not bring somebody some good.'

But the grim Arctic cold of that 1895 winter brought no such concomitant of calamity to the crofters of Glendale. For there was no plumbing. Like their counterpart in far-off America, there was only a primitive backhouse for the calls of nature and the shallow well nearby for fresh water. Just think of the folks, especially the aged, having to go out for ablutions in the unrelenting cold of that winter!

That winter, John, the eldest of the brothers came home for the New Year, possibly because of the restrictions which the ice brought to the ports. He was already a young officer on a merchant ship and his visits to the old home in Skye were a rare event. One evening the cold was so intense that repeatedly, the boys would go out to the peat stack for fuel to keep the fire blazing in the hearth. John followed his two young brothers Donald and Angus outside into the dark of the night. Snow lay on the ground and gave some kind of light to the scene. John saw the canvas wrapped round the feet of my father, his little brother, the only pitiful protection to cover his feet. For he had never owned a pair of shoes or boots in his life hitherto.

The oldest brother paused reflectively in the lee of the stack as he observed my father's feet. He knew only too well from earlier days, the grim aspects of deprivation, for he had lived through the unrelieved years of want when the potato crops repeatedly failed; when the eye of the potato was dug out before using for food, so that it was kept for seed.

Things had improved since these dark days. The new home was built, a world of difference from the old 'black house'. There were only the three young brothers, Ewen, Donald and Angus left at home to draw upon the meagre income of crofting and fishing. The girls being older had by now left home. John was silent as he saw my father's shoeless feet. My uncle Donald told me when I visited him in the 1950's, how John turned to my father and said,

' *'Se so geamhradh ma dheireadh, 'a theid thusa mach dh'an a chruach, as eughmhais brogan. Tha mi gealtuinn dhuit, 'n uair a thig mi dhachaidh a rithisd, bheir mi paithir bhrogan ur dhuit'* (This is the last winter that you will go out to the stack without boots. I promise that the next time I come home, I will bring a new pair of boots for you).

It was a nice sentiment and a sincere one no doubt. But more, this was a powerful reminder of the dark side of deprivation and what many would regard as the absence of the basic necessities of life. John was not able to visit his home in Glendale for several years after that. By the time he did, his youngest brother also had left home.

Separation

In the wonderful day of the motor vehicle and the jet-liner, when an ordinary person can leave Canada after supper and have breakfast in Scotland, it is hard to visualise the separation that distance caused between loved ones. Angus's father worked as foreman on the Mallaig Railway in the 1880's. Although the distance to his home and his family in Glendale was less than two hundred miles over sea and land, it required leave of absence from his work of three days to make the different steps of the journey by the connecting transport. The double journey therefore required almost a week of travel. No allowance for travel time was made in any holiday arrangement. And indeed, no holidays were built in to the system of labour. Furthermore should anyone absent himself from work, another was given his job. This included that of foreman, the position which my grandfather held.

My uncle Donald, when I visited him in the old family home, told me of these early days as I inquired about my grandfather. I knew little about my grandfather, except that he was an elder in the church, and was absent from home during much of the childhood of my father and the younger siblings. This visit was shortly after my father's death and I was conscious of this omission of information from my father also. It was as if the father of the younger boys was little known to them. Now my uncle Donald told me the explanation.

His father, John Angus MacKinnon, foreman on the Glasgow-Mallaig Railway project, was home only three times in nine years, to share a few days with his wife and family in Glendale. I repeat, for those who think of union contracts, or conditions of labour, this foreman could get home for a holiday to see his loved ones only three times in the space of nine years. And the distance was less than two hundred miles. Just think of that separation. It is true that my grandmother did go off several times to see her husband where he was working between Glasgow and Mallaig. But the little boys had only a very slight acquaintance with their father. My uncle Donald lingered over this theme, as I conversed with him, when he was then an old man in 1957. As we shared the memory together, and felt vicariously the pain endured by our forebears and the sacrifices they made to provide for their families, he spoke of a New Year occasion when his father was home on a visit.

Words spelt out the picture like the image appearing on the screen of our modern computer, as the keys are pressed. Here was the explanation. It was the second visit home for the father to see his children. And here before him was his youngest child, Angus, a little black-haired boy of seven years of age. His father holds young Angus at arm's length and looks at him. He draws his youngest son to his breast, a hand on the young boy's head. He holds him in this embrace, the child responding to his father in a wordless experience, that these things should not be. You could understand it if the father had been across the ocean thousands of miles away, or fighting with troops in some far corner of the Empire. But surely not this unnatural estrangement right there on the west coast locality in Scotland! There are no words that could describe the emotions of that fleeting exchange between a father and his little son, whom he had not seen for three years. And these momentary visits of a father to Glendale, meant that the young boys grew up, hardly knowing their father.

No wonder polarised capitalism has driven the working man to seek new answers in atheist socialism, and turn away from historic Christian orthodoxy! No wonder workers across the globe united to try and change the political system that not only permitted such cruel social and labour relations, but reinforced this by legislative coercion! No wonder millions have turned from the Christian religion to seek humanist answers when the inequities of society were stamped with the Church's approval and moral sanction! Even within the Church, ministers like George Macleod of Govan and the Iona

Community and James Currie were stirred in the inter War
years to think in terms of socialism in the face of the grim
redefined forms of slavery in the Glasgow industrial area. No
sentimental slush of pseudo-spiritual sublimity of thought
projected in benevolent poetry could hide the grim picture.
One thinks of Robert Browning's poem on the working girl
who had one day off from unrelenting drudgery in the silk
mill. Her joyful appreciation of the one day off, 'the holy
day' is beautiful. But it merely accentuates the contrast of the
industrial slavery of which she was at a young age already a
victim.

What wistful longings, what heartbreaking yearnings for
the Edenic joys of freedom in a world that the Creator
designed to be a habitat of joy. It does one good even to dwell
upon it, as Browning depicts the little girl skipping over the
hillside, picking daisies, her young voice singing sweetly in
unison with the singing of the lark.

> The year's at the spring,
> And the day's at the morn;
> Morning's at seven;
> The hill-side's dew-pearled;
> The lark's on the wing;
> The snail's on the thorn;
> God's in His heaven -
> All's right with the world.

(Pippa Passes 1.)

Here in my grandfather's case was a concentrated
instance of one man's situation, even as a foreman of a

working group of men. Multiply the situation and you have a powder keg of social/labour injustice. The tragedy is that the answers of atheist socialism in the extreme projection of political philosophy as Communism, exposed the flaws of human nature equally as evident as the structured Capitalism that it sought to replace. Political philosophy or any humanist-based formula for man's ills can never work. The rot is a spiritual deficiency, a bent projection of human perspective. Redemptive enlightenment from the Divine source of the Christian Revelation alone can effect a remedy. And that is the challenge of the Church both to advocate in words and to exemplify in action.

Chapter 6

Leaving Home

As the 19th century gave way to its successor, so much of that past way of life would also give way to the new age. This would be a motorised age, an age of momentous events, far beyond the dreams that filled the minds of many with unbounded optimism, and as different as night from day, in the nature of the predictions from pundits, in church pulpits, political platforms, or the polyglot voice of the up and coming 'newly educated' scientific age.

The new prophets were already swiftly replacing those of the traditional thinking in the intellectual world of church and state. There was a mass movement to relinquish the old with its premise of theistic thinking. In the new philosophy, people were fed with dreams of unlimited possibilities of a wonderful Utopia. Already the rose of scientific secularism was budding. The world waited for the petals to open. People were already intoxicated with the scent. Across the board, from the common man to the highest intellectuals, they anticipated a new day, a century of miraculous progress. This would not be just a second Renaissance, but such a basic giant leap into the future, that the glory of the original Eden of Adam and Eve would be established universally. And the dreamers, so gullibly believed by the masses, promised a vast improvement on that first effort of God himself. The crystal ball of the new sages promised that man would succeed where God failed.

The prophets of the new age had a simple theory. First you make the external environment into a place of beauty and prosperity. Then, so the reasoning went, the individual persons of mankind, *ipso facto,* by relating wholeheartedly to the products of the new form, would achieve the goal of happiness. This would be a collective of fulfillment, an automatic unthinking gift of man-made creation of secular science. Adam would be allowed to return to the Garden, without the nasty requirements of the 'sweat of his brow'. The work of God himself would be reversed, Man would get out of the hole himself. And already as the sign posts of Christian history were being taken down hurriedly, new ones in neon lighting accompanied by bewitching psychedelic music were being prepared for erection in their place.

There is no doubt that many subscribers to this view were sincere and also that there was some substance to the idea. Pragmatism is certainly more promising than idle 'idealism.' But a glance back over the past century shows that the leaders of the new secular thinking, and the army of lesser lights that became disciples presented a mirage as reality. The verdict on that retrospective glance at the 20th century where human genius and product met together, could well be that the latter represents a landmark in human history, staining it with shame. For the most powerful image is a record of achievement in the inventive genius of evil and the proving of its tenets in the research laboratory not just of Auschwitz and Belsen horror camps, but the selected theatres of war.

The 20th century could well be classified as the cemetery of secular hopes, with its record killing power of millions of men, women and children, using mindless, irrational detached, efficient, weaponry of cowardice in the new wars of the enlightenment, the secular age, the sophisticated century, the day that man kicked God himself in the teeth and took over the controls to create a super-society. In the new prospectus the machine would replace man, and the soldiers so detached from the concomitants of death, the sickening stench, the cry of the helpless, the collective carnage of civilians in whole cities and all so objectively expedited, that no conscience would condemn the killer. Killing one or millions by remote control, by the press of a button, gave a creative excitement to the new reign of the scientific and technological age, that would make the 20th century a monument to human disaster, or ominously a rehearsal for one greater to come.

When Angus MacKinnon, the young Highlander a century ago looked out on the world, like many people he had no idea that the world would go so far off track. Resilient optimism insists on illusions and he stepped off the edge of the old into a wider world, full of anticipation and for him a world in which he well knew that he would have to start the climb to success from the bottom rung of the ladder. He had no part in the intellectual revolution that would bring out the new formulas and translate the blueprints of the secular visionaries into the practical fulfillment of technological perfection. For him, the next decade would be a physical rather than an intellectual education. Yet this experience would not be lost on his receptive mind. No experience of life, even the apparently negative is without merit. Rather it becomes 'grist for the mill', where there is an ongoing resolution, and evolution of purpose related sensitively to the particular challenges and needs of our generation.

Like most young people, my father left home for seasonal employment. For this he looked to the herring fishing as it took place in turn right round the coasts of Britain at different times from spring to the fall, from Lerwick to Lowestoft. The fishing industry was in its hey-day in the late 19th century, and especially the seasonal harvest of the 'silver darlings', the herring, and contributed much to the survival of the family, in coastal towns and villages.

The boats were chiefly of the *zulu* type, which was a well- balanced sailing vessel. The full size was usually about seventy feet in length, with eighteen feet beam, and drawing eight feet in the water. The last of these, the Research, is preserved in the Scottish Maritime Museum in Fife. She was so streamlined in her under-water profile that it took relatively little horse-power to drive her hull, compared to that of a boat not built as a sailing vessel. In these full size boats, a single mast had its heel on the keelson not far from the stem. It rose through an elongated slot, when raised. In diameter the spar was about eighteen inches. A huge loose-footed lugsail had its tack at the stem. When the boat changed course, the top spar holding the sail was dipped to take round to the other side of the mast, hence the designation, the 'dipping lugsail.' To raise the mast and heavy sail, and to deploy ground tackle such as anchors, there was a windlass on the foredeck. This was driven by a steam donkey engine.

My father served as deckhand on such fishing boats for several seasons before and after 1900. He enjoyed this life. Like others he was contracted for a certain amount of money. If the boat did well, he received his money and was paid off. His brother Donald was working with his father one summer day on the Glasgow Mallaig Railway, when a familiar voice was heard, calling to him. It was my father. He had been only three weeks away at the East Coast herring fishing. The boat had been unusually 'lucky', and the West Highland youths had been paid off in full. It would take Donald a long time, working the standard twelve hours a day, at the manual work of building the railway, to make the same wages.

A Brush with disaster

While working during the West Coast herring season in the Minch the boats fished out of Stornoway. On one occasion my father left port aboard a full-size east coast boat. She was a Fifie. An earlier design and distinct from the zulu, she was equally powerful and very fast. The stem and the stern were vertical—in contrast to the zulu, where the stern swept downwards at an angle cutting off the heel. The later zulu had been conceived to obviate a tendency in the Fifie to be caught in a following sea and broach to. You can understand this as a following sea could catch the large expanse of the keel at the heel and throw the boat sideways.

On this occasion, a ferocious gale sprang up from the south west. The huge sail filled and drove the boat before the wind north-eastward. There was no hope of turning back nor indeed of entering a harbour. The only course followed at the time was to 'run before the wind' until the storm abated or the wind changed course. There were several boats, especially the full-size Fifies, that had presumably foundered as they were wheeled round sideways or 'broached to'. The key was to keep the boat before the wind and use the wideness of the ocean until the storm was over.

The boat passed Cape Wrath. The seasoned skipper knew the score and what he had to do and what he could not do. In order to make passage through the Pentland Firth, he would have to change from a starboard tack to a port tack, a deadly hazardous operation, with gravely predictable probable results. This he could not risk even trying in the vicious seas. Anyone who knows the ferocity of a howling wind and the way the sail presses against the mast, when a ship is running, knows also that it is nigh impossible to take down the sail. Just think how much more difficult to take down the huge heavy spread of canvas, all in one, that powered these big 70-foot boats.

The skipper chose therefore to run north east round Orkney and south of Sumburgh Head in the Shetlands and so into the North Sea. For two days, the storm continued and the boat sped onwards, the crew well aware that their lives were continually in peril. But they had a great skipper, a decisive one, who held to his resolution as they reached north towards the Lofoten islands. Then one morning, the wind lost its venom, the seas abated and with a change of wind, the fishing boat, turned south and west to make port in the harbour of Wick in Caithness.

A subtle change came over my father after this close call, this brush with death. That was not a quick flash of a warning light. That was a protracted experience of waiting for something to happen, in the timeless experience of the sea's fury. In such a trauma, for that it surely was, the individual sees life in a different perspective, from that of every-day life. It is one that brings to the consciousness the reality of spiritual values, the accountability all have to their Creator and the brief opportunity to fulfill life's mission and purpose, while we are spared on earth. In short, that experience triggered off cosmic rather than parochial thinking, that led my father to think of his Maker and consider what life was all about.

Chapter 7

Life in Canada

In 1908 my father joined the tens of thousands from Britain and the mainland countries of Europe, in the great ocean passage westwards, to seek a new life in North America. He was just twenty-three years old, with no learned skills for life, beyond the manual physical familiarity associated with sailing vessels and fishing boats, and the art of making a bare living on the Highland croft.

Montreal, that great city beckoned the new immigrant with its sparkling lights and matchless natural beauty. Here was the gateway to inland America, a thousand miles up the St. Lawrence River, with the unimagined magnitude of a whole continent stretching beyond across the vast central provinces of lake and prairie, not to mention, the Shield of the Rockies, opening onto another ocean, the perpetually blue Pacific. Montreal was the hub of the new colonial nation called Canada, still joined by the umbilical cord to her birth mother Britain with the sinews of commerce and trade. That is to face the reality by which the French were affected in face of the British Empire's dominance. Now the latter, at its zenith, would reign yet for a few short years and then race downwards in a graph of decline, like its predecessors in history. But the age of the new world had come, and immigrants crowded into North America to seek fulfillment and share in the excitement in this new virgin land of opportunity.

Montreal was the gateway to this new life in Canada. There was a continual traffic, excepting the ice recess in winter, where ocean ships loaded up at the long lines of docks and carried the wheat to ports all over the world. The city was a seething mass of volatile moving life. Tens of thousands of immigrants from Europe filled the streets. It was in effect a 'clearing house' for the recruits to the new nations of Canada and the United States. The turn of the century was unprecedented in the huge numbers that continually came across the ocean from Europe to the New World.

Young Angus easily found his place in the ever changing labour market, working at the docks. For apart from the wheat trans-shipments, there was a continual unloading of imports from the more established industrial world of Britain especially and the mainland of Europe in general. Here for a period he joined the crowds of newly arrived immigrants. Here was the Exchange, the great junction, for which hopefuls to the New World studied the next step forward, which would offer the best prospects in the fulfillment of their ambitions. The young Highlander was not alone also in that for a period he had his older brother Ewen with him, and there were many Gaelic-speaking countrymen, who found a new life in Canada and the United States.

Although there was a new freedom, this was more physical or geographic than social/economic. In fact, for the most part there was little autonomy. It is justifiable to say, that the New World was as stereotyped as that of the old. Options for new immigrants, apart from those with professional standing, or those with Colonial business connections, usually led them westwards. There they found their place as first generation Canadians and Americans in the labour- intensive work of farming, lumber and fishing, and the ever greedy vortex of large scale engineering projects, chief of which was the extension of branch or ancillary railways from the mainline arteries that crossed the continent from the Atlantic to the Pacific ocean.

For a while, my father engaged in fishing on the large schooners which reaped the rich stocks, especially of cod on the Grand Banks just south-east of Newfoundland. There was a basic division of labour on these famous fishing-boats, many of them about one hundred and thirty feet in length, the most famous of which would be the Bluenose of Nova Scotia almost synonymous with Maritime Canada. There was the ship's crew, manning the ship. Then there were the dorymen. The schooner carried dories each about twenty feet in length, fitting into each other on deck, like stacking chairs. The schooner was the mother ship which took the dorymen out to the fishing banks. Each day, given suitable weather the dories were launched, fished and brought back their catch to be salted and packed aboard the schooner. The Grand Banks had been the larder for Europe since the Middle Ages. The harvest of the sea was the counterpart of the harvest of the prairies, making Canada potentially one of the richest countries of the world. It is strange that a century later, in the international money market, Canada carries an enormous proportion of debt. A further anomaly is that the Maritime provinces, with such huge generic resources from the sea, are left far behind on the economic scale.

But we must go on. My father left Newfoundland and spent some time fishing in the Hudson Bay. He spoke to his children one evening long afterwards as they gathered round the open fire in the family sitting room of the manse in Aultbea.

'Tell us a story, Dad,' one asked. 'Tell us a story of your adventures in Canada long ago.'

And here he was shown an atlas used for school homework, showing the different provinces of the far-off Dominion. The memory lingers, the map with the contrasting colours and the bite out of the middle, the Hudson Bay. He smiled as the child's finger pointed to it and said slowly, 'alright', as his mind went back in time. We all waited for the mental mechanism just as modern children wait for the computer screen to respond to the program impulse on the keyboard. All eyes looked to him, willing him to bring out the excitement of the past, a past that he shared with multitudes in an earlier age and a very different one from that of the middle of the century now drawing to its close.

'Yes, I fished on a big schooner on the Hudson Bay. I made several trips. There's one trip I made that I'll always remember and it was my last.' And so he showed his children a word video of an adventure, where the pictures were graphically etched, with every animated nuance on the fertile and incomparably effective screen of their young minds.

There were Portuguese, Germans, Japanese and Norwegians as well as Scots, who comprised the crew. Inevitably this led to misunderstandings, because of language. Men just could not come to agreement on some particular point regarding the catch of cod they brought back to the mother ship in their dories. There was a dispute among several on deck. Others crowded round and it was clear that there was an alignment of compatriots. Tension built up, as the limited vocabulary of the newly adopted language failed to express any shades of compromise.

Suddenly men came to blows. There was a swift and explosive exchange. That was not necessarily a bad thing. It had the potential therapy of release, a crisis that called out for some solution, if not by compromise among the men, then by the final arbiter on a ship according to law, the captain. People often do this and after a while the air is cleared and a problem is addressed and solved amicably. It would be good if more disputes came to fisticuffs with this happy effect. And it would have been good if this were so on the deck of that fishing schooner on the Hudson Bay. Alas, the fight was unequal. Clearly bigger men were still on their feet, and others, in spite of pugilistic virtue, were felled to the deck.

An anxious face looked to Dad and a voice piped out with concern from one of the girls, 'Where were you, Dad; were you hurt?'

My father paused for a moment, maintaining the drama of the story, to give it out to his audience, slowly in instalments. Why, this was a break from homework, and Dad revelled in the role of the story-teller especially when he related first-hand experience. He then went on, 'I was standing back near the helmsman on the poop deck at the stern. You see I was part of the crew which sailed the ship, not one of the dorymen who fished. I recall it clearly. The sun was sinking in the west, its rays shining on the scene like a searchlight as men fought with one another. There was now an anger taking hold of the different nationals, especially

among those clearly at a disadvantage, whose compatriots had
been knocked down. The fight got ugly, with hard looks on
the men's faces, cold eyes and snarling sounds. Something
made me look towards a fallen man on the deck. He was
getting up, like a tiger crouching, about to spring on his
victim. The sun glinted on shiny metal in his hand. It was
the deadly blade of a knife. He had fallen, and lay near the
scuppers where there was a fishing knife used to gut the fish
when it was taken aboard the schooner from the dories. In a
moment he was on his feet. He lunged forward and thrust
the knife at his antagonist. In that moment, the whole scene
changed into a deadly fight. More knives like magic could be
seen in the hands of others. Size and strength were now not
the deciders, and the bigger men well knew it. They too turned
to knives as their weapons. Some men went down, big men
and small men. Blood spilled over the deck.'

'What happened then Dad. Were all the men dead?'

Dad broke the tension, looking at the children, and realising that consternation and distress were on their young faces.

'No, no,' he said. 'Just then, the skipper a weatherbeaten
old bearded sea-dog took out two longbarrelled colt pistols—
the same as cowboys have in the Wild West. He raised the
pistols and fired several shots in the air right over the heads
of the men. The fighters got a start. In a moment, the ship's
bo'sun, a huge Norwegian, with a face that showed the marks
of fights from which he had come out the winner, was now
at the scene. He grabbed two men by the neck with his huge
hands. He lifted them up and brought their heads together
with a crack, so that they fell like limp sacks to the deck. In a
moment it was all over. One and all came to their senses. The
skipper spoke to them as they stood there. All left, even those

with knife wounds. That night, the schooner, now full of fish, made for port.'

Thus ended one drama, an excerpt from the life story of young Angus from Glendale as he pursued his uncertain fortunes in the new land of Canada. And the children, their minds stimulated and relaxed, returned to their homework.

That was the last trip Angus made on the fishing schooners in the Hudson Bay. Like most immigrants, he decided to make his way westwards. The Canadian Pacific Railway now stretched across the continent from the Atlantic to the Pacific. Each day thousands of immigrants filled the rough railcars, many hitching an illegal ride—a tolerated infraction, excused in the pioneering atmosphere of development of the newly adopted land. Many of the rail-cars, loaded with wheat from the Prairies for the ships at Fort William, now called Thunder bay, went back west, empty, to cities like Winnipeg and Regina. Thus the youth from Skye found himself in mid Canada, in a strange new world for him, an inland environment, where the sea with its familiar though volatile and ever changing moods was far off. In place of this, all round was endless farmland or forest, both as seemingly wide as the ocean.

He now was united in part to his family, spending some time near Winnipeg, with his older sister Katie. She had come out to Canada as well and was married and settled down with a young family on a farm. Katie lived her life on the Prairies, like tens of thousands of immigrants who settled the western states of Canada, the rich wheatlands of Manitoba, Saskatchewan and Alberta. The wheatbelt was served by the trans-Canada railway. This was the backbone of the new country and the vital link that joined the country together as a nation, from Nova Scotia to British Columbia. It would be nearly half a century later before Newfoundland would severe links from Britain and merge with the other provinces to complete Canada's geographic territory.

Farm life did not appeal to Angus. He teamed up with his elder brother Ewen, joining him in the burgeoning city of Calgary, an exciting location with all the activities of a city at the frontier of a new age. Here he met many Highlanders. One of these a Lewisman told how he applied for a job on a huge ranch. Asked about his experience with horses, he answered that he knew them well. He was put on a horse in a paddock, the gate was opened and the unbroken stallion bounded out like a rocket with the Lewisman holding onto his back. He was found a quarter of a mile away bruised but alive. There was no sign of the horse. Oddly enough, in spite of this, he was given a job and became a top cowboy, before moving on to fresh pastures. It's only a Lewisman who could do this.

Ewen and Angus were very attached to each other and even though physically separated, kept in touch by correspondence. They separated after a while, each with his own vision of life goals, and the way these could be achieved. Ewen was artistic. He had an inventive talent and saw the growing industry of home improvement and servicing as a field of possible success. He took out several patents, and became a member of the Patentees of America, an association still extant in the 1970's, where his name is honourably recorded, but of course the patents have all run out. He had invented among others, a baking device, which was in production for many years before the Second World War and continues to be made in a modified form in the United States today. He had licensed several designs for the production of wallpaper for homes. He achieved some considerable success until the Depression that hit the West in the 1930's. From then on, he became disillusioned, and made his way across Canada eastwards, to take ship from Halifax, back to Scotland and his home in Skye to live with his widowed brother Donald. It turned out that he did not recross the Atlantic. While the train was stopped near Truro in Nova Scotia, Ewen heard voices outside the window of his carriage. He looked out and there saw a group of workmen. They were conversing in Gaelic. He was greatly taken aback. He called out to the men,

'Co as a tha sibh, agus sibhse 'cumal comhradh ann an cannan mo bhreith?' (*Where do you come from, you who are speaking the language of my birth?*)

One of the men paused and looked up to him, replying,

'Buinidh sinne do'n Eileann Ceap Bhreatuinn mu thuath. Tha sinn an a so ag obair air a rathad iaruinn. Co as a tha sibh agus c'ait am bheil sibh dol? Gabh mo leisgeul, a faighneachd.' (We belong to the island of Cape Breton to the north of here. We are working on the railway track. Where are you from and where are you making for? Pardon me for asking.') The man's name was Rory MacNeil from Iona, Cape Breton. He related the story of my uncle Ewen, my father's brother, to me in 1972.

The end result of that meeting was that Ewen joined the workmen when they returned to Cape Breton. There he lived on, happily merging into the Gaelic speaking community from Catholic Iona to Presbyterian Little Narrows. He built a little house near MacKinnon's Harbour at Ottawa Brook. He was made to feel welcome with Highland hospitality in every home right to River Denys, homes of such families as that of the Kennedys and MacKenzies and Camerons in River Denys; Calders and MacKinnons and Gillies's in Orangedale; MacDonalds and Kennedy's in Alba, MacLeods and MacDonalds in Estmere; Mathesons and Ross's, MacIvers, Nicolsons and MacKinnons among others in Little Narrows. He was respected and liked by all the people. Sadly, being troubled with deafness, he was struck down by a train at the Alba crossing near Orangedale in 1949 at the age of 67. He is buried in the churchyard at Little Narrows. His funeral service was conducted by the Presbyterian minister, the noted Gaelic-speaking Rev A.D. MacKinnon, DD. By this strange turn of Providence, Little Narrows would become from then on, to the MacKinnon family from Glendale, as a kind of second home, a counterpart in the new land of Canada.

Angus, now in his mid-twenties, joined a party of immigrants, for the most part from Europe, working with them, laying the branch lines of thousands of miles of rail track, the feeder lines of the central arterial railway line from the east coast to the west coast of Canada. In this capacity, he contracted along with others to work, laying track, felling trees, building bridges, in the whole process of providing the necessary network of transport for a viable commercial economy, where there was fusion between the vast agricultural resources and the urban centres that serviced them. In direct ratio to the implementation of this process, could Canada thrive and prosper, in meeting the insatiable appetite for grain, primarily in Europe, and the world at large. He worked intermittently, as all construction workers in Canada did, subject to the constraints of a climate of hard cold winters and short warm summers. He spoke in later years of this period of his young manhood in Canada, before the Great War.

Several hundred men worked on a stretch of railway. It was always outward from a town centre. Thus rails, ties and all supplies for the workers' camps were brought forward as the rail line progressively was extended. As a rule all went well, as the work party met the corresponding one from the other location.

On this particular occasion the winter was coming on. There was no work party, working its way to meet them. In anticipation of stopping work on the section, the supplies were already loaded on the cars to take them back. Whether by intent or by accident, the steam engine left with the cars, leaving the work party behind. The labour force chose to walk rather than wait, and led by some who thought they could reach a town, over a hill and therefore by a shorter route, they set off. The journey lay over the hill, but one valley after another appeared for them to cross and one hill escarpment after another. They walked through forest and over the ground now hardening with an early winter frost. At last snow lay on the ground. There was no shelter from the cold and no food for the three hundred men. My father several times later in life retold the story of that great trek, each of the three days, covering about sixty miles. There could be no loitering. Winter was every night tightening its viselike grip. They stayed alive relying upon the few tins of corned beef carried in their packs.

At night wolves howled continually. Bears could be seen prowling, their black coats making them visible in the early morning. At first the men travelled, close together, giving all a sense of collective security. Then the column lengthened.

Some, the stronger moved forward at a greater pace; the weaker ones began to lag behind. This was a formula for trouble.

Wild animals, the wolves and the bears boldly dogged the stragglers, as they struggled to keep up with the column. Then it happened. It was evening. The sun had set. They were skirting round a forest and had almost cleared it. The pace had quickened as lights of the township ahead now began to appear. My father was in the middle of the column. He heard a murmur of men speaking out spontaneously in European languages. He looked back and saw a scene that stayed vividly in his memory, for the rest of his life.

A straggler had faltered as they were leaving the forest behind. Just then a large black bear came loping out of the woods, coming directly towards the men at the rear. Everyone who could, hurried forward for fear of their lives. The straggler just couldn't make it. His hands reached forward and a cry filled the air, the desperate cry of helplessness. Everyone froze on their feet as they witnessed the animal pick up his victim and carry him off into the darkness of the forest. There was a sense of utter futility, as they could do nothing to help. By midnight the column reached the town. The great trek was over. It had claimed one human victim. On the positive side, had the winter unleashed the fury of an early snowstorm, the loss of human life could have made this a far greater tragedy

My father spent some time in the growing city of Calgary. On its outskirts it had the air and smell of the Wild West but already at the centre tall spires and blocks of commercial buildings were in evidence. The Highland youth from Glendale did not tarry there for long. Perhaps, born to the sea, it was natural for him to reach westwards to the Pacific coast. Eventually he arrived in the new bustling city of Vancouver. Into this city, still in its infancy, but dynamically alive, in the huge export business of Canada's natural riches of timber, fish, wheat, and mining products, Angus came, finding work in the warehouses of the port. He also worked at the extensive lumber yards where massive trees, the best of hardwoods from Canada's virgin forests were being exported to countries like Japan. My father worked in this one-way trade for several years. His forte was in securing the massive timbers for lifting and loading on ships. It thus carried responsibility as well as personal risk. The skills learned back off the British coasts in the big zulus, and his experience on the schooners on the Grand banks and on the Hudson Bay, served to make him a key man in the movement of the massive logs. Later in life he would speak of this period and the comparative relaxed life of a working day, exercising his skills as the foreman slinger.

Having a regular occupation and an orderly routine, he now turned his thoughts to the city about him. There was a large complement of Gaelic speaking Highlanders in Vancouver. It was natural for him to meet them, and the Free Church was the chosen weekly location of sharing the fellowship of their heritage and worshipping in the language of their birth. In the course of a relatively settled life for several years, my father was drawn more and more into the spiritual stream of the church's life. The seed sown in child-hood germinated in the atmosphere of his adopted city. For truly, his attachment to Vancouver became a lifelong one, after he was to leave it. Life here became a school of experiences. He had been transplanted from the nursery of his birthplace and now was being continually enriched, far beyond the physical parameters that curtailed his growth and development within the structured limitations of old Scotland, and especially the Highlands and Hebrides.

Chapter 8

Spiritual Focus

Now the Spirit of God spoke to this young exiled *Daileach* (native of Glendale), so that his perspective matured with spiritual understanding. Now grace, saving grace, visited his heart, through the orderly communication of the dynamic Word. Already much of the latter was ingrained in the cells of his photographic memory and as the Spirit flowed into his mind, all the memories of godly servants of Christ, all the treasured recollections of his parents' prayers at family worship, the supplications of his spiritually-minded mother, heard as she knelt at the Throne of Grace—all these caused the soul to thirst, to hunger for living truth. And the Spirit did its work in the heart. So that now the soul of this young man was satiated with fatness, the meat and drink of the Living Bread, the central resource of Mercy from the Redemptive Work of Christ and His Saving Sacrifice on the Cross.

Now his poetic nature, with its heightened sensitivity, hungry for the inner peace that only the forgiving love of the

Heavenly Father can bestow on a wayward son, caused him
to respond to the dynamic overtures of Mercy. Grace for the
soul is like good food for the body. It will not 'keep'. This
has a three-fold effect. The soul must be fed every day on
Christ; the soul therefore can be filled with the joy of
spiritual food; the soul does not need to worry, or be
restrained, as it feeds and drinks abundantly from the
heavenly provisions that we call grace.

Thus young Angus MacKinnon found a new identity, or
should we say, a renewed identity. The beauty of holiness in
the mirrored image of the Saviour produced in him a
transformed nature. He now saw his life in a new perspective. He saw the broken pieces that needed to be put together,
rebuilt to the design of heaven so that his life could be used
for the purposes of his Maker. Brought up in the God-fearing
community of his childhood, the highest Christian virtues
instilled in his mind as 'man's chief end' in order to 'glorify
God and enjoy Him forever', he now had a first-hand
experience of that dynamic change, by which the meaning of
life is found in spiritual realization.

Round about him, men's lives fell apart as they lived for a
day, and made shipwreck because they had no spiritual
purpose to integrate the different faculties of their being, and
synchronise their energies in a dynamic unity and singleness
of purpose.

We mentioned that my father was a born poet. Reserved
by nature and humble by disposition, he would rarely speak
of his own personal experience of saving grace. But the poet
in him would not be suppressed and he now gave singularly
exquisite expression to his own spiritual encounter with His
Lord and his return to the bosom of his Heavenly Father's

forgiving love, in that avenue of poetry.

Secular poetry fades in comparison, when the art of verse delineates the unseen spiritual motions of the soul in its transactions with heaven. Words, prosaic and ordinary, take wings as thoughts of the incomparable love of God are caught in the poetic language of human communication. Can one say that no language on earth touches the sublime as does the language of the Gael? It is illustrated vividly in the poem that the recruit to Christ's service now composed, under the title of *Mac Stroghail*, the Prodigal Son.

You may recall, when a little child, naively taking an armful of peats from a neighbour's peatstack nearby, my father expressed his contrition and conviction when upbraided, by answering a question in verse. Now, with his soul exercised in all the agony of conviction of sin, yet brought to a saving assurance of Christ's redeeming love, he encapsulates his testimony in a poem of dynamic and exquisitely beautiful content.

Am Mac Stroghail

1 'Se dhol do thir na fadachd as, thug creachadh air mo mhaoin;
'Se 'n truaillidheachd 'san d' ghabh mi tlachd, dh'fhag mi am mhac na daors'
Do bhrigh mo lochd tha mi ro bhochd, 's le ocras a dol aog,
Gun sunnd gun sult a measg nam muc,'sa feitheamh air am plaosg.

2 Dh' iarr mi mo mhaoin air m'athair graidh, 'ce dh'fhag sud e rium an gruaim,
Dh'fhag mi dachaidh bheartach bhlath, far nach robh cas no cruas,
Bha m' anamiann ag iarraidh sath, bho nithe graineal truagh,

Thug mi gu lar fo smag mo namh, 'sgu dorsa bais is uaigh.

3   Eiridh mi 's theid mi air m'ais, a dh aideachadh mo bhron,
Le colunn ruisgte is poca lom, 'sgum bhonn agam am' dhorn,
C'arson a bhiodh mo chridhe fann, 'smo chnamhan gann do fheoil,
'Sgu leoir ra sheachnadh aig gach am, aig m'athair na thigh stor.

4   Mu'n d'thainig mi do m' athair dluth, chunnaic a shuil mo chas,
'Snam codhail ruith, is phog e mi, 'sna ghlachdadh mise dh'fhaisg,
An aite corruich bhi na ghnuis, se bh' innte ciuin is blaths,
Is fhuair mi deagh-ghean 'n aite diomb, is gabhail rium na ghradh.

5   Dh'iarr e culaidh dhomh a mach, bu taitnich' bha   'na bhuth,
Is rinn e maiseach mi gun dail, le fann 's brogan ur.
Is fhuair mi sath de'n fheoil a bearr, de'm bheil am faileadh cur,
S'bidh mi gu brath le aoidhean graidh ag ardachadh a chliu.

Translation:

The Prodigal Son

1   'Twas going to a distant land, that robbed me of my wealth
Taking pleasure in a low life made me destitute.
My sin has made me poor, with hunger, like a skeleton,
Without cheer, without joy, left among the swine, waiting for their husks.

2   I asked my inheritance from my loving father, and that left me melancholy.
I left my rich warm home, where there was no hardship or want.

My negative desires craved satisfaction from reckless and
ignoble sources.
I was brought to rock-bottom, enslaved by my enemy,
And reached the doors of death and the grave.

3   I shall arise and return, confessing my sorrow
I'll go shame-faced, with empty purse, and nothing in my
bag.
Why should my heart be faint, my bones now stripped of flesh,
And always an abundance in my father's store!

4   Before I reached my father, his eye took in my straits,
He ran to meet me, kissed me, his arms about me close.
In place of anger on his face, was only calm and warmth.
Instead of wrath, he showed goodwill, embraced me in his
love.

5   He ordered out a coat, most pleasing in the store.
He dressed me up without delay, with ring on hand and shoes
on feet.
And I was filled with best of fare, the richest flavours known.
And I'll forever sing God's praise with all the guests of love.

About the year 1912, my father was working in a lumber
yard where large timbers were being loaded from railcars.
The work was dangerous, as logs were wet from months of
lying in rivers after felling in the forests in the upper hinterland
of the province. The work of the 'slinger', the traditional
name given to my father's job, though similar in principle,
lacked the refinements and safeguards that have been made
possible through more modern technology. For instance, the
communication between the winch operator and the slinger

was by visual signals. Today the same is helped by precise and explicit vocal exchange on portable radio. Further, the cranes used early in the century were in their infancy and were driven by steam winches, a less precise and controlled power than geared electric motors. Not only so, but now with electrical power, the slinger controls the lift precisely himself with a remote control which is operated in his hand, like a cellular phone.

It happened one day as my father was working that, for some reason, the rope on the pawl of the capstan slipped momentarily, causing the load to jerk in the air before the lift continued. That was enough for a wet log to come loose and fall to the ground. An end hit the ground. But the other hit my father on the head, felled him to the ground and the heavy log came to rest across his back.

The accident caused him to be badly injured, so that he could not continue physical work. Given nominal compensation, he left Canada and returned to the family home in Skye. There he settled, the youngest of the family, with his widowed mother. On a visit to Glendale in the 1950's, uncle Donald showed me the small shop with the counter which his young brother operated for a very short time. Alas, he was not a success in his business venture. In any case the scene on the wider stage of life was swiftly changing. A voice was beckoning him to leave the old declining past and find his way in the new. Already, within him, intellectual and spiritual dynamics called out to be given precedence.

Nations were on the brink of war. Western society in the pampered exclusiveness of the privileged and rich, was being already cracked by a new radicalism. This could be seen politically in the first appearance of the Labour movement as a party at Westminster. Technology, with potential gain for the masses, stood at the door of the new century, impatiently waiting its chance to throw out the obsolete cumbersome machinery of a past age of economic and social drudgery.

An economic interpretation of the Great War did not exclude the need for an explosion of international violence to break the steely grip of the old imperial feudalism of Europe. Within forty years and two outbursts of total war, the high felt top hat and the white lace mutch, the everyday symbols both of class and servitude would vanish before an avalanche of social change and revised conventions of a new egalitarian society. This would be like a store swinging its doors wide open and inviting one and all as the big stores do, to rush in and grab bargains in a 'first come, first get' mêlée of pretended equal opportunity.

The Call to the ministry

Personally, my father had already reached a new maturity. Now he saw before him a life where the spiritual commands of God were leading to the full-time ministry. The inner work of grace made a lasting impression upon his life. In turn, this called for expression in service to his generation. With the poet's eye he saw graphic images of God's work, rescuing, redeeming, seeking, finding, those who once were lost and were strangers to heavenly things and the glorious blessings of the children of God. He saw himself as an alien, chosen and brought by the elective will of God, to become a citizen of heaven, and given to be filled as a vessel of honour for the Master's use. Already he conducted services as a lay preacher and was favoured with much acceptance on the part of his hearers wherever he preached. Quiet, humble and unassuming by nature, he had a receptive disposition. With this, people saw in him a sympathy, a face of kindness and a seeming limitless compassion. Thus those in any distress of mind or soul could relate to him and draw out from him the comforts that were sent from heaven and disbursed to needy recipients through the distribution and exposition of the Word.

Chapter 9

My Father's Family

Like many families in the Highlands, my father's brothers and sisters had to leave home and make their way in the wider world. Here we speak of a few of my father's siblings and events relating to them.

John, the Captain

A telegram arrived from John, the eldest of the family, asking my father to meet him in Glasgow. John had risen to become a captain of a large ship. He had served throughout the War since 1914, having been torpedoed twice, losing two ships, but so far his life had been spared.

My father went to Glasgow, and they spent a full happy day together in a mini-family reunion at the home of their sister Annie, who had married a Raasay man called Donald Nicholson. Later in life my father spoke of that memorable day of shared happiness, a fleeting interlude of family fellowship, in the midst of conflict and uncertainty. The usually tough steel-like sea captain appeared to have a special gentleness and warmth that the others had not known before.

It is true that as the youngest, my father hardly knew his eldest brother as there was a long age gap between them. When the day was over the two brothers took leave of each other at the Central Railway Station, where John would take the train south and return to his ship in Southampton. John, who was a man of few words, now said,

'Angus, I wanted to see you this time. I wanted to know you for a little while as we scarcely knew each other before now. Mother told me in her letters about you and the change in your life. I want you to speak to mother and to all the rest of the family.'

The big, rather stern, uniformed captain paused, and then went on, 'I want you to tell them that all is well with John. It's tough going, with the E-boats like sharks, lurking under the sea, waiting for us, night and day. It's been going on now for three years. You understand, I've been in the water twice, with two ships going down under my command.'

Again he paused, the strained face softening as a wistful note came into his speech. He went on, 'I'll not see you again. I'll not be coming back from this trip. I feel inside that I won't make it.' Again a pause. His eyes turned to his youngest brother. My father told me long afterwards, that there was a kind of shining in that look from his brother, a kind of serenity, as if inside, his soul was already seeing another world, a better one, a very different one from the harsh rigour and cruel treachery that was his lot to face from the newly conceived evil inventions of war that now stained humanity. He went on softly in the Gaelic tongue, 'Tell mother, when the news comes, that I have rest in my heart, and my soul is at peace with God.'

They parted, a strange new gentleness linking them

together. This was a spiritual bond, a union greater than that
of the physical. It was something spiritual, that reflected their
membership of a greater family, those whose destiny was
sealed in Christ and whose possession was life eternal as
citizens of the commonwealth of 'Israel' and the household
of faith.

True enough, John's ship was torpedoed in the English
Channel. This was the third time his ship was torpedoed. All
the officers and crew got away as the merchant ship listed.
All except Captain MacKinnon.

Sequel

In 1958, while I was worshipping at a service in Leith, an
elderly Highlander introduced himself to me at the close of
the service. He would then be well into his seventies. When
he had confirmed my identity, he said he wanted to tell me a
story about his early life. The two of us made our way, on
foot, up Leith Walk, the long avenue that leads from Leith to
the city of Edinburgh. Usually I would board a tramcar. But
this veteran Highlander, who by his Gaelic speech and accent,
was clearly a native of Skye, was precise and decisive, as he
said, 'We'll walk. I want you to hear this.' I record his story
as best as I can.

He began with these words. 'I was mate on the three
ships that were commanded by your uncle John. We shared
nearly four years together, crossing the Atlantic and made
several trips to Saigon and Singapore in the far East for
cargo and especially rubber. (There were no synthetic tires
then, all was made from grown rubber trees in the plantations.)
It was near the end of the War.

'This third ship was more of an old tramp steamer, with

an open wheelhouse. We had left Southampton and were running down the Channel, the English Channel. We had passed the Casquets and the Channel Islands and as we were about to turn to port to clear Brest, suddenly without warning, the torpedo hit us. It struck amidships. Then a second one hit us further aft. It came right through the hull and exploded at the ship's boiler. The night was now on us and we knew that it was the end of our ship. She shuddered and a roar of steam and rushing water could be heard as we peered down from the bridge. There was no panic. We saw the silhouette of the enemy submarine some distance away. She was on the surface watching her victim in its death throes. The deck lurched to lee under us so that we were almost hanging over the canvas covered rail of the bridge. The captain, your uncle, calmly gave orders. Within one minute, two lifeboats in the davits on the lee had the 'falls' loosed. There was a command from the captain to those crowding near the third lifeboat still in its davits. I heard him say clearly, 'Cut the falls!' The lifeboat dropped into the water, I remember, with scarcely a splash, as the sea was now coming over the gunwale. I saw the boats pull away to avoid getting trapped as the ship would inevitably overturn.

'What should I do? I thought. The answer came from your uncle. He turned to me for a moment only. There was something noble in his face, the true Highlander who left the Hebridean hamlet in Glendale, and rose to be captain of his ship. But there was no sentimental softness in the tone of his voice as he spoke in an unmistakable command, 'Falbh thus', a Dhomh'll. A nis.' (You go, Donald. Now.) By the tone of his voice, this was an order. I ran down the ladder and threw myself out into the sea and swam away from the sinking vessel. I was picked up and found myself in a lifeboat. I turned my eyes towards the ship.' Here the old man paused. He could not speak. Emotion welled up as he sought to compose himself.

'Yes,' he went on, ' I saw him still standing on the bridge. He was scanning the deck below as if looking for any of his crew that might still be there. It was the last time I saw him on earth. Within moments, the ship overturned, right over so that the keel could be seen. The bow followed the stern as the ship dived backward and went under. There was nothing but a faint outline of a whirlpool of water, with the gurgling of swirling eddies.

'We waited for a while. Then we rowed the lifeboat back and fore in the dark. But your uncle had gone done with the ship. He was the last man on the ship as she sank, and he could not get away, this third time that we were torpedoed.'

The old man had finished. We had been walking up Leith Walk. Soon we would come onto the great bright lighted world thoroughfare of Princes Street in the beautiful city Edinburgh, with its Greek-columned public buildings and its unfinished landmark of half-built monument on the Calton Hill, flood-lit high above us.

The old Skyeman, stopped and turned to me and said. 'I always wanted to tell someone of your family about this. I know your own father is now dead, but I am very glad that I was able to see you and tell you.' He paused again, and then went on, 'I want you to know this. I count it a great honour to have served under the command of your uncle. He could have gone on to greater things, if he had lived. He was a born leader of men.'

We parted. Thus one more chapter was closed for me,

regarding my father's immediate family.

A man called Peter

The second oldest of the boys was Peter. He became an inspector in the police force in Argyll. I met him only once. He was retired then in 1947 and in fact, bedridden, having had a stroke—a common family affliction. I was taken there by my sister Rachel. My uncle kept looking at me, repeating, '*Gille Aonghais, mac Aonghais.*' 'Angus's boy, Angus's son.'

His son Kenneth became the youngest chief constable in Scotland, and successfully steered the crisis in the militant demonstrations against the American nuclear submarines being stationed in the Gareloch on the Clyde. True to the family trait of peacemaker and diplomat, there were no fatalities nor even injuries in the many confrontations between the Protesters and Police, at the gates of the Gareloch base. Compare that with the many confrontations since across the world, like that in the United States against the Vietnam War where many students were slain by police, and the grim toll of human life when the Chinese army cleared Tiananmen Square with gunfire.

Donald

Donald was the next youngest to my father. He lived his life, for the most part, in the merchant service as a seaman in coastal shipping. He was in touch with my father and our family off and on throughout his life until he died. Losing his young wife in childbirth, he followed the sea as his profession for many years. His one daughter, Mary Ann, married Donald MacKenzie, a childhood sweetheart, living next door in Shiadar. They made their life in Glasgow, but

especially since retirement, continue to spend several periods
of the year in the old family home in Skye. On a visit from
Canada in the spring of 1996, my wife Mary and I had a
wonderful time meeting them. I have to include here for the
record an account of a 'crisis' that occurred an hour after
reaching the quiet usually undisturbed peace of the hamlet,
now invariably designated as Galtrigil, by the Postal
authorities. The name Shiadair is officially dropped to avoid
confusion with another hamlet of the same name in Uig. I
relate it as it happened.

Next door was Donald's brother John, and his good wife
Chrissie. They also were home from Glasgow for a holiday.
The day was beautiful, the sky a deep blue decorated with a
few frills of little white clouds. It was warm and dry. It was
ideal weather for the traditional season of 'heather burning'
which took place all over the Highlands. The reason for it
was to burn the heather so that the grass would grow for the
sheep. John had seen fit to set fire to some grass round his
house—a kind of easy substitute for mowing. The fact is that
there was no lawn mower in the village and never had been.
That is a new invention in the long list of expensive 'musts'
that the new age demands that people buy, to keep the whole
economic cycle turning. In the Highlands, sheep were used
to keep the grass down, right up to the front door of the
crofthouse. On reflection John could have used a mower this
glorious day. But then, all would have missed the excitement.

We had not previously met John and Chrissie. Now we
did, and without any time for conventional courtesies. Within
minutes of our arrival at the old family home, the excitement
began. My cousin, Mary Ann, heard a shout. We rushed out.
The grass fire at our neighbour's house on the other side of

the road had spread through a fence. The slight breeze from the south west was blowing gently, but firmly. The fire was catching the heather. A line of crackling flames was reaching out in a widening arc up the hill and in the direction of other homes on the other side.

John was trying his best to join up a long hose from the tap in the house, to try and extinguish the flames. Chrissie was on her way across to ask for help. The law in these circumstances is not to panic. Panic, and you get calamity. Fire brigades were a distant hour long answer, if you could round up the volunteer crew to come from Dunvegan. I could hardly believe what was happening. We had arrived, for a quiet interlude, away from the madding crowds and the trauma of incessant noise and activity in the feverish modern world. And here, in Glendale in the uttermost corner of north west Skye, clouds were filling the sky and flames were hungrily licking up the heather, clearly intent on making for the township of Skinnidin and the rest of Borreraig.

Gaelic punctuated the sound of the wind, and blended into the air itself in a musical mixture of excited concern and suggested solutions. A twofold strategy was at once pursued. The hose was 'man-handled' by the dynamic feminine pair, Mary Ann and Chrissie, neither of them physical weaklings and both with irrepressible assertive personalities. One would have to say that they were a match for any man. Their part was to unroll coils of two long hosepipes from the house to the 'front line' where the enemy was steering its way round every rocky outcrop in the uneven escarpment behind John's home. There was a continual exchange of Gaelic comments and advice. There was some difficulty connecting the hose to the tap but this was overcome. But this method of fire-fighting, dousing the line of flames was clearly too slow, and too feeble. Steam would rise and flames burst out again, time after time, fanned by the breeze.

There was a continual chorus of questions, from Chrissie and Mary Ann. 'What will happen? What are you going to do, John? What are you doing, Donald? It was all in Gaelic, a kind of long distance exchange as Donald and John were trying to dowse the flames. These were moving further up the hill. It looked as if outside help would be needed. I heard one call, 'It's getting away. We'll have to phone Dunvegan and get the firemen. '

I heard an answer from John, *'Na can sin. Cha bhi feum air.'* (Don't say that. There will be no need of it). *Agus co-dhiubh, cha neil gin duibh aig an tigh an drasd.'* (And in any case, none of them are at home just now)

The two men, now retired, John and Donald, had shovels and were beating out the line of flames, each with a stretch of what was nothing less than the war front. My holiday was changed into a full working day. A shovel was thrust at me. There could be no malingering, no excuses. Everyone, able-bodied or not, had to pitch in. My section was up at the top of the hill behind John's and Chrissie's house. This would have been about a hundred and fifty metres long. I had to stop the enemy from spreading at all costs. The imperative in a case like this, is to quickly assess the situation. The method of beating out the flames is a proven one. Success would come by finding the right pace so that you could go on without tiring. If you rushed, you would be exhausted and fail. If you found the right pace, you simply continued at that ongoing pace. This tactic, namely dowsing the flames with the shovel at an even pace, was followed. For the most part, everyone was occupied. The note of alarm gave way to a quiet exchange of helpful comments and encouragement, with here and there an extra piece of advice. There was one moment which could qualify as the exception.

I had to stretch forward over a high rock to beat the flames in nests of grass and heather. Below me was a big drop of about thirty feet to the road. As I reached over, Chrissie saw me. She was standing below on the road. Chrissie was somewhat upset that I, whom she had not met formally or informally before this, presumably a soft visitor from abroad, should get this reception in Galtrigil, being rushed into a crisis and put to work, even before she had made my acquaintance. With true Highland courtesy and reserve, she could not bring herself to call me by my first name, although the others were using it of me all the time. Chrissie like all of the women there, has an irrepressible animation. Even the heather burning crisis could not keep her down. She now added to it all, when she spotted me. Her voice was directed up to me in grave concern.

''Thoir an fhaire; tha feagal orm; tha'n aite sin cunnartach, Maighstir MacFhionghuin. Bhroinean! Tha mi'n dochas nach tuit sibh.'

(Take care, I'm apprehensive; that is a dangerous place, Mr. MacKinnon. Dear me! I hope you don't fall.')

I thought I had been handling the situation very well up to that point. But suddenly seeing Chrissie's upturned face full of anxiety, coupled with the powerful intonations of her expressed concern, magnified tenfold in the Gaelic, I wobbled, almost overbalancing, as my foot slipped. For a moment it was touch and go. I almost lost my balance. I say almost. I could well have hurtled down, possibly only with Chrissie to break my fall. I quickly composed myself and assured her that all was well. At the same time I retreated from the edge as fast as I could.

It was nearly two hours before the All Clear sounded. The crisis was over. We all retreated into John and Chrissie's house for a rest. There Mary and I were officially introduced. It was deemed timely to partake of some Highland refreshment. Truly, though our acquaintance was brief, we all felt we had been friends for a lifetime.

And what has that to do with my father and his life, you ask? Yes, this. As I sat down to restore my equilibrium after the crisis, I was also sitting in the house of 'Ceit Alais,' for whom my father brought home the minister's sermon, word for word, repeating it from memory, a long time previously.

What a joyous visit that was for me to cross the ocean and meet my relatives and touch again, however briefly the roots of my *sloinneadh*, my clan name. In the hands of my cousin Mary Ann, the old MacKinnon home, all spruced up, extended and modernised, seems destined to be an enduring source of joy and holiday renewal, barring calamity, for another hundred years.

A Close Call for brother Donald

My uncle Donald told me this story about his own life when I was visiting him in 1957 in Skye where he was then retired and happily content in the old family home. He told me how once he was on a ship leaving Newcastle-on Tyne. It was dark and raining, a winter's night. He was working on deck, putting the heavy hawsers or ropes in order at the stern. These warps had been used when the ship was tied up while loading a cargo of coal at the pier. Now, there was a loop of rope hanging over the side. All was slippery and wet, with the temperature on the freezing mark. The rope would not come inboard. He leaned over the gunwale to free it. Somehow when he stretched, his body slipped over the smooth ice-glazed rail near the stern. In moments, he toppled helplessly overboard and found himself struggling for his life in the dark and cold of the winter sea. When he surfaced, his ship had gone. No one was there when he had fallen over. It might be some considerable time before his absence was noticed, so that he was now left to his own resources. Just think of it, a fully clothed man in the oily and filthy waters of the Tyne on a dark winter's night. He had fallen overboard in the middle of the channel. Now there was a double danger. He had to struggle for his life to stay afloat, but he also had to face the grim challenge of avoiding being run down by one of the big ships that continually passed up and down the seaway. Two hours later, he was still in the water. He was now well down stream from where he fell in. He was trying to pull in from the central lane but the current kept taking him back. Every ship that passed was a threat to his life, as he feared he would be run down. A ship was slowly making its way upstream. The captain had difficulty keeping a course as the vessel was empty. Donald could hear the huge propeller thrashing the water at the stern. It was half out of the water and the blades scarcely getting a grip of the water.

He was near the end of his resources and he knew it. Soon he would be in the estuary of the dark swift industrial river, the Tyne where the river broadened as it met the incoming sea, and rough water. On the other hand, this ship was very close to him. Its bow was turned in to the centre of the Channel and the captain was trying to get the bow round so that it would again face upstream.

At this point Donald found himself near a Channel buoy. No sound came from the steam engine as it turned over the propeller, thrashing the water. He felt that as the stern came nearer and nearer to him, he would shortly be drawn into the lethal motions of the propeller. In a wave of last minute desperation, he opened his mouth and cried out. Men were at the time looking over the gunwale, peering at the buoy. A search light was shining on the buoy. When he cried, the light moved and crossed over him in the water several times. He raised his hand and cried once more. The searchlight returned slowly this time and stopped right on him. My uncle Donald recalled that moment, the light shining on him and blinding him. He was a reserved man, but that moment was marked on his mind forever. His life was spared. He was taken up out of the dark greedy river, his body blackened by the filth of the busy channel, one of the busiest in the world, linking the coal capital of Britain, if not of the world, Newcastle-on-Tyne, by an endless traffic of colliers to every country, near and far.

It is strange, but one apparently negative factor was really a blessing. His whole body was covered in black coal dust. But the water was an oily liquid. This served to coat his body with an insulating cover, which kept out the cold. This could well have been the deciding factor in his survival on that dark winter's night.

Life had been hard for him from the beginning. He was married to his young wife for only three months when he was parted from her as he went off to sea again. She died in childbirth. When he returned, it was to stand at her grave in the historic old cemetery in Dunvegan near the castle, the seat of the MacLeods. His life at sea gave him little opportunity to see much of his little girl, Mary Ann, as she grew up in the home of a relative until she was seventeen years. When he told this story to me long after it happened, it seemed as if he felt that God's love did not exclude him and as he looked back to that incident when the searchlight found him in the water, he linked it to the saving mercy of Jesus, the Light of the World.

Note on Katie in Canada

One last glance at my father's sister, Katie, who had emigrated to live her life out on a farm on the Canadian Prairie. There she raised a family. In the 1950's a young pretty nurse, a grand-daughter, came over to Scotland and made herself known to her relatives. We have now given the background of my father's life, his experiences in his youth. We have included glimpses of contemporary life and took the liberty of relating these to events in their historical setting, in the background of my father's life. To some these may be regarded as digressions. We chose to see them as necessary concomitants of his progression through the years to maturity and his preparation for his life work. Our inclusion of short biographical notes on his sisters and brothers, seems natural for they surely are not separate from the life portrait of their youngest brother.

Chapter 10

First World War

Angus MacKinnon was just under thirty years of age when he joined the British army at the outbreak of the Great War in 1914. Physically he was immensely strong and healthy, in spite of hard physical experiences, not least of which was the accident in the lumber yard in Canada. It was believed at the time of his accident that it was his great strength that prevented the fallen log from breaking his back before it was lifted from his body. Though he had not lost consciousness, the glancing blow of the log had torn the flesh on his head. This left a large ragged scar which was hidden under his flowing locks of thick black hair. Regrettably there was something basically wrong with his vision. His children in the years to come would try on his heavy thick reading glasses. Apart from being unable to see anything through the lenses, the effect was to cause loss of balance, and induce a severe headache. This deficiency became a 'cross' for my father, throughout his life. He was accepted by the army, but not for service in combat duties. Unfit for this, he served as postal courier, itself a role hardly less hazardous than being in the trenches.

There is little to say about my father's war service. As
mentioned already, his eyesight prevented him from a combat
role. That could be interpreted as a blessing. But it did not
prevent him being part of the horrors of war.

There is one anecdote linked to his army days which was
made known posthumously, some three years after his death.
It was like this. At the close of the evening service in the Free
Church, Lochgilphead where I was preaching as a student, a
man spoke to me and made himself known as a retired Baptist
minister. I recount our conversation as well as I can remember.

He said, 'Your father was Angus MacKinnon who became
a minister?'

'Yes', I replied.

He went on; 'It was your father that led me to Christ and
God used him to give my life in his service as a minister in
the Baptist Church.'

'How was that? ' I asked.

'It was like this', the old man continued, adjusting his
thoughts to bygone days, picking up the strands of memory,
so that he could explain to me what he meant.

'I was in a company of soldiers in training on an army
base in the south of England. We were led into a barrack room,
about thirty of us in all in the long hut. It was the time for
retiring, and the room was full of young soldiers, each in
various stages of getting ready for bed. There was continual
banter and a great deal of profanity. I had come from a devout
evangelical Christian home. But here I was in another world
as it were, the real world. And I thought to myself that I
would just have to leave my religion back home and be part
of this. There was this constant noise, as I said, swearing and
cursing all part of it as if this was the way of it.

Suddenly a silence spread right through the hut. I looked up to the further end. There at his bunk, a soldier was kneeling. His head was bowed forward, his hands clasped in prayer. All eyes were turned towards the praying soldier on his knees. I remember how the profane language of young men close to me faded away, so that you could feel the hush over the whole company. Faces, each a mirror of their thoughts, signalled the profound effect this soldier had made on the company. Yet he had not spoken a word.'

The old man's voice faltered. It crackled with emotion as he took a grip of my arm and blurted out, 'That was your father. That hour was the moment of decision in my life. Your father was not afraid to show that he honoured the Lord and nothing would stop him kneeling down at the Throne of Mercy and Grace, before men. Because of his testimony, I gave my life to serve the Lord forever.'

The old minister parted from me that dark winter night as the streetlamp lighted up the stonework of the old Free Church. His last words were, 'God bless you. I am so glad to have met you to tell this story that changed my life.'

That meeting still stays in my own memory. What a thought for us all. My father never spoke of these days and possibly never knew the profound effect his silent witness had on this young man and possibly on many others that night the soldiers stayed in the transit camp. Maybe this moment seems insignificant to many readers. But you think of the circumstances. These men were on their way to battle, and for many, this was to mean death in Belgium or France shortly thereafter.

How little we know the influence for good or evil our behaviour, our actions, or our words have on the lives and very destiny of other people, even our silences! What a powerful effect one silent act of Christian witness can have on the life direction of another.

Such an anecdote seems to indicate a calm and dynamic faith now entrenched in the fabric of this young Highlander, a calm that implied the maturity and strength of a man who in spirit was already the 'servant of the Lord.' Behind this were many influences for good, chief of which was that of a devout mother. When he had returned to Glendale from Canada, a changed man, spiritually awakened, he lived in her fellowship and his spiritual experience was seasoned as a living and working faith for everyday life. These two years were a kind of seasoning period for his faith and a maturing of his thinking--a kind of shaping out the rough but positive course to pursue, by which his life would be a fulfillment of God's will to which he was completely committed to seek and to follow.

Speaking of his mother, she herself was a woman of spiritual stature, albeit, not allowed to shine overtly in public because of conventional restriction of women. Yet no social nor ecclesiastical stricture could deny her worth, a widow in Israel, like so many more devout anonymous women, whose lives are betrothed to Christ, and with the Church, have their Maker as their husband. Just about the time my father finished his studies for the ministry, his mother, then in her eighties, passed peacefully to her rest. What a completeness to a life, to leave earth's scene, for the glorious tryst she had with her Saviour. And the grieving of her youngest son Angus was qualified by immeasurable thanksgiving, as the remains of his mother were laid to rest in the ancestral burial ground of the MacLeods in Dunvegan.

From this period forward he composed sacred verse. He

wrote many poems in long-hand and these lay for years at a time before being brought to the public in several publications. As he grew spiritually in the midst of the real-life context of war and the restraints of the physical discipline of the soldier, he found harmony in himself and positive purpose in using his poetic gifts to express his faith. This was not just an inverted egocentric process of escapism. This is illustrated in several poems which he composed about this time, including the period of his studies for the ministry immediately after the cessation of hostilities, and extending to the time of his ministry and well past the end of the Second World war. One on the theme of grace and glory reflects that spiritual perspective of realism where any observer of the war scene, with its mindless slaughter of the 'flower of young manhood' in the muddy battlefields of northern Europe, could not miss seeing the grim diminution of human worth, in the falsely called 'enlightened' new world.

Smuaintean mu Ghras is mu Ghloir

1

O m'anam duisg, is beathaich fein
air aran Dhe, 'se ni dhuit feum.
'S e bheir seargadh air an fhein,
's a bheir do'n eug mu dheireadh i.

2

O amhairc suas ged tha thu fuar,
is sin thu fein a chum na duais'.
Faic an-t-Uan, 's e dol suas;
gur sona 'n sluagh tha maille ris.

3

Dh-fhosgail e 'nt-slighe troimhe fein,
is chaidh e steach troimh fhuil na reit',
Is chrath e i an lathair Dhe,
is ghluais gu leir na flaitheanas.

4

'Se tha tagradh 'sle a shluagh;
ni e saoradh o gach truaigh.
Chan fhas iad sgith a bhi 'ga luaidh,
cha chaochail buaidh na fola ud.

5

Chaidh e dh'ullachadh dhoibh ait',
gu bhi maille ris gu brath.
Ni e cumadh ris troimh ghras,
's cha bhi namh no camadh ann.

6

Bith am fireantachd cho ard,
'sgu bheil an t-iomlan dith o ghras.
Bith i na h-iongantas gu brath,
a thog gu aird nan aingel iad.

7

Cha tig briseadh air an slainte',
bith iad iomlan anns gach pairt.
Cha bhi osna ann no bas;
bith 'nt -Uan a ghnath 'gam beathachadh.

8

Ni iad aoradh dha gun sgath;
bith ant - Uan am measg 'n tamh
Bith 'n anam lan de bheatha ghraidh,
's i teachd o shraid na cathrach ud.

9

Gheibh iad uile crun na gloir',
's a chlach gheal tha 'g innse 'n coir.
Fosglaidh ant -Uan dhoibh na stoir
le iuchair oir na h-airidheachd.

10

A' seinn a chliu gu siorruidh buan,

mu bhuaidh is eifeachd fuil an Uain;
   Rinn e an ionnlaid anns ' chuan,
rinn righrean buan is sagairt dhiubh.

11

Is sona 'n sluagh a fhuair gu sabhailt',
   steach do chala sin na samhchair.
   Bith a ' ghrian aca 'na h-aird',
cha chlaoidh na sgailean tuilleadh iad.

12

Ged fhuair iad earlas de an oran,
   mu'n deach iad null thar Iordan,
   Cha robh an clarsaichean air doigh,
gus 'n d-fhuair do'n ghloir a ghealladh dhoibh.

13

Ach a nis tha 'n cupan lan
   's ag cur thairis le a ghradh.
   Cha chaill iad sealladh air gu brath,
oir cha bhi amhghar tuilleadh ann.

14

Bha iad sgith a dol troimh 'n ghleann,
   ach bha neart aca 's a Cheann.
   Bha corp a bhais 'g an cumail teann,
ach thainig ceann mu dheireadh air.

15

Bha cuid dhiubh 'nduil an tus an cuairt
   gun coisneadh iad an t-slighe suas.
   Ach ruisg an Spiorad iad 'na thruas,
thug teagasg buan na fola dhoibh.

16

Thug dhoibh sealladh air an Uan
   'guilan peachaidhean a shluaigh,
   'S e toirt riarachaidh le buaidh,
an aite shluaigh a shealladh ris.

17

Fhuair iad creideamh nach robh fann,
   fhuair e cleachdadh anns an am.
   Bh an aimsir dhoibh 'na gradh

'n uair thuit gu lar an t-eallach dhiubh.
18
'S iomadh namhaid bh'air an toir
anns an t-slighe dh-ionnsuidh gloir',
'G iarraidh an tarruing o an choir;
'S e gras is gloir nach mealladh iad.
19
Cha tuigeadh iad, a 'ruith na reis',
cuid de na nithean 'bha cur eis.
Ach dh'oibrich iad an ceann a cheil'
chum maith gach cre a bheannaich e.
20
Dh-fhag iad sinne anns a ghleann,
far nach eil an t-amghar gann;
Ma bhitheas sinn ceangailt' ris a Cheann,
bheir e gu ceann mu dheireadh e.

Translation; (I have taken the liberty of converting the literal translation into a form which to some degree reflects the rythmic flow of thought rather than sticking to the literal words used to express it.)

Thoughts on Grace and Glory

1.
My soul awake, begin to live
for Heaven's Bread will nourish you.
Then self will shrink, a withered plant,
And vanish in decay.
2.
Look up, though hostile is the sky,
Reach forward for the prize to grasp.
Behold the Lamb who now is Risen,
How happy those who now are with Him

3.
Through Him the Way is opened up
That leads man through the Blood of Peace.
He sprinkled it before the Father,
And now to Him belongs dominion.

4.
A Pleader for His people, He
shall free them all from chains of ill.
They'll never cease their praise to give,
For endless virtue from His Blood.

5.
A place for them He came to make,
for them with Him to rest for ever.
By grace He makes them like Himself,
No evil can that bond now sever.

6.
Their righteousness He will exalt;
a need of grace they no more have.
The wonder of eternal skies,
That angels raised them upon high.

7.
No breach will mar their happiness,
For now they live in perfect peace.
There cannot be a sigh nor sorrow.
The Lamb will always succour them.

8.
They fearlessly shall give Him praise,
The Saviour with them giving rest.
Their souls are filled with life-long love,
Straight from the throne above.

9.
A crown of glory for each one,
In the white stone that speaks of truth.
The Lamb will feed them from His store,
The key to this, His Worthiness.

10.

They sing his praise for ever more,
the Blood that brought them victory.
They're washed and clean as in the sea,
And now made kings and priests of heaven.

11.

What joy for those who reach the harbour,
and know the shelter of its peace.
The sun for them is at its height;
The shadows flee before its light.

12.

An earnest of the song they knew,
Long before they crossed the river.
For then their harps were not in tune,
But Glory brings them all fulfillment.

13.

Now the cup is overflowing
with the fullness of His love.
They will never lose the vision,
For no clouds obscure the sky.

14.

Uneasy, walked they through the valley,
finding strength in Christ their Head;
Weak they felt like every human,
they overcame and now are with Him.

15.

Some thought at first and took the view,
that they could earn their place of rest.
The spirit taught them in their hearts,
Alone to Christ they all did owe.

16.

They saw the vision of the Lamb,
upon the Cross their burden bear,
The thousands and ten thousands with them,
All Israel owning Him their King.

17.

The faith embraced was one of power,
placed in the One who faced the Hour.
In the experience of his love,
when they were from their burdens freed.

18.

Many a hostile foe pursued,
As they on heaven's road now fled,
seeking to strip them of their robes,
the robes that Christ Himself had won.

19.

They'll never fully understand,
all the pitfalls in the sand.
But all things worked to them for good
Even when sorrow's pain to them was food.

20.

We are still within the valley,
Where there's no scarcity of pain,
But if we're joined to Christ, our King
He will bring it to an end.

The Glendale Communion

Angus MacKinnon returned from the War and spent some time each year at home with his mother in Glendale, where he worshipped in the church of his childhood. He now had a new love, far exceeding the natural and nostalgic ones that bind us all to our roots. Now these natural feelings were magnified with the enriching ties which bound him to the spiritual destiny of believers.

We speak elsewhere of his love for the Glendale people. In the following poem which he wrote in 1918, he articulated his ties to the church of his fathers, yet the reader notes that this poem embraces affection for Christ's church at large. It is also true that the poem is not without the need for interpretation. The references to St Paul and Timothy must be looked at as a reflection of his keen observation of the ministers present, assisting the Glendale host at the communion.

Traditionally there was an older minister who was given seniority in the duties of the services in connexion with the ordinaces. The other would be considerably younger and take a secondary yet full role. It was rare indeed for a younger man to show any resentment towards the older minister. Yet this is implied in the poem. The names of the ministers there at the time are not disclosed. In spite of this unquestionably specific criticism, the poem exudes a spiritual feeling that strikes a chord in many believers and fits the pattern of their own relationship to their Lord and the precious seasons of His presence through the ministry of the Word and the fellowship of His people at the Table.

Deireadh Ordugh Ghleanndail

1

O tha mi muladach,
Ag ionndruinn na chunnaic mi
Dol dhachaidh do na teampull.
'S bho shamhlaichean fhulangasan.

2

Gur mise bha gu bronach,
Air Di Luain an orduigh,
Cur m'aghaidh air an otrach
'Sgun deon agam pilleadh ris.

3

Nuair sheall mi air mo shulthaobh,
Bha'm pailluin air a dhunadh,
Thug sud na deoir o'm shuilean,
'Smi 'g iondrainn na chunnaic mi.

4

'Nuair sheall mi air gach taobh dhiom,
Bha 'n co-thional air sgaoileadh,
Bha sgapadh anns na caoraich
Ri aodann nam firichean.

5

Bha fear na cuiream 'na lathair,
Toirt cuireadh do na brathraibh,
'Scha mhor nach togainn pailluin,
Dha fein, 'sdo Mhaois, 'sdo Elias.

6

Bha ghras 'gar deanamh laidir,
Bha anail a'cur blaths oirnn,
'Sdhe aodach thainig faileadh
De'n alos, mhirr, is chassia.

7

Ach tha mi 'nise craiteach,
'Smi air a chuideachd fhagail,
'Sgum fheudar teachd do'n fhasach,
'Smi tearnadh far na beinne ud.

8

Ach ithidh Mephiboset
An comhnuidh aig mo bhord-sa,
'Se sud mo bharrant dochais
'Smo chomhnadh ro bhunaiteach.

9

B'e Pol is Timoteus,
Bha roinn an arain neimhaidh,
'S cha'n fhuiligeadh Timoteus
Gun Pol a bhi air thoiseach air.

10

Bha Pol gu h-ealamh eudmhor,
Toirt cuireadh do na feumaich,
'S bu teth gu deanamh sgeul e,
Air sheudan na flaitheanais .

———————————

Translation:

At end of Glendale Communion

1

O, how sorrowful I am,
Missing what I saw,
Going home from the church
and from the symbols of His suffering.

2

'Twas sad I was indeed
On the Monday of the Communion,
Seeing the dunghill of the world
Without any desire to return to it.

3

When I looked behind me,
The church was closed
This brought tears from my eyes,

Just missing what was over.
4
As I looked on every side
The congregation was dispersing
'Twas the scattering of the flock
Turning their faces to the moorland.
5
The master of the Feast was there
Giving his invitation to the brethren.
I feel I 'd like to build a monument
To Him to Moses and Elias.
6
Grace was making us strong,
The breath of the Spirit gave warmth,
And from His clothes the perfume fell,
Of aloes, myrrh and cassia.
7
But now I am desolate,
Leaving the great company.
Now I to the desert turn,
Far from salvation on the Mount.
8
But Mephibosheth will dine
Forever at my house.
That is my hope and confidence,
And lasting habitation.
9
Both Paul and young Timothy,
Did break the Heavenly Bread,
And Timothy would suffer not
Saint Paul to be ahead.
10
Paul was keenly zealous,
In offering to the needy,
Devoutly making mention of the stones
The precious Sovereinty of His grace.

In all the many ways that express our response to the love of Christ, from self-sacrifice to all outgiving, praise remains the umbrella of all witness and the enduring expression of our Christian calling beyond the limits of our stay on earth and going on forever in the habitations of the Redeemed. Thus my father revelled in articulating the devotional thoughts not of himself only, but of the corporate church of which he saw himself as a humble and privileged member. What greater way of living than to use our time of worship, rehearsing for the choirs of heaven in the longing and assurance that we will be allowed into that numberless multitude that praises the Lamb, our Redeemer upon the Throne of the renewed world, forever and ever! It is this theme and elevating purpose for living that motivated the young man from Glendale who was 'saved on the Mount', to bring others into the compass of God's Redeeming Love.

Chapter 11

College Days

W hen discharged from the army at the end of the Great War, my father prepared for the Scottish University entrance exams, studying at Skerries College, Glasgow. Having matriculated for an Arts course in Edinburgh university, he completed this pre-Divinity course as prescribed by the Ministry Committee of the Free Church of Scotland. Subsequently he took the regular Divinity course at the theological College of the Free Church in Edinburgh and graduated from it with credit in 1923.

Until the end of his life he held a high regard for the professors in the College, and spoke highly of them as men of great integrity and high principle, an inspiration as role models for the students studying in their classes. His professors were Messrs. Alexander, Bannatyne, Kennedy Cameron, Moore, MacKay, MacLean. There was an English gentleman scholar, Mr. Simpson who did tutorial work for the students. Mr. Bell, a relative of Alexander Graham Bell gave elocution classes, a significant and beneficial adjunct to the curriculum, which my father greatly valued.

The principal of the College was Mr MacCulloch. This patriarch had lived through church controversy, but had a peculiar gentleness, yet resolute firmness. He remained a prime figure in the mind of this young student from Glendale. At the same time Principal MacCulloch was senior minister of Hope Street congregation in Glasgow. Now well up in years, he was only in the College in Edinburgh on special occasions, and gave addresses to students at these times. It is of interest that he was the minister at Latheron in Caithness nearly fifty years earlier, and preached at the induction of Rev Ronald Dingwall in Aultbea. My father could not know then that he himself would also be inducted into that charge as its minister.

There was one other in a responsible position for whom students had a high regard. That was Mr. Salvage, the College custodian. This man made a deep impression on all students who went through the rigours of study at the Free Church College. My father kept referring to him as a wonderful reminder of common humanity. Mr. Salvage's facial appearance was striking. He had a broad intellectual forehead, a long powerful nose and a direct, sharp, penetrating look. He had a large head of hair which rose sideways like a Dickensian wig, with traces of sideboxers, in part camouflaging big powerful ears. He regularly smoked a long pipe, with the aroma of a mild blend, which did not offend. He would look speculatively at the budding student ministers, his long pipe stem still in his mouth. Then out of the mouth came the pipe with a deliberate flourish, and there followed words of advice, wisdom or wit, rarely unappreciated.

Maybe a place like a sombre theological college needs someone like this. He becomes a foil to the sometimes austere and lofty untouchable image that students have of their professors. Though my father did not smoke, the smoking room in the Free Church College was a great place between classes. A visit from Mr. Salvage at these times was a happy relief to all, just to hear one little witty story from him, and such anecdotes would not exclude a friendly tilt at the professors. It is well known that the latter were known as much for their eccentricities as for their theology.

It was a happy experience for me to return to Scotland and find that a subsequent incumbent of the office, Mr. William Anderson has more than filled the role for which Mr. Salvage set such a high standard. Mr. Anderson, apart from his warm helpful personality, has a great love for old Edinburgh and its history. In his tenure over some twenty years, he cooperated with the National Heritage of Scotland in the necessary steps to preserve the College building with its special features, the Presbytery Hall and the Chalmers Hall. These with their ornate ceilings now restored are truly a treasure. Now the College with its own special historical contribution is marked as a 'must' for any serious visitors to old Edinburgh in planning their itinerary. Mr. Anderson through his love and dedication has produced a lasting image of the College's history, in published form, an exquisitely fine volume in pictures and script.

These post-war years left many men scarred by the grim experience of war. At the same time for many it was not altogether negative. Rather, that experience was like the firing of a clay vessel in the furnace. Men matured quickly with profound convictions. A large number of Highlanders were in this category. With others in the wider sphere of thinking realists, they saw that there could be no dream world of happiness without the Coming of God's kingdom, 'on earth as it is in heaven.'

Others who were too young to serve in the War, learned vicariously—for war's horrors and sorrows touched everyone. The whole population in Britain as well as in Europe and the Commonwealth, were deeply marked by the shattered ruins of humanist myths and illusions of a man-made Utopia. What a heap of ruin now comprised the conglomerate of Charlemagne's Europe! What would that 9th century potentate think if he could look on the post-Great War scene? Is not the perennial enemy of man nothing more than man himself, not generically but in that he seems so often to be the slave of Satan, and struggles to fulfill aspiration, handicapped by 'every weight and the sin that so easily besets him.' [1]

In the conservative circles of the church, there was a reaffirmation of 'eternal verities'. Switzerland's Karl Barth and Scotland's John Baillie to a lesser degree, took up the broken pieces of a shattered Protestant theology, projecting on the ecclesiastical scene a working syllabus for a new church. There is no doubt that both were intellectual giants, and at the same time did have a vision of the Divine redemptive mission of the Incarnate Son. But the academic world and the humanist adherents so prolific in church quarters from the early 1920's, began sniping and whittling away at the newly structured edifice of 'orthodox' historical thinking. Some aspiring pundits found it tedious and prosaic and out of step with conquering the new frontiers of the new world. Therefore many turned to esoteric mysticism, or dug up Existentialism especially in the dormant diaries of the eccentric Danish theologian, Soren Kirkegarde. Resurrected and given 20th century respectability, the Danish theologian was hailed as a

1
Hebrews 12:1

modern saviour. Climbing up on the shoulders of Kirkegarde, Paul Tillich in America and lesser lights supplied fashionable theological inventiveness and rose to man-made stardom, in the sheltered world of theological fabrication, thereby condoning the humanist idea of infinite man-made resource.

Here you have the equivalent of confusing road signs. The result was a mosaic of many different colours of theology, an almost impossible situation for any earnest seeker to make an inspired choice, and even identify the distinction between the mandatory premise of belief and the concomitant of human reasoning. Especially was this a dilemma, as the giants of theology appeared to have their signature on the opposing options of decision. In the middle ground occupied by the middle class of theological students of which the church in Scotland was comprised, William Barclay in Glasgow produced a synoptic handbook of theological tenets. This was cognitively simple, with the Apostles' Creed still intact and no great intellectual effort required to grasp this working structure of Christian thinking. The system worked smoothly for many years right up until the 1960's. Then Dr. Barclay, in an interview with the Edinburgh *Scotsman,* disclosed almost casually, that he personally did not believe in the affirmative truths of the Apostles' Creed, singling out for special denial, the Resurrection of Jesus Christ. Whether or not his words were misinterpreted, or his age had brought injury to the process of his thinking, he did not see fit to clarify. Many people were very shattered, and unease again ran free across the land.

The fact is that faith and reason do not in fact conflict with each other, where both are components in a life lived in union with the triune God, and where Jesus Christ in his

Lordship is primary. Furthermore it is not a good thing for the
thinking of the church to be split into the elitist of academic
votaries and the mass of followers on the ground, ministers
and congregations of people. In 1936 in spite of, rather than
because of Dr. Karl Barth's efforts, though he was not there
in person, there was the ineffectual Barmen Conference and
Declaration of the Protestant Church in Germany in the face
of Hitler's racism especially linked to Erastian theological
thinking. In that year in Scotland a book was published, where
leading notables in church circles subscribed a batch of suitable
questions which ideally required an answer, to get a tolerably
clear picture in the confused thinking of that unenviable period
of history.

One of these contributors, the distinguished Rev Dr.
George MacLeod when confronted with this book, some thirty
years later, at first failed to recall that he had written anything for the book, until his contribution was shown to him
from my library. Then, true to his character, he was decisive.
He declared emphatically that a book of questions could never
comprise a solution for a confused and lost world. **It had to
be a book of answers.** I cannot forget the way he left the
new church in Out-Skerries. He asked us to bow with him in
prayer in the church before he left the island by the fishingboat
St. Clair on the Monday morning. The phrase in that prayer
from that radical and redoubtable hero of the battlefield, military and spiritual, that lingers, is this, 'Sovereign Lord, may
we give all diligence to make (our) calling and election sure.'[1]

Historically the Free Church in which my father was to
be a minister, left the frontiers of speculative theology
unchallenged. Its professors and people revelled in the
historical role bequeathed to them, to hold the fort, in the name

1. II Peter 1:10

of past heroes, Reformers and Covenanters. They were never alone. Though reduced to a minority, often incurring the mockery of lesser men raised on the shoulders of fashionable and gullible enthusiasts, they, instead ploughed a straight furrow, looking to their Master and serving Him in their generation. Thus, taught by like-minded teachers my father and his fellow- students gloried in the Gospel of Grace and were filled with a sense of mission to work in the vineyard of the Master and 'gather in the harvest for the Lord'. To this purpose his whole energies were directed. With the poet's eye, my father often scanned the horizon of a renewed future, reaching in spiritual thought into the heavens. Personally he would indulge in this and often unite with the Gaelic poets like Peter Grant and Dugald Buchannan in the exquisite tenderness projected by the former and the profound views of spiritual insights of which the latter was the master recorder. And then, there were the hymns of the Apostle of the North, Dr. MacDonald, which were ever dear to my father and which he would often quote at length from the full and ordered shelves of his memory.

But the young man on the threshold of life as a minister, was no dreamer. Rather he leaned to pragmatism. His inner life percolated, as it were through his being, and was not by any standard a substitute for reality in a mistaken polarized dichotomy between the flesh and the spirit. He saw the world about him as the theatre of God's operation. He was profoundly exercised by the political philosophies that gave birth to the disasters of his day in Europe, in the vividly first-hand acquaintance with war. He believed in seeking answers within the framework of accepted social patterns. He did not live in a postwar sequel of futility or bitter resentment at the *status quo*. Rather he believed in bringing a change to society by change first taking place within people. While he saw the external machinery of the church as essential, there was a sense in which its nature to him was secondary and academic. Let it stand or fall on its usefulness and effectiveness. This was a pragmatic approach which relieved him of burning up energies on petty ecclesiastical questions, that affected or infected the weak conscience of others. At the same time, he saw essence or primary value in the need of people who govern or are leaders in both church and state.

My father's conviction was clear from his actions. He inter-related with his peers or counterparts as leaders in secular society as opposed to those in the church. To change people 'at the top' can lead to profound and effective change in the multitudes of the mass of citizens. Bring the Christian message to bear upon those who govern as well as governed. Change people and you change society. Watch a flight of geese as they fly across the sky. They form a big 'V'. Where the leader flies, so do the rest. Night and day through storm and sunshine, where the leader goes, the others follow. My father, had no time for dismissing people in places of influence. He saw his role and pursued this all through his ministry, to bring round those in leadership positions locally and nationally, to the maturity of Christian perspective. For him, though he was not dogmatic by nature, this was singularly the only viable way that would lead to a happy society.

Brought up within the limited privileges of his childhood environment, his approach to life was philosophically universal. Only occasionally did he get stuck on some particular sectarian side-road. He preferred to think of society in a broad sense, where some were already on track, others were coming on line, and there were yet many still to come out of the side-roads and byways. He saw this Highway with the church representing those who were already 'being saved' and those yet to be redeemed, travelling to Zion. He liked to keep a trans-historical perspective in which all the centuries of time are seen coalescing into one pilgrimage, an oblique photo of humanity, of past, present and future. In this, the words of our Lord, 'But strait is the gate and narrow is the way,'[1] in the metaphorical contrasts of narrow and broad roads, relate to failure, to pessimism, a world where there is regress, where the projection of truth as it is in the Biblical Revelation, is distorted and its teachings bent like the rays of refraction that reach our little planet from the sun. For him, he saw it differently. He dwelt upon the possibilities, the practical possibilities of the Church's potential to bring in a transformed world, a faith that could move mountains, and the unlimited betterment that would follow from the adoption of the Christian formula for society. That was Jesus' projection of the potential of a world that would follow him. [2]

This perspective did not come automatically. He had lived through the subsistence environment of his childhood, where repressive action on the part of government kept the lid on human liberty for the many and locked the doors of privilege for the benefit of the few. For him, the differences of ecclesiastical structures of external government, hierarchical or democratic and all the shades in between and all the varied time-wasting interpretations of them all, to a large extent were simply academic, an indulgence for intellectual hobbyists or churchmen who have a restricted spiritual vision or mission. Reared and conditioned as a Scottish Presbyterian, he accepted this as a happening of providence, a coalition or

1   2
Matthew 7:14   John 14:12

synthesis of historical evolution, if you like and that mysterious element, the Divine Will.

My father spoke of the ingredients that made up his beliefs and fashioned his perspective. He would speak of his years in Canada, rubbing shoulders with fellow immigrants from every country in Europe, as a period of enlightenment. This was not an arm-chair education, but a real life one in which he consciously assimilated and digested the data. This became the premise for a clear and unambiguous approach to other people, in high or humble positions. He saw people in the basic texture of our common humanity, with weaknesses and strengths. In this every man is a beggar, every man is a king. We are debtors to all, and all are debtors to our Maker. He was Highland, but easily accepted identity with the Lowland Scottish poet in his verdict, 'The rank is but the guinea stamp; a man's a man for a'that.'

He would go out to the 'spiritual front' of his calling, with many cobwebs of prejudice and selective preferment brushed away. This was a man of the people and for the people. Respect would be given where due. Labels, whether social, military, political, ecclesiastical, academic or even spiritual, he would acknowledge—they have their uses—but the discerning servant of God would see beyond these, like an X-ray machine. In this, his attitude would not be to demean any, in a cynical and negative levelling of human infirmity. Rather he would see others, great or small, as inherently valuable and capable of the greatest potential. Humbly he saw himself in the uniform of balanced and modest social, professional and spiritual maturity, born on earth, but of heaven, a child of Christ's kingdom. As such he could be used as one building block in the edifice of a new and redeemed world. To this end he dedicated his whole life.

Chapter 12

Week-end Preaching

Students attending the Free Church Divinity Hall in Edinburgh combined their academic studies with regular trips right to the west coast on weekends to conduct services. This was both a part of their training, and provided an ongoing source of 'supply' for pulpits in small congregations that could not afford ministers. There was also the opportunity to preach in some large urban congregations, especially in Glasgow, where there were large gatherings of exiled Highlanders, who filled the Gaelic churches like Hope Street, Govan, Duke Street, or Partick Highland. Here we speak of the Free Church, as in the Highland Gaelic area people were at that time predominantly the continuing heirs and followers of the Disruption of 1843 and the segment which continued this heritage after 1900. In Edinburgh some students were regularly occupied conducting services in the largely Highland congregation of Fountainbridge. This amalgamated with another, the church of the distinguished preacher and social reformer, Rev Dr. Thomas Guthrie. It was known thereafter   as St. Columba and the venue of the General Assembly of the Free Church of Scotland.

Among the rural congregations to which students used to go to do supply, I would mention Shiskine, on the west coast of the island of Arran, the last regular Gaelic preaching station on the island. It was vacant for a period when my father was attending the Divinity Hall. (In the 1920's, services on the Sabbath day were still conducted in Gaelic in many of the Small Isles as well as the Outer Isles.)   Therefore my father, being a Gaelic student, preached there during the vacancy several times on weekends.

 I now ask the reader to step forward in time some years to the post Second World War period. The MacKinnon family had connections in Arran. The oldest, Rachel Mary, was married to the Free Church minister. He was Alastair Gollan, son of exiled Glasgow Highlanders from Applecross and Erbusaig in Wester Ross. He saw service in the navy during the Second World War and afterwards studied for the ministry. His first charge was in Shiskine. During his ministry there were still a few old people who had the Gaelic, but Gaelic services had been discontinued. In his stay in Shiskine, a lovely new church was built to replace the large edifice that had been erected almost a century before at the Disruption.

During a visit there in 1951, before the new church was built, I had a look round the glebe. The manse was of traditional design, with harled walls, a large comfortable residence in keeping with the rather privileged status of the country minister in a past Victorian age. A large garden and thick broad hedges with scent of honeysuckle and the hum of insects—these are memories that linger. My mind was occupied with a certain curiosity about the church. There used to be Gaelic services. But having gone through the church and searched in cupboards and the many now unused pews especially in the gallery, I found no sign of any Gaelic Bibles. In most churches where the Gaelic services were discontinued (I think of Delny and Ferintosh and Rosskeen in Easter Ross, Scotland, or Whycocomagh, Lake Ainslie or Mira Ferry in Nova Scotia, Canada), there were many old Gaelic Bibles, worn and now a curiosity. You could compile a list of families in the past who worshipped in the language of their people and heritage, for their names were written on these Bibles.

A building behind the large church caught my eye. It was surrounded by some trees and almost hidden by overgrown bushes. It was a stone cottage-type building. The roof was slate and apparently still weatherproof. It gave the appearance of being mellowed with age, retired from use, as if its work was done. I was attracted to this silent monument of a former day. Even as I approached on that summer afternoon, a certain stillness, a kind of hallowed atmosphere obtained. As I pushed whinbushes aside to get to the door, there was a feeling that I was on sacred ground, crossing over into a sanctified scene of time past and by-passed by the clamour of a new age. But there was no hostile opposition as there would be to a stranger. For was I not a Gael through and through, whose whole being was the embodiment of all that this building had once represented! It seemed to me that I was welcome, as one born out of due time, yet belonging, a citizen of a new age, but whose roots were deeply embedded in the past.

I was filled with expectation, as one on the brink of a discovery, an answer to my questions. I knew that here the book of the past was closed. But for a moment, it might open for me to see a glimpse of its recorded memories. As I prised aside the prickly branches, I reached the wall. The door was closely shut so that it could not open. I cleared round a small window. Numerous cobwebs could be seen like a network decorating the corners of the window panes on the inside.

The sun shone in midday brightness from behind me. I cupped my hands over my eyes, like the blinders on a horse, so that I could get used to the darkened interior as I peered inside. For a while I could make out nothing. But gradually the dark within gave way to shapes. As I continued to concentrate, the silhouettes became three-dimensional. Then it seemed as if I found myself looking at the sacred interior of the Gaelic meeting-house, unused and now a forgotten relic of a past culture, people and language. For me it was a photograph of yesterday, a picture whose every feature spoke with significance, so that in a sense I myself the observer, was carried back in time and drawn into the experience of which it spoke so vocally. I did not resist the drawing power, the spirit, that carried me out of the fast lane of the hurried new age where there is less time than ever to muse, to think, to reflect. Now I was in another day, and one which has been left behind, and its incomparable values discarded on the great heap of history, judged as obsolete in the computerized judgment of an impersonal society.

This was a church in miniature, a typical 'meeetinghouse.' Objectively each feature could be seen distinctly. There was a pulpit raised at the end, with a precentor's box for two in front of it. Right up to this, the rest of the hall had rows of long pews or seats. A large Bible was closed, resting on the bookrest in the pulpit. In the pews, all along the book rest of each pew, there were small Bibles. They were worn, with dog-ears on the corner of the pages.

The picture before me was speaking to me. The message was unmistakably clear. This was a meeting-place of yesterday, but one with a perennial subject, the meaning of human life, the tragedy of a broken humanity, and the message of Redeeming love in the Covenant of Grace. By this, the lost could be found, the fallen lifted up, the ashamed given a new self-esteem, the estranged find a new or renewed communion with the Creator and Redeemer, through a Crucified and Risen Lord, even the Son of God.

In my mind's eye, I saw the scene of long ago, as it must have been in my father's time. I merged with it as if I was part of it. Time and change, I must admit, could never erase the essence that shaped me long ago when I was young.

The pews were filled with people. The women's faces were half hidden under their hats. Men, quite young, with dark hair still on their heads could be seen at the back, manly, with tanned faces. I could see the white teeth of several as they sang the psalm. There were some boys and girls with a Bible open in front of them with their heads down. One girl with a pleated pig-tail protruding from her bonneted head, was looking up, a thoughtful look on her face, her mouth was moving as the cadences of the Gaelic psalm filled the hall. On the front pew, there were two men, one with a beard. The latter was well up in years, a patriarch. He wasn't looking at the Psalm book in front of him. Yet he was singing. He knew the songs of praise by heart. Beside him was a refined looking, high-cheekboned companion. He was younger. There was no beard but a moustache. The hall was animated with the music of the Gaelic singing. A precentor put out the line. It even seemed to me that the tune was Ballerma. I could not identify each person present with a name, yet the names came to me, Bannatyne, Currie, Murchie. It was as if here was a representative microcosm of the church's witness over the past centuries, an authentic video of something precious and somehow irreplaceable.

The precentor had a psalmbook, the big flat one held up in one hand. The other hand was gripping the stand in front of him. The precentor's face was lifted up so that his voice presented the words like free gifts to the people. He was singing in Psalm 36.

Le saill do theach is t'arois phailt
sasuichear iad gu mor;
A d'abhainn lan de sholasaibh
deoch bheir thu dhoibhr'a h'ol.

They with the fatness of thy house
Shall be well satisfied
From rivers of thy pleasures thou
wilt drink to them provide.

Tobar na beatha tha gu dearbh
agadsa Dhia nan dul
Is ann ad sholus dealrach glan
chi sinne solus iul.

Because of life the fountain pure
remains alone with thee;
And in that purest light of thine
we clearly light shall see.

There was no sense of hurry. Dare we say, the scene evoked a sense of the timeless, even of the eternal. The singing came to an end, the melody still lingering in the air. It was as if the voices, used to praising God, blended together with a particular unison and that harmony brought the worshippers together as one body of people in the presence of God. There was joy and a sense of triumph at what God had done. There was an air of reconciliation, of victory. And this victory was of grace, from a God who is just and holy, but at the same time without any contradiction, the God of supreme love. Here was the sacrifice of praise presented to heaven, a sweet savour, an acceptable offering to the Redeemer, whose

Covenant Mercy in Christ Jesus, gave hope to the sinner and
expectation to the terrestrial traveller to Zion.

It was the prelude to the sermon. I could tell. There was
a pause, a hush. I waited. There was no hurry for me. In a
way, I ceased to be conscious of this transport of spirit into
the past. I looked with the people towards the pulpit. There
was a young man, beginning to preach. His hair was black,
his forehead sloping back above his broad face. He wore a
white collar and black tie with a dark single-breasted suit.
Strange but comfortable emotions filled my being. This was
a student. And the student was my father. There was no
mistaking him for another. Younger than I could ever see him
in life, the voice that read out the text was unmistakably the
same. I had heard such Scriptural quotations all my life a
thousand times as his voice rose and fell with melody, almost
singing the immortal life-giving riches of Scripture, especially
those texts from the heights of spiritual verities and clothed
in the incomparable poetry of the Hebrew prophets and the
invitations of Christ himself. My father's reading had an
unmistakable beauty. It conveyed conviction, compassion,
urgency, the urgency of the evangelist. 'Come,' he seemed to
say, 'here is a provision for you for life's journey. It is ready,
prepared. Take it now while it is fresh. It is specially suited
for you in all your human needs.'

He read the text in Isaiah. Then he paused. The people
waited. His head was turned down and he stood almost sideways, a hand on the open page in front of him. Then he turned
round, his face lifting up as he faced the front. His arm was
raised up and his hand stretched out to the people. I could see
him, his dark hair swept back, the white cuff clearly visible
on his outstretched arm. And on his lips, the invitation through

the prophet, the words that never lose their exquisite import of hope for those who are tired of the broken cisterns of this world that hold no water for the soul. Thus he began his sermon, enunciating his text, making it the fulcrum of his thoughts and the focus of the waiting people's expectation.

> 'Ho! gach neach air am bheil tart, thigibh-se chum nan uisgeachan: agus esan aig nach'eil airgiod, thigibh, ceannaichibh agus ithidh; seadh, thigibh, ceannaichibh, gun airgiod agus gun luach, fion agus bainne.'   (Isaiah 55:1)

Translation:

> 'Ho! everyone that thirsteth, come ye to the
> waters, and he that hath no money; come ye,
> buy and eat; yea, come, buy wine and milk
> without money and without price.'

The words lingered, like a glorious missive from heaven, words that carried the nuances of the spirit, the refined shades of the preparations, provided by the Divine apothecary for all the wounds and hurts of the heart and the perennial needs of the soul. Here was the premise of letting go the hopes of the world. Here was a compelling reason to reach out with open and empty hands, in response to the invitation of the Word and the unction with which the young student preached. There was a persuasive embodiment of inclusive benevolence reflecting St. Paul's description of the depth and height and breadth of both the wisdom and power of God. And as the fullness of heaven's provision was displayed to the worshippers, it was as if they were closeted in here in this little Gaelic meeting-place, at a banquet. And one felt that without pretending to articulate the motions of the soul, the thoughts going through the minds, the emotions of the hearts, old and young would have this shared testimony. 'It was good for us to be here.' They would recall it as a treasured experience, one carried in the suitcase of memory; one that they would take out and look at and speak about to friends, until their earthly journey was over. And who knows, that they would also carry to the great beyond, where the Redeemed, are kept in perpetual wonder. For there, all the promises of God that they accepted by faith here on earth are being continually fulfilled.

Time passed; I lost count. I moved my feet; a cloud behind, cast a shadow over the window. I looked again. The pulpit was empty; the pews had no people. I drew back into the present. I had seen a capsule of time in the church's past. Surely this was a glimpse of one of the multitude of cells of human testimony, from the 'north and the south and the east and the west,' of human witness to the saving grace of our Lord.

Shortly after this, a new church was built in Shiskine, a fine new smaller church, which was designed by Mr. Eric Shilton, a Glasgow architect, who gave freely of his time and talents in supervising the erection of the new building. Making another visit sometime thereafter, I noted that the old Gaelic hall, the 'meeting house' as it was called in the Highlands, was no more. But there is no past for the shared worship of generations. That worship rises continually in the centuries of time to the Throne of heaven. Such memories when my father like others led the worship, mingle in the ever-present of the Church's experience, that signifies for all in the Covenant of Grace, life, life that shall never end.

Chapter 13

Locheweside
Historical Background

W e cannot speak of Aultbea without some brief reference to the historical setting of which it was a
part. Until the 1820's, the parish of Gairloch was
treated as one ecclesiastical charge. There was only one
minister with the manse at Gairloch. There was a church in
Gairloch, and one in Laide, two miles from the Aultbea centre.
These churches, the ruins of which can now be seen in the
cemeteries, go back to the Reformation, and possibly earlier
times. They are now stripped of their roofs. But carvings of
the stonework round the Gothic arched windows can still be
seen, though stones have been dislodged in the ruin.

 On the Poolewe side, the south and west arm of Lochewe,
you have hamlets, Boor, Naast, Inverasdale, Fyremore and
Cove. Services were held in the last-mentioned place, Cove,
where there was a commodious cave. On the Aultbea side,
services were held in a cave at Idrigil, very close to Laide.
The caves were used for worship right into the 19th century.
One virtue was that the minister could not keep the
congregation too long, as the incoming tide dictated the time
to bring the service to a close. This depended upon the time
of the month and the strength of the tides.

 Since the church was established, even after the

Reformation in 1560 when churches were often built at the whim of landowners, there was a large discrepancy between the provision of churches and the population. Landowners, including the monarchs, also presented ministers, their own personal choice, men who, with noted exceptions, 'piped to their tune'. This was the universal law of patronage as practised in England. Increasingly, governments towards the end of the 18th century saw how unsatisfactory this provision was, in the scarcity of churches and also of ministers, a trend clearly visible, both in England and Scotland. It's not as if politicians were suddenly concerned for the spiritual welfare of the people. But they saw, in the increasing radicalism of the secular, a similar stirring of disaffection in the church, established by law as the one church, on both sides of the Border. Such a disintegration of the 'system' that preserved the traditional class privileges, would have to be addressed.

It is odd but the established church in both England and Scotland just could not accommodate the evangelical life that people craved. In England, in spite of every effort to keep within the established church structure, the Wesley brothers were forced to dissolve historic ties. The result was Methodism, a parallel but contrasting dynamic spiritual church.

There were numerous secessions, which in turn threatened the basis of the Scottish national established church, and undermined the accepted principle and premise, namely, a single denomination in each parish. In principle and practice, the Reformers projected this basic tenet, one Nation, one Church, one Parish, one Christian school. Over and above that Church/State liaison, there might be religious freedom privately, but it was not envisaged that the outward unity of the Church would give way to unlicensed and often unscriptural 'do it yourself' parochial alternatives. The political Settlement of 1688 had guaranteed freedom of religious expression. This could be interpreted as a recipe for ecclesiastical disaster. You could say that it was the easy way out, a legislative expedient which seemed to solve all problems. It was something like a classroom of scholars, each wanting a different lesson or subject to be taught. The teacher gives up in the face of pressure. He abandons the timetable; only one subject can be taught, the official one. Since his authority to do this is challenged, he solves the problem, by writing on the blackboard in a pseudo-authoritative show, 'Let everyone do that which is right in his own eyes.' That may be freedom of religious conviction, but it is a denial of freedom of true religion. But in practice, it took a long time for people to realise people-power.

Spiritual freedom is not a *carte-blanche* for all kinds of groups, some no doubt good, and some overtly evil. Religious conviction relates to the impression upon the individual; religious liberty relates to the expression made upon the collective of society. The first is a true right. The second is a responsible privilege. The church as a vision of an established, continually reforming entity, universal, catholic, call it what you like, identifies with geography. Scotland was divided up into segments, identical with presbytery, which was a collective of parishes. These in turn were identified with congregations within the parish bounds. The authoritative historical and Scriptural principle identified the church, one church with one geographically based presbytery—we are speaking of Scotland. Read also St. Paul's letters. Repeatedly, he speaks of the church at Corinth, or the church at Ephesus.

John speaks in Revelation of the church at Sardis, or the church at Philadelphia. The underlying principle clearly taught in Scripture is that the Church, irrespective of liberty of conviction, must maintain ecclesiastical unity and relate politically to responsible government in a partnership of decisive and authoritative mutual co-operation.

The tragedy is that the secular powers felt, justifiably or not, that they could not produce a formula that would please everyone. Thus, the secular powers, in the guise of a law guaranteeing religious freedom, washed their hands of any more responsibility clearly mandated in Scripture and incumbent upon the civil magistrate, to promote the Christian teaching according to creed and authoritative historical precedent.

There is always a confusion between people-power, or political liberty, a coveted human privilege, and on the other hand what we might term, Pentecostal power. No one would argue that the former is a right. Many would question that the latter is a right. The Settlement, supposed to guarantee everyone their religious liberties in 1688 was called a Bill of Rights.

But you cannot command spiritual Pentecostal power. If it is of the Spirit of God, which is premised on true orthodoxy of doctrine, then the spark, the genesis, the subsequent collective awakening and expression of religion, must also come from God, in a continuing dynamic, a quiet ongoing influence permeating, not an exclusive cell in society, but the whole of the community in the everyday intercourse that makes happy villages, towns and cities. The role of the church is not to be judged by its apparent external image. Like the central heating system in a home, it may be functionally efficient yet little seen. But seen or not, overtly as visible to the senses, in impressive centrally placed churches, or in the intercourse of social life, it will be judged by its fruits.

It would take the lighting of the heavenly flame to bring redress to the ills of a secular and sinful society. But it required the secular partner of the State to provide the context of an ordered church. It is a bit like a garden. You cannot have a proliferation of plants jammed up against one another. Their multiplicity negates the growth of any to fulfill its purpose. Because the State—look at England—defaulted in social legislation to protect the poor workers in the 'dark Satanic mills' of the Industrial Revolution, you had the 18th century break-away from the Establishment, in Methodism. The spiritual dynamic came first through the preaching of the Wesleys, and the charismatic Whitefield. It is well known that the Wesleys had reluctantly to accept the fracture and separation from the Established Church. Why? Yes, because the Established Church had such a cosy relationship with the secular that it failed to demand of the secular the social reforms and enlightened mandatory legislation necessary to curb the avarice of powerful greedy capitalists.

In Scotland, it is easy to see a parallel. It could easily be called Chalmers' Choice. Dr. Thomas Chalmers reluctantly, if decisively, led a third of the Church to form a separate segment called the Free Church. But he made it plain that this was temporary, a Protest, like a strike, until the constitutional situation was rectified in London. But in Scotland there was a difference. The issue was not one of social need. It was the right inherent in generic human liberty for a congregation to chose their minister. Within the *status quo*, there was room for several ministers to be considered, and thus the people's choice to obtain. That was illustrated in Knox's concession to practical necessity in appointing bishops in 1572. To avoid any charge of episcopacy, which had earned a rather negative reputation, these were called 'superintendents', viz. Bishop Carswell of Glasgow. Critics gave them a shrewdly accurate designation of 'tulchan bishops'. This was borrowed from a deceptive expedient in dairy farming to trick a cow to give its milk, thinking her newborn calf was sucking her udder. But then necessity dictated the expedient. And perhaps that in the last resort describes all variations of church government in the whole range from hierarchical to congregational. At the end of the day, whether a bishop appoints, or a congregation choses, the whole issue rests on the person who is chosen. A congregation can and does make a bad choice as often as does a bishop. The maxim is often true that a congregation gets the minister it deserves. The spiritually-minded people will seek out a like-minded minister who will keep them spiritually alert; a worldly congregation will seek out a time-server who will flatter them in ease.

The Gospel awakening came to dark Scotland, as it had done in the dis-established Wesleyan church in England. As in England the dynamic spiritual life came first. Then followed the politics of ecclesiastical separatism. That could be construed historically as a tragic development, the fruits of which are reaped every day in the loose and lost ties that should unify a community. Add to this the breakdown of ecclesiastical authority, the multi-voiced church often sounding contradictory notes. And not least the sheer waste of the givings of people, keeping up a multiplicity of church buildings, a pure material venture that is often stripped of spiritual value except for denominational egotism.

Contrast the situation in the Highlands over a period of a century. Visiting a Highland parish in 1830, you would see there was usually one denomination, the established church. If you visited the same parish a century later, in 1930, you would have three if not four Presbyterian churches, plus a possible Scottish Episcopal church or a Roman Church. Had history evolved on a straighter course, ecclesiastically and ideally, without the erosion and undercutting of magnified hair-splitting, and arguments over such issues as the date of Easter, unity, at least as a golden Scriptural and social goal, would be retained. And there is little doubt that many of the negative aspects of subsequent development in the church's history would be obviated. It is interesting that revival, even that of the historic Reformation, began within the structured unity of the Christian Church. Many claim the separatist denominations were the progenitors of the religious awakenings. Far from it, the splits and subsequent denominational entities, were consequences of revival. And though clearly of benefit, also generated their own 'sins'.

But much of that is speculative and must remain hypothetical. History, good and bad, is reality. By the 1820's and onwards, religious revival among the people in Kilsyth and elsewhere, spread to glen and to strath, and across the water to the western Hebrides, like the traditional clan call to war, the 'Fiery Cross'. It found a ready response in the hearts of the people and took deep rooting in the Highlands. The *one church, one parish* rule no longer worked. Many new churches throughout Scotland were being built outwith the established church. Population also was growing. If the established church was to continue, more churches had to be built with extra ministers to serve the people's needs. It could be said that the greater working population of the cities was lost in part through the inertia of the established church. The legacy of the state church's failure to reach the urban working people left these looking elsewhere for life's answers. Here was a similar pattern to that obtaining in England, where the Church of England in its constipated security left untouched the millions that migrated into the cities to bend under the burdens of economic slavery.

But we must speak here of the Highlands, and particularly the charge that would be my father's sphere of spiritual labours. The Government split up parishes, just for ecclesiastical purposes. Thus Aultbea and Poolewe became a separate parish from Gairloch. The new churches built were called Parliamentary churches. One was built at Poolewe. In Aultbea, where the greater number of people lived, the place of worship was still the cave at Idrigil, where the church building was a roofless ruin. The 'uncommon' worshippers, though few in comparison had not only a nice new church built for them in Poolewe, but plush red cushions laid on their pews, and the raised backs padded with the same, all paid for by the British tax-payer. The patrons, the landowners, sat on their little thrones at the side of the pulpit of these churches, usually in the gallery. If you sat in one of these, you would see how separated these worshippers, the rich, the privileged, were from the rest of the people.

Often, the ordinary people when they worshipped in church, had to take their own stools, if they wanted to sit down at all. Remember Jenny Geddes, some 200 years earlier in St. Giles in Edinburgh, who impatiently threw her stool at the minister who was using the Royal Prayer-book. The first Free Church place of worship, built after the Disruption in

1843, had no seating for the congregation. In the 1940's an old woman, 'Bel' MacIver from Buailnaluib, told the manse children that she used to carry a stool, as did all the people, in order to be seated for worship. It is true that many churches had eventually been furnished with pews. Indeed the cost of these was collected from each family every year and provided a return of expenditure by the patron on keeping the church open. The collection of pew rents was carried over into the dis-established churches, particularly the Free Church. I think of Aultbea in the 1930's where this was still collected, albeit for the congregation's funds.

The central ecclesiastical question behind the Disruption was not appointment of minister by bishop or congregation. The issue was one of appointment by a secular patron or a congregation. To illustrate how the church situation was unsatisfactory, think of the Patronage presentee to the parish of Gairloch, Mr. Russell, in 1802. Here was a parish where Gaelic was the language of every day life. Yet the minister had not acquired a competence in preaching in the common language, nor an ability to converse in it with the people. This favoured the *status quo* in which relatively prosperous English speaking visitors came on holiday. In fact the Presbytery took note of complaints that the minister used Gaelic sermons which were written by the schoolmaster. Not only so but the minister could not read these sermons properly. But he suited the incoming visitors who were there on holiday chiefly during the summer, to catch their salmon.

An energy-less laid-back style reminiscent of the 'Dark Ages' followed the relatively dynamic live excitement of the 17th century. The national witness of the people of Scotland, signing their allegiance to Christ, even with their own blood in the Greyfriars' Churchyard in Edinburgh, the bright witness of the Covenanters, and the martyrs' testimony, lighting the nation with its spiritual flame, during the 'Killing Times'—all this had a reaction, a very negative reaction which began with the Crown Settlement in 1688 of King James's daughter Mary, and her husband William, Duke of Orange, as Protestant incumbents on the throne of the United Kingdom. The slumbering inaction associated with the subsequent years ceased with the rupture of the English Established Church in the Methodist Revolution. In Scotland the national scene of passive inactivity and spiritual lassitude ended with the dynamic impulse, politically and spiritually, in the Disruption of the Scottish Established Church in 1843, almost a hundred years later.

It is possible to see the Disruption in part, as a political phenomenon, a restless impatient action by the votaries of the new age, children of the Industrial Revolution. Dr. Chalmers had his new manse in Fife fitted for gas lighting, long before gas lighting using coal byproduct was available. It is true to substantiate this view, that the Free Church was aligned with the current resurgence of Liberalism. This was colourfully personified by Ewart Gladstone, prime minister and the 'grand old man' of later 19th century politics, connected by family with Dingwall in Ross-shire.

But political interpretation alone could not fully account for the dynamic movement in church, education and general social philanthropy and structural public care that swept Scotland into a new era of comparative prosperity and progressive social development. Sadly the influence of the powerful neighbour south of the border caused Scotland and indeed the Free Church, to retain, if not formally the

Patronage of the old, at any rate the class characteristics of the latter. To a large extent, the class system was scarcely dented. The wheels of industry ground on, in spite of the few enlightened Christian visionaries like David Dale and his son-in-law and like-minded practical Christian Robert Owen, in the New Lanark Mills, with socialized factory provisions for workers, in clean houses, schools and sickness insurance. His experiments at Blantyre, that town identified with the immortal name of David Livingstone, were shrugged off in the contemporary rush for riches. Dale pioneered economic reform in experimental mills in Oban and in East Sutherland in the Highlands. Sadly such efforts pettered out, for want of support. And, like it or not, the church, even in its new radicalism, stayed put, in the comfortable conservative social structure of the old.

There is no doubt that the Disruption was the channel in which a revived spirituality found expression. Apart from the documented explosion of practical Christianity in education, and the medical sphere, this could well be the primary dynamic which it represented. Thus the Free Church brought to Scotland and the Highlands particularly, a new vigour. But the personalities were bigger than the principles. Gifted men found fulfillment in promoting intellectual development rather than the spiritual. Inevitably, the fire of spiritual fervour would decline and not surprisingly the denomination itself lapse into a new 'moderatism', a 'laissez-faire' variety of flexible doctrinal compromise. Within twenty years of its inception, cracks began to appear in the credal fabric of the Church's beliefs. Swayed by the exciting biological rediscoveries of a minister's son on a scientific Government-sponsored study of tortoises in the Galapagos islands in the Pacific, the

Scriptures were reduced to being a source-book for faith, rather than authoritative text-book of God's Revelation. Once the rot set in, the inerrant Nautical Tables for taking sights to keep people on course on life's voyage now became an optional accessory in the toolbox of God's tradesmen, apprenticed and officially qualified as journeymen in the building of Christ's Church. Now the 'bright' students did further studies in German universities—a kind of 'finishing' school for the top Scottish professors and ministers, who in turn would share their 'enlightenment' with their lesser brethren, and the ordinary folk in the pew.

Little wonder that as church spires multiplied, at the same time the church, United Presbyterian and the Free Church with the fringe branches, not forgetting the old Parish Church itself still lumbering on, laden with teinds and legal securities, presented a kind of toothless image of impotence. The Free Church like its sister patrons of voluntaryism, craved the privileges of the imported Victorian age. After all only a veneer of education, social manners and graces, a posturing of accent and behavioural pattern were required to fool the crowd and confirm the myth that God had created men equal, but that some were more equal than others. The corollary of this was an impasse where the dynamic of spiritual promise associated with the revived church, was unfulfilled. In spite of the many positives, in relation to social action to right the many obvious wrongs in the secular sphere, the hopes entertained for the church were not realised as an enduring witness.

If that conclusion is unwarranted, there is no doubt that somewhere in its nursery stage it ceased to reach maturity, irrespective of its self-image and denominational reputation. The fact is, the church of Christ is at its best when it is least heard of, and its greatest achievement is to humbly influence the world about it, without fanfare or demonstrativeness. No flourish of ecclesiastical activity, bursting out and evolving under the skillful leadership of Dr. Rainy, chief architect of a new ecclesiastical structure, outwardly amalgamating with every historic secession in a synthesis of false national regeneration, could animate the dead carcass of a collapsed, top heavy orthodoxy. Sadly if statistics are correct, attachment to the conglomerate of the 'national church' and the remnants of secession still extant, now is reduced to a puny fraction of Scotland's population.

The 19th century story of the Scottish Church with its focus on the Free Church, is in many ways, in spite of great worth, a repeat of earlier church history, the rape of the Celtic Church, using the excuse of an Easter bonnet and the English influence of sweet Queen Margaret. Now, the label of another queen, that of Victoria, stamped even the Scottish scene, ecclesiastical as well as secular with its pompous hypocritical image—the 'Victorian Age'. And for Scotland, floods of Irish Roman Catholics swelled the city of Glasgow and its satellite towns. The result, maturing throughout the 20th century, is a profound statistical change. In church and universities, in business and sport, the once treasured Sabbath as the hall-mark of a God-fearing nation has been exported and scuttled in the ocean. And that pillar of Scotland's history, the Preaching of the Gospel, the whole Word of God, is often reduced to a diluted nursery talk.

Eighty years after the Disruption, this Highland parish of Locheweside embodied the best of Scotland's ecclesiastical history. Here, perhaps insulated to some extent by the rugged geography of the surrounding mountains, where the golden eagle soared in lofty and exclusive solitude, was a preserved example of the historical community, not unlike the projection of Scotland's John Knox for every parish. If there were disparate views and attitudes, these healthy differences were not asserted to form rival substitutes for the collective historical unity of the church and the community.

Aultbea - Locheweside

Now that we have taken a wider look at the church and mentioned interpretively these salient points of note, we would return to this example, namely Aultbea, which was to be the scene of my father's labours.

The parish of Gairloch had two main divisions. These followed the geography of the northwest coast. The township of Gairloch, with Strath as the chief concentration of people, was centred on the short squat sea loch of Gairloch, translated in English, 'the short loch.' The other division was the collection of hamlets round the larger Loch Ewe referred to as Locheweside. This loch has the special feature of a large island, giving the northern side a shelter from the prevailing southwest winds. Here is Aultbea the chief township, a small port with a large populated area round about it, with clusters of crofts, namely Tighnafaoline, Bualnaluib, Ormscaig, Mellon Charles, Culchointich, and Badfearn. Extending to the back of the north arm round Greenstone Point, Aultbea includes Laide, Idrigil, Slaggan, Achgarve, Mellon Udrigil, Sand, First and Second Coast and Gruinard. Added to these as components of the parish, was the extension mission at Little Lochbroom, with its hamlets of BadLuarach and BadTrailleach and others beyond to Dundonell.

More hamlets stretch right round the south and western arm of the loch, the chief of these being Poolewe. This village has been historically given precedence over Aultbea, chiefly because of the unsurpassed reputation of the river on which it is located. This one mile long waterway joining Loch Maree to Loch Ewe is one of the best salmon rivers in Scotland. You can understand why Poolewe attracted the rich sportsmen, thus enhancing the township's reputation artificially over that of its greater and more populous partner Aultbea.

With the parish split into two, a Government church and manse were built in Poolewe, about 1828. In 1843, Rev Donald Macrae signed the Deed of Demission. Mr. MacRae, married to the daughter of Mr. Russell, the incumbent of the south Gairloch parish church, was left in a technical dilemma. While most of the people joined the new Free Church, the Established Church would not release the building of manse and church—the new *quoad sacra* church given to them free by the Government some thirteen years earlier. Such is law, and such is vindictive entrenched evil. In the dark offices of Church and State, orders were crisply sent 'down the line'. The policy to be followed is clear. 'Lock the people out of the church and the minister out of the manse,' or in common jargon, 'If we can't use it, we will make sure no other will either.'

Until at least the outbreak of the Second World War, the parish church and also the manse had a dark sinister appearance. Both were shrouded in a circle of trees, presenting a secretive aspect to the outside world. Ministers who were placed there from time to time seemed to share an anonymity, in which they scarcely ever impacted spiritually upon the community. An English academic, H. F. Wilson from Cambridge, on holiday in Poolewe, wrote a poem on the subject of the Ewe river, in 1885. He adverts to the parish church in this couplet,

'A kirk too ample in extent
To house the 'shrunk' Establishment.'

The law of Scotland had a dark side to it. It appeared at any rate that the hand of the Established Church and that of the State had clasped in a bargain made by none other than the devil himself. The pattern was repeated throughout Scotland. Even the landowners, influenced by Edinburgh, refused sites for Free churches. It all was shown up as a public scandal, when the people of Strontian had a large church, seating six hundred worshippers, built on the Clyde and towed up the west coast by a steam tug. It served as the Free Church, anchored off the shore for many years, before a site was granted outside the township to erect a permanent building on land. The people still worship there to this day. (I would have to say that while preaching there in the1960's, invited to a communion by the minister Rev Robert Park, there was an atmosphere of peculiar spiritual liberty and blessing.)

    But let's get back to the particular situation of the Free Church in Locheweside. Now several events followed. Mr. Russell the parish minister died in Gairloch, a broken man with only a few stragglers for a congregation. Mr. MacRae accepted a call to Tarbert, Lochfyneside. Just think of it, the unyielding iron will of the State Church keeping the church and manse locked so that the people, eighteen hundred members and adherents worshipped at outdoor services for seven years, and that in a part of Scotland where most days make you think of the Niagara Falls, and the continual spray of mist and water that linger in the air as the river plunges over the vertical precipice. Think of the calibre of the new Aultbea minister, Rev James Noble, minister in a relatively comfortable charge in Edinburgh, who ministered and preached for two years before a new church was built in Aultbea and in Poolewe, and a manse built at Aultbea for him and his family!

From then on, with the vast majority of the people living in the Aultbea area, you now have the manse and larger church built in Aultbea, and the minister residing there. In practice the change over from the Established to the Free Church meant no doctrinal change. The issue was one of polity, or church politics rather than spiritual principle.

We cannot omit reference to the Gairloch congregation. Though its minister, Mr. Russell, remained in the Established Church, the great majority of the congregation left to become the Free Church. Rev Duncan Matheson came from Knock, Lewis, to be the new minister of Gairloch Free Church, south. There were only three ministers in that congregation from 1843 until 1923, when my father came to Aultbea. Duncan Matheson as mentioned, John Baillie and William MacKinnon. Baillie was the father of the two distinguished theologians, Donald of St. Andrews and John of New College.

In Aultbea, Mr. Noble worked until he was worn out, bringing the ordinances to the people, and pursuing the new conscientious pastoral work that was the hall-mark of the Evangelical movement to which the Free Church gave witness. Aultbea was realistically recognized as the central locus of the extensive charge. Poolewe retained the character of a ministerial congregation, but in a shared concessionary deference to the greater congregation of Aultbea. It had to be happy with a resident missionary or catechist, who alternated with the minister in taking the services. Rev James Noble died in Aultbea in 1864 and was mourned by his people. He had come from a Gaelic Free congregation in Edinburgh, to be the first minister of the Free Church's new charge, Aultbea and Poolewe, the north parish of Gairloch. He was a man of high calibre, leaving the city for a large scattered charge, while there was still no manse or church. A potato crop failure, similar to that in many parts of the Highlands and in Ireland, over several years brought destitution to many. In this situation Mr. Noble laboured for some considerable time, enduring hardship and separation from his family, his wife and children having to be domiciled in Inverness, until the new manse was built in Aultbea.

He was buried between the church and the manse in a grave surrounded by an iron rail. That first church is no more. But the grave is a reminder of the church and the minister. The cast iron memorial gives a record of the love and regard with which he was held by his people.

Mr. Noble's successor, William Rose, was called one of the 'three greatest preachers in the Highlands,' by none other than the distinguished Dr. Kennedy of Dingwall. In 1872 Rev. Ronald Dingwall, a native of Kingussie, succeeded him. Dingwall identified with the people as had his predecessors. His medical knowledge made him physician for the body as well as for the soul. A man of many gifts, he thought it not demeaning to do any work of carpentry necessary for the manse. The kitchen table used as late as 1950, was made by him. It was perfectly put together with tenon joints and proved its maker's workmanship by standing up to the tough use and abuse of the eight lively manse children. Mr. Dingwall also had a large extension added to the manse, with indoor plumbing. With this, came a bathroom, scullery and washing-room, vital requirements for a large family.

With the Disruption, a large Free Church place of worship was built rather hurriedly in Aultbea, not a stone's throw from the new manse. The location was right in the centre of Aultbea. There was a basic fault. It was built facing due east. In Aultbea, whether by accident or design, most if not all buildings faced the south. There is no doubt that with the gable facing the east, the body of the church and one side of its roof were exposed to the unrelenting wind and rain from the south west. The plantation of birch trees in front of the manse did nothing for the first church, in this respect. For the second, still presently standing and as good as ever, this an excellent wind-break. This first Free Church building proved to be inadequate and had structural problems which could not be corrected. When Rev Ronald Dingwall became minister, as successor to Mr. Rose, this was recognised and the building, now only just over forty years old, was demolished. The church gable at the front with the arch of the doors and part of two arched windows were left standing for the next century. This monument was part of the childhood habitat of succeeding families of manse children and still remains indelibly ingrained in memory. But with Mr. Dingwall at the helm, the trustees and Deacon's Court looked to the future. The new church would be built not only to accommodate the large congregation, but it would be built of the best materials available, a fitting edifice to the glory of God, in the centre of the township. It still stands more than a century later, witnessing to the vision of the people and to the spiritual priorities which undergirded their lives.

It is logical, if a people are Christian and the fabric of their lives is woven in the texture of Biblical Redemptive teaching, this centrality of the people's beliefs and faith should be boldly reflected in the visible architecture and location of their church. The Christian Church should be the central edifice in every community. This rule should not be abrogated. In another pattern, the Christian place of worship obeying the same rule or principle of centrality, should be situated in a location central to several townships whose people it serves and who travel inwards towards it like spokes of a wheel. This practical principle or indeed laudable expedient was clearly implemented in the building of the new church in Aultbea. With the spiritual guidance and practical commonsense shared by Mr. Dingwall the minister, and the office bearers in Session and Management of the congregation, a great day of celebration and thanksgiving climaxed the completion of the congregation's desire.

Opening of the new Free Church at Aultbea

This handsome and substantial edifice was opened on Thursday, the 21st inst, this being the Fast-day in connection with the dispensing of the Lord's Supper in the parish. The services were conducted by the Rev Mr. McCulloch, Latheron(the minister-elect of Hope Street Free Church Glasgow), and the Rev. Mr. Baillie, Gairloch. On each of the five days of the Communion, there were crowded congregations. On Sabbath there were no fewer than 1300 persons present. All the passages were supplied

with forms, and many had only standing room,
even the stairs to the platform being crowded.
The principal entrance to the building is in the
south gable, and about a dozen yards from the
high road. The gable which faces the bay, and
principal thoroughfare, has, with its belfry, an
imposing and pleasing appearance. The front
of the building is in square rubble. The free-
stone has been conveyed by sea from the East
Coast, and the rest of the stone was procured
from the Isle Ewe Quarry. The platform (which
is placed at the north end of the building) and
its surroundings, including precentor's and
elders' seats, are of pitch pine, as is also the
front of the gallery. The seats, which are roomy
and comfortable, are of redwood, and the whole
of the woodwork being varnished and partly
stained, the interior presents a warm and
comfortable appearance. The acoustics are
perfect. Though the church is large, the
preacher's voice is distinctly heard in the
remotest corner. There is a large hall at the north
end for congregational and other meetings. The
work has been altogether very satisfactorily
executed, and reflects great credit on the
architects and contractors. The architects were
Messrs. Maitland and Sons, Tain; builders,
Messrs. Maclean and MacKenzie, Dingwall;
plasterer, Mr. Munro Tain; plumbers, Messrs.
Tolmie and Mackenzie, Dingwall; painter and
glazier, Mr. Ross, Dingwall; ironwork, Mr.

MacIntosh, Tain. The whole work is estimated to cost something over 1800 pounds (sterling).

By the completion of this church a greatly felt want is supplied to the inhabitants of the district. The old church was hurriedly got up shortly after the Disruption, and it fell— not by neglect, but by sheer natural decay, in spite of repeated repairs —into such a dilapidated condition as to be scarcely safe to meet in. On stormy days, which are not infrequent here, wind and rain freely entered during the last winter, and people, especially the aged, attended the means of grace at considerable inconvenience to themselves. The lasting gratitude of the congregation is due, and it is most heartily accorded, to the generous friends who have so readily responded to the calls of our minister in liberally subscribing to the new building. The people are not, however, at all out of their difficulties. This parish is so wide and populous that two Free Churches have been since the Disruption required by the congregation, in each of which the minister preaches on alternate Sabbaths. The able, respected and beloved catechist of the parish, officiates in the one church when the minister is in the other. The Poolewe Church, the timber of which is of home growth, is in a ruinous state, and steps are in progress to have a new church built there this summer.

The opening services at Aultbea were listened to with rapt attention by appreciative audiences. Mr. McCulloch and Mr. Baillie both preached impressive discourses.

(Extract from Inverness Courier, 29th March 1889)

This building, thoroughly maintained over the years by a competent Deacon's Court and responsible Trustees, is still used over a hundred years later. If its walls could speak, what glorious anecdotes of preaching and prayer, of Christ's love and the Spirit's liberty could be told in all the transactions of grace in the hearts and lives of the Aultbea people! You will note that the Aultbea new Free Church place of worship was of considerable size, designed to accommodate normally, a thousand worshippers. Of the same design but about half the size, a similar church was built on Riverside, Poolewe, as adverted to in the newspaper article above. It also was of the same high standard of workmanship and materials. It is there a hundred years later, still giving testimony to the centrality of religious foundations upon which the community is based. We will speak further on the meeting-houses which formed a network of locations for religious purposes in the smaller hamlets that comprised this extensive charge, and which has been aptly designated Locheweside.

Into this hallowed sphere of spiritual labours, Angus MacKinnon would be inducted as minister. He would be designated ever after as 'MacKinnon Aultbea.' His name and that of the place in which he laboured would merge into one. His heart would be there because he would become so identified with the people in all their varied experiences, their sorrows and their joys, that like a tree transplanted from its nursery, the past chapters of his upbringing would find maturity and flourish in the glorious privilege of ministering to a great parish congregation.

The cords of affection to Glendale, so strong in his nature, would now be woven round the lives of his parishioners and the homes and families to which he ministered. There was something elusively mystical about his presence, by which he communicated spiritual affinity with his adopted family, his life-long family of the church in Aultbea. This was related to his personality.

This trait of personality was noted by one minister who watched him greeting the people of Glendale after a service when both were there assisting at a Communion some years later. These ties to his birthplace and people could never really be broken. But generically the location of his lifework would also have the same ties of affection. It was the occasion of a communion in Duke Street, Glasgow, where he was assisting the minister, his college friend and fellow Skyeman, Rev Archie MacDonald, who had just been called from Strathpeffer. My father was surrounded by Skye people, many from Glendale, who of course he knew from his childhood. The host minister saw that time was swiftly passing and he was getting just a little bit impatient with his visiting colleague in the never-ending reunion with friends at the front of the Duke Street church. He was heard to remark:

'*Tha e na's fhasa am biodh a' thoirt as an fhaochag beo na Aonghas MacFhionghuinn a ' thoirt air falbh bho na Daillaich.*' (It is easier to pull the food out of a whelk as it is to separate Angus MacKinnon from his own people of Glendale.)

The same unusually strong ties of affection would be reborn in the context of his lifelong ministry to the people and the place. Only the people of Aultbea would themselves be responsible for a reciprocal loyalty, born and nurtured for a century previously, as we will illustrate later.

Chapter 14

David and Goliath

L et us trace the sequence of events from 1900, leading up to the settlement of Mr. MacKinnon in 1924. Mr. Dingwall, the minister in 1900, joined the disciples of a new *instant* ecclesiastical union set up as a rival to the historic Parish Church of Scotland. Infiltrated with ideas of a new radicalism in politics and theology, their leaders in the academic world promised them, ministers and people, the prize of intellectual maturity and theological respectability, and also bewitched them with a glittering mirage of a new century of Utopian humanist fulfillment. They called themselves the United Free Church.

It is very puzzling that Mr. Dingwall, who for twenty three years was the esteemed pastor of Aultbea, and himself a man of balanced judgment and mature learning, separated from his people when the Free Church broke up in Edinburgh in 1900. He of all people should have known the mind of the congregation of Aultbea and Poolewe, who almost all remained in the Free Church.

One can only think that the good minister of Aultbea, like hundreds of others, was tricked by the clever church politicians into believing that those who did not leave the Free Church would be put out of church and manse, irrespective of what the people wished. It had happened in 1843, and now as 1900 approached when the decision would be made at the General Assembly, the church lawyers advised that the same ruthless undemocratic power politics would apply again against the people. Many good men were tricked besides Mr. Dingwall. One thinks of good men like McAskill, successor to Dr. Kennedy of Dingwall who capitulated to political pressure and also lost his congregation. Dr. Alexander Whyte of Free St. George's West, Edinburgh, with others like his protégé, John Kelman, followed Henry Drummond with sincerely held views bordering on delusions. Such ephemeral hopes for a scientific Utopia would be summarily dissipated in one brief moment of naked venom as the Kaiser's guns opened up, spewing death and destruction over Europe in 1914.

In Aultbea, great anguish and pain attended the rupture of the pastoral tie between minister and parishioners. Sadly, Mr. Dingwall was assured from the new disciples of an alien Voluntaryism— another mischievous 'ism'—that, although he left the Free Church, he was legally still minister of Aultbea and therefore had title to the church and manse. But his own dutiful didactic ministry and that of the ministers and catechists before him, had given the people and especially its leading elders, maturity of judgment and the historic spiritual and ecclesiastical values, which gave them a rocklike unity of conviction that they should remain steadfast in faithfulness to their national ecclesiastical heritage.

Now, as Mr. Dingwall returned to Aultbea from that fateful Assembly, he was brought face to face with the consequences. The minister was barred from entry into the church, to the great distress of both parties. The congregation were forced into this unnatural confrontation with their minister. And the minister was faced with the humiliation of losing his congregation and his living. The stand-off was not a source of pride but grief to both. The congregation held to the beliefs for which their Church, the Free Church of Scotland, came into being, through the leadership of Dr. Thomas Chalmers, a mere fifty seven years previously. Furthermore they had accepted their minister and the sincerity of his preaching in the espousal of the historical verities, cherished by the Reformer, statesmen, like Knox, Melville and Henderson. They had just built their new church and manse. Nearly every home was still with them.

There followed in Aultbea, what could only be described as the first big 'sit-in', pre-empting the many sit-ins in the open political and social setting of a later day. With practical wisdom, the congregation now set about holding on to their beloved church. Until the law of justice was recognised they would have to use every non-violent means to prevent being steam-rollered, as it were, by the new contrived consortium, fabricated by ecclesiastical artifice, that for the second time in just over half a century would seek to rob them of their common heritage. The leading elders, men of unquestioned calibre, by nature and by grace, called the people to fight the ecclesiastical giant of legal darkness. The people responded. Relays of families took turns to occupy the church day and night. There they worshipped the God of their Fathers; there they prayed, led by mighty men in prayer. Night and day, the oil lamps of the sanctuary were literally and metaphorically kept alight as the people held on to their beloved church. Outside, hawks circled about, but not the native breed of the surrounding Highland hills.

These were ecclesiastical hawks, mysterious legal
emissaries and officers of the law, cold, smooth faced hard-
looking men in dark coats and top hats, with sheriff's officers
to do their bidding. They waited, hiding in the local hotel,
biding their chance to occupy the people's church, if given
the opportunity. There was no violence, no hint of civil
disobedience, no excuse given for action by police. For three
months, the stalemate continued. The people stood firm. With
them was right, with them was God himself, with them were
their local leaders, men of conviction, men of spiritual stature,
without equal, with their natural gifts amplified by grace to
make them dynamic, spiritual, and yet convincingly and
authoritatively reasonable.

God provides a person for every hour of need. Aultbea was
no exception. A dark hour of unspiritual cold now chilled the
people's hearts, as an eclipse of the sun brings shivers to people
on a mid-summer day. Their link with the constitutional church
in Edinburgh was the spiritual and sinewy strength of Rev
William MacKinnon, Gairloch. Rock-like in his convictions,
without any trace of fanaticism, he took over the oversight of
the congregation in his authoritative position as interim-
moderator of Aultbea, now bereft of its pastor. He assured
and encouraged the people of Aultbea to hold on against the
encroachment of the powerful ecclesiastical and secular forces
arrayed against them. And at last they prevailed. They held
the line. One and all shared the triumph. Even the people
from Poolewe, and those in Inverasdale and Cove, and the
big Grants from Isle Ewe, and the Grants from Mellon Udrigil,
with all the rest, joined in as a resolute team, like a 'tug of
war' team. They held their ground and held on to their beloved
church. There was nothing like it. Without any violence, they

beat the bureaucratic ecclesiastical machine that had become a juggernaut, and the perverted statutes of the historic liaison of church and state, linked to Scotland's character as a nation. The tide turned. Second thoughts and opinions and more seasoned objective perspectives were brought to bear. The nation at large, in spite of attempts to suppress the injustice imposed upon the Free Church, realized that little David was up against a Goliath, the new instant church, now given the name of the United Free Church. We leave the readers to read their history. Enough to say that the Free Church were supported by none other than the Archbishop of Canterbury and a huge mass of goodwill from the secular and ecclesiastical world. At last even the House of Lords vindicated their constitutional rights as heirs of the Disruption, and the physical endowments that belonged to it.

In the dramatic confrontation in Aultbea, eventually realization dawned, and the tiny minority conceded defeat. The 'pack' was called off, and the congregation came back to normal. But the wounds were there and nearly a hundred years later the scars are still there, with the mischief then brought to this singularly happy united people where synthesis of secular and sacred was void of division—the visionary embodiment of the nation's historic reformers and statesmen.

Mr. Dingwall went away a broken man. There is no doubt that he had shown uncharacteristic mistaken judgment. It remains to this day a puzzle how he could possibly have been taken in by the ecclesiastical politicians in Edinburgh. What joy to hear that his family still love Aultbea and have a holiday home in Bualnaluib, the home of 'Maggie the Bridge', not far from the local school, to which they come every year. If the situation of Aultbea had occurred a hundred years later, the Press and Television would have zoned in on this ecclesiastical confrontation on the ground, in contrast to the academic isolation of the Assembly Hall in Edinburgh. The pros and cons would have been quickly sorted out in a wide and informed debate. The ecclesiastical ruse of Dr. Rainy and associates would have been exposed.

Consider the Model Trust Deed passed in law some twenty years earlier. By it all congregations were invited and encouraged to centralize their property deeds in the safety and security of the central church offices in Edinburgh. A thousand congregations from all over Scotland, and missions on every continent, especially in Africa and in India responded, and were thus tricked. Once the central church had the deeds, it could control the ministers and congregations in subsequent ecclesiastical manoeuvers. This was exactly what the ecclesiastics were already engaged in, uniting with the voluntaries, the newly formed United Presbyterian Church, largely placed in the Lowlands and the East Coast. But Aultbea and Gairloch and Dingwall and the Free North in Inverness and, indeed, all the congregations in the Highlands did not fall for the ecclesiastical trick. Hence the people in 1900 were supported by the law of the nation in the highest court of the land, the House of Lords, and retained title to their buildings.

Remember that in Aultbea and Poolewe memories of the injustice were still fresh, namely when all the people came out of the Establishment in 1843. Just think of it, eighteen hundred people dispossessed and left to worship outside in rain and cold and snow for seven years without relenting by the church and state lawyers. Think of the cruelty and the vindictiveness, as the Parliamentary church in Poolewe, built by taxpayers' money, was now used only for the relatively few and exclusive rich visitors who came for the salmon fishing in the summertime.

There is every ground for believing that the supposed ecclesiastical union, was contrived, albeit with political skill comparable to that used to formulate the European Union a more than half a century later. One would have to add, that in spite of it being church politics, the skills employed were no more scrupulous.

Just think of the contradictions. The Free Church was in principle tholed to the historical position of the Established Church in its spiritual liaison with the state—a reciprocal partnership of spiritual responsibility of both, to God and His Word, not to each other. Given this historical and credal fact, it was an act of breach of trust and betrayal, for Dr. Rainy and his ecclesiastical 'Cabinet' ministers to mislead the greater part of the Free Church into a union of professed Voluntaries hostile to the idea of Establishment.

It must remain hypothetical, but it would have been rational for the Free Church in 1900 to join with the old Parish or Established Church of Scotland. There is no doubt that the remaining constitutional part should have returned to the fold. The law would not have faulted them for that. And further it would simply be the natural corollary of the 1843 Disruption, which Dr. Chalmers saw as a temporary ecclesiastical rupture.[1] The latter, that is the Established Old Parish Church was still ticking over like an old grandfather clock. Aultbea especially was, although denominationally separated, really the Parish Church. There was no Established Parish church in Aultbea. The mischief of interfering ecclesiastics, pushing their

1 See appendix

irrational schemes upon the church in Scotland can hardly be overemphasized. Just look at the proliferation of church buildings, nearly all Presbyterian. They have divided the 'House of the Lord,' sown discord among its people, and caused the material resources and ministerial personnel to be exhaustively misused. The end result by any observation at the end of the 20th Century speaks for itself as a tragic social and national consequence.

Here there is a grim picture of a land that has lost the spiritual structure identified with its history, and an alienation from its ecclesiastical heritage of four fifths of its population.

The Aultbea people were strengthened, as we said in their hour of crisis by their neighbours in Gairloch. Mr. Baillie had died in 1890. He was succeeded by Rev William MacKinnon, a native of Skye. Mr. MacKinnon was a highly erudite and able minister. He stayed with his people and church and became an anchor for the area of northwest Ross-shire. Apart from playing a leading role in the ecclesiastical affairs of the Church at large, he became a kind of foster parent to Aultbea and Poolewe, the North Gairloch parish. Rev Donald MacNaughton came as minister to Aultbea in 1914. But MacKinnon Gairloch retained a special place in the hearts of the Aultbea people. He was there in 1900 when the congregation rocked like a ship in a storm. He was there on the bridge of the ship, and his advice had the authoritative ring of a captain's commands.

Now the years had passed well into the 20th century. The Great War was over and when MacNaughton left, the congregation waited for a new minister. Thus it was in 1924, that a class finished in the Divinity Hall, a class of which Angus MacKinnon, another Skyeman from Glendale, was also a graduating member. At thirty-eight years of age, he had a wide experience of life behind him, a reasonable, if belated, formal education which he would assiduously continue to improve upon in his profession. He had special gifts, natural and spiritual, altogether making up a composite human potential that would be shaped and used, for the glory of God, as a parish minister.

We have sought to illustrate how this young boy from Glendale was prepared in Providence with all the seasoning maturity of life's experience and the transforming dynamic of the Spirit, for a lifework as a Highland parish minister. We have equally sought to illustrate how the congregation of Aultbea was also prepared as a place for his labours. The church is likened on earth to a bride. Christ would be ever the bridegroom. Ministers are as the word implies, just servants of the bridegroom. Yet in virtue of their calling there is a vicarious aspect in their pastoral relationship. When a minister is inducted in the midst of a people, to care for their spiritual welfare, and himself find fulfillment of his vocation, there is a union which cannot exclude a contract with the overtones of heavenly sanction.

In the Fall of 1923, Mr. MacKinnon Gairloch asked the student probationer to preach for several Sabbaths in Aultbea. In July of the following year, when he finished his studies, the congregation intimated their desire for him to be their minister. Congregation and minister appeared designed for each other. The student at once according to old elders, speaking of that time, seemed to follow in the footsteps of the gracious ministers, all loved by the people, who had previously laboured faithfully among them. It must not be overlooked that after Mr. MacNaughton left, MacKinnon

Gairloch chaperoned Aultbea. He was not alone. Apart from the able elders in Aultbea and Poolewe, the missionary, Mr. Angus MacAulay, a man of competence and great humanity, was an able lieutenant. There was no hint of congregationalism in the assertion of people power in the parish of Aultbea. There was a generic acceptance of the national church—as long as that church honoured the spiritual as taking precedence over the temporal. Thus, elders never, as far as I recall, preached. They kept the church open should a minister or missionary not be there, but they filled the hour of worship with Scripture readings, prayers and singing. There is a place for this kind of service, one in which the individual and his subjective peroration is omitted.

Meanwhile the clock of history ticked on. The student was licensed to preach the Gospel, by the presbytery of Edinburgh in June 1924. The call from Aultbea with 650 names of adults, 'members, subscribers and regular worshippers', was processed by the Presbytery of Lochcarron, of which Rev Finlay MacRae Plockton was clerk. The call was accepted by the licentiate. Within months a date was set for his ordination and induction. Minister and congregation would be joined in a contract of mutual assent. The resultant union between congregation and minister would bring benefit to many souls in Christ's vineyard and evoke rejoicing among the angels in heaven, over the years to come.

Chapter 15

Aultbea

There is no place in Scotland quite like Aultbea. For scenery it has its undoubted rivals. It is true that its neighbours, Gairloch and Poolewe have stolen the limelight over the years. And both of the latter have indeed a justifiable fame. Gairloch, with its historical and ecclesiastical identity, its west Ross-shire seat of the Clan MacKenzie, its great hotel, and its prolific output of illicit whisky as an unpublicised yet significant part of the economy, inevitably took precedence. According to the 'grapevine' the stills of Melvaig in Gairloch provided the potent base for numerous unofficial blends in outlets far afield, in the same manner as the malt distilleries at Tain and Invergordon. The parallel of the religious and the secular was harmonious. Never twain did meet. Yet each version contributed to the 'spirit' of community life, giving the special texture that warranted Gairloch's unchallenged reputation as a place to be reckoned with. This is not to imply that Aultbea was 'dry'. The sub-division of Laide was the locus of a thriving distilling activity which served the needs or wants of the community and also provided for more cautious communities to the north, in west Sutherland.

The whole parish had a thriving industry of poaching. Venison, God's provision for the common people, traditionally the morally entitled users of wild-life on land and sea, was commonly on the menu. Equally, salmon was on the crofter's table as often as it graced that of Flowerdale House, Cliff House in Poolewe, Inverewe House, Kernsary or the Lodge at Drumchork and Gruinard—all these being the dwellings of the landowners.

Poolewe also has outshone Aultbea, some would say rather unfairly. Ecclesiastically it tended to be a failure since early history, though given a last chance in the *quoad sacra* church and manse built by the Government in the early 1830's. With the Disruption it may be said that Poolewe found its rightful place, and that was secondary to Aultbea which had the main church and the manse. In other respects, its mile-long river gives it an enviable reputation that still merits Poolewe as a special place. Also the Inverewe Gardens are a guarantee of continued attraction, on an international scale, for tourists.

There is every ground for believing that a treasure of some considerable worth is hidden on Isle Ewe. Factual historical evidence supports the view that a carrier with a bag of gold for Bonnie Prince Charles, on his flight from the Whig Government Redcoats after the defeat at Culloden, buried the money on Isle Ewe. Some associate Mellon Charles with the Prince's presence there when he was dodging the notorious Captain Ferguson in the frigate 'Furnace.' Certainly the name 'Charles's hill' makes sense of this interpretation. Especially is this so as a tradition associated with Bualnaluib, makes this the locus of a battle. Strictly speaking it was more of a small skirmish between the Redcoat soldiers who came ashore and rudely sought to search the homes of people. They were convinced that Charles and 'Flora' were in hiding there. But the men of Mellon Charles and Bualnaluib put them to flight. Just about the beginning of the Second World War, a British navy cutlass was brought to the school at Bualnaluib. The local boy, my schoolmate Alick MacIver said that the sword came up while his father was ploughing. The sword blade was still razor sharp. The schoolmaster Mr. John Murchison blunted the blade with a file, to prevent any one being accidentally cut.

But even without that peep into local history, Aultbea is still full of undiscovered treasures. One of these is the reward given to those who stop there instead of passing it by. Many travellers have missed out by omitting Aultbea on their itinerary and going on from Poolewe to Ullapool. But those who turn down the road at Drumchork junction have their reward. Aultbea responds by showing them a treasure of scenic beauty that equals that of rivals. This was brought home to me as a visiting exile in 1996. I motored down through the hamlets past the main village, through Ormscaig, past Rudh' a' Choin in Mellon Charles. There from the hillock above the cemetery where my parents are buried, I surveyed the surrounding scenery. The sun had travelled round so that it shone from the southwest; the sky was an azure blue with speckled white clouds decorating nature's ceiling. All round was a breathtaking panorama. This was a scenic view from inside, a view that none could have unless they looked out from Aultbea. This is part of Aultbea's secret, a discovery waiting for all, but only for all who do not pass by, who stop on the Poolewe-Laide road at the junction and turn west to north Locheweside.

It is still, to some extent, a virgin world. Near at hand, the topography with its gneissic hillocks, its almost lunar little valleys has been likened geologically to 'the ends of the earth.'

The seas sparkle and foam in an endless assault upon the coast, carving alternating rocky promontories of jagged rocks and caves, and on the other hand, there are inviting inlets of golden sands, that make it a swimmer's paradise, from Mellon Charles, past Leac an Dona to the Bay of Slaggan. Islets like Fura and Sgeir-an-Fharaig, with Inverasdale and Cove in the south background, lead the eye to the big Isle of Ewe, dominating the loch in the near distance. Seton Gordon naturalist and writer, described it thus:

> The green Isle of Ewe, sparkling like an emerald in the summer sea.'

It reminds one of Ile Madame near Quebec in the St. Lawrence River in Canada; both are matchless in their beauty. The eye takes in Aultbea and the populous hamlets between, Ormscaig, Bualnaluib, Cul-choinntich, and Badfearn and Drumchork beyond. The mountain road from Poolewe, locally called the 'tops', can be traced, weaving in and out of the hillside, making its mark on the rocky escarpments as an engraver would impress his line on a metal vessel.

Then there are the walls of the whole parish, the ring of mountains that rise with their majestic peaks like guards, round Little Loch Broom, through Gairloch and to the south side, made famous in their geological designation by the 'Father of modern Geology', Hugh Millar, as the Torridonian Sandstone. There is a sense that here is a privileged world, a different world from that beyond, a world of special values, safe, secure and enduring, the creation of a relatively timeless historical evolution where that of place and people evoke something of the eternal.

It is also true to say that Aultbea shares with the whole of the parish of Gairloch the history of its people. While there

has indeed been some natural partisan rivalry, the parish in
the full civil sense has a definite unity among its citizens.
The parish is identified with the MacKenzies and the House
of Seaforth. A close relation is the clan MacRae, a clan with
a wild reputation as fighters, a quality that made them valuable
friends. One of them—apart from Donald MacRae, minister
at Poolewe at the time of the Disruption—also a minister,
was a distinguished preacher, born in Lochalsh. In every way
this Free Church minister justified being called 'the Big
MacRae.' There were also many MacLeans, MacAulays,
MacDonalds, Chisholms, MacLennans, MacIvers, MacLeods,
Urquharts, Gunns, Camerons and MacLeays, as well as other
clan names of others, who came into the community over the
years. One of these was the name of Grant. Their presence in
Aultbea has been traced to Strathspey from which one man
came to the district, to the remote hamlet of Slaggan after
the 45'. Many Grants individually joined the Jacobite army,
in spite of the Duke of Atholl's refusal to do so. The
significance of this incident is in the fact that this man was of
large and powerful physique. Needless to say, he married
and had children and children's children. So that there are
many Grants in Aultbea, especially in Mellon Charles, Mellon
Udrigil, and also on Isle Ewe. And what's more, they are
with rare exceptions unusually big men.

You see how Aultbea is a hidden treasure, an untapped
source of great interest, overlooked to a large extent and
unrecognised for what it is, a wealth of enriching anecdotes.
But it is also something else. Gaelic history and literature,
including Gaelic poetry, *bardachd,* owes much to Aultbea.
Here was the birthplace of John MacKenzie, a refined
musician and poet. He did something unique in his short

life. He translated several devotional books of sermons, then
popular in the 19th century revived church, into Gaelic. Thus
McCheyne's *Sermons,* and Guthrie's *Christian's Great
Interest,* Bunyon's *Pilgrim's Progress* among many other
devotional books, came into every Gaelic home. He produced
a volume of the Songs of Duncan Ban MacIntyre, a prince of
Gaelic literature. And for generations to come who would
value the language and seek to preserve it when they were
scattered round the globe, part of the Greater Highland
Diaspora, there was the McAlpine's Gaelic Dictionary, a work
from Gaelic to English and English to Gaelic that university
students also would use with confidence, in their Celtic classes.
Just think of his academic achievements, and his education
primarily received in the home in Mellon Charles, in the little
school among the trees on Isle Ewe, and in the parish school
in Gairloch.   He also brought together the best of secular
poetry in the 'Beauties of Gaelic Poetry,' *Sar Obar nam bard
Gaidhealach.* This is uniquely valued in the Gaelic academic
world. When it is remembered that John MacKenzie died at
the young age of forty-two, and in his short life produced
over thirty books, edited or written by himself, surely we have
in him an example for all the young aspirants who claim
handicaps of limited opportunity, to 'redeem the time' and
seek fulfillment, not in length of days, but in qualitative
service.
     The birthplace of the author, Aultbea, has for the most
part gone unacknowledged. Surely Aultbea is a place of
undiscovered treasures, elbowed out by more aggressive
competitors! But a quiet humble unassuming disposition is
characteristic of the place and people. There was a cultural
leaven here where music and song were acknowledged and

given their justifiable place as part of the religious/secular fabric of community.

Life is many-sided. One aspect of the charge of Locheweside which was particularly suited to anyone who loved the sea was the fact that the sea loch as well as the inland loch, Loch Maree, touched every part of the parish. And though no one had as yet thought of the new form of transport, the motor car, except for the mailcar, Aultbea congregation had a boat. Yes, this church had its own boat for the use of the minister. She was a substantial vessel, planked in larch—the wood that loves the salt water. In dimensions she was about thirty-nine feet long with a beam of fourteen. She was a modified 'Fifie' with a strait stem but a rounded forefoot. She was a half-size fishing type boat. (A full size fishing-boat would be about seventy to seventy-five feet in length.) As a traditional double-ender she came in at the stern which was raked aft, something between the stern pattern of the Fifie and Zulu. The Aultbea people were proud of their boat. She was rigged like a cutter with bowsprit, two jibs and a gaff mainsail. It was the joy of people, to join the minister on trips to Isle Ewe, to Inverasdale, to Poolewe, on parish work and for services. And now and then visits further afield were undertaken, especially in the summer round Greenstone Point to Loch Broom. and also to Ailligin on Loch Torridon. And in the summer too, the Aultbea boat with a full complement pulled in at Gairloch for their communion. There, friends met friends, long before telephones became common in homes. *Sgoths* from Raasay, from Torridon, from Kishorn and Plockton and from Portree tied up at the pier, or at times anchored off the shore not far from the church. Then people all dressed in their Sunday best were ferried to the shore just below the church. Only when weather was inclement were the summer communion services held in the church. For the most part, visiting people would join the multitude at the historic location of worship outside the old church, the *'Leabaidh na ba bana.'* What savoury thoughts of these glorious days come to the mind, even the simple human aspect with all its natural happiness, quite apart from the spiritual joys that were linked to them!

One last note on the congregational boat in Aultbea. At last her day of seaworthiness was over. But like other boats it was not the end of her usefulness. Until the end of my father's ministry, she could be seen not far from the church close to the main street. It had been turned over and raised on stone walls. The boat became a weatherproof streamlined roof. It was known as the 'black shed'. There were many stories about the *black shed*, for here the coffins were made by the joiner, Muey, and latterly his successor, Aonghas an Eileinn', Angus Isle Ewe.

But we must not linger. The cultural texture of the community was reflected in other noted bards. There was Murdo Grant, the *'bard mor'* from Mellon Charles. Like all Grants he was big. He was six feet six inches in height. Aultbea is happy to share with Poolewe and Gairloch, identity with other poets. Chief of these must be William Ross, who had national stature and must be classified with the 'greats' like *Rob Donn, Alasdair MacMhaighstir Alasdair* and *Ian Lom*, the transmitters of the Gaelic secular heritage. His mother came from Gairloch, herself a daughter of the well-known *piopaire dall* (the blind piper) from Gairloch, official piper to the MacKenzies. William Ross touched the deepest springs of natural emotion in his love songs, especially those reflecting unrequited love for a girl in Stornoway, the experience of his own life. Leaving earth's scene at twenty-eight years of age, his death was attributed to a broken heart. His memorial is in the churchyard at Gairloch.

Alexander Cameron, born at Inverasdale, was highly esteemed and is known as the bard of Tournaig. A monument to him was erected just after the Second World War. It can be seen by the traveller beside the road near Inverewe Gardens. Instrumental in this endeavour was Captain Ian Moffat Pender, who more or less adopted Poolewe. Though an Australian he commanded a company of Highlanders from the district, the Seaforths. He testified that there was none in battle like the men from Ross-shire, the county of the Seaforths.

And *bardachd* is still alive in this century. A native of Inverasdale, resident in Aultbea, Ian Cameron, a relative of the Tournaig Bard, has also shown the same gifts of the Gaelic language and culture. There is one song that exiles have loved to hear on the radio, that triggers off thoughts and emotions woven in childhood round beautiful Aultbea and all Lochewe-side. *'An Inbhirasdail air taobh Lochuibhe.* 'Inverasdale on the side of Lochewe.'

Chapter 16

A Man for his Times

There was great gladness throughout the wider area of Aultbea. Many already knew their new minister. He had interned among them the previous summer. There was a completeness about the settlement as if all felt it had indeed the divine benediction. The whole area needed a new strong and younger man to carry the heavy spiritual responsibilities of this extensive sphere of labour. MacKinnon Gairloch was now well over eighty years of age. He had to hand the reins of spiritual responsibility over to another. He had lived through ecclesiastical turmoil and kept the two charges of Gairloch and Locheweside respectively, almost intact, through the stormy ecclesiastical new era of the 1900 Schism.

Amazingly, the mantle of ecclesiastical leadership would fall upon another Skyeman, and one of the same clan name. With the coming of the motor car age, his successor would have greater facility in travelling round the whole parish from

Little Lochbroom to Kinlochewe and Ailligin. Now it would be MacKinnon Aultbea who would be the unofficial bishop of this Wester Ross 'diocese' and instead of extended vacancies in Aultbea, these would obtain in Gairloch. Nevertheless, Aultbea was not another Gairloch nor its minister a copy of his predecessor. There was a special character about Aultbea and its minister that was unique.

It could well be said that Aultbea, as a charge, represented the zenith of Free Church life in rural Highland communities. As a spiritual force, the church was the basic dynamic of society. It is not that there was a theocracy, as in Old Testament Israel. Here there was still the civil and the ecclesiastical. Yet there was a reciprocal relationship, in which the temporal was strongly influenced by the spiritual. At the same time the church was cognizant of the civil and conscious of the practical and temporal, without which the spiritual would necessarily be irrelevant. Jesus himself was a pragmatist. Did he not overtly imply this when he said, 'Give the starving man bread first so that he can live. Then give him the spiritual food for the soul.' There is no question about it. Whatever obtained elsewhere, the spiritual permeated the community of Locheweside, giving it a texture of unsurpassed quality.

Thus the presbytery of Lochcarron inducted the new minister into a very special charge. Here people knew whom they served and understood what they believed in. Here was a religiously 'educated' charge, one in which the people, old and young, were tutored in the truth and the eternal verities, that undergirded society locally, nationally, and in the catholicity of the universal church on earth. Here in an isolated quarter of Scotland, the people were subject to the full range of the church's influence, making old and young active members of a spiritually accredited community life, and an integral part of the Covenant people of God.

We quote a report of the Ordination and Induction as it appeared in the Free Church Record in 1924. The article was written by the interim-moderator, Rev William MacKinnon, Gairloch.

The ordination and induction of Rev Angus MacKinnon over the united congregations of Aultbea and Poolewe took place on the 17th of July, and great interest was taken in the services within a wide district, from Little Lochbroom to Kinlochewe, indicating the desire of the people of the Free Church for the settlement of ministers.

A large congregation assembled—many being present from Gairloch—who are very pleased to see a minister settled in the neighbourhood. Rev. R. Fraser, the young minister of Ullapool, preached and presided and conducted the ordination service. The other members of the Presbytery present were Mr. MacRae, Plockton, and Mr. MacKinnon, Gairloch, and some elders. Rev. Dr. MacLean, Edinburgh, being at present in Lochcarron, came a distance of at least sixty miles to countenance and encourage one of his students, on the occasion of his settlement. The Presbytery and the people were very pleased to see the Dr. present, but the hurry of the party to catch a train, at Achnasheen, prevented the people to thank him for being there.

The Clerk made a statement regarding the steps taken for the settlement of Mr. MacKinnon there, emphasizing the cordiality and unanimity of the people in the three large districts occupied by the congregation, Poolewe, Inverasdale and Aultbea. By far the largest portion of the congregation is in Aultbea and the manse is there. After the ordination and induction, Mr. MacKinnon, Gairloch addressed the new minister, and the Clerk who was himself appointed to do it, asked Dr. Maclean to address the people, and wise counsels were given to them by him.

The congregation kindly entertained the Presbytery and friends in the manse, under the kindly and efficient superintendence of Mrs. MacAulay, the missionary's wife, and there showed their great kindness by presenting testimonials to three persons who seemed to feel uneasy for the enormous expense of the people in connection with the settlement of their minister. These parties were the newly settled minister, who was addressed by Mr. Roderick MacDonald, elder, Cove; the retiring Moderator, who was addressed by Mr. Murdo Maclean, elder, Mellon Charles; Mr. MacAulay, their missionary, who was addressed by Mr. John Maclean, elder, Mellon Charles. These men were presented with beautiful purses full of bank notes.

Rev. Angus MacKinnon was settled with great heartiness and hopefulness, he being a very promising young man, and it is the prayer of all concerned, that he will do great things among a very kindly and interesting people. In the west we are not often, if at all, accustomed to a great flourish of trumpets, and this account is not meant as such, but as bare truth, which would not be complete without some personal reference to Mr. MacAulay, who was missionary there for some years. Mr. MacAulay was ever very diligent in labouring among the people, often working alone in the two congregations. Mr. MacAulay is a sound theologian, and the people there know his worth and they are most anxious to retain his services in the charge, to help the minister, for one man can never carry on the work alone.

(Rev. Wm. MacKinnon)

This was one of the last services that MacKinnon Gairloch attended. He was a patriarch of the Church, an old soldier of the Cross, bearing the heat of battle in troubled days, and pastoring with signal success in the many quiet years of peace as minister of Gairloch. Now, with a young minister taking over in Aultbea, the north Gairloch parish, more suitably called, Locheweside, Rev William MacKinnon could rest. Soon like Elijah he would pass from earth's scene having seen the Cause in the whole ecclesiastical area committed to another Elisha. He could let go the reins and did so in a calm and serene peace. His work was done. He had ploughed and reached the end of his furrow. Now a younger man would begin the next. Rev. William was known as *MacKinnon, Gairloch*. Rev. Angus would be known for over the next three decades, as *MacKinnon, Aultbea*. Within a year MacKinnon, Gairloch died in his manse. In keeping with the succession, all the books of his large library were given as the working tools to the new minister in Aultbea. And there in the parlour/study in the Aultbea manse, the enlarged photo of MacKinnon, Gairloch would hang on the wall, the benign and benevolent face looking down with the blessing of divine benediction upon the large family of children. And behind those kindly eyes, the indelible memory of his own loss many years before, of his one and only child, a darling little girl.

As the mantle of honour fell upon the new minister of Aultbea, so also would the burdens and responsibilities, far beyond those of an ordinary settlement. For a decade, Gairloch would be vacant, adding almost double responsibility to an already unusually extensive charge. But the new minister was young and strong. He was equipped and ready. He was seasoned by life's experiences and both physically and spiritually, as he now turned to the work the Lord set before him. And as he did so, with the support of a willing people and mighty men of spiritual stature, along with devout women, there began another phase in the congregation's life, of sowing and reaping and hopes and expectations, but also with fulfillment of promise.

The new minister had no illusions. There's no heaven on earth. But then, there were people that made one think of heaven, for they were on their journey to the 'celestial city.' Aultbea was very much part of historic Wester Ross. Even the names on the Call to the minister—there were 124 MacKenzies, — reminded one that this was the land of the MacKenzies. Powerful ministers like *Maighstir Lachlann Mor,* Rev. Lachlan MacKenzie, Lochcarron, came easily to mind. To work for Christ's kingdom, in this area held forth both the challenge of preaching to the unconverted, and the promise of fragrant spiritual fellowship of seasoned disciples. The very reason for an evangelical ministry presupposes an on-going need for the craft of 'fishers of men.' Knowing in himself the waywardness of the human spirit, and the passions of the 'flesh', the wiles of the devil, whose chief end is to subvert the church of God, this new MacKinnon brought a wealth of seasoned experience of human nature to the responsibilities of his calling.

To this he also brought a uniquely warm human touch, in which the Gospel was brought before the people. All preachers have their own special gifts which are brought to bear upon their listeners from week to week. MacKinnon Aultbea brought the fullness of grace and glory, in their inexhaustible variety, like parcels of good things, like pictures of attractive beauty. In these, Christ in all his suitableness, in all his sufficiency, was depicted graphically in the context of our common humanity.

It is well known that in every community there are two parallel entities the religious and the secular. The 'religious'

covers all that positively pertains primarily to the spiritual or
the soul. The secular covers a multitude of aspects of human
life, good and bad, relating to the physical and the sensual.
Sometimes the religious dominates, making the community a
kind of victim of apparent suppression. In other cases, or at
other times, the secular wins out. The upshot is that the church
representing the religious, is often thrown on the scrap heap,
or simply ignored. In Aultbea my father found both currents.
They were both virile and one could say healthy. They co-
existed. There was a kind of mutual respect for both. At times
there would be definite differences and even conflict. But there
was a continued *rapport,* to which the community returned,
after any 'difference', in reconciliation. There is no doubt
that the continued health of the community was believed to
hinge upon the right balance, where both aspects, the religious
and the secular, dove-tailed together in a co-existence of
peace, if not always in accord. It is here that a minister is
proved. He must not blend the religious and the secular
together. Yet he must achieve a balance where both have their
place. It goes without saying, that he is unambivalent in
projecting the religious as primary. In Aultbea, both currents
were strong. Just as the religious had a healthy and influential
colour of spiritual health, the secular life was also often
dramatically alive. Aultbea was not an anemic community. It
was normal, with many shades of excitement reflecting human
nature. We observed that the religious was primary and it was
the minister's responsibility to maintain the precedence of
the latter. One instance of this is illustrated in a situation which
happened much later on, sometime after the Second World
War.

The winds of change were by then blowing across the

mid-20th century Europe, and these blew north into the glens and hills of the Highlands, stirring the cultural and religious landscape, as history had not known previously. Many good people, were carried away by this atmosphere of accelerated change and   recklessly wanted to throw away the enduring and tried ways that had premised daily life for generations. Modern technology and communications brought these winds of change. And in direct contradiction to this shrunken world of instant news on radio and later of television, some would have the Sabbath secularised, and shops opened and newspapers, specially loaded with the more salacious national gossip, sold for secret reading, in place of the Bible and public worship on the Sabbath day.

A new retail proprietor, came to the community, a good Scotsman, but one who did not realise how much the Sabbath meant to the Highland community. He began selling Sunday newspapers, opening his shop which was close to the church for a period, in order to do so. Several of the people remonstrated with him. There was a kind of subterfuge involved, which suggested he knew that he was importing a foreign ingredient into the fabric of the community thinking. Thus it was several weeks before this new public commercial behaviour was notice taken of. He was challenged by local people who were not slow to point out that he was eroding the community standards honouring the 'Sabbath day to keep it holy.' He became more intransigent, and hardened with patent defiance. He sought to justify his action on the basis that the newspapers were printed on Saturday, while the Monday newspapers were printed on Sunday. There was a logic in what he said and many saw his point. But there was an underlying fallacy. Two wrongs do not make a right.

Society would collapse if you transferred the 'ethos' of one area and imposed it upon another, unless there was a reciprocal action on the part of both.

To give an other illustration, it would be nonsense to stop using an ambulance to take the sick to hospital, on the basis that the oil was extracted and converted into combustible fuel and transported from an other part of the world, where the Sabbath was looked upon differently. The binding moral imperative or simply the obligation to give obedience to a commandment relates to our situation, the first person singular or plural. The obligation relates to our life as given by God and our reactions to his law and his love. Our obligations to God do not hinge upon the actions of another. It could be said that morality has to do, laterally with our human society, and vertically to do with God. Both are essential in the equation. It follows that if we look to the situation of others, as a premise for our own actions, we are remiss. God will not condemn us for breaking a common religious rule, based on the Decalogue, for instance 'not to do any unnecessary work' on the Sabbath, or 'not to steal', provided the reason for such is the fulfillment of the great commandment, namely 'to love God and our neighbour as ourselves.' If the liberty we take does not reflect obedience to that universal obligation, our liberty is egotistical licence.

Bearing this in mind, let us now follow the mini 'crisis' in Aultbea. The Sunday Newspaper seller felt boldly justified. And with the shop being opened even for a short time on the Sabbath day, clearly this was the thin edge of the wedge, a crack in the engine block or the chassis of the community. Soon, a modern new alloy substitute of diluted morality would take over, and the community conscience would go to sleep. I speak by anecdote. No shopkeeper had hitherto even considered opening for business on Sunday, although if there was necessity, it is certain that any would have given a person what was urgently required. Now the pattern was broken. But not for long. Our new shopkeeper, getting bolder by the day, was now already adding cigarettes and other little items to his sales list, all unofficially of course. It was time to act. Some thought it was too late. The shopkeeper was becoming more confident, and sure of his ground. He was heard repeatedly saying, ' We are in a new age; you've been all behind the times; you are entitled to freedom; you don't want to be kept down by the church.' More and more people were seen slinking in to the shop for that Sunday newspaper.

It was time for a visit from the minister. Several people were witness to that visit on a Monday morning, when the shop was open. The minister was rarely known to do any local shopping. And he was always seen in public in his full clerical attire. His presence therefore walking along the road towards the shop immediately became the focus of attention. Word reached the shopkeeper before the minister reached the shop. Word was relayed to him, ' The minister is coming in.' Some shoppers scattered, especially any who felt guilty. Now the minister came into the shop and greeted the shopkeeper. He asked if he could speak to him in private. A shopgirl was left to serve the customers. Proprietor and minister were more than an hour, secluded privately in the house next to the shop, the old Montgomery home, bought now by the incomer. They were seen, shaking hands as the minister left.

No shop opened on the Sabbath day after that as long as Mr. MacKinnon was minister in Aultbea. If newspapers came to Aultbea on Sunday, they were brought by individuals who received them by transaction, meeting a van somewhere on the public highway, as it made an itinerary outside the township of Aultbea. This illustrated the wisdom that Mr. MacKinnon exercised in a community crisis. Whatever he said to the shopkeeper, it worked. He was not unique. Many ministers have done this. It should be said that two other factors obtained here. The vast majority of the people wanted the *status quo*. Also it must be conceded that the proprietor, though not professing to share the same mind on the subject, was intelligent enough to accept that he could not succeed in business and at the same time trample upon the spiritual values of the people. There is something else that was clear and unusual. It was this. The minister did not make a victory sermon on Sunday. Neither was one word heard from the proprietor in public, except one outburst of exasperation to one of the manse children. Apart from that, the matter became history and Aultbea sailed on serenely, sensitive to the contrary winds that now sought to change society, but holding steadfastly to the course of which the fourth commandment is one of the salient points to take its bearings.

There is no doubt that there was a continued confrontation between the Christian community and the eroding forces of pretended innocuous innovation. But at the same time, Aultbea did not turn and run before them or capitulate to their pressure. Rather she sailed on in a quiet obedience to the tenets of a common Christian faith which made Scotland's greatness. And as she faced the contrary winds, she still moved forward, using discretion and skill. And who was at the helm, but a master seaman who had sailed the oceans and weathered the rough storms of life. He was a skilled minister who was both the ambassador of glad tidings for the soul, but also a diplomat who kept the community together with the common sense that Christian wisdom required. The course was set, a city whose builder and maker is God, and minister and people moved on to that city of celestial light. But the journey was important, the life journey, as people rubbed shoulders together in community, in all the diversity of personality and not inconsistent with the fundamentals of human liberty. Therefore they looked forward to the Christian Zion, the New Jersualem and at the same time, lived on the way to that fulfillment, in the corporate fellowship and obedience of a Bible-regulated society.

Chapter 17

A Bride for the Minister

For the first two years, the minister's niece Katie Cameron, filled the role of hostess in the manse in Aultbea. But my father soon found his life partner in the person of a young Christian woman from Stoer in the parish of Assynt in Sutherlandshire.

CatherineMatheson was marked out as a child for her adult role as a 'lady of the manse.' When very young she was conscious that the hand of the Lord was upon her. As she played on the croft on windswept Raffin in Stoer on a summer day, she felt the breath of heaven touch her cheeks. She knew it was the Lord and she did not resist the overtures of grace. She turned her face to heaven so that the Spirit filled her soul. It was not long before it was clear that heaven had laid claim to this young girl and that her life would become irrefutable proof of elective love. Christ was her lover from an early age, she could not say when. She was born to witness for Christ as surely as she knew Christ died for her redemption because of his love for her. In contrast to the dry legalism that often brought spiritual paralysis to the church, in an ambivalent testimony to personal belief, she professed an unqualified conviction that she was saved by grace. Her soul delighted in meeting her Saviour in her secret tryst, that bower of prayer, the 'secret place' where humans, whether in palace or in prison, in times of prosperity or times of persecution, may savour the riches of grace, and their minds dwell upon the glorious inheritance bequeathed to them as heirs of God and joint-heirs with Christ.

Recovering from an illness when she was a young teen-ager, she came to a spiritual turning-point in her life. Indeed her life was itself in the balance. She was laid up at home with a great fever, and was not expected to recover. The shroud was already ordered by her parents and had arrived by special messenger to the home. She lay, hovering in semi-consciousness on her bed. This was the prelude to a special visitation from her beloved Saviour.

Speaking of the episode to her children in Aultbea many years later, she recalled the scene. The dawn was breaking; all was quiet in the household as others slept. Some time before, she was aware of her mother, bending over her, her hand caressing her cheeks and passing over her fevered brow. Now there was no one in the room. The candle on the bedside table had burned out. Suddenly she knew someone was in the room, yet the door had not opened. A fragrance, a heavy perfume now pervaded the sickroom. Her eyes opened to see the figure of a man. He was gloriously clothed in white and shining before her. He was standing at the foot of the bed. His face was turned to her. It was radiant and animated as with heavenly passion. She told her children about this incident several times, when gathered together on a Sunday evening in the sitting-room after church, when, as was quite frequent, our father was away at some Communion. The children would look up to her expressive face, as it reflected the memory of that experience. They would say in a chorus, 'What happened then, Mamma?' She would respond as she had done often before,

'He spoke to me. He spoke to me.'

'And what did he say?' one of the girls would ask.

My mother would then continue, the children's eyes rivetted on her face.

'He spoke to me and looked at me, and he said, "I will come for you but not now. You will not die. You will live and make a home for a minister and family.'

Such was the woman who 'broke the church barrier' and 'went forward' taking with her, her first cousin Jessie, several years her senior, to sit at the Lord's Table. There, before the large adult congregation, under the loving ministry of Rev Farquhar Matheson, with two favourites, her own relative Rev Dr. Donald Munro, Ferintosh and Rev Norman Campbell Dingwall as visiting ministers, the young blonde radiant girl broke the theological barrier. This was an assertion of Christian right and privilege, not unlike the social and political counterpart played by the Pankhursts and followers in the Women's Suffragette Movement in London. No one on earth should or could keep a child of God from witnessing to her Saviour's love and her love to her Saviour, at His Table.

This was the woman the new minister of Aultbea courted at a Communion in Coigeach in 1926 and shortly thereafter married and brought to Aultbea.

The occasion was marked by a social on Friday, 10th December, 1926. This was truly a celebration of a happy event which filled the hearts of the people with optimism and expectation for the ministry already begun.

Here is an account of the evening as recorded in the Record:

Aultbea Presentation

A very pleasing function took place in the Free Church Manse, Aultbea, Ross-shire, on Friday, 10th December. It was the home-coming of the minister with his young bride. The congregation showed their affection for their minister, and most heartily welcomed his young wife into their midst by presenting each of them with a very handsome wallet of notes. The congregation contributed towards both presentations in a very hearty and generous fashion—a token of the esteem in which the Rev. Angus MacKinnon is held throughout the whole district. Incidentally it may be said that the Aultbea and Poolewe charge is one of the largest and most loyal in the Free Church. The presentation was made by Mr Murdo MacLean, elder, Mellon Charles, on the motion of Mr D. MacKenzie, Inverasdale.

Mrs MacKinnon, the minister's wife may be assured of the affectionate loyalty and help of a warm-hearted and generous people. Miss Cameron, the minister's niece, whose genial kindness and hospitality have endeared her to the whole congregation, was present and it remains to be said that she will be remembered with affectionate regard by everyone who experienced her kindness. Mr MacKinnon is a native of the parish of Duirinish, Skye, and is the youngest son of the late Mr John MacKinnon, Shiadar, elder in the Duirinish congregation of the Free Church. P.M.

Quite apart from her natural graces, my mother always retained an attractive feminine look which all the menfolk unquestionably appreciated. This included elders and ministers among all the rest who were privileged to know her--what normal man does not appreciate a beautiful woman! But there was something extra about her. Her beauty was more than external. Her experience of God's grace permeated her whole being so completely that there was a radiance in her disposition that had a spiritual quality, making her in many ways unique. She had a combination of gentleness and spiritual strength that would serve her well in taking over the heavy responsibilities of the manse in a large parish, besides raising and nurturing a large family of boys and girls.

Rev Angus MacKinnon was well aware from the beginning that his young wife was a woman of unusual faith and spiritual power. His children also lived in the assurance, the double assurance that both their parents were special servants of God with all the privileges and blessings that this brings to human life. Children everywhere remember parents like camera prints in different scenes from the past. We describe one of these that springs from early life in Aultbea, to us that perfect place of childhood. It was a recurring scene and a description of daily life connected with upbringing and that powerful unselfconscious interplay of influence, especially in the parent-children relationship. It stays as such as an indelible print in memory.

A place of prayer

Until her health broke, mother took the full concern for the domestic scene, including the vital one of the welfare and husbandry of the animals. She loved all animals as she loved humans--with the exception of the usual aversions. Regularly she milked the cows, morning and evening in the old byre not far from the manse near George MacIver's shop. I have no recollection of her doing so in later years when the old byre was abandoned in favour of the modern building of the estate on the far side of the glebe behind the doctor's house. There was no public delivery of milk in Aultbea. The manse dairy herd comprised as a rule, three cows with two of them usually 'in milk'. *'Bleoghainn a chruidh'*, or 'milking the cows' was therefore of great importance. One reason that my mother did this herself, while other chores might be done by others, was her concern for cleanliness, an essential in days when there were few if any safeguards against dairy-related disease and in the absence of refrigeration.

After milking, my mother did not leave the byre immediately. If you were near, you were drawn to the door where you looked in. She was there on her knees at the milking stool, now taken apart from the cow stalls. She was now in daily therapy, that exercise of spiritual sinews that was surely in part the secret of her power with God. Her hands were clasped in prayer. As she prayed, the expressions on her face changed, matching the divisions of prayer in all the range from humble confession, pleadings for grace, praise and thanksgiving, to the ultra exquisite devotional transactions with heaven where her soul was being filled with the sweetness of Christ, the Bread of Life. You could hear her in earnest pleading with God, reflecting the many practical needs and burdens of home and family, and community.

Such is an immortal portrait of a minister's wife in her greatest role. Such was the young wife Rev Angus MacKinnon claimed for himself as his closest partner in the team work of the ministry in far-off Aultbea in the Scottish Highlands.

In 1941, my mother collapsed in the stairway of the manse. She was pregnant with her ninth child. Her body was worn out with work and concern aggravated by the increased burdens and cares brought on in the home by the War. The doctor was called immediately. She was laid gently on her bed. She was worn out. How much can one take? Her physical strength coupled with her condition could not match her will. She was utterly spent. With great tenderness she was taken down the stairs on a stretcher. The doctor saw that her life was in the balance. Thus the golden-haired beautiful mother, who kept the heart of the manse beating, was conveyed to hospital in Inverness. She gave birth to a little girl who was to be named Helen. But within a week the child died. Mother slowly recovered. She was not fit to go back into harness, in the heavy role which was her lot in the Aultbea manse. She was put into a Nursing Home for several weeks, a quiet restful place overlooking the banks of the River Ness.

Some weeks later, father accompanied by his younger son, arrived to take mother home. She ought to have been given six months to recover and ideally should have left to renew her strength in a sunny land rather than in the dark damp climate of the gloomy Highlands and the taxing demands of her responsibilities as minister's wife. But that could not be. And her husband was counting the days if not the hours when Mam would be back home again at his side. The Aultbea manse just could not function long without her.

Father and son ascended the steps and rang the bell at the Nursing Home glass-panelled door. It opened. Father spoke to a nurse. Within a few moments, a thin, aged woman appeared. She was wearing a long blue silk dressing-gown. On her feet were red slippers with white woolly puffs. Her hair was streaked with grey, almost white, and flowing down her shoulders. The little boy did not see the face. Then the woman embraced his father. The little boy was confused. Then his beloved mother, for this was her, the shadow of her former self, now turned to him. She bent down to her nine-year old, who was always with her in the byre, helping with the cows, who from a little child claimed a seat in the manse pew beside her so that when sleep overcame him he would rest his head on his mother's lap. Now he felt like weeping. Pain rushed through him, a stabbing pain of sorrow. Was this his beautiful mother? How could they, who ever they were, have done this to his mother? Here was a shadow of what his lovely mother had been just a few weeks before. But that could not be reversed.

Again for the second time in her life she had come back from the gates of death. But now the winter frosts had prematurely blown away her health. Her natural physical beauty was now stripped off her and she was left like a leafless tree. Her face was gaunt and lined and now framed with gray hair. But somehow the spirit broke through. It was still Mam, the centre of the family, and the woman of great and indomitable faith, whose life was Christ-powered. One had to adjust to reality, this almost criminal change. And when this took place, she was seen still, her head held high, her posture straight and upright as always, and in her eyes, that irrepressible light that radiated from her soul and could not be hid.

Turning-point

From then on the minister's wife struggled on stoically to fulfil the many responsibilities of the manse and to bear the burdens of her large family. But already the new world was replacing the old. No longer was there the help of a nannie. One remembers the last, a lively competent girl, Mary Morrison, from the island of Harris. She had been in the manse for several years, as also was another Harris girl called

Chrissie Morrison. I have a clear recollection of her as she pushed the pram up the brae past the present-day community centre, built as a cinema during the War. My sister Ina was in the pram. I was walking. Being a bit plump, and still a little fellow, I found it hard going to keep the pace, up the steep hill. Like all little ones, I had good lungs and used them to make my situation known, and in any case I was a bit of a drag as I was falling somewhat behind. At last after several vocal Gaelic attempts to placate me failed, Mary whisked me up like a bag of peats and 'plonked' me in the other end of the pram. I was content. In front of me was my baby sister Ina. We were like twins now in the pram. My irritating persistent penetrating fog horn now was turned off until my next mini crisis of getting my own way. And Mary Morrison that stalwart girl from Harris was there pushing the pram and at the same time singing softly, a Gaelic song.

But that day was past. The older girls now helped run the household. They also were diligent at outside tasks. The marriage of a Skyeman and a women from Sutherland had produced a bevy of physically strong girls, who were more than a match for many boys of their age. All six manse girls were lively, each with their own separate personality. The older ones tended to be more aggressive, pre-war products of a more affluent and socially privileged day. The younger ones were more subdued, conditioned by humbler circumstances to which all had to bow, in the stark, psychologically and physically uncertain conditions of War. Just remember, Aultbea tasted the War first-hand.

The point we make is that all children who were little ones and heard the thunder of guns and huddled in shelters in wartime are to some extent affected. At any rate the older ones in the Aultbea MacKinnon family had by War-time reached some maturity. Rachel and Katie, both who were later to marry ministers, had to curtail their secondary education in turn, although bright and promising scholars, being called home to help keep the domestic machine going, because of the new do-it-yourself economic situation, and my mother's now chronic indisposition.

The two boys in turn milked and looked after the cows, until they also left home on scholarships to a private school in the south. After that, it was a new world, a new economy. All but one of the cows would go, all the cows we loved as if they were members of the family, Grayag, Reddy, Whitey, Spotty, Blacky. All were called conveniently by their colour. Latterly there was only one. It came from Laide, a lovely easy-going cow that was gentle and always 'gave the milk,' tolerant of the different hands that milked her. She was given the name of Laidey. Many cows are very fussy and just will not 'give the milk' except to their regular milker.

I would have to say that the byre for me as a little boy was a wonderful haven of delight. I would stay there happily, absorbed in the many forms of animal life. There were numerous cobwebs, out of reach in the high ceiling. There were mice to chase along with the faithful and competent cats, when the oat straw was disturbed in the loft. There were rats that peeped down, watching while the cow was being milked. And the byre was so warm on a winter's day. Often it was a delight to cuddle down beside the cow with an arm round its neck. I especially remember as a little boy, talking to Grayag and Laidey, while they kept up a rhythmic tranquil beat, chewing the cud. And always that enduring identity, the byre was the meetingplace of heaven and earth where mother brought all the needs and concerns of home, family and people to the Throne of Grace.

The memories of my mother and the manse barn and the byre are as vivid as ever. They have a kind of religious immortality. I see her yet, kneeling down to pray. I hear her yet after sixty years, her face turned heavenward as to the sun. I see the dew of grace upon her brow and the beams of heavenly light making her face to shine. I see her rising up renewed and invigorated, to return to the manse and its duties, refreshed by communion with her Lord and her God. And then, I realise that there is no contradiction here. Was not our Lord in his visit to the earth, born in a stable, with the cows happily eating their food from the manger and chewing the cud in the metronomic regularity that speaks of perfect order and contentment!

Getting the minister's ear

Men are as a rule as reluctant to confide in their Protestant minister as they are to go to their Catholic priest for Confession. It seems ironic, but there it is. Just as most women related more easily to the minister, male members or male adherents, even the elders, felt more at ease, speaking to the minister's wife. In this sense, here was the line of communication by which the minister kept his finger on 'the pulse' of the congregation and knew the current trends of thinking and incidents in the community that continually were of importance for true parish preaching in the weekly services. Though this was an informal link, it was very effective. Thus it was that Mrs. MacKinnon would linger outside, in what was called the 'clothes garden', after hanging up the baskets of washing—no mean task. She could be seen at this task by the crofters from Tighnafaoline, one of the little hamlets or sub-divisions of Aultbea. These were fine men, like Ali *Shim* MacKenzie, Allan MacLeay, *Mur'chadh ghreadhaidh* MacIver, *Mur'chadh glic* MacIver. Sometimes they were working on their crofts. It was common for one of them by some chance or contrived excuse to hail the minister's wife from over the wall. Then followed a lengthy exchange of views, the Gaelic voices carried gently in the still atmosphere of a summer day.

It was the same when Murdo Cameron or Roddie his brother, Inverasdale men, came up to the manse door with MacLean's grocery van. There was a steady queue, on duty or not on duty that found some excuse to engage in conversation with the minister's wife. Somehow it was easy to speak to my mother. She was known for her resolute faith, not by formal confession of creed, but by the sheer attractiveness of her life pervaded by that incontrovertible quality of grace which is called Divine essence, even love, in its highest connotation of virtue. The list goes on, Donny the postman, *Willie Deus,* with the coal lorry, Simon with a free load of turnips from Ian MacLean for the manse cows. And one cannot forget a visit from a seasoned and honourable poacher like S*tutan* from Second Coast with that most acceptable gift, wrapped in burlap, so much appreciated in the manse at the communion and blessed by many godly divines with a secondary blessing for the gracious 'giver'. Stutan was modest. He would at other times tell a son of the manse to call in at Coast for 'something'. It coincided with the partition of a goodly horned stag in the barn, downed by the gun from the rugged hills at his doorstep.

All the men loved to talk with the minister's wife. Probably this is a general rule, but here is objective observation of Mrs. MacKinnon. There were a few who, having taken a glass too many at the local hotel, looked up and saw that the minister's car was not in the manse garage. Such a one then made his unsteady way up the drive to the manse. Then Mrs. MacKinnon was seen in both a motherly role and as a counselor.

The Proof of Prayer

The great advantage of living in contact with God through the Spirit dwelling in a believer's life, is the corollary, guaranteed in the Scriptures, that we have 'power with God', especially for emergencies. There are many times when God keeps people, even his most devoted followers, waiting at the Throne of Grace. They are seeking, knocking, waiting for the door to open so that they can see the face of their Lord and then ask an answer for their petition. It is true that the answer may not even be positive as they see it, but at the End of the Ages, it will have served to sanctify them and to fulfil the purposes of the Divine Will. But there are other times when there is an emergency. God is as it were, 'put on the spot.' There is no doubt that this has no relation to presumption, or exploiting religion for selfish ends, or shoring up a religious egotistical reputation, or building up an inventory of spiritual victories in order to qualify for sainthood.

You recall that the War brought a mini-crisis to the economy of the Scottish manse, and particularly as we speak of here in Aultbea. These were the days of tradesmen, serving the community with their skills. One of these was *Eachann an greusaiche,* Hector the shoemaker. He was a vital factor in a family of eight children whose feet were rarely still and whose boots and shoes were worn out quickly on the hard gravel roads, or on the rocky shore.

Hector usually came up to the manse on a Saturday. On this particular day, Mrs. MacKinnon was in the kitchen, baking at the time, when daughter Cathie announced that Hector the shoemaker was at the manse gate, and was at that moment untying a parcel of repaired boots from the carrier on his bicycle. For a second my mother seemed visibly taken aback. She flushed as she said, 'I'll have to pay him, and I have no money. What shall I do?' It would be only a matter of a few minutes at most before Hector would be at the back door. For my mother, clearly this qualified as an emergency. The younger ones of the family were round her. She was everything to them and above all they knew her faith. They saw it at work. But this time, it looked as if time was not there for it to get into action, far less for God himself to give an answer that would prove his promise. '*And all things, whatsoever, ye shall ask in prayer, believing, ye shall receive.*'[1]

She knelt down right in front of them at one of the kitchen chairs. The scene is a never-to-be-forgotten one. If there are portraits of the church's praying people in glory, that must surely be one of them in the galleries of heaven.

Her face was drawn upwards in supplication; her hands were clasped in an unusual manner so that her long fingers crossed, as if they were gripping some unseen, or was it 'someone' unseen. She was at the feet of Christ, in that peculiar intimacy that is known to all who frequent the 'secret place' for their deepest needs and their greatest joys. Now her lips moved in urgent intonations of soft Gaelic pleadings to her Lord and Redeemer.

There was no time for waiting. Her prayer was a

1. St. Matthew 21:22

compulsive imperative for the God who loved her. Further there was this. In her case as with those who live 'near the Lord' as a way of life, there was no need to introduce herself. She knew the Lord intimately and communed day and night with him. But more than that, the Lord knew her intimately as one of his chosen ones, and his Covenant people. Why! Was she not here as minister's wife because the Lord had ordained that she live to fulfil the role according to the heavenly vision of His Presence, which she saw as a young girl at the very gates of death, long before, in her home in Stoer!

The seconds ticked away on the kitchen alarm clock, a tinny irritating reminder that it would soon be too late. Thus the children viewed things, with a kind of shattering impact upon them, as they saw that there was no possibility of an answer, even from God himself. They experienced a kind of pain as they witnessed the mighty faith of their mother at last being shown up in this instance as a failure. The knock came to the door when mother was still on her knees. Ina, the third youngest, called from the back door lobby as she opened the door, 'It's Hector with the shoes.'

The minister's wife suddenly rose and stood upright. Her face was calm and serene, as if relief flooded through her very soul. She brushed her hands across her eyes, softened by spiritual emotion. An inexplicable smile broke across her face, so that it took on a radiance of seemingly incontrovertible assurance, which one associates with winning. As she walked towards the open door to confront the shoemaker, the youngest daughter, Donalda, a little blonde replica of mother, less than four years of age, ran past Hector, right to mother's knee.

Her words were part of the drama. 'Mammy, Mammy, Lena Gunn gave me this.' And saying that, she thrust a pound note into the hand of her mother.

Mother accepted the brown paper parcel from Hector. On the paper covering was written, 'The manse, 18 shillings.' She handed him the pound note and took the two shillings change from the shoemaker as she thanked him.

Hector had no idea of the remarkable way in which he was paid for his work that day, by the lady of the manse. For Hector was almost stone deaf.

Back in the kitchen when the shoemaker had gone, the children looked at their remarkable mother. They were always familiar with her fearless witness, her clear unambiguous belief in a God who was Saviour of the soul, but also Provider for the necessities of life here on earth. Here again her power with God was indisputable. This was not the prayer of self or a variant of psychological auto-suggestion. This was no relation to religious cant. Nor was this in any sense related to some kind of spiritual self-stature. Mother would indeed often wait long in prayer, pleading for blessings upon home and congregation, for soldiers, sailors and airmen away in war, and always for God to break through in a visible coming of his kingdom on earth, the Heavenly Jerusalem that cometh down from above. But here they were witness to a short emergency prayer, a whispered call to the Throne of Grace, a flash of light on the screen of Omniscience, and an answer of power from God, her God who knew the request before mother knelt down at that kitchen chair.

This was surely a triumph of God's power made known unmistakably in that mundane incident of Hector the shoemaker coming to the Aultbea manse door with the parcel

of repaired boots and shoes, when there was no money to pay
for them. That moment was turned into a dramatic enactment
of God's power, a transaction of practical religion. Here the
dynamics of grace synchronised with a faith that was already
coded and keyed in to the Master computer of heaven.

This scene is symbolic of my mother's faith and her unusual
power with God. It links the spiritual with the pragmatic.
Examine it in its pure simplicity and who can not be touched
by the vividness of its message for each and all, who ever
they may be, who read this, far from the shores of beautiful
Lochewe, in their life journey through this world!

Chapter 18

Getting into Gear

There were no more than a dozen cars in the whole community in the 1920's. Add to this, MacLean's lorry, John Alick's van and in Poolewe, Colin MacKenzie's two big black charabancs. For public vehicles, there was the Achnasheen Mail bus and the County road maintenance lorry. After some years there would also be Dr Hunter's Armstrong-Sidley, a beautiful car but one which caused a lot of trouble as it had an American-type hydraulic transmission.

The County lorry was seen, as a rule, every day, going round the roads filling in the many ruts and generally keeping the surfaces, such as they were, in commission. This lorry was an Albion. It had a high cab, with oval windows on the doors at the sides, and along with every other motor vehicle, was the wonder of the children. A MacKenzie family had traditionally provided passenger and mail service before the Mail bus displaced the natural horse-power. John Alick was a son of this family. He had a shop in the village and also a Ford van.

To get round his wide parish, my father decided that he would take the plunge and do what no minister had done before. Hitherto, a gig and horse was provided by the congregation for pastoral duties, along with the services of the ' minister's man,' though often the minister drove the gig himself. Since the end of the Great War a few years previously, the Mail coach was now a motor vehicle, introduced to Aultbea because of the traffic of navy personnel from the rail station at Achnasheen to the Aultbca naval base. (Aultbea was used in both World Wars as a vital naval base.) On Sabbath a local entrepreneur ran a charabanc, the early type, taking the missionary to services from his residence in Poolewe. There was a vacuum with regard to the requirements of the minister. A new day had come, and by default, the minister would have to find an answer to his transport needs. If not, his ability to fulfil his obligations would be very strictly curtailed.

The new minister was decisive. He needed transport. He would buy a car. The manse gig and old horse called 'luath' (swift), exactly what it was not, were both now retired. Their day was over. Aultbea was now entering a new age, and the minister was at the front. Off to Glasgow he went.

Having listened to various advisers, all of whom had little or no mechanical knowledge, the minister was led to make a choice from the various makes. The result was that he returned to Aultbea in his own vehicle, a sparkling new Clino. This was a hardy little car with a canvas hood. She was very well built and everyone who had a Clino spoke well of it. You must remember, that roads were very different from the smooth paved highway at the end of the 20th century. They were narrow, one way, with a deep ditch on either side. There was a natural hump in the centre that provided grass for sheep. At times this was yellow with dandelions, and rabbits often had their lunch on it. Many sheep liked this for a siesta as well as for a free meal. You see traffic was minimal. A car making its way along a road between the hamlets was quite a novelty, and every one was identified and known for its particular make and shape, sound of engine and sound of horn and of course for its owner. In 1924 the minister was one of the first with his Clino.

The Clino, though a quality car, was, by modern comparison, rather primitive. It had a magneto for electrics plus a six-volt system. It had a gate gearbox of three forward ratios and a reverse. There was no synchromesh in first gear. Changing gear was therefore a formidable skill which could only be acquired after much experience. Also the roads were so steep and demanding that the low revolution long stroke engine did not have the revolutions to   keep going as level road and hills alternated.

It is interesting that the steam car at the beginning of the century, had a huge advantage in this respect. It had instant power because of the immediate high torque. Furthermore it didn't even need a gearbox. Just think of that. And it made no noise, just a very pleasant hiss of steam, like a steamship. There is every reason to think that had the later advancements of technology been applied, the steam car would have held its own against the internal combustion engine which has starved the habitat of man of oxygen, and brought the threat of ecological imbalance with ominous portent to the 21st century.

Also think of these sheep, and the minister's car coming across them on the road to Mellon Udrigil, probably the only car that passed along the road that day. It was not uncommon for stubborn sheep to refuse to remove themselves from their comfortable spot in the middle of the road. Then it was

necessary to get out and order them off with the help of a
healthy but harmless kick. Later as cars increased and roads
were paved, sheep were frequently killed by lorries or cars
which came across the animals in the dark.

The Clino did its duty faithfully. But it was left behind in
the great race of capturing the market in the automobile
industry. The new motor industry would have many
casualties. The company went bankrupt. Parts could not be
acquired for it and the car became obsolete.

John Alick MacKenzie was one of Aultbea's outstanding
characters. Flamboyant and humorous, he could be relied upon
to help the minister in every possible way. Thus he was the
minister's man, when it came to getting from place to place.
Nothing would get John Alick down. His presence changed
serious situations into occasions of humour and easy
possibility. To illustrate how he took everything in his stride I
quote just one incident. He was travelling along the main road
in the village and was just turning to the right to go up the
road to Tighnafaoline, when his van suddenly lurched
sideways, threatening to tumble off the road into the shore,
and came to a grinding stop in a cloud of gravel dust. A rear
wheel had come off, as the van made the right-hand turn.

My friend Kenny and I were just there at the roadside when
it happened. John Alick had come out of the driver's seat to
survey the situation, muttering about this being an unfortunate,
though not unusual, delay, and clear evidence that the van did
not want to go up to Tighnafaoline, for some reason or other.
At the same time he shifted his eyes from the van hub, now
resting on the gravel road, to the rebellious wheel that was
bouncing its way down over the seaweed. It continued its way
at speed to the stony part on the shore. The tide being out,

there was a large area of sand. It now hurried off away down towards the line of the tide and the incoming sea, about three hundred metres distant. It looked as if it was a wayward servant who decided that it had enough, and was determined to make a life of its own. When John Alick spotted us, he quickly had us run down to the shore and bring his wheel back, for which good deed we received a special large sweetie from the van. Finally after backtracking along the gravel road, we also recovered three of the four wheel nuts and soon with the erring wheel back on, John Alick was on his way up to Tighnafaoline.

John Alick, who also was unofficially the local veterinary surgeon and was called upon if a cow was under the weather, became indispensable for the minister and his transport. On winter days, the Clino became unsteady and one could say alarmingly unsafe, as the winds blew strongly in fierce gusts. The canvas hood would lift, threatening to raise the car into flight, like a modern hang-glider. My father took two precautions, especially when motoring over the high road called 'the tops', twisting its way along the coast between Aultbea and Poolewe.

First, strong rope was wrapped round the hood and attached to the car sides. When that was not considered enough, John Alick accompanied the minister, sitting beside him as ballast in the light little car. It all presented a comic Flintstone appearance, the early car making its lone way along the road with the minister at the wheel, and John Alick with his elbows out the side, holding on to ropes from the hood, with both his hands. The seven mile journey to Poolewe was often a hair-raising adventure, frequently with a stop on the roadside to change a wheel because of a puncture on the hard road-metal surface.

1932 was a calendar year in history. Momentous events were taking place in a readjustment of nations to a new age. Adolph Hitler gained office on his road up the ladder to become the king-pin of international tragedy for Europe and indeed the rest of mankind. In Aultbea, Mr. MacKinnon had another son. This increased the family to five. The Clino could not cope with such numbers. A new car was necessary for the manse, one which would do for professional use and also serve the needs of the family. In that summer, my father went south to the General Assembly in Edinburgh. For some unknown reasons, again he was misled by advisers. Instead of buying an economical ordinary car, tried and tested on the British roads and already proved by public acceptance, he was persuaded to go off the beaten track and buy a French Citroen, a large heavy fourteen horse power model. (The Clino had been a nine.) One should not think that this horsepower rating was the same as that spoken of seventy years late. In recent times engines are rated for their brake horse power, that is the power the engine develops at speed. In the early days, engines were rated by their stop horse-power. In other words the 14 horse power Citroen of that time could develop four or five times that of brake horse power.

As a car, this was clearly one of the finest of its day. It also was a saloon. It was therefore warm and dry for travellers in contrast to the coupe before it. The wide chassis, and its low centre of gravity gave it a rock-like stability. Unfortunately the car was really too low for the roads and often you could hear the bottom scraping the central ridge on the very uneven road. Inside, the coachwork was beautifully crafted, with facia and surrounds of polished wood. The rich brown leather upholstery and the fashionable blinds on the windows plus the sliding sunroof, reflected a certain degree of luxury that made the car stand out among the more common ones. And the price was high, too high for a parish minister and his limited stipend. Yet my father bought the car, and drove it north from Glasgow. The Clino had served for six years, only failing because of lack of available spares. It was the same with the Citroen. The car served the minister well for ten years. It traversed the rough gravel roads without letting the minister down. Its engine with its long stroke rarely failed. It putted along in a seemingly unstoppable mood, as if it would go on for ever. We all loved the Citroen.

Yet there were however irritating limitations. One was particularly frustrating. Before starting, the bonnet or hood had to be raised in order to switch on the petrol tap. The minister was drilled by advisors, that if the petrol tap was left on, the car was certain to flood the carburetor and catch fire, when it was next time started. There was no ignition switch. The ignition took place when the self-starter was pulled or when the engine was manually cranked, a frequent necessity. I often wonder, was it really necessary to switch off that petrol tap with all the bother this entailed. Surely the float system in the carburetor would obviate this necessity, as it does in all other cars since then! Another limitation was the six volt electrical system. This was never adequate in a motor car.

But the fact is that the big Citroen became a familiar sight on the roads. It travelled every sideroad; it carried the family near and far. It took us on holidays over to Aberdeen, to Pitlochry, to Edinburgh. The minister would take it to Glasgow and come back with a carfull of grocery stores on a large scale—an essential, where he had so many mouths to feed.

My father was always reluctant to trouble neighbours by asking for the use of horse and cart for the work on the glebe land unless absolutely necessary. One year, he had the seats of the car removed—not a difficult task—and then he drove the car on to the glebe and filled the car with mown hay. Back and fore the car went to the barn. All this was just great for his big family of children. All went well until the heavy car stuck on the field in a soft place. The rest of the day was a commotion, getting the car unstuck. The ruts made in the land remained for many a day afterwards to remind one of the experiment.

Sixty years later, we still have vivid recollections of holidays at Pitlochry or Queensferry camping grounds. On these holiday occasions, my father again removed all the seats, even front ones, every night, so that the whole family or those born to date, slept or at least rested through the night hours. What thoughts of stories told by Dad still linger in the memory, fragrant and wistful thoughts of a past day and a happy and privileged childhood. We will never forget the Citroen and the many happy experiences that are linked to it. But there was always a longing for an ordinary car, a Morris or an Austin or a Hillman or even a Ford, or the Rover, the latter coveted by ordinary people as the working man's Rolls Royce. These were seen in increasing numbers. They were well-proven and ruggedly suitable and easy to maintain on all the roads in Britain. There is no doubt that my father was misled and incurred much extra expense in buying both the Clino and the Citroen. Exclusive and luxurious, the Citroen was quite unsuited to the minister's requirements for the Highland parish and family needs. Buying and running such incongruous vehicles brought a constant financial drain upon his limited stipend in a day when expenses for motorised travel had not yet been invented.

Chapter 19

Friendly Rivalry

The Free Church manse in Aultbea was relatively big. Built at the Disruption it had two upper stories. If you included small rooms like the scullery and the lamp room and the clothes room, there were twenty-two rooms in all. Mr. Dingwall had supervised the building of two extensions towards the rear. Dormer windows gave light to the front top storey bedrooms. Later these were replaced by skylights in order to stop leaks. It did not work and southwest storms exploited this weakness to soak the house with rain and give the minister's wife one of the many continual bugs to put up with.

Meanwhile, as time went on, the Aultbea manse resounded to the cry of newborn babes. They came in quick succession, sometimes an annual event. There was Rachel Mary, Ian Angus, Katie, Catherine—four in five years, not bad at all by any standards. Aultbea was delighted. The manse had been full with children before. Now the tradition was continued. The house was big, and here the new minister was on the way to bringing it alive as nothing else can, with the life and laughter of children and in so doing, beating past records and all since then.

Some were of the opinion that the minister's family was now complete. But that illusion was soon dispelled. A new principal came to the local school. He was Mr. Murchison, a native of Lochcarron in southwest Ross, which is a favourite resource place for the professions, especially ministers, school-masters and doctors. (In Prince Edward Island, Canada, the name Murchison is connoted with the pioneer spirit, and at least one location near Belfast, P.E.I. is called by the name. In Scotland, Murchison Point is well-known to those who follow the sea, between Kyle of Lochalsh and Balmacara.) This new headmaster in Aultbea married a Scots-Canadian, Mary MacIver, of Lewis parents, an attractive nurse who came back from Canada. She came as a bride to the Aultbea schoolhouse at Buailnaluib in 1931.

Soon the schoolhouse echoed to the sound of its own little children. Thus began a parallel augmentation of the local population, MacKinnons and Murchisons. First there was a boy, Murdoch, in 1932 and there followed a bevy of four beautiful girls over the coming years. In the manse another son was born—that was the year the minister purchased the big Citroen. Now he would need that big car, for his family kept increasing. He had a head start on the schoolmaster with four children already. After 1932 it was all girls in both manse and schoolhouse. The local people were intrigued. The world situation was not a happy one as the Depression spread a malaise and gloom over the land. But here in Aultbea there was a real-life race. Lovely little babies were brought year after year to the big church for baptism. The Baptismal sacrament for the manse brood was always administered at the Communion season. This meant large crowds. You can understand everyone wanted to be present on these occasions.

Thus the minister and the schoolmaster were caught in a kind of race. It became an ongoing sensation. They were running 'neck and neck'. And they were all girls, from manse and schoolhouse, healthy strong beautiful girls. Big families were the 'in' thing in Aultbea and here the people were delighted at this conformity to current convention. And so the years followed one another with this friendly rivalry. In the manse there was Ina and in the schoolhouse, Margaret; in the manse there was Joan and in the schoolhouse, Lilian; in the manse there was Alda and in the schoolhouse, Mairi; in the manse there was Helen (she died as a baby) and in the schoolhouse, Alina.

About then, the Second World War broke out, and the minister and schoolmaster called it a day. You could call it a draw, an honourable tie. Their families were complete and they turned to face with others the grim race on the international scene, between the forces of Freedom and those of Fascism. Aultbea itself would feel the impact, for the naval base was situated on the natural locked-in safe anchorage of Lochewe, and would be marked out as a target for German bombers, seeking to destroy the large American convoys of merchant ships, rendezvous-ing there after crossing the Atlantic, loaded with war supplies, before they sailed off round the north of Britain to Murmansk in north Russia.

The link between school and church was of a deeper and more significant character. This was a partnership that shaped the nature of the community itself as a Christian entity.

There is always ideally a strong liaison between religion and learning. By the Education Act of 1872, the schools in Scotland were taken over by the State. Nevertheless this did not mean secularisation. That misconception is at the root of many problems in modern education. In Scotland, it was clearly understood that the State was simply fulfilling its role in the partnership, if you like, of the secular and the religious. Education means 'leading out of ignorance' with the corollary of 'leading into knowledge'. Briefly education is the process of learning to become a good, useful and happy citizen. You do not get education; you become educated. It is not a commodity that is purchased at a mercenary institution of learning. Rather it is a process that takes place when a person is assimilated into the community of other citizens, consciously adjusting his or her perspective to harmonise with the 'ideal' or basic model. It is something like the production of a car. The model is recognisable by appearance and performance. But there are infinite grades of sophistication just as they appear, in the modification of the basic model of the car. Some may be saloons for the family. These may be graded from the basic model upwards. The vehicle may be a van; it may be an ambulance; it maybe a police car with a strengthened chassis and a bigger engine. There is no limit to the variations on the theme. But in all this the car is basically the same in the thoroughness in which principles of dynamics and engineering leave the drawing board and come off the assembly line of the factory.

Is that not seen when education follows the same pattern, and principles, vertically as spiritual and laterally as collective, extending to the relatedness of the individual right out to the perimeter of human society! Both secular and religious combine as vital factors in the equation. Newton's penetrating mind saw no conflict between the mathematical universe and the continuing creative power of God.

John Murchison was neither parochial nor clinically

humanistic. An intelligent man, he projected a concept of the natural world, as a reasonable corollary of belief in a dynamic Creator, whose greatest work was the redemption of fallen man. He was superbly suited to influence children for good. If you look beyond mediocrity, it will be seen that historically the greatest thinkers in all the realms of knowledge rarely become parochial or narrow in their views. And if someone suggests this means that one is not being objective, surely this is a fallacy, as all knowledge requires the conscious mind of a human being to validate its reality. The universe is full of facts. But these cannot be classified as knowledge until assimilated by man. And history and the contemporary world with its global mistakes, is 'scientific' evidence that reason or the 'secular' is not enough. There has to be the 'religious' and the faith factor as well.

There are strong grounds for looking upon the Aultbea situation as a model or prototype for a good Christian community. The Murchison family was brought up with the highest Christian aspirations of service, expectations which were fulfilled. Both parents were devout Christians and their influence extended throughout the community. In the Scottish tradition, and according to the vision of the Reformed Church, the liaison of religion and learning obtained. It was a happy occasion when the schoolmaster conducted the evening English service in the church in the minister's absence. He did not do this often, but memories are still fresh of his humble presence and his quiet devotional address on the 23rd Psalm. Being also brought up by the sea, he was also very fond of boats and shared this with the boys in the school. As a teacher, he was unorthodox. He had a wide view of education, but did not divorce this from reality as a philosophic exercise of the mind and spirit. He gave a very thorough grounding in the different aspects of world geography. The inter-war years and the war years also, lent themselves to this. The world situation presented a kind of animated, contemporary curriculum, an ever changing pattern of living, exciting historic evolution. The nations were not dead words stamped across the big oilcloth maps on the walls. Rather they were dressed up, in the uniform of their national armies, the identity of their aircraft and the singular and identifiable might of their capital fighting ships. The whole contemporary scene of the war fronts became a chessboard in the classroom, as the Allies fought the Axis forces in Europe and elsewhere. Not only did his pupils in the 'big room' learn a detailed knowledge of nations, their cities, rivers and industries, plus their various histories, but also soldiers' skills with rifle, and signalling in Semaphore with flags and in Morse with the Aldis lamp became a regular exercise. Mr. Murchison had the knack of bringing pupils to their peak performance in class competition and in oral questioning for mental arithmetic. Also he developed a systematic and easy way for memory work, using short cryptic poems. These, used for history or geography gave life-long results. He was certainly unorthodox but experimentally refreshing and stimulating as a teacher. Here is one example for remembering events in British history.

> With Edward Sixth, King Henry's son,
> The Reformation still goes on.
> Mary of Blood comes to the throne;
> At the Stake, the Protestants do groan.
> Latimer, Cranmer and Ridley,
> Were burnt because they did not flee.
> The next to rule as queen was Bess.
> King James did rule in 1603,
> And for main Plot, locks up Raleigh.

> At Hampton, the Puritans deride,
> And with Episcopalian Version side,
> Twenty Pilgrims sailed far over the Wave,
> Although the Parliament did rave.
> In '88 to Devon Strait,
> Came Mary and husband Bill,
> To Louis XIVth, James fled in fright,
> And William signed the Bill of Right.

And even after fulfilling his teaching obligations all week, he still had the dedication to teach a large class in the Sunday School which met in the afternoon in the school. Such a teacher made an indelible impression upon many of his pupils. In this way there was continuing co-ordination and co-operation between church and school in the nurturing and preparing of young people for adulthood.

Chapter 20

Return Visit to Canada

In 1930, with three little ones already born in the manse, the Aultbea minister took off on a trip for the Church in Canada. He had a great love for Canada, after spending so long there before the Great War, and this love did not leave him for the rest of his life. In retirement he would often advert to the experiences of his young days, and all the adventures that made the New World synonymous with a greater freedom and virility of life. But there was something else. As related earlier, it was in Canada that he came to experience the saving grace that became the dynamic principle in shaping the subsequent course of his life. There the love of Christ, the incomparable love of Christ, laid hold upon him and there was a metamorphosis of soul, mind, affections and body itself, a transforming work of the Spirit, call it what you will. The fact is, there he became a changed person. The carnal became spiritual. *'To be spiritually- minded is life and peace.'[1]* The glance back over the subsequent course of his life was one of few regrets. The commitment to his Lord filled him with sweet memories of that saving experience of God's forgiving and redeeming love, the love that in Christ

1. Romans 8:6

surpasseth all other aspects of knowledge, because it has the spark of Divine dynamics. And only divine dynamic can bring life to the dead bones of prosaic orthodoxy.

He had already used his poetic gifts to express his testimony in the autobiographical poem, *'Mac Stroghail'*, the Prodigal Son. This he composed in the context of his spiritual awakening and his early life in Vancouver. The gift was always there in him. He had composed many poems and songs of sentiment and romance in his youth in Skye. But none of these matches the chords of exquisite tenderness which he achieved when he applied the bardic gift to express the experiences of his soul in the way God's love sought him and found him in the 'far country.' Now as he left Greenock on a liner for Canada to do a year's service for the Church there, he put his thoughts again into verse. The reader will notice that although the theme of the poem is spiritual, it is graphically anchored in the context in which it was composed.

This is the hall-mark of real *bardachd*, poetry. You can see this in the social economic poems of the classical poems like those of *Ian Lom*, *Alasdair MacMhaighstir Alasdair* and *Rob Donn* among others. The poem my father now composed while on the ship centres its verse on the immediate, the simple human factors of home, of congregation, of nostalgia and physical separation. It brings out the spiritual experience of the poet by contrast with those aboard the ship who find fulfillment in diversions. At the same time the spiritual is not contrasted with the concomitants of nature, so dramatically impinging upon the human consciousness, on the ocean. Rather the poet sees the cloudless sky and the favourable weather as a harmony of heaven's blessing. He speaks of this as symbolic of God's kindness and linked in providence to the prayerful goodwill of the congregation that he left for a season.

He uses Scriptural and direct metaphors not as a substitute but as a parallel of his own experience. In this way, over-spiritualising of human social events, even of Hebrew history is avoided. Here is the poem that was written as he returned after twenty years to Canada.

It has an unsurpassed poetic perfection in Gaelic. We give an English translation where a wider readership can share in the imagery of his thoughts and identify with the common human experience.

Imrich Cuain

1   'N uair fhuair sinn uil' air bord na luing
     Gun d'fhalbh i leam gu subhach,
     A fagail as a deidh gach tir,
     ''S dh fhag sud mi fhein gu tuirseach.

2   Bha cuid ri cluich 's bha cuid ri ceol,
     Bha luchd an oil ri sugradh.
     Bha mis' mar phelican leam fhein,
     ' Smo chlarsach a's gun durd aic'.

3   Oir dhiadh air m'inntinn mar gum b'oidhch',
     Is rinn mi caoidh fo sgaile.
     A chionn gu'm b'fhada bhuainn 'n Allt-bheithe,
     ' Far am bheil mo phobuill gradhach.

4   'Far am bheil mo cheile shamhach shuairc',
     'Smo leanaban luachmhor aluinn,
     'S aithne Chriosd a's maith a shluagh
     A bhuadhaich orm 'gan fhagail.

5   'S cor dhuinn fulang air son Criosd,

'Sna thiodhlac E dhe gradh oirnn.
'S cor a dhol do thirean cein,
A sgaoileadh sgeul a Shlainte.

6   'Dol thairis air a Chuain an Iar,
Bha aimsir bhreagha 's ciuin ann,
Bha gluasad mall am measg nan tonn,
'S na bh'ann do ghaoith 'nan culaibh.

7   Bha 'nt-adhar shuas gun ghruaim, gun neul,
'Sa 'ghrian a deanamh iuil dhuinn,
'S thubhairt   iomadh uair rium fhein,
Tha sluagh mo sgir' ri urnuigh.

8   Is thainig mar gum b' oiteag bhlath,
An aireamh bh'air an gluinean,
Thug orm gun 'd'thubhart mi fianuis chaich,
Tha neach no dha dh'am ionndrainn.

9   Air teachd do'n t-Sabaid air a cuairt,
Cha d'fhuair i ach a reubadh.
Ach mhothaich mi gun robh an cuan,
'S ant-adhar shuas toirt speis dhith.

10   An sin bha mis' mar Israel,
Air gheugaich chroch a' chlarsaich,
An Sion 'nuair a chuimhnich mi,
Aig sruthaibh coimheach Bhabeil.

11   Ach bha an Cruithfhear dhomh dluth,
'Gam urachadh le grasan.
Oir anns an uamh leis na fithich,
Nach do bheathaich E am faidh!

12   Criochnaichaidh mi a nis   mo rann,
Tha long air tighinn gu traigh leam,
'S innsidh mi dhuibh sgeul na tir,

'Ma 'se gun till mi sabhailt'.

Translation

Crossing the Ocean

1   When all of us had boarded ship,
She bore us off with pleasure.
Behind her leaving all the land,
And in my heart a sadness without measure.

2   Some played at games, some took to songs,
Some took to drink and indolence.
In sadness like a pelican, alone,
I sat with harp in silence.

3   My mind was closed as with the night,
And in its shadow now I wept;
When I recalled far-off Aultbea,
And all my loving people.

4   My serene and beautiful wife is there,
My precious lovely little ones.
It's Christ's command and for His flock,
That led me now to leave them.

5   It's right we suffer for our Lord,
Whose gift of heaven's love He gave us,
To travel far to distant lands,
With the Gospel of salvation.

6   While crossing now the Western sea,
The weather beautiful and calm,
The gentle hollows in the waves,
The zephyr wind behind us.

7   The sky above a cloudless blue,
            From which the sun it cheered us.
            And oft I thought within myself,
            ' My people don't forget me.'

8   It came to me a warming thought,
            Of those who now in prayer were bowed,
            As if I heard their witness voiced,
            That some among them missed me.

9   And when the Sabbath now came round,
            No thought for it was given,
            But in my heart I felt the sea,
            In honour with the sky, received it.

10   Then I was like God's people Israel,
            Of old who hanged their harps,
            On branches at the riverside,
            In strange and far-off Babylon.

11   'Twas God Himself sustained me,
            Renewing me with His grace.
            Likewise with ravens in the cave,
            The prophet He sustained with food.

12   I'll close the verses now I write,
            The ship has come to harbour.
            I'll tell you later of the land,
            If I return in safety.

Once again he found himself on the shores of the New World. The last he saw of it was twenty years previously, before the outbreak of the Great War. Much change had taken place. It was a new age. He himself had changed. He was now a minister and it was a joyous thought for him to return especially to places and people he had known right across the great country from East to West. The man they once knew as an immature young immigrant from Gaeldom was now seasoned by War, matured by spiritual realisation and transformed by applied study to be an ambassador of Christ and a 'fisher of men'.

Now he returned to this vast Dominion as a minister. In Montreal he met his brother Ewen who was domiciled there at the time. On this visit to Canada, my father had a set itinerary, by which he visited the Free Church congregations in Toronto, and Fort William (present day Thunder bay). Then on his way by train to Vancouver, he stopped off in Manitoba to stay for a week with his sister Katie,who was married there to a farmer on the Prairie. He spoke later on to his children of his return to Vancouver and the incomparable view of the blue Pacific on the other side of the North American continent.

The changes since he had last seen the city struck him forcibly. Now Vancouver was a large relatively modern city. Tall buildings were everywhere, stamping the city as the western centre of Canadian commercial activity. Sailing schooners and barquentines sprouting tall masts had all but vanished. In their place were coasters, tramp steamers, large grain ships and merchant ships. But he noted that many large buildings were still unfinished, with scaffolding rusting in a network round their skeleton structures. There was a kind of languishing, as if a blight had stilted economic growth. Then of course 1930 was right in the middle of the infamous Economic Depression. Many in Britain think this was only Britain's calamity. Canada and the United States suffered equally, if not more. Tens of thousands of farmers on the

Prairies lost their homes and liveliehood and migrated into the cities to swell an army of unemployed.

My father made one significant observation which is relevant in today's ecological controversy. The Railway Terminus was a vast spread-out system of side-lines and feeder lines, with a continual activity of engines shunting wagons and flat railcars back and fore. The harbour was identified by a plethora of long black funnels of ships. These continually emitted steam, a seemingly innocuous spasmodic evaporating mini-cloud. But a closer look at the funnels would show a steady slow effusion of coal smoke from the boilers deep within the hulls. The boilers on the ships tied at the docks and also on the large fleet of various vessels at anchor in the bay were not allowed to grow cold. Rather their fires were alight so that they could be stoked up in short notice to get a 'head of steam', when called upon to do so.

The air was strange to my father's nostrils. He remarked how this contrasted to his experience in earlier days at the turn of the century. Then there was a a great smoke from all the wood-burning mills and also from household heating. Now however this was increased at least a hundred-fold to compound the atmospheric pollution of the commercial and maritime activity. Coal with its toxic smoke of inefficient steam generation and the not so invisible grime associated with the increased industry, now brought Vancouver, that beautiful city, one step closer to being just another industrial city, like Glasgow, Detroit or Newcastle. And Vancouver had a special handicap, a corollary of its geographic location. The rising shield of the Rocky Mountains at its back trapped the clouds of toxic air so that it tended to hang over the city, much like the notorious smog that stubbornly rests like an

Rachel MacKinnon nee MacPherson, Glendale

Captain John MacKinnon

Childhood home, Shiadar, Glendale

The old manse in Aultbea.

The old manse and church from Pier Road

Inside of Glendale Free Church circa 1880.
Meeting of the Land League.

Free Church College - Session 1922-23
Back row: Alex Fraser, Jonathan Campbell, Alex MacLeod, J.
MacPherson, Angus MacKinnon. Middle row: R. MacInnes, A.
MacDonald, D. Ferguson, J. MacIver, D. MacKay, A. MacDonald, W.
Fraser, M. Maciver, J. Shaw
Front row: Prof. R. Moore, Prof. J.K. Cameron, Prof. W. Alexander,
Prof. J.R. MacKay, Prof. D. MacLean, K.C. Bell, Elocution Lecturer

Rev. MacKinnon (left) with colleagues at wedding in Glasgow. Rev. Ewen MacRury Shiskine, a Gaelic scholar and Rev. Duncan MacDougall, Dunoon, a minister in Vancouver and also served as newspaper publisher

Allan Macleay, the church officer. 'Tha e na s fhasa ant-searmoin a thuigsinn a's a Ghaidhlig' Donald MacIver, the Precentor. 'A voice that brought both skill and reverence to the worship of the sancturary'

Aultbea Free Church

Poolewe Free Church

With bride, Catherine Matheson from Stoer, Assynt

Family Photo in 1936
Mam and Dad
Cathie, Angus, baby Joan in mother's lap, Rachel Mary, Ina, Katie, Ian Angus
Inset Donalda born in 1938

umbrella over Los Angeles, a few hundred miles to the south, on the same coastline in the United States.

Still, my father found it a great joy to visit the city after a twenty years' absence. Many had known him long before, in his youth. The welcome he received was overwhelming. Now in his prime, and stimulated by the eager receptiveness of the large body of exiled Highlanders, for the most part first generation, he preached to large congregations. He was in his element. Here the whole spectrum of human thought and emotion came together, as his mind grasped the metaphors of absence, separation, longing, of new beginnings, of homesickness, of resignation, of natural expectations, of hope and the many forms of adversity. This was the stuff for Gaelic preaching. His facile use of the Gaelic language enabled him to use the latter as a vehicle to match all the varied colours of the human experience. Thus in his preaching, the language flowed through the arteries of human thought and touched the deepest emotions. Of course such preaching had a purpose, that of waking people to spiritual life. For the soul, the inner spirit of man is not impervious to the empirical *stimuli* of the human situation. The spiritual has no meaning outwith the context of ordinary human life. The soul has no existence in a vacuum, but generically is identified with the individual person in all the seemingly trivial and ordinary trappings of our common human life. And the great thing is that God uses this to implement His election of Grace.

But equally MacKinnon Aultbea was affected in himself by the same emotions. The difference was that he was now just on a visit, and his immediate family as well as his congregation were a continent and an ocean's distance away. After some six months, overcome by a sense of longing, he felt he had to get back to Aultbea. With great reluctance on the part of the Vancouver people, and with the acquiescence of the Church Offices in Edinburgh, it was agreed that his visit be curtailed.

In the last service in the Vancouver church, an old Highlander who was there, spoke of the spiritual Presence and the human emotion in the service. Few were untouched as the preacher, who was 'born again' in that city, led his hearers to the 'mountain-top', and focussed the people's attention on the King in his beauty and 'the land that is a very far off.' Mastery of the Gaelic language, his gift for illustrative imagery taken from every day life, and his own personal acquaintance with the Love of Christ, made that night an experience of spiritual immediacy not soon to be forgotten. Many hearts were filled to overflowing and souls tasted of exquisite joy.

Thus he parted from them, like St. Paul of old from Ephesus. Though he left for Aultbea where his heart lay, he would never forget Canada, and throughout his subsequent life, he would from time to time advert to his Canadian experience as a very positive and enduring element which was profitable to him in his Master's service.

Chapter 21

The Minister as Teacher

Teaching was not only implemented from the church pulpit. My father had a circuit of religious education throughout his charge. There were at least six locations where prayer meetings were held by elders in each hamlet. Also the minister visited these in turn. On these occasions, he administered baptism, or held the 'catechising'. Undoubtedly this was the secret and still is, of a religiously educated community, namely the institution of Catechising.

In the 1990's the Roman Catholic Church has given a lead to the Christian world in producing a revised catechism, which is being assiduously applied and accepted, in a world where the religious signposts have been for the most part taken down and the teaching machinery of church life dismantled. If there is one clear reason for the church's failure in both the Catholic and Reformed sphere, it has been the discarding of this vital practice as an out-dated archaism.

We will look in, as it were, on one of these meetings of congregational education. Come with the minister to Mellon Charles and see the synthesis of Prayer, Sacrament and Teaching as these three basic elements co-relate together in the integrated order that makes this a premise for quiet dynamic efficiency in a Christian community. The minister's car pulls in at the top of the hill. It is Saturday evening. Lights glow from the windows of the plain meeting house. But all can see this meeting house, alive and patronised by the people. For it is situated on top of the hill, and now the light from it shines like a beacon of witness and testimony, compelling evidence of the Christian character of the community.

Inside the people are waiting. There is no hurry. They are not slaves of time. Time is their servant, giving them opportunities to redeem it and invest in it for spiritual dividends. The hall is comfortably full. The lamps shed their yellow light from the walls. A tilley lamp at the pulpit end gives a brighter white light for the minister. Pews are full with families, parents with their children, aunts and uncles, brothers and sisters. You can see the youngest clinging to the arms of their mothers. The others are sitting upright, the girls with their bonnets and pigtails sticking out behind them. The boys are subdued, dressed as best they can, their faces freshly washed, their spiky hair betraying the rough haircut given to them by their dads, now rebelliously sticking up. There was no Bryl cream in those days, nor fancy shampoos to tame their windblown hair. All the women sport bonnets, streamlined, a safe defence from strong gusty winds. The men are dressed in homespun tweeds. If you studied them closely, you would see that they were not dressed in their best suits. This is a weekday and it is natural for them to gather together from the houses round about. Here you have MacKenzies, MacLeans, MacRaes, Beatons, Camerons, Chisholms, MacLennans, Grants. There are not many families of other surnames in Mellon Charles and Ormscaig, its little Norse-named neighbour.

My father has come in. He sees them all before him, one segment of the large flock over which he is shepherd. Here there is no paucity of people, but a gathering of appreciative parishioners in one fold with one shepherd. For there is no other church in sight and no other shepherd to care for them. As a rule this regular prayer meeting on Saturday is conducted by the elders. This evening it is given over to the minister, yet with the elders fulfilling the duties of their office as the minister's lieutenants.

This is a big event. There is a baptism of an addition to the MacLennan family of *Ali Abi* (Alick son of Abigail). The child's mother is Flora, and the family live in their house not more than a hundred yards from the meeting house.

Here the Sacrament of Baptism is not taken lightly. It is projected in its symbolism but linked to the Word. The meeting opens with the singing of a psalm, with readings from Scripture including the authoritative warrant from the words of the Lord, and vicarious prayer. Then the minister refreshes people's minds in recalling the significance of the Sacrament. There is no ambivalence. It is presented as parallel with the symbolism of Old Testament Hebrew circumcision but signifying chronological historical sequence by which membership of the Old Covenant is superseded by something greater, even the glorious New Covenant of which Christ Jesus is both the Foundation, the Means, and the Head. It is the minister's joy to demonstrate this in the dimension of the New Testament, which transcends the old.

The mother hands the child, dressed in the christening gown, to the father. Now the glorious blessings of heaven are called down upon the newborn addition to the family. The minister engages in prayer. The appropriate questions are put to the parents. There is no need to grill the parents. They have been here before when the older siblings were brought into the fold of the Covenant of God's people to be the beneficiaries of its privileges in the diversity of the means of grace in the visible church. Obedience to this is a fundamental premise of baptism, namely an obedience of faith which through grace leads in God's sovereign will to the fruits of the Spirit and the maturity of faith.

You can feel a visible change. The whole building packed with people becomes one in spiritual expectation. It is as if the doors of every heart are open in obedience to the Creator, the God who has given to them as a people the privileges of His Covenant and the Mercy of His everlasting love. There is no holding back. Everyone assents in participating in this Divinely ordained appointment, this sacred enactment of faith, this simple yet profound dispensation where a newborn of this world is brought by a community to the church's door to be touched by the breath of heaven as a child of promise, according to the inexhaustible riches of Christ.

The kerosene lights frame the scene, while the white light of the tilley pressure lamp on the side wall accentuates the drama that Christ himself instituted, *Go ye therefore, and teach all nations, baptizing them in the name of the Father, and of the Son, and of the Holy Ghost.*[1]

Then follows the baptism, and as the water is sprinkled over the little one's head, and the sacramental blessings are poured upon it, there is heard a cooing sound from the infant. Every one, even the old veteran elders, turn to look at the little face, the face of another generation, born into the world, and the mirror of the future yet to unfold.

Now the meeting continues in the familiar sequence. The

1
Matthew 28:19

vicarious act of spiritual reception, carried out by the minister, is followed by the Aaronic blessing.

> Gu'm beannaicheadh an Tighearna thu,
> agus gu'n gleidheadh E thu:
> gu'n tugadh an Tighearna air ' aghaidh dealrachadh ort,
> agus gu'm biodh E grasmhor dhuit:
> gu'n togadh an Tighearna suas a ghnuis ort,
> agus gu'n tugadh E sith dhuit.

Translation:
> The Lord bless thee, and keep thee:
> The Lord make his face shine upon thee,
> and be gracious unto thee:
> The Lord lift up his countenance upon thee,
> and give thee peace.
>
> *Numbers 6.24-26.*

Somehow, you sense that here the minister is in his element. He is 'at home'. This is not work, but a calling. Time, gifts, endeavour, sacrifice, energy—the outgiving of these bring to him unspeakable returns. There, with his people in far-off Mellon Charles, Rev. Angus MacKinnon is truly wedded to his flock as an under-shepherd of His Master.

Then follows a specific prayer for the home, for the family, thanksgiving for a mother spared in childbirth; a prayer for strength to cope with adversity, and the blessing of God's grace to make the child a blessing to the home. The prayer closes with a supplication for all the community, and that every want might be met and every difficulty overcome through the grace of the Lord Jesus Christ.

With the Sacrament over, a highlight has passed. But there is more to come, and yet this is not an anti-climax. The tone of the meeting has been given a fragrant note, a species of spiritual perfume, the loveliness of the newborn child, the hopes and promises of God's blessing upon it, the solemnity of the sacred Word and the holy atmosphere of spiritually-minded prayer, by ruling elders and the teaching elder, the minister.

Now the mind of the people is addressed. For them the Westminster Catechism is the 'blue book' of doctrinal and religious knowledge. It is in two parts, the Shorter Catechism for children and the Longer Catechism for adults.

Here in Mellon Charles all the religious exercises of Sacrament and teaching, prayer and praise were in Gaelic. An elder gives a list of names of those who have said they are ready to be examined for their religious knowledge in public. Adults now rise in turn as their names are called out to answer the primary and secondary questions of the Larger Catechism. The minister commends those who answer well. He has a way of encouraging those who need coaching. Where there is hesitation, he reiterates the answer himself so that all can hear clearly, adding explanation of any obscurity.

When it appears that all are finished, John the elder stands up, leans forward and speaks to the minister. All can hear.

'Mr. MacKinnon, there's one more with us this evening, whose desire is to be asked a question from the Larger Catechism.'

The minister turns his face towards a pew in the middle of the hall. Informally, he addresses a little girl, Rhoda MacKenzie, the youngest daughter of Duncan the mason. She is only six years of age, a little girl with rosy cheeks and pigtails sticking out from under her Fair-Isle knitted bonnet.

The minister says, 'Rhoda, I am told that you are ready to

answer a question in the Catechising. We all rejoice that you have given such diligence so that you can do this. ' He puts two questions, the first two in the Larger Catechism, the first eliciting the belief; the second eliciting the reason for believing it. We give the Gaelic as was used then and the English translation of questions and answers. The reader who is acquainted with the Shorter Catechism will notice the amplified difference from the Shorter Catechism usually addressed to children.

Minister puts question:
Ceisd 1.   Ciod i crioch araid an duine?
(Question 1   What is man's chief end?)

Girl gives the answer:
 Is i crioch araid an duine Dia a ghloireachadh,   agus a lan-mhealtuinn gu siorruidh.
(Man's chief end is to glorify God and to enjoy Him forever)

Minister puts the second question:
Ceisd 2. Cionnas tha e soillear gu bheil Dia ann?
(Question 2 How does it appear that there is a God?)

Girl gives the answer:
Tha 'n solus naduir sin fein a tha 'san duine, agus oibre Dhe, a taisbeaneadh gu soillear gu bheil Dia ann ; ach is iad 'fhocal agus a Spiorad a mhain, a tha foillseachadh Dhe gu diongmholta agus gu h-eifeachdach do dhaoinibh, chum an slainnte.
 (The very light of nature in man, and the works of God, declare plainly that there is a God; but his word and Spirit

only do sufficiently and effectually reveal him unto men for
their salvation.)

There is a sigh of relief in the hall. There is more than a
hint of a smile on many faces. This is for real. No protocol of
generation gap is absolute. No rules or regulations are allowed
to suppress the greater end for which they are ultimately
introduced, namely to regulate but not dictate the privileged
expression of people's faith, old and young. Why! Are not
old and young all members of the church? You can feel how
proud people are of this little girl. The eyes of the old elders
search her face with their keen and intelligent discernment.
All share in a kind of special happiness that a little girl should
acquit herself so well. Before she sits down, the minister
articulates the feelings of the meeting for her perfect
performance. He commends her, and   encourages her by
saying that she has given joy to everyone.

Let us join in the closing psalm. There is nothing like this
on earth. The precentor, himself a lover of Christ and loved
by all who knew him, brings the voices of everyone together,
blending them in the sweetness of this familiar tune so that
the words also have a peculiar preciousness. You see, this
Psalm stresses the importance of instruction, instruction in
the laws of God and the doctrines of His Word. For they are
indeed food for the soul as they are food for the mind.

From Psalm 19

1   Eagal an Tighearn fiorghlan e,
           buan-mhaireanach a ghnath:
           Fior agus cothromach air fad,
           a bhreitheanais a ta.
2   Is fearr r'n iarraidh iad na'n t-or,
           an t- or as fearr air bith:

Na's milse na a'mhil ta iad,
no cir mheala r'a h-ith.

3   A faotainn rabhaidh fos a ta
d'oglachsa uath' a ghnath,
'S 'n an coimhead curamach gu dearbh
mor-thuarasdal a ta.

English:

1   Unspotted is the fear of God,
and doth endure forever:
The judgements of the Lord are true
and righteous altogether.

2   They more than gold, yea much fine gold,
to be desired are;
Than honey, honey from the comb,
that droppeth sweeter far.

3   Moreover, they thy servant warn
how he his life should frame:
A great reward provided is
for them that keep the same.

My father returns home to the manse in Aultbea. What might be considered an evening of tiring duty has filled his spirit with renewal and encouragement. What a preparation for the next day, the Sabbath and the duties before him in ministering to the congregation in the public worship of the sanctuary!

If you were to multiply this several times throughout the charge in the staggered order according to requirements to fit in his spiritual duties, you can have some idea of the permeative influence of a didactic or teaching ministry. There was no co-ercion in this; there was no fear. No one was afraid to go there to be shown up, to be humiliated before others. There were some who, humanly speaking were not disposed to stand up in public and answer questions. All was done in an orderly way. A list was given by the local elders of those who felt able and were willing to take a vocal part, that is of men and women. It was considered a privilege and an honour and a justifiable profession of competence as well as of faith, to acquit oneself well in this participatory role in the teaching/ learning process.

You can understand how the Catechising was a bridge within the structure of the church. There was no polarised rigid divide between adherents and communicant members. There was no sacred privilege permanently written over the church door, 'For members only.' Membership, in the community or parish church, without diluting its spiritual significance, was one of degree, rather than division of categories of people as believers and non-believers. One speaks of the ideal. It would be pretentious and misleading to suggest that right thinking was maintained by everyone in this respect. Polarise the distinction into absolute terms or dilute the difference and you have the source of many problems endemic and apparent in the church in history and the contemporary church of today, near the beginning of the 21st century.

There really is no secret here. Those who were born in the community were also born into the flock of God's people, to be nurtured and brought up in the 'fear of the Lord', just as surely as the children were born into the homes of the Israelites, as a composite pattern or prototype for the new Israel, on the catholic or world scale of the New Testament. The little ones were brought to public baptism or baptised in homes when circumstances warranted. But that flexibility only reflected the willingness of the church, through the sagacity of the minister and the elders in presenting the people as the church, and not the church as the people.

In this context, the minister saw the church taking form, not as an abstract entity of evolving history, encapsulated in the burdensome chains of prolific and ever increasing ecclesiastical legislation, but having reality, born of the people, given accreditation through God's love to them and the responsive love of the people to God, in living in obedience to His law. As their Father in heaven, there was a perpetual awareness of the God of Providence even in the little mundane matters relating to the daily lives of people. Thus it was no burden to honour the Sabbath day and give it over to the things of God. People consciously valued it as a gift given by God to them, to give them a break from the ordinary toil of the weekdays, and as an assertion of the spiritual needs, as primary over any compulsion of legal compliance by the rules of the secular state. In Scotland, there was and is in the religious heritage, a binding obligation for the civil government to partner the church in the structured framework, which qualifies the country to be called a Christian nation. Bring a cessation to this basic historical thinking on the part of the representatives in responsible government, and you spell the death knell of all the hopes and promises of divine benediction represented in the Christian vision of society. And 'Where there is no vision, the people perish.'[1]

We stated that there was continuity from the birth of the child through adolescence and then to the maturity of adulthood and full membership within the church. You can understand how the community religious structure lent itself

1. Proverbs 29:19

to this. The person who grew up with the knowledge of religion was   no novice, when he asked to be received into full communion. The child was taught in the secular and Sabbath school and also under the nurturing influence of the Christian home. As an adult he or she graduated from the Catechising. As a concerned seeker, he or she then started 'following'. This turning to spiritual things, was apparent outwardly by attendance at the weekly prayer-meeting. Couple this with a perceived diligence at the public means of grace in the worship of the sanctuary, a visible marked change in the person's life, in the absence of the profane, there was no surprise when that person came before the Kirk Session on the Saturday, the day of Preparation, of a Communion season.

What a triumph of orderly transitional standing for the child of yesterday, baptised into the household of God, taught in the church, in school and home, at last to profess that grace had won the heart! Hear Scripture, both Old and New Testaments concurring in their assent to the terms of Divine blessing for a community.

'And all thy children shall be taught of the Lord; and great shall be the peace of thy children.'[1]

We are here looking first-hand at the Locheweside charge, but there is no doubt that the situation here was replicated throughout the Highlands. Especially was this so within Wester Ross to north and south of Aultbea,   from Plockton, and Lochcarron, south Gairloch, and Lochbroom and Coigeach to the north.

My father was zealous for his people. He loved to be asked to preach in other congregations and to have fellowship with colleagues in the church at large. But his greatest joy and source of satisfaction in his calling was found when he was

1. Isaiah 54:13; John 6:45

among his own flock, feeding them, nurturing them, steering them from life's pitfalls, gathering them, rejoicing with them. We have sought to demonstrate this in that aspect of the parish ministry specifically linked to the Catechising. The current of communication was maintained in a purposeful intercourse of pastor and people, the teaching ministry of religious knowledge.

There are many ways in which the purpose of schools and education are obscured. Essentially, schools and education are vehicles for learning to live full and happy lives, helping one another in a Christian community. Aultbea represented the pattern of responsible educational policy by the happy liaison of church and state as followed in the Highlands generally.

In the public school the Bible was taught each day by the teachers. At least once a year the local Presbyterian minister or ministers examined pupils in Scripture knowledge, in co-operation with the teachers.

Many who might not otherwise shine in school lessons, redeemed themselves with a high standard of response when the oral examination took place. There were three classrooms in Bualnaluib Public School, a central location for the Aultbea area. Roughly a hundred pupils were enrolled. Teachers like Miss Beaton, Miss MacCann, Miss Nicholson, headmasters like Mr. Murchison and his successors like Mr. Thomas and Miss MacKenzie, were all highly proficient in the discharge of their duties. They were grounded in the cultural character that gave substance to the Scottish education system, with its historic regard for the integrity of learning.

The minister was given real V.I.P. treatment. Pupils were fascinated by the clerical clothes, the contrast of black and the white dog collar. To many, he was like someone from another planet. They were used to church services, to seeing him away up there in the pulpit. But here he was right there in front of them. And he was talking to them, without the austere-looking elders sitting in the latron between him and them and without the great company of adults, dwarfing them and crowding them out as a necessary minority with little significance. The presence of the minister in the formal clothes of his vocation, the identity with the lofty pulpit, the adult nature of the church life, now in the 'flesh', right there in the children's exclusive world of the classroom, had a profound uniting effect upon the children. They felt a certain child consciousness, but through this interaction, this 'class' consciousness was mitigated or reinterpreted, in their thinking, so that they felt part of the whole of society. And more, that God himself was interested in them. This was proof of it. Why! Was not His servant, his ambassador right there in their school, the school where they spent most of their young life and where they met just a handful of adults, their teachers. The only other adults that one can recollect were the inspector of schools and the dentist on their annual visits.

The religious curriculum was objective, directed to the minds. It was not conceived as the teacher's task to communicate in teaching the spiritual subjective nature of the Gospel and the nature of belief in the process of thinking that is allied to the feelings of the heart. Even the Christian ethic was the composite form presented in the Judeo- Christian code of the Ten Commandments. The qualitative nature of the latter in the greater light of the comprehensive law towards God and our fellowmen, centred on the definition of communicative love, was not touched upon. This gave the school a kind of easy atmosphere where no pupil felt any self-consciousness. You could literally be a communist, if that was the philosophy of the home, and yet feel perfectly comfortable in the classroom. The school was not there to teach theology nor was it there to proselytize. It was there to confirm what already exists and is obvious to any sane intelligent reasonable person, that we live in an intelligent universe. In this, it is natural to give identity to all created beings, from primitive life to highly sophisticated forms—a wasp is a highly sophisticated life-form. Equally it is natural in such context, to assume the premise of Creator. Religious instruction was not there to prove anything. Rather in its acceptance of Biblical authority and derivative of Catechism material, its task was to inculcate awareness of evolving history, premised upon knowledge of Divinely initiatory creative beginnings.

There was no dichotomy between the religious and the secular. There was no divide between evangelical or liberal, between religious and humanist. Here no forces pulled the children of the community apart, left them bewildered by imposing choice upon their immature minds before they were ready to make decisions based on knowledge. Here the school was used as an expedient of society to give the children a world family consciousness, of which their national heritage, religious and civil was a part, and of which they ought to be intelligently aware and also rightly proud. Here there was no place for power games of alien cartels beaming their atheist views or perverted theist speculations, upon the formative and sensitive minds of the young. Neither of course was there the distorted subliminal message of humanist exclusivism and pretended scientific certitude from the daily persuaders on radio and television. These mischievous forces let in, by traitors to Scotland's national good, now ruling the minds of multitudes with their laser -like pervasive influence on the sub-conscious, were totally absent. Thus the cellular structure of a unified society in its sequence of growth from childhood to adulthood was maintained and confirmed.

Here in Aultbea you have a system that has this testimonial—it worked. What a happy day this was, as the minister broke the ice, asking a few well-thought introductory questions. These were specially designed to put the pupils at ease. Hands would shoot up from every direction, some snapping involuntarily with their fingers, in their enthusiasm to answer. Thus the classroom was tuned up with the silent 'hum' of young minds, happily conscious of their opportunity to prove their knowledge. At this point where the minister seemed so gratified and pleased, he would then turn to the teacher and leave him to elicit answers covering the whole syllabus for the year. This would mean selected areas of memory work and comprehension from the Ten Commandments, the Psalms, the Beatitudes, passages from the prophets like Isaiah 53 and the epistles like that of Paul in 2 Corinthians 13. Then there were questions on biography of main Scriptural characters, like Abraham, Moses, Jacob, Joseph, David, Jesus' disciples and the Apostles. Doctrine was objectively taught as memory work from the Shorter Catechism. With the syllabus in his hand, the minister would make himself comfortable, very comfortable—some pupils believed he was asleep—in the chair specially provided for the purpose.

This was all deliberate on the part of the minister. He wanted the children literally to forget he was there so that they would have no inhibitions in responding to their teacher and thus give their best. Somehow the children ceased to be aware of him and unself-consciously responded to their teacher, doing just that.

Then, suddenly coming to life, the minister stands up, glancing towards the teacher, he commends a pupil for an answer just given. He then draws out some added colours to clothe the subject with the immediacy of warm humanity. Then with a carefully worded comment closely related to the classroom performance, he commends the pupils and encourages them to redeem the time of their school years as a valuable preparation for their adult life. He would pause, looking down at his notes. A rather pregnant silence would ensue, the classroom waiting expectantly for a 'pass' or a 'fail, like a court waiting for the jury spokesman's verdict. There was a sense of great relief, when the minister, looked up from his notes, then turned to the headmaster, and informed him that he was satisfied with the examination and the performance of the pupils. By the time the whole of the school was examined, most of the afternoon had passed.

The school day was crowned with joy as the minister left in the car. By tradition, the school day was now over and the teacher dismissed the pupils absolving them from any new homework for that day.

Chapter 22

Purposeful Preaching

T he Sabbath evening service in Aultbea every fortnight was, as a rule, given over to the work of the evangelist. Then in a crowded church my father cast the net far and wide, right out, away from the boat. He was not content with a few people gathered in, the mature, the seasoned believers. His vision of the Gospel was one of multitudes being saved. And his work was to bring them in for Christ, so that His house would be full, so that the seats would be occupied, so that the banquet of heaven's provisions won on the Cross for defaulters, would not be prepared for them in vain.

Yet this is not to disregard individuality and the personal responsibility that gives people the profound and sacred privilege of human liberty. Thus the preacher appealed to old and young, to every kind of individual. For he stressed that while God's kingdom is designed and is being built for the multitude, they enter in individually, through the Door which is Christ Jesus. Because the congregation were already numbered in the visible church, with the outward marks of God's people, especially that of baptism in the church, every one was within hearing of the Gospel. My father spoke of the net of the Gospel, bringing before people the image of the nets of the fishermen on the sea of Galilee. But he did not go into detail about the kind of nets used there. Instead he spoke of the nets that were commonly used in Aultbea itself and were known first-hand to many of his hearers.

Picture the big Aultbea church. The autumn is just giving way to winter. The evening is calm. The minister is 'at home.' Churchgoers make their way along the roads all converging on the place of worship situated right in the centre of the township. People are walking. Old folk are leaning on a stick. Mothers and fathers walk together and their children walk some way behind them. Dozens of worshippers arrive on bicycles. They come from the north hamlets of Buailnaluib, from Tighnafaoline, Cul-choinntich. They come from the west, from Ormscaig, and Mellon Charles. Others arrive from the east and northeast, from Badfearn, and coming from the Laide road there are many families from Achgarve, Mellon Udrigil, Slaggan, Sand, Second and First Coast, right to Gruinard.

There are a few cars. Each is well known and treated individually according to the reputation of the driver. A large black car arrives from Mellon Charles. It is a taxi. Sam Turner from the Lowlands, married to a MacLennan girl, has acquired this huge American car and uses it as a taxi. It is not unlike those used by the Mafia in New York. It's a Buick, with a tanklike front and a sun visor—probably designed to shade the view of the black-coated occupants who used these tanklike cars for their nefarious calling in New York and Chicago. As the big car stops, no Mafia characters come out, but black-coated worthies, Godly women, who exercise secret power in the community, but the good kind, the 'power of prayer.' Women may be debarred from church office by convention, but none can bar them from the throne of grace and the powerful ministry that brings blessing to every aspect of community life that has God's sanction. Equally, these very women are fearless in asserting the mandatory obedience to the given religious duties of churchgoing and Christian living that premises God's blessing upon old and young.

There is another car coming from the direction of Mellon Charles. It sweeps in to the village centre, rushing down the small brae past the Pier Road junction, past Murdo Aird's house. Before it reaches, the growing crowd of people at the front of the church on the roadside scatter and hasten to give it a wide berth. It comes to a stop with a jerk. A woman is driving. She has forgotten to put the gear lever in neutral, so that the engine stalls. She has turned the three mile trip from Mellon Charles into an exciting hair-raising experience for herself and the ladies that follow her out of the car. Her driving, having begun late in life, lacks certain fundamental skills. Clearly her understanding of the horseless carriage is only in part. Those who are brought up in the motor age cannot begin to realise the adjustment required in earlier days, for those who learned to drive in their twilight years. Also, with the cars of that time, without synchro-mesh gears and the refined fuel systems of carburation and injection, coupled with the unrefined petrol mixture, plus the narrow, uneven gravel roads—well, frankly one could well ask, would many of us have done any better?

Apart from the cars which were really difficult to drive for the inexperienced, the roads were narrow and twisting with short steep braes and dangerous curves. There were often sheep ensconced in the middle and not uncommonly also the driver had to contend with a deer jumping suddenly across the road with its mate following. This was rather like an obstacle race and motoring for these brave pensioners was more like stock-car racing, rather than quiet uneventful country cruising. No wonder the bystanders gave these and other cars in Aultbea, especially church-goers, a wide berth.

The fact is that some of these drivers just could not pass the official driving test. They carried Learner plates on their cars for years. They sat tests time and again. New driving instructors came to put them through their paces. But alas, time and again, the result was negative. Many driving instructors had 'bad' experiences. The test itself hyped blood pressure and the performance was likewise spectacular. Everyone in the area knew of the test. It became a periodic event, matching a boxing match for excitement. Before the car moved, there was a loud roar as the accelerator was unnecessarily pressed by a nervous foot. There was an ear-piercing scraping noise from the transmission being engaged in first gear. Then a pause, and a sudden rush forward. You could see the driving-instructor's head shoot back and glimpse a grimace on his face. But, the comment all round among watchers was, 'She did it; she got away; she did it without stalling' And off the car went having kicked up a smokescreeen of gravel dust. We will not follow, and will not speculate on other aspects of the 'performance'. The miracle is that these dear people drove their cars for many years. It's true they had many incidents, but they survived them all. I have to say that I am convinced that the Lord is good, preserving those who trust in him.

I think of three good people in Canada whom I have known, who had only one eye and indifferent sight in the remaining one, who regularly drove to church and by some miracle did not come to grief. One of these was Charlie Hancock in Murray River in Prince Edward Island. In 1960, he kindly took me, as guest preacher, in his ancient Ford to a church service in *Sobhal* or Desable, where there was a large old Scottish Church. Charlie had very little sight but he had an advantage. I was sitting in the cramped backseat. It was summer, a very hot evening, and the canvas hood was down. Charlie's wife was beside him. All along the route, she gave instruction, 'Slow down', 'Keep to the right', 'Watch out, the lights are red'. Time after time, instructions followed so that they merged into a blur of noise, as wind and engine competed with Charlie's good wife for the driver's attention. And this was the miracle. We actually arrived safe and sound and in good time. I recall yet when we reached our destination I was taken to a house and the kind people looked at me oddly. I must have given some reason for them to think that I had just had a nightmare. I was led to a bedroom and told to lie down and rest and recover before taking the service. I say, this was a miracle, because Charlie Hancock, apart from being one-eyed, a First World War veteran, was also stone deaf, a result of the same shell explosion that practically destroyed his sight. It is totally amazing to me, the faith his wife had in him and the obvious belief that her computer-like instructions worked.

We cannot leave this subject without giving some explanation for an unresolved official problem. After many years, at last these 'special' drivers in Aultbea were no longer asked to sit a driving test. In effect, there was a total silence on the question. It was said by some that no driving instructor would come to Aultbea or Gairloch for these clients. It is certainly true that the local police sergeant treated these drivers differently. They were given a special license for the purpose that they desired. And that was for 'going to church.' These people did not want to join the stock car feverish activity of the modern motor age. They had no desire to drive in the fast lane. No, all they wanted was to use the expedient of the car to enable them to be in the House of God to worship their Maker and Redeemer, on the Sabbath day, and go to the Prayer-meeting—and of course all the special services, with possibly a little shopping thrown in on the side on a weekday.

There was something else that made the situation in Aultbea a relatively safe place, in spite of the fact that the roads were single track with only passing-places to use when meeting other cars. The reason for this was that on the Sabbath day, the whole community as a rule went to church. Therefore traffic was one-way, like that on a Saturday when crowds make their way to Murrayfield in Edinburgh for a big international rugby match, or to Hamden in Glasgow for a Soccer match, or, if you like, to Maple Leaf Gardens in Toronto for a big hockey game. It was therefore unlikely that any cars would be going the opposite way, to meet them to cause a crash. And there is this. The policeman himself was in church, and made a point of being one of the last, so that he was not seen to be part of the illegal drama. The authorities would like to prosecute, to fine, to imprison these defaulters, these highway deviants. But the 'wise' sergeant knew the score. He was ruled by common sense, so he adjusted the law to fit the special circumstances of Aultbea. Yet do not for a moment think that the policeman let everyone off with crime. He was uncompromising in prosecuting poachers, forced to act, by pressure from landed interests. And young boys with motorcycles were a target for his suspicions. As I reflect on these times some fifty years ago, I wonder do they still have special dispensations for churchgoers in far-off old Aultbea!

Meanwhile, there are other features to take note of at church time. Men cyclists pull in at the church entrance and lean their bikes against the cast-iron railings. They bend down and remove the bicycle clips so that the trousers of their good Sunday suits are allowed their natural shape. All the bicycles are the upright models and many carried a raincoat strapped to the handlebars or neatly folded on the carrier behind the saddle. You note the cycle lamp on the front of the bike. It will be needed as the dark will overtake the worshippers before the service ends, and they make their journey home.

The calm of the evening is broken by another noise, a gentle leisurely throb of a marine engine. A boat has turned in round the pier, about a furlong from the church. It is a fishing-boat with its Kelvin quietly pushing her along as she is skilfully drawn up alongside the jetty. I say, skilfully, for there is no reverse gear. This is the Grant's boat from Isle Ewe. Already several families of MacLennans and MacKenzies have come to land in their own smaller seaworthy boats, rowed with long oars by big strong men.

It is now twenty minutes to the hour of worship. Many worthy people go straight in to the church. Crowds of others remain outside. They have fellowship, gathering on the 'bank' jutting out on the sea side of the road.

In the relative quiet of the evening, someone points to the

seaweed lifted up by the tide that is nearly full in. There is movement in the seaweed. All eyes of those nearby keep staring. They are rewarded. A salmon, a big one, has leapt up in a graceful Olympic jump. Who could not appreciate this perfect example of nature's wonder, even the staunchest Calvinist, on a Sabbath evening! And in any case, God, the God that made the Sabbath, also made the salmon. This leads to some comment. A self-made prophet says for all to hear, *'Feuch thusa, bith' bradan sin 'air bord a' mhansa ma's tig deireadh an t-seachduinn.'* (Watch you, that salmon will be on the manse table before the end of the week). And I have to say that it is possible that he was right. For on the Tuesday following, a large twelve pounder with most beautiful glittering scales came into the manse trammel net just between the church and the doctor's house—a perfect spot for salmon, when the trammel net was set close to the shore and when the tide was right

But we must go on. The hour of worship approaches. Men put out their pipes and tap them on the heels of their polished boots, so that they are empty of tobacco ash. Soon all have gone in to church. The elders who have had their dinner in the manse after the morning service, have left much earlier. Now they are in the latron in front of the pulpit, each in their specific seats, an arrangement that would only be disturbed when the whole latron would fill with many elders from elsewhere at communion seasons. I can see them yet, as if in a film recording the passing sequence of the years of my childhood, John and Murdo MacLean, from Mellon Charles. You cannot mistake them with their striking appearance. There is *Morty Mor,* Murdoch MacLennan, from Laide, a tall man with a full expressive face. Also you see Alexander Grant from

Bualnaluib. He is a handsome fine looking man, who spent some of his working life away. He is still fresh and vigorous and it is not long since he crewed on one of Sir Thomas Lipton's huge yachts that tried to capture the America Cup. With them are others, such as Alasdair MacLean who would yet be lay missionary in succession to Donald MacIver. There is Murdo MacKenzie also from Mellon Charles. And to the left of the pulpit, is a very finely dressed elder, Kenneth MacLean from Mellon Udrigil. He is elderly but not a patriarch like the brothers John and Murdo. *Coinneach Liza* as he is known, is a true gentleman, loved and esteemed by old and young. Without exception, it appears that those who are ordained as elders in the church live up to expectations. There is something about them as representatives of the people and the specific different districts of the congregation, that both merits the commendation not only of God but also that of the community.

The large church is now comfortably full, with faces old and young. Women's hats and bonnets, interspersed with the bare heads of men, make a chequered sea. A few bright coloured hats can be seen, giving relief from the dark colours traditionally used. Two of the old school remind one of an age that is almost gone. The two ladies are Mrs MacKenzie, Laide House, and 'Bel' or Mrs MacKenzie, Bualnaluib. Both are well into their eighties. They sit erect, clothed in black with a kind of sash-like band at the collar held in with a large Cairngorm stone. The faces are almost pure white. Deep lines can be seen on that of old Bel who is close in front of us. Perhaps these represent the furrows of sorrow for the several children of her large family that were now in their graves. Framing the face of each of these ladies is a large Victorian hat. The women's hair is swept up underneath the hat, and straps come down the sides of the face and are tied under the chin.

The eye is raised to see the galleries at the sides and back. They are dotted with people, mostly younger ones. Those in the front seats lean forward with their elbows on the balcony, seemingly eagerly curious as the pageant of their religious culture is enacted before them. By their presence they are part of it, but for some, commitment is reserved and yet to be realised in the conscious personal experience of saving grace.

The twilight still lingers, with varied hues of coloured light beams filtering through the stained glass windows. But the church officer has already lighted about thirty kerosene pressure Tilley lamps. They hang from walls and balcony, with two large circular ones hanging from the ceiling about the centre. There is a constant hissing sound from the lamps. You get a commanding view of the whole scene from the manse pew, at one side of the pulpit. The congregation is a cross-section of the community. Families are identified by their pew for which they pay by tradition the annual pew rent.

Now the stage is set, the people are all in their places. The side door opens and all eyes are on the minister, clothed in dark clerical dress, with the distinctive frock coat, as he enters from the vestry, and characteristically with a hand on the rail, turns and makes his way up the steps to the high central pulpit. The door is open and he enters, bringing the door closed behind him. The top of the door is broadened out and covered with the deep red cloth. The result is that both doors, one on either side, appear an integral part of the pitchpine panelled pulpit surrounds.

The minister now adjusts to the situation. He, like all

ministers, knows well the cold winter days when storm and
snow can decimate church attendance and leave the big church
with the proverbial remnant of hardy faithfuls in the pews
before him. But tonight it is different. Before him is a sea of
faces of old and young. On the three sides of the galleries, a
goodly number complete the setting, making the church the
place to come to for which it was designed and built—namely
to be fed with the Word, sanctified by the Spirit, and presented
in all its sufficiency to needy humans, for spiritual
nourishment.

Quietly, the minister makes the call to worship, 'Let us
worship God.'

From now until the benediction is pronounced, the order
and sacredness of worship according to the Directory for
Public Worship, will govern the scene. Congregation,
precentors, elders and preacher are closed in like the final
preparations for flight as a jetliner is ready for its flight.
Now, as the precentor Donald MacIver stands to lead the
singing, there is a pause. The beadle, Alan MacLeay has closed
the big church doors at the front of the church and takes his
seat on the far side. One side door is left open for the inevitable
stragglers who may arrive in the following fifteen minutes.
It is an unwritten rule, that latecomers may arrive up till the
end of the first pastoral prayer. After that it is considered
disruptive and somewhat unseemly to join in the service.

With seasoned skill, Donald MacIver strikes the right key,
lifting up the Psalm book professionally before him with his
face also raised upwards and his voice directed forward in a
commanding posture of natural leadership. The acoustics are
ideal. There are no echoes, as often obtain in a near empty
church. Instead the church suddenly bursts to life in song,

'All people that on earth do dwell.' The service is in English. All present are 'taught of the Lord.' And all sing unto the Lord. Say what you like, and many have indulged in at least gentle criticism, the Free Church has saved for the Scottish nation, Psalm Singing and that without the proverbial 'kist of whistles.' If you go to the corresponding fellowships in the New World, the same praise form is used. There is even a fellowship of American Indians who use the Psalms in metrical form unaccompanied by musical instruments. But that is not to say that there is not music. The melody in the heart and the nuances of the human voice are the ultimate in expressing musical content. Is it not true that the technology of instruments seeks to simulate this, and undoubtedly often succeeds in doing so in synchronising the varied blends of the human voice. But here is pristine worship. No bellows, automated to drive by electric power is relied upon, only the human lungs.

A Sunday evening service in Aultbea was like the rendering of a human orchestra. Old and young, uninhibited by drowning wails from an organ or fleeting notes of a piano, and not put off by imposing colours of choir uniforms, sang together in the confidence of knowing what they sang, and led decisively to reach the extremities of blended musical beauty, which the human voice at best can attain to. What a beginning to an evening service—a big congregation lifting their voices in the pristine purity of collective praise to the tune Old Hundred! Here was not a narrow national parochial or sectarian presentation of presbyterian exclusivism. This was the church in its truly generic catholic outreach, calling all people on earth to praise the Lord. No wonder the Chicago Football stadium reached its greatest moment, on the occasion of the Papal visit in the 1980's, when sixty -six thousand people broke out in one great offering of praise. And what did they sing? None other than Psalm 100. 'All people that on earth do dwell' to the tune Old Hundred.

Now in a distant Highland village, there is the same sense of universal inclusiveness. Somehow, the whole building is filled with the music. The acoustic offering rises like incense to the lofty ceiling, fittingly blending in with the architecture of the Gothic arches through the pillars, that complement the galleries, both in the structural and aesthetic perfection of the architect's design. The congregation come to their feet, as the minister says,

'Let us call upon the name of the Lord. Let us pray.'

There follows a prayer with the seasoned phrases of the church's liturgy. There is no slavish formality. But, though unwritten and unread, the phraseology is familiar. The minister draws on phrases appropriate to the time of the year, the circumstances of people and nation, and even the time of the day. The minds of the people are lifted up, to dwell upon the triune God, Creator, Redeemer, and the Divine Dynamic, the Father Son and Holy Spirit—facets or roles of the architect and builder of the universe, the one living and true God.

The prayer does not tell God anything. It acknowledges His Omniscience. The minister leads people straight to the Throne of Grace. He leads them, himself, like a guide bringing before them the glorious options of Heaven's provisions. These are displayed before the shoppers as the perfect answer to the varied needs of the human dilemma. Here the lost, the sinner, the fallen, the hurt, the persecuted, the tried, the sorrowing, the backslider, the careless, the thoughtless, the waster, the misguided, are brought face to face with the options that have the stamp of Divine origin. Then the prayer takes a turn. This is identified in the changing tone of the minister's voice. There is a peculiar note introduced which words cannot fully express.

He has stopped before the Person of Christ Himself. The prayer becomes a shaft of light as it rests on the imagery of the Godhead, the Word made flesh, and the 'express image of the Father, full of grace and truth.' The prayer dwells upon Christ, the efficacy of His shed Blood, the matchless love when he poured out his soul unto death, bearing the sins of the world, alone on Calvary's Cross, to set the sinner free and restore the fallen so that there would be hope for a new or a renewed humanity.

The prayer turns outwards to encompass the needs of the world in a shared concern of our common humanity, in the current specific tragedies, special issues of war and peace, of famine and human failure. In all there is an irrefutable assertion of the Sovereignty of the Most High.

This evening the minister declares the Forgiving Love of God, the Father. His text, Luke 15:20, 'But when he was yet a great way off, his father saw him...' makes the prodigal a contemporary human being and the image of the father, a vivid portrayal of the unfathomable nature of divine mercy. The preacher uses the poet's gifts to bring the whole story alive with a powerful immediacy. His language paints the privileges given to the son; his choice which led to profligacy; the penitence that led to pardon.

My father could never leave this theme of heaven's love, as it was manifest for one person. He has drawn his hearers this night, into one of Scriptures' greatest dramas, and the meeting point of heaven and earth, God's mercy and man's sin, man's misery and God's salvation. The exposition is over.

The minister's voice now is thrown out in the musical chant called the 'seis' There is something persuasive and wistful about this form of communication. Preacher merges with the Scriptural witnesses, using their language for the greater part in the sublime expression of immortal truths as they relate to grace and also to glory, to human emptiness and divine abundance. Hearers lean forward, faces turn upwards in a collective consciousness of a shared spiritual experience. In this, the Gospel table is set, the provision is made, the host himself, none other than Christ is already there as graphically and Scripturally he is presented by the preacher. All that is required is for penitents to return to their Heavenly Father's house. There they will meet His love. There they will be washed and made clean and the hardness of their sins dissolved by the Blood of Christ. There they will be dressed anew in the righteousness worn here by faith and forever in glory. Here shoes, those of the therapeutic Gospel of peace will enable them to ascend the steepest hill of challenge and by wearing them, guide them in the paths of righteousness. Here the ring of betrothal will be put on their hand to signify their acquiescence with the terms of restorative grace and full pardon, as redeemed members in our Heavenly Father's House.

The lights flicker across the scene as all eyes follow the preacher. The darkness has come outside, but the lights of the sanctuary have come into their own, filling the beautiful building of listening people with light, in spite of the fact that some of the lamps have lost their pressure. And there is no doubt about it, there are young and not so young this night upon whom the glorious light of heaven has shined as well. It is all so graphically clear. The voice calls from the pulpit, with an unqualified invitation to one and all to partake of heaven's redemptive provision. The minister walks from one side of the large pulpit to the other. His white cuffs mark his raised hands as he recites the terms of free pardon and the efficacy of saving grace.

But time has passed. The minister glances at the large clock especially placed on the balcony at the side so that he can read it even with his imperfect sight. His voice drops. There is a pause. He looks out to the people and closes his homily with the invitation given by the Lord himself. His voice is quiet and tender, matching the pregnant stillness of the church.

> Come unto me, all ye that labour and are heavy laden, and I will give you rest.
> Take my yoke upon you, and learn of me; for I am meek and lowly in heart: and ye shall find rest unto your souls.
> For my yoke is easy, and my burden is light.
>
> Matthew 11:28-30

Suddenly, the minister's hands go up, with the accompanying words, 'Let us pray.' With the people now standing, a short prayer seeking God's blessing on the preaching of the Word follows. Then the church fills with music, the music of the closing Psalm on the lips of the people. There is a peculiar beauty and glory about the singing. Hearts have been touched. People have been brought to the door of the kingdom.

With the pronouncement of the benediction the minister leaves the church and the congregation disperses. He ascends the steps from the church through the tall green painted gate and makes his way to the manse door. Behind him, the church officer is already making his rounds, turning off the Tilley pressure lamps. The beadle's itinerary within the building can be traced, as one by one, the large windows of the lighted church darken and at last merge with the darkness of the night.

Now, back at the manse, the minister would sit in his favourite chair in the sittingroom. All he asked for was quiet, which he did not always get, surrounded as he was by a healthy lively brood of sons and daughters. Then he shared with his wife thoughts on the service, or news of people in the congregation. The sermon would also be discussed. Of course there were times when a service seemed 'flat', ineffectual, as if the spark was not there, as in a car which does not start no matter how much you turn the engine; or like a plane revving up on the tarmac, which does not reach enough revolutions to get airborne. Every minister is only too aware of these painful negatives and my father was no exception. Then the corollary would be disappointment and sadness, and a sense of futility and self-blame, and self-searching and self-doubt.

But it was different this evening. Now the children sought their father's face. They too shared in the 'spiritual high' of the event. Whenever there is a sense of spiritual liberty accompanying the preaching of the Word, even a child is conscious of the 'glory' being present and knows that this is a 'special occasion.' Little ones now vied with one another for their father's attention. Lovingly, they unlaced his shoes and replaced them with his slippers, first warmed at the fire.

Then the call is given by the older girls, that supper is ready. Already it is set on the table behind the armchairs, in the parlour, the family room. Round it, all take their place and first bow in silence as father asks God's blessing.

Afterwards there is a pause for thanksgiving or 'returning thanks.' Then follows sweet family fellowship. The lamps have long been lighted, the duties of the byre with its animals have been discharged, and even the hens have now retired and have fallen asleep in rows on their "spiris", the raised perches in the henhouse. The Sabbath evening closes with family worship, the manse family like others all over the community, lifting voices in praise and prayer round the Scriptures, the source of their structured community Christian life.

Now the candles and lesser paraffin lamps are lighted to guide everyone to their bedrooms upstairs. Soon all is still.

The minister has fulfilled his remit from his Master. He was the servant of the Most High, and he never forgot the purpose of his commission as a preacher, namely to declare the Gospel of Saving Grace.

Chapter 23

The Sunday Circuit

With the onset of the War, my father was appointed chaplain to the naval Base. This involved a lot of correrspondence. There were several trips out on a service vessel for burial at sea. He conducted mandatory services each Sunday. This meant an addition to the statutory services of his parish, but he did not hesitate to take up this challenge. Now consider his preaching schedule on alternate Sundays, that is, when the assistant, resident in Poolewe exchanged pulpits. This arrangement lasted for the five and a half years duration of the War.

Sunday began for him at his usual time of 6 a.m. At 10 a.m. he was in the naval base. His daughter Rachel, until she went off to High School in Dingwall, or Katie, next oldest daughter, helped chose the hymns. This was co-ordinated with a naval serviceman who was a very competent organist. It's amazing how there's always someone with the necessary gifts for God's work.

The new chapel at the Aultbea base was beautiful yet simple, as becoming the strong unadorned structure of Reformed theology. Though Presbyterian, this chaplaincy covered other Reformed denominations and contrasted only with the Anglican fellowship. The Presbyterian service of the Church of Scotland roughly coincided with that of Methodism. Add to this a fair sprinkling of Congregationalists, who as a denomination, shared a strong evangelical fellowship with the Free Church.

The chapel was outwardly not dissimilar to the many wooden huts surrounding it. But inside it was quite otherwise and beautifully furnished to reflect the Christian heritage. Artistically, a window on each side of the chancel portrayed the twelve apostles with our Lord as central. A blue carpet covered the raised platform on which the pulpit stood.   All woodwork and furnishings were in light oak. The pulpit stood out as a work of art, an exquisite example of craftsmanship from the Base workshop, a stone's throw from the church. Falls with the Burning Bush, the symbol of Scotland's Established Presbyterian Church, along with Bible marker tassels, framed the Bible Rest, in an open style without a pulpit enclosure surrounding it. A carved communion table with a blue cover gave the setting for the brass cross, the visual focus of our Lord's vicarious sacrifice and redeeming formula for a rehabilitated humanity.

The church was filled as Navy men and women filed in to sit in the pews. Here was a congregation of young people, going through a traumatic experience which would be part of the texture of their whole life. For more than one, their compulsory attendance at church would be blessed to them, both as a contrast to the grim enterprise of the genocide of the human family of which they were in Providence participants, and in the personal shaping of their life pattern, through their subsequent adulthood. It is false to separate all the elements that comprise the picture of these times. Therefore while one visualises the uniformed young people, ratings and ranks, non-commissioned and commissioned, one thinks of the world about them. Guns pointed skywards from many locations right round the loch, one battery, two hundred yards away at Aird Point.

Portsmouth of the North

Aultbea was called the 'Portsmouth' of the north, an allusion to its role as Naval Base. The loch had many service ships, with a large hospital ship with the Red Cross conspicuously painted on its white superstructure. In this protective shield, huge grey battleships hugged the steep cliffs which dropped to the sea like the walls of a dock. This loch, as in the Great War, was the natural shelter for the navy. Huge ships of the line, whose smoking guns knew exchange with the 'enemy', struck a pose of invincible might as they lay to their anchors. Destroyers and lesser corvettes surrounded the great leviathans and a continual traffic of liberty or service vessels, commandeered fishing boats, including a large number of steam drifters as well as diesel ringnetters, about a hundred in number from the Scottish east coast fishing ports, plied between ships and pier.

How can one omit mention of the aircraft carrier H.M.S. Ark Royal? Then there was the H.M.S. Nelson, with its long foredeck and massive long barrels of its big guns. It's a pity that it was crippled after sailing back from the Far-East, just when it was entering Loch Ewe, reputedly hitting one of the British navy's own mines. This caused a crisis and great excitement on a local level at the time. Boom boats tied alongside and great pumps laboured night and day to keep the massive battleship afloat as she crawled in to the loch to anchor in the lee of the 'tops', opposite the *'guallan mhor'* big shoulder of the island. Divers worked furiously to try and patch the gaping hole in her hull. A floating dock was despatched from the Clyde, towed up the west coast by tugs. Of course the ever watchful German reconnaissance planes read the picture. On two successive nights, their bombers gave Aultbea an unfriendly visit. Equally the defence artillery sent a wall of gunfire skywards. The sky was lighted up with searchlights and tracer bullets to the accompanying discordant *aria* of droning enemy planes, the constant gunfire and exploding shells, high in the night sky. A *sortie* of fighters from Stornoway brought an end to the attacks. There was also the fact that the long distance from their airports in German-occupied Norway meant that the bombers could not carry too much fuel for a protracted attack. They had a long way to get back home.

The H.M.S. Hood with its complement of thousands of men dominated the loch, a mighty floating fortress with its central castle of guns and funnel, rising in silhouette above the outline of the island. All but three or four of its crew would lose their lives, when the German Scharnhorst's salvo of lethal shells dropped down through the funnels and blew up the warship's magazine. There was the newly commissioned modern battle cruiser, called after the king, George VI, father of Elizabeth II. This new battle-cruiser would come to Loch Ewe after a major 'kill' in contributing to the destruction of Germany's greatest naval predator. The whole of Aultbea, on land and sea would celebrate, with Churchill himself secretly repeating his visit there during the Great War. And always, there were scores of merchant ships comprising the convoys that continually ran the gauntlet of German U-boats and dive bombers on the Murmansk supply route to Russia.

Sadly these convoys would hardly be out of the mouth of Loch Ewe when the sound of explosions and gunfire would mark the grim destiny for many of being sunk, with great loss of their brave crews. This was the background to the service on the Sunday morning in the Naval base in Aultbea, considered by many as the 'Portsmouth of the North.'

Thus the minister conducted the service of worship on Sabbath morning in this vital northern base, in the supply chain of military logistics to the Allies' partner, the U.S.S.R. In the sermon, the minister linked political imperatives to the prosecution of the War. He sought to put it all in perspective, leading his congregation of regimented listeners, to see some pattern to make sense of the many contradictions. The service triggered off association of homes, local churches, and the general norms of the Christian heritage of which the Scriptures and hymns were witness. Thus the fellowship of worship renewed them and made correction to their perspective, that they were not abandoned. But family ties were still strong; everyone was in this together and God loved them. There was a great earnestness as all sang, filling the chapel with hope and a certain shared conviction of faith and love, in the synthesis of prayer and praise in hymns like 'Eternal Father strong to save.' It would be difficult to match the scene and sound in that chapel, full of young people for the most part. By the last verse, all were drawn into the singing, giving the service a certain kind of completeness which complemented the minister's pronouncement of the Divine benediction. One recalls the last verse of the hymn:

> O Trinity of love and power,
> Our brethren shield in danger's hour;
> From rock and tempest, fire and foe,
> Protect them where so'er they go:
> Thus evermore shall rise to Thee

Glad hymns of praise from land and sea.
(William Whiting 1825 - 78)

The minister's first service is over. He has three to go. He hurries home to the manse a short distance away, driven in a naval car. Refreshed by a cup of tea, soon he is off to Poolewe, to Riverside, for the noon Gaelic service.

The church here is a smaller version of the big church in Aultbea. Inside, its beauty lies in its architectural symmetry. Pitch pine and varnish, brass lamps, the skilled use of natural light, the centrality of the pulpit, these impinge upon the observer and lend themselves to the atmosphere, reflecting the historic Christian faith. Even the church's location, beside the fast-flowing river with its prize salmon, links nature with the spiritual, and the staple reason for Poolewe's fame as a salmon-fisher's paradise with the greater redemptive hope of which the ecclesiastical building is the visible symbol. The service is traditional. There are two main precentors, Angus Cameron and Kennneth MacKenzie. Both are tall lean-looking men. They are ex- service men from the Great War. Angus Cameron had been face to face with evil, like all the Allies on the European Front in the Great War. His was a special legacy of being gassed. He might have succumbed had not the wind changed in Providence, making the Germans recipients of their own diabolical weaponry.

Today an old elder, Ailic MacLennan is present and he precents one of the psalms. He is one of the last of an age. Though well into his eighties, his presence is animated, his spirit strong. He has lived through many wars, having been born shortly after the Crimean War ended. He is not embittered by life and the many aspects of social and economic change

that swiftly passed him by. Instead he is refined by life, like
the pebbles that are smoothed by the angry waves and are
tossed up on the shore of the bay from the wild and wintry
coast. He is tall and dignified. His bearded face is now
lifted up. His voice grasps each line and raises it in musical
harmony before the people, like an offering that his own
soul delights in. Young children love him, both in his home
where they visit him and know his gentle friendship, and here
in the House of God. It is as if for him, every word is precious
and every line is a golden thread that he likes to linger upon,
as he sings. Then in turn, the congregation follow. The Gaelic
lends itself, in the rising and falling cadences, to nuances of
language and feeling that blend in with the grace notes, not
divorced from the music of the bag-pipes. In introducing the
psalm, the minister had specified that three verses would be
sung, for Gaelic Psalm singing, putting out the line, takes
extra time even for a few verses and four verses are the
maximum in the liturgy of a service. But the precentor does
not stop after the third verse. The minister had risen in the
pulpit to begin his sermon. A little put out, he returns to his
seat. He cannot even tap Ailic on the shoulder with the psalm
book, an expedient commonly used especially during
communion services. The reason is that Ailic is not in the
precentor's box but in the elders' latron. He accepts the
situation philosophically, hoping Ailic will come down to earth
soon. There is no doubt that the old saint is caught up in the
spirit. Though he holds the psalm-book out in front of him,
his eyes are closed as he puts out each line. For his soul looks
to heaven and the spiritual experience of praise is his delight.
The image of his gentle Christ-like face is stamped on the
memory even of those who were children.

Guth gairdeachais is slainte ta
am pailliunnibh nan saoi:
Deas lamh Iehobhah uile threin
fhuaradh gu treubhach i.

English:

In dwellings of the righteous
is heard the melody
Of joy and health: the Lord's right hand
doth ever valiantly.

                                    Psalm 118:15

What matchless scenes some of us have been privileged
to witness on earth as a foretaste of the glory that is before us.
Here was a veteran believer, still full of the joy of his Lord,
while praising the Saviour in the sanctuary. He was ordained
an elder, not so much for any inborn abilities, but for the gifts
of grace which adorned his life, a kind of aura of heavenliness
that lingered over his person and blunted the often perceived
comparative harshness of religious restrictiveness and
imagined censoriousness. The faith that he espoused when
young at the beginning of his pilgrimage, was in his old age
still evergreen, untarnished by time, undiluted by compromise,
undimmed by bitterness, still shining like a lamp in the witness
of its Christian joy. One cannot forget him and his singing
that day, when he carried on beyond the required verses.
Maybe there was a special reason for it. Very soon after, he
passed peacefully from earth's scene, to fill his destiny along
with the Redeemed, gathered in through Christ. There Ailic
would be 'at home.' There would be no curtailment of praise.
He could go on singing all the verses of the psalm day and
night, praising the Lamb upon the Throne, even His Saviour,
forever and ever.

After the service the minister has dinner, beautifully prepared by the missionary's wife in the mission house. At three o'clock there is a second service in English at Poolewe, after which the minister is off again.

The fourth service for the minister is alternately held in Cove or Inverasdale. Today it is the turn of Cove, the furthest away of the villages. As the minister drives along, the evening is near. The northwest wind ruffles the seas as they run inland bringing in the cold north Atlantic swell, even into the loch. The car passes Boor, a bleak unused three-storey farmhouse with some small farm buildings in a hollow round it. Then through Naast—literally meaning a 'nest for boats.' The car climbs the hill on the other side and the minister changes back to 'top' gear. Were he preaching in Inverasdale, he would stop to pick up Ali Alasdair Urquhart, an elder. This man had a warm kindly personality. His son would follow him as a Christian witness and be known as *Ali Ali Alasdair.* Alick the son of Alick the son of Alasdair. The Citroen shakes as it reaches thirty miles per hour. The gravel road has now become even narrower. It is little used. Grass grows unhindered in the middle. It is twilight, a bad time for seeing, especially as the car-lights have blinkers on as a war measure, to avoid any help to enemy aircraft. The driver has to watch out for Inverasdale sheep who have a special predilection for sleeping at night on the road, possibly receiving residual heat absorbed from the daytime sun on the gravel.

The sloping croftland of Inverasdale with its sub-divisions of Mid-town, Stirkhill and Braes is reached. An elderly lady, Mrs. Macleod is taken aboard. She looks to the minister's visit as a bright moment in a life that has known much adversity which is clearly recorded in her kindly but sad face.

She is one of Christ's close disciples, sustained by his grace. Anonymous, like multitudes of the redeemed on earth, her name is known in heaven and is on the roll of the elect, who are washed by the Blood of Christ. The car progresses, through Midtown, past the bridge with its snug little harbour sheltering two small fishing boats. The car passes the big stone building to seaward, whose ground floor is the Inverasdale meeting-house, where the minister will preach the next time. The road is now level and comparatively straight across the spread-out croftland and then it crosses the peaty moorland, with its dark mounds of treasure—the community's fuel supply of peats, provided by nature—and so on westwards.

The twilight is still there, as the chassis of the Citroen, always a low car, brushes over the grass-covered hump in the middle of the road. Now it gains speed as it passes Firemore. There is a gun battery military station here, overlooking the convoys of merchant ships, darkly grey and unlighted, all with their bows facing the same way, the North West, at anchor. Firemore has a sandy well-drained appearance with a promontory jutting out on the right. Here is the neat well built home of a Matheson family. One of the family, Kay a young school teacher caught in the elixir of patriotic fervour would help to bring the Scottish Stone of Destiny, back to Scotland, from Westminster in 1950 for a short-lived holiday. The stone, used in crowning Scottish kings, and stolen by England's king Edward I, some six and a half centuries earlier, was symbolic of Scottish sovereignty and autonomy. Seers predicted that when it would finally return, Scotland would again assume its national status of freedom. The fact that the stone was returned, peacefully and voluntarily, by the British Government on the 700th anniversary of the theft, in 1996, makes many optimistic about the fulfilment of this prediction.

At last in the waning light of day the minister's car reaches Cove, the last hamlet on the southwest arm of Loch Ewe. The land is buttressed by rocks, battered by the Minch over millenniums of years, carving out caves and weird rock formations. Some have likened this to the primeval topography of geological beginnings or that of the end of the world, a kind of ultimate scenery, that related to origins or the final consequence of expired creation. In the previous century, worshippers gathered in a cave nearby as the inexorable seas kissed the gneissic basalts and split the strata into indented irregularity, leaving projecting cliffs and under-cutting rocks to form several commodious caves. One of these was very comfortably furnished as a place of worship. Its acoustic excellence made it a competitor for a cathedral, with its own orchestra of maritime music, as the 'swell' engineered musical patterns, a perfect natural accompaniment to the Gaelic psalms. Mendelssohn might well have been inspired to record a companion composition to that of Fingal's Cave, had he known of this.

The meeting-house appears suddenly. The scene here this Sabbath evening is one of contrasts. The wintry night is closing in, with its shroud of darkness, and the harsh pitiless elements. Dimly you can see the outline of the lime-washed crofthouses dotting the hillside, where somehow over the centuries the hardy people scraped a living from the shallow ground, in conjunction with the harvest of the sea. And now the minister pulls in to a stop on the left near the meeting-house. The car joins the two others, that of Roddie Botlan and that of Neily, large taxi-like Austin saloons that took elderly folks from Inverasdale to church here in Cove. All other worshippers come on foot or on bicycle. The hall is now almost full. Before the War, the two back rows were full with the young men of the community. Now these rows are conspicuously empty. These young men are absent, away in the Navy, the Army and the Air Force. Yet in the service, even as they were continually remembered in the hearts of their loved ones, so the minister would include them in worship, seeking God's protective care for them, in the prayer of supplications, the list of prayerful needs, brought to the Throne of Grace, to the people's God, and the God of all people on earth.

As the minister walks up from the door to the pulpit, families, old and young sit solemnly quiet in the wooden pews. No organ prelude is needed here; nature outside provides its own prelude. The wind whistles on the roof, sweeping up over the rocks; the waves can be heard as they beat incessantly upon the shore. But something has happened; the minister is there in the pulpit at the front. All eyes are turned to him as he stands and faces the congregation. All else, the concomitants of war in the ships in the loch, the guns arching out their defensive barrels of death skywards from the gun pits near the church, even nature's orchestra of wind and wave, they all are some how pushed aside into the retaining shelves of background thought. Now the minds and hearts are directed to the spiritual and the things of heaven.

There is now a hush over the congregation. The minister stands up, pauses for a moment and then opens the service:

'*Toisichidh sinn seirbhis an Tighearna, a seinn chum a chliu* ...'   We shall begin the service of the Lord, singing to his praise ...'

Then the psalm number is announced and the verses to be

sung are read. Ruaraidh Iain Doigh precents the psalm. After the introductory first two lines, he then chants out the others in turn, with the congregation following. Old and young sing out. Grace notes interject the regular melody, enriching the singing like the various components that contribute to the rendering of an orchestra. Tunes like St. David, Dumfermline, Martyrdom, Bedford, Kilmarnock are used in turn and often linked to a precentor who loves a particular tune. Outside, the wind has freshened as the night closes in with the resultant rising noise, a synthesis of wind and sea. But within, the human orchestra prevails. There is a mingling of sound. Rising and falling cadences of human voices fill the House of God with praise.

The contrast has a spiritual lesson. Without, the forces of nature vie with one another, giving the winter night the character of struggle and antagonism. Within, all is brought together, the clear voices of the children, the wavering soprano of the aged women, the deep-throated bass of the men, all infusing the melody with a rich variety of notes. All is woven into a pleasing synthesis of harmony, a spontaneous yet ordered sacrifice of Praise to God, reflecting the reconciliation of Redemptive Love.

The church here is an extension of the homes which comprise the congregation. Families worship in the same idiom in their homes at family worship. Thus they celebrate here together that which they believe and seek to implement as Christians. That is the shared heritage of Christ's church the world over, the efficacy of Calvary and the Finished Work of Christ in His vicarious sacrifice, and the grace by which the people are strengthened and sustained by the Spirit, as they live out their lives an ongoing pilgrimage through this world.

Now in the pulpit of the rustic meeting house in Cove, the little church became in effect a cathedral where the minister himself was spiritually invigorated. All the 'exercises' of the day had brought him to a pitch of readiness of mind and soul and even of body. In this, reception of heavenly thoughts and familiarity with Scriptural narrative, especially the language of devotional thought, were brought to a vivid clarity and spontaneity. He was the messenger of God, in the immanence of His presence in history, God incarnate in Jesus Christ, the projection of pure humanity. As John recorded, 'And the Word was made flesh, and dwelt among us, and we beheld his glory as the only begotten of the Father, full of grace and truth.[1]

Eagerness was writ large on all faces, now turned upwards to him. There was expectation and anticipation. It was as if the minister could hear the people saying,

'Look, we have come out from our homes tonight to the house of God. We value the means of grace. We come, desiring the Bread of life. You have shown us already that we can take freely of the Divine gift, the comforts for our sorrows, the strength to bear our burdens, but above all you have shown us views of God's love, redeeming love. Now we want to meet Him who is the 'express image' of our heavenly Father, to embrace him, so that our souls may rejoice in him for His own Name's sake, so that our iniquities are pardoned. We come with empty sacks like Jacob's sons, to Christ the Joseph of the New Testament that we may go away from the granary of heaven, with abundance and overflowing, with enough and to spare to share even with others that they might rejoice with us.'

Now you have a perfect setting for the greatest work in the

1. John 1:14

288   The Sunday Circuit

world, namely setting Christ forth in the context of community in all the efficacy of saving grace and in every conceivable context of the human condition.

The minister was made for this. As a gifted preacher, pastor and poet, he faced the challenge, that seemingly superhuman challenge. He did not withdraw into safe, self-saving preservation. He responded as he always had done and would do until his strength failed him. He would give his all.

Thus he pronounced his text from the Scripture narrative of faith on trial, in that mightiest example of Abraham where he was ready to sacrifice his own son, Isaac before the Lord. The words he chose to take as the fulcrum of the drama were these, even the command of God whose sovereign will, Abraham   accepted as his own:

> And he said, Take now thy son, thine only son
> Isaac, whom thou lovest, and get thee unto the
> land of Mount Moriah; and offer him there
> for a burnt-offering upon one of the mountains
> which I will tell thee of.'   (Genesis 22:2)

For my father, time was at a premium. He preached here only once a month at the most. Therefore   his sermons necessarily concentrated on the great themes of life. He consciously opens the covers on the stalls in the outlet of Scripture, the community store for this scattered coastal settlement. Then he lays out the rich and varied menu of heavenly fare.

Faith is the evidence, the conviction of the unseen.[1] This is illustrated in the Scriptural drama. The minister recounts the story, tracing the sequence. Abraham ascends the mountain with his son Isaac. They pass the foothills to the appointed peak. They leave below the busy life, the milling

1. Hebrews 11:1

crowds of daily crowded life. They come apart. Faith requires this, coming apart, and also time. Faith requires thought or reflection. These three are prerequisites without which faith cannot begin even to grow strong. Cut them from our spiritual experience each day of our life, and it doesn't matter what else occupies our time and energies and thinking, our faith will suffer and the garden of our soul will dry up and wither.

He has made a sketch, an outline; he has brought it before the people, like the artist's preparatory outline of the painting he will yet present in completeness. Thus he introduced his canvas. Faith demands we come apart. Our action is a corollary of God's command. He has spoken. He has given his command, 'Go to Mount Moriah.'

The minister has done his work. All the parts are in their place. The obedience of faith has been complied with. Then the human touch. The question of Isaac, the only son.

There is the altar and there is the fuel. 'But, Father, where is the sacrifice?'

And that heartrending reply, 'Son, God will provide the sacrifice.'

Here is effectual preaching. There is no unlicensed torrent of words. Rather there is a dialogue in which the minister speaks, but gives time for listeners to think, to digest, and it is as if the minister waits for a response, albeit an unspoken one, before he goes on. Time ceases to count in the meeting house. The attention of the people is riveted on the face of the minister. They themselves are part of the picture. Their minds are active, receiving the stimulus of vocal messages in the graphic imagery of the minister's preaching. There is a sense in which each one is somehow also detached, pushed as it were into considering his or her own life situation. The soul or inner human spirit reads his or her own mind. The person's spiritual and intellectual machinery are co-ordinated in a constructive process. The 'food for thought' is stamped with the signature of Heaven's redemptive Mercy and explicitly and irrefutably manifest in the Covenant of redemption. And who can demur as all is sealed with the shed Blood of Christ, the ultimate proof of love, paying the penalty of sinners, with the sacrifice of a sinless life.

The minister's tone alternates, rising with the varied intonation of the Gaelic tongue, falling into a near whisper, with the tense intimacy of the drama that is now shared on the screen of their minds. Familiar with that great story of one of Scripture's immortals, the waiting people hold their breath as the drama is enacted anew like the one of Shakespeare's plays.

The minister uses the graphic brushes of the linguistic artist to paint the picture. He amplifies the imagery of the human characters, the incidental ones and the central ones. At last the picture is complete. The congregation share together the reconstructed scene, that immortal scene that surely is unsurpassed in the drama of human faith in the living God.

Even as Abraham raised the knife, God spoke:
'And the angel of the Lord called unto him out of
heaven, and said, Abraham,Abraham.'
(Genesis 22:1,11)

The eyes of the patriarch see the ram, the mountain sheep caught in the thicket, by the horns. Rejoice, says the minister, God himself has stepped in. He has given his answer. He has provided a sacrifice.

My father pauses; he gives time for the people to reflect, to take it all in. The tension is released in the congregation.

The minister's voice rises in triumph. God has done it. It is his glorious work. He had not broken his promise. In Isaac Abraham's seed would be blessed for all the nations of the world.[1]

Here in the down to earth simple meeting house, faith is seen enacted amidst the shrouded mists of the Hebrew desolate mountain. Faith stands vindicated, a possibility for all because it is placed in a God that never fails.

Now the time has expired. The minister peers at his watch and says,

'A chairdean, cha'n uireann sinn a bhi fuireach n'as fhaide. Feumaidh sinn na smuaintean priseil eile fhagail, air son am eile. Cuiridh sinn crioch air an seirbhis a tairgse dhuibh cuireadh ann an ainm Chriosd, dhoibhsan uile a bu mhath buadha a chreidimh agus aoibhneas slainteil an Tighearna, aithneachadh 'nam beatha. Gabh ris agus gheibh thu beatha gu saor agus an asgaidh. Agus ge be air bith an suidheachan a tha air thoiseach oirnn, bi so fior, a reir a gheallaidh, 'Gheibh sinn tuilleadh agus buaidh, tridsan a ghradhaich sinn.[2]

('Now friends, we cannot wait any longer. We will have to leave other precious thoughts for another time.

We would close with an offer, the invitation in the name of Christ, to all who would know the triumph of faith and the joy of the Lord in their lives. Accept this, and you will have life free, without price. And whatever situations are before us, according to the promise, 'We are more than conquerors through him that loved us.')

The orchestra of wave and wind outside can now be heard as the sermon ends. Then the closing psalm is sung, a triumphant assertion of the spiritual and the eternal. In Cove

1. Genesis 21:17   2. Romans 8:37

there is no haste to disperse. The people here want to linger in the gathering this Sabbath evening. They have come to a feast and they were not disappointed.

There follows the usual routine at the close of a service. People meet the minister informally. Elders consult with him and exchange thoughts regarding homes and situations of families in the congregation. But all is brief. The business of the congregation ecclesiastically is cut to the minimum of necessity on the Sabbath day. No organizational interests must break the chords of spiritual dynamics which brought the animation of the Spirit to the House of God. Then, as the minister turns towards his car, he is accosted and prevailed upon to delay his journey home by having supper in a house not far from the church. The invitation is a compulsive one which he just could not refuse. The house is that of Mr. Urquhart the Road Surveyor.

The Highland crofthouse has an extra grace and sense of adequacy. Within, the fire burns cheerfully in the hearth. The table is already set, beautifully prepared over the white lace tablecloth with silver and crystal. This must have already been done before the service as all the household were in church. Surely faith even in this respect is vindicated.

A grown daughter lovingly and enthusiastically soon brings out the food. It is the best, prime salmon, cooled and dressed on the ashet at the centre of the table. The flames of the peat-fire flicker on the walls and the light of the Tilley lamp cheers the room, so that it is like a banquet hall.

There are no regrets on the part of the minister that again he stayed for supper at the home of Duncan, the road surveyor. A son   and grandson of this home would also carry on the torch of Christian witness each in his generation. Too soon he takes his leave. He drives off into the night, carefully steering over the road with hardly a foot to spare at each side for the broad Citroen. After being stopped at two army checkpoints, at Poolewe and Tournaig, at last he brings the car to rest in the manse garage in Aultbea.

He had risen at 6 am. It is now almost 10p.m. He has given out all day, sparing nothing, withholding none of his energies, giving himself completely in the Master's service. But somehow he is not spent. In his heart there is a song. His soul is full to overflowing, stirred up to bless and magnify the Lord. At such times of sheer completeness, MacKinnon Aultbea would not have exchanged places with a king, nor the riches of his spiritual happiness for all the wealth of this world. For he was a courier in the service of the King of kings and he had just delivered to his people another consignment in the provisions of Divine love. How true the word of the prophet:

> 'How beautiful upon the mountains are the feet of him that bringeth good tidings, that publisheth peace;'
>
> Isaiah 52:7,8

Chapter 24

Only by Boat

Within a year of Rev Angus MacKinnon coming to be minister of Locheweside of which Aultbea was the centre, the adjacent and equally extensive charge of Gairloch became vacant with the death of Rev. William MacKinnon. My father had two assistants in his own sphere of service, one in Poolewe and one in Little Lochbroom. Gairloch was roughly the same as Locheweside in the responsibilities of its minister. While the minister did not have an assistant in the charge, he was interim-moderator on a permanent basis for two peripheral locations, both enchantingly beautiful, Kinlochewe and Alligin. Because of Rev William MacKinnon's death, in effect, my father's responsibilities were doubled almost from the moment of his induction. But more than that, this situation would obtain for the next eleven years, the time it would take for the next minister, the young probationer Rev. Hector MacRury to be inducted there as its minister in 1936.

This extra responsibility entailed a great deal of

ecclesiastical correspondence. My father was always writing letters. Remember there was then no phone. He had to ensure weekly supply for Gairloch itself, that is three to four services, held every Sabbath. Calls for pastoral care, maintenance of Kirk Session and Deacon's court meetings in the regular framework of both his own congregations in Aultbea and also in the Gairloch charge, engaged his energies and demanded his continual attention. The demands upon his time and energies were unending. Though assisted by the lay missionaries and elders in his spiritual office, there were clear-cut distinctions which were always respected as belonging solely to the office of the minister. My father still had duties on Isle Ewe where there was a viable community with its own side-school, and teacher, Mary MacLennan, a native of Gairloch. Though not more than a mile distant from Aultbea at its nearest point, the island community had a character of its own. A little township nestled not far from the southeast end, amid large lush meadows and fields of arable cultivated land. The homes were sheltered by a cluster of trees, a contrast to the greater area of Aultbea and Mellon Charles opposite, which were exposed to the prevailing wet southwest winds from across the Atlantic.

Here were MacLennans, MacIvers, MacKenzies and Grants, occupying a location over a mile distance to the west. Isle Ewe was part of an estate belonging to one of the MacKenzies of Gairloch of whom Kenneth and Osgood MacKenzie were the best known. The family held a baronetcy. The people on the island were tenants of the land, large tracts of farmland, which in fertility and in size contrasted with the fragmented strips of croftland on the mainland. The Grants, like all Grants, were big powerful men who worked the land and fished the sea. They alone have stayed on the island and the two sons, Ian and Donald, when they came home from the Second World War, married local girls, raising families, who also stayed on the island to enjoy their life in this unique and idyllic setting.

You can understand that there was no monotony in my father's ministry. Just think of it; the minister's visit here was like an excursion on a summer day, albeit with his spiritual duties to perform, but nevertheless a happy occasion, with the experience of being rowed over to Isle Ewe, in its matchless location, itself sitting tranquilly in the expanse of the loch, with the mountains of Loch Broom, Loch Maree, Gairloch and Torridon, rising like protective sentinels on the elevated horizon of the landward ridges. And there was something else, something precious and strengthening for both minister and his wife. The visit brought to the minister and his family the love and esteem bestowed upon them, and the bonds of the pastoral tie, flowing like a current of appreciation between them and the people.

But let us go with the minister on his trip this summer day to Isle Ewe. He is taken swiftly along with my mother accompanied by one of their children in an island boat. The course was a straight line about a mile distance between the Aultbea pier and the east jetty below the hamlet on the island. Mr. MacKinnon, who himself loved boats and the sea, was delighted to be free from worry about the car and the rough roads that so often punctured the tires.

He was 'at home' in the beamy boat with the cross-thwarts and the stones in the bilges for ballast, visible through the slatted floorboards. There was no need for him to take an oar. The broad- beamed double-ender, commonly known as the *'sgoth'* was now powered by four big men rowing with their feet pressed against cross piece stops. This gave them the purchase power necessary for oar propulsion. A slot with a galvanized iron bracket on the reinforced stem thwart marks the spot where the mast is placed with its base on the keelson, when the large brown lug sail is used. Muscle power or manpower is the rule of the road for the crofter fishermen especially for those who live on Isle Ewe. Often an easy crossing on a fine day can change into a battle of rowing against the elements on the return journey, demanding the sustained effort of seasoned strength and experience. It was a common sight to watch this from the manse.

If I may digress, one such memory is that of William Grant alone in his little boat which he loved to use when he was then well up in years and retired. He was rowing back to the island from the east jetty at Bridgend, a sheltered spot where the mountain stream from Gooseloch came down to meet the sea, giving Aultbea its name, 'the burn of the birch trees.' The wind had risen sharply since he had crossed to the mainland. Now the waves were short and steep so that the little boat was pushed almost vertical as William Grant kept her head pointing directly into the southwest wind and his island home. Viewers on shore watched discreetly for nearly an hour. The wind was increasing; the waves were getting bigger as they stretched over the open water of the exposed bay. But never once did the rower's stroke change; never once did the rower falter. Evenly, rhythmically, the oars dipped and rose, the blades feathered to meet the wind and the spray. Inch by inch the little boat crept forward. At last the island veteran won. His was the reward of endurance, of perseverance, the prize of seasoned experience and skill.

William Grant had reached the weather shore and the sheltered lee of his own anchorage on his island home. He had prevailed. It's strange how he loved to cross over in his own little clinker boat, with the frequent challenge to his waning natural strength for a man in his eighties. It was his choice, for he could so easily have crossed over in the big Kelvin powered family fishing boat, used by his equally strong sons, Ian and Donald.

Now back to the pastoral visit of MacKinnon Aultbea to the Isle of Ewe, a sparkling green emerald rising out of the summer sea. The boat is now moored at the main stone jetty on Isle Ewe. The sea is a pool of calm, as transparent as glass round about the boat. Little fish swim happily, safe in the knowledge that they can dart into the shelter of the seaweed growing round the jetty stone wall. Green crabs stroll lazily across the sandy bottom, ultra visible in the purity of the water some eight feet below. A big brown rock crab, the size of a big man's hand, stirs up a cloud of sand kicked up by his thrusting legs. He chooses to walk quickly backwards.

The visiting party disembark, to walk a few hundred yards to the cluster of houses that comprise the hamlet. The minister is a welcome guest. He enters several houses in turn, those where age confines a family member to the house. There he prays with them and gives a blessing, reminding them of the Love of God that joins the believers for ever in the Covenant of Grace through Jesus Christ our Lord.

Visitation, which for a minister is a prerequisite for enjoying the liberty of God's Spirit and the power of preaching at the Sabbath services of worship, is here confined to three homes of the aged and infirm. But these are part of multiple generation families. The result is that even with these visits, the minister has close contact with the rest of the island homes. There is tea for the visiting party, with scones and pancakes, fresh home-made butter and crowdie and jam. If the minister wished, he could have sat to a feast as he is offered every kindness and hospitality.

The island people have now gathered in the school, called a side school, where the pupils are all taught by the one teacher. What vivid and sweet recollections come back to people who were there that evening as the minister conducted the Catechising and prayer meeting. Happily, a visitor can still return and find families of children's children on Isle Ewe, all springing from the family of William Grant. In 1995 the annual Sunday School outing of the Aultbea church took the form of a family picnic. Several motor boats carried the large number of adults and children over the sea to Isle Ewe, the Emerald Isle. Surely this must rank as one of the most delightful rendezvous and experiences for a Sunday School outing anywhere!

One recollection that characterizes the relationship of the congregation to its minister in Aultbea is never forgotten. Mrs. Sandy Mackenzie lived in Isle Ewe. She had boys in her family, one of whom Kenneth, known as Kenny Sandy , would become a captain of a giant ocean supertanker, with his son Roddie succeeding him in the nineteen sixties and onwards. Memory flicks over some pages from this visit to the island, and stops in the manse early during the War years. One day Mrs. Mackenzie arrived at the manse with a parcel of gifts. When opened, it contained fresh butter and crowdie. That was commonly brought to the manse and was welcome in augmenting the supply from the glebe. What stays in memory as a strong subjective impression was something else. There

were four pairs of stockings for the manse boys. These were
long and thick with reinforced heels. What a wonderful
present! Woollen stockings did not last long without the need
of darning. I think Mrs. Mackenzie had a special love for
boys, possibly because of her own, both now away at war.

With the evening shadows lengthening, it is time to
return. The boat is ready at the quay. The happy visit to Isle
Ewe is over.

We now turn to another occasion where the minister has
a baptism that takes him to Letterewe, on the far-side of the
shores of Loch Maree. This is a house baptism of a family on
the estate, where the man is a gamekeeper.

The minister drives his car through Gairloch, past
Flowerdale and Kerrysdale, where there was the 'Big House'
now covered in ivy with its circular stone staircase leading to
the main door. In its earlier days it was called the 'Tighe Dige'
and had a thatched roof. It was the western home of Sir
Kenneth MacKenzie and his related family of Brahan in
Easter Ross. A scion of the family, Sir Osgood, wrote a book,
'A Hundred Years in the Highlands'. This covered life for
the lairds of Gairloch to a large extent in the 19th century.

The minister's car pulls in off the main Aultbea/
Achnasheen road, a few miles before reaching the Loch Maree
hotel, famous as a fishing venue. The car is parked at the
side of the highway, and the side road is taken, a rough road
down to the jetty at the loch side some two furlongs distance.
My father had a fetish for punctuality which meant that he
was never known to be late for a duty, in the same consistent
way that he was never known to have a common cold. This
trait meant that on this occasion he was again early. The
estate settlement of Letterewe, meaning the 'steep sloping

place', could clearly be seen on the other side of the loch. The minister's car was spotted, for almost immediately a boat left the shore and made its way across the three mile distance to pick the minister up and ferry him to his rendezvous on the other side.

The boat, as befitted a boat made for the tideless inland waters of Loch Maree, was a beautifully varnished launch about thirty feet in length with a very moderate beam. It had comparatively slender scantling for its carvel planking. This was compensated for by several grown heavy frames and a strong keelson, making the vessel stiff, though having a shallow draft. It could not match the rugged powerful traditional Highland and Hebridean 'sgoth', a mature product evolved over the centuries since the Viking longboat and the chieftain's 'birlinn', designed for treacherous seas of the Minch and the northwest Atlantic and the North Sea, and built not primarily for a motor but for sail.

Two estate men crewed the boat. But there are many who would have put greater trust in the sinewy strength of the Isle Ewe men and their long oars, rather than the iron and brass gas engine of this refined and relatively sophisticated rival. As the boat neared the shore, this was clearly the territory of the rich and privileged, or the energetic and ambitious, who had used their talents instead of marking time or even burying their gifts in a kind of resigned fatalism.

It is true also that here was the locus of the 'landed' class, in this case leased out by the MacKenzie lairds to parties from the south. The MacKenzie family remained close to the crofting tenants, intermixing with them in their daily life. Several spoke Gaelic fluently. I think of Sir Osgood MacKenzie, referred to above, and also Mrs. Sawyer of

Inverewe House who made sure she became fluent by conversing with her nanny and the estate personnel. She and Mrs. Matthews of Drumchork Lodge sponsored annual Christmas parties for the schoolchildren. When these ceased on the coming of the Second World War another benefactor continued this kindness to the children of the community. She was Mrs. Maclean, wife of Ian Maclean who became proprietor in a large part of Aultbea as well as being the chief local businessman. Mrs. MacLean put on memorable Christmas parties at Drumchork farm. She herself will be remembered, for her loving, kind deeds for children. Many homes of the needy were recipients of her generosity. Her religion was her life and her life was in all its loving outgoing kindness, the witness of her religion. The manse and the minister's family could never forget all the extra gifts of groceries, or the truckload of turnips dumped at the barn, for animal sustenance in a late spring.

But back to Loch Maree and the minister's visit to Letterewe. On reaching the farther shore, the launch glided out of the sunlight into a covered boathouse, high and ample with its own quay for easy disembarking. Remember here there was no tide so that there was no awkward height disparity between boat and quay, always a cogent factor to reckon with in a coastal harbour. Suddenly the soft voices of the Gaelic-speaking Highlanders became amplified in the acoustic enclosure of the high cathedral-like boathouse. Nearby were long slim clinker- planked boats, some four in all. There was another motor launch as well. While the motor boats served as ferries for goods and people to the main road and the outside world across the loch, the long slim rowing boats were designed for fishing parties serving summer residents. Most of these boats used for hotels and lodges to serve fishing parties here throughout Wester Ross, were built by the MacDonald boatbuilders in Alligin. A lesser number were built by Fraser, the boat-builder in Inverness. The Alligin boats had a straight vertical stem as a rule. In contrast, Fraser's boats had an overhang, with the foot of the stem cut away.

A holiday here on Loch Maree, with the exclusive Loch Maree hotel as base, was unique. Even Queen Victoria could not pass it up. She had to sample the breathtaking beauty of fishing under the lee of the surrounding mountains, Slioch, Beinn Lair or Beinn Airidh Charr. She also had to join the long queue of pilgrims, the saints and the curious to alight on Isle Maree, the island of Saint Malrubha, with its reputed burial place of Danish kings There also was a visit to the island of the 'lucky' tree now the heaviest tree on earth for its weight, with thousands of copper pennies embedded in its trunk and branches, the proof of wishful thinking by visitors over the centuries.

But the really big lure of visitors even for royalty was the fact that Loch Maree contained not salmon but trout. These were not little fish. It was not uncommon for the connoisseur fisher to bring in a twenty pound trout. At least one over thirty pounds was brought in and preserved in a glass case. With such trophies to grace their homes, visitors all finished their holiday on Loch Maree, feeling like royalty. A plaque at the roadside near the hotel commemorates the visit of Queen Victoria and her husband Prince Albert.

Now over on the far side of the loch, the land is seen to be rich green verdure, rising steeply to merge in with the rugged scree slopes that cover the ancient generic mountain core of igneous rocks and metamorphosed Torridonian

Sandstone. Letterewe 's location is due to the relatively small narrow level area beneath the mountains and the confluence of more than one mountain stream. There are large forestry plantations of larch and Scotch pine. In the immediate vicinity there is some arable ground and the evidence of sheep husbandry. A sheep fank can be seen situated some distance away. There are hundreds, if not thousands, of beautifully white newly clipped and dipped animals, now relieved of their shaggy woollen coats after a rigorous winter. The air is filled with the bawling of ewes and the bleating of lambs, so that this resembles a kind of cheering welcome from crowds of people, to greet the minister as he is led to the estate car, an immaculately polished black Lanchester, with heavy chrome over its brass radiator and headlights; it has a long slick hood and beautiful sloping wings, clearly built to last indefinitely. Here everything exudes the atmosphere of the 'privileged.' Here was a timeless unchanging world, blissful for the rich who were served, and also for the humble who catered for them, the experts in estate service with the specialised skills acquired in a long apprenticeship and tradition.

There are several houses of gamekeepers for the prolific deer and pheasant or grouse hunt, foxes, hare and wildcat. Here is the controlled habitat for these perfect examples of God's exclusive creative power. It is a positive observation that only in the apparently ruthless class division reflected in the economy of the 'Highland estate', that nature in all its wildlife and topographical beauty is preserved for generations.

The car is now on the road. The canvas hood is up, but the scenery is vividly clear as the car very slowly makes its way along the narrow gravel road. Trees mask the 'big' house, but not enough to hide its appearance of traditional opulence.

Cottages of shepherds and fishing gillies appear, sometimes two joined together. They were built with windows and door frames of hewn stone with slate roofs, small but comfortable looking. In an age of precarious economic opportunities, many young people were attracted to service on the Highland estates for nominal remuneration. Their's was a sheltered life with loyalty as the prime requirement along with unquestionable competence in the specialist skills related to caring for fishing parties and hunting wildlife, as well as the fine art of domestic service where etiquette and food preparation provided the choicest of provision for host and visitor. The fact is that wages were in a large measure 'in kind' here, where meat, mutton venison or salmon and every other kind was shared without rationing and was the daily fare of the humblest worker.

But now the Lanchester moves on. It swings up from the lochside road and climbs a steep road on the hillside, then comes to a stop beside a cottage nestling peacefully on the roadside. The prospect for the visitor is breath-taking, even for the minister and his little son who accompanies him. To the southwest, the matchless beauty of the view was manifest, the loch some hundred feet below the elevation of the cottage, stretching to the eastern extremity towards Kinlochewe, 'the head of Loch Ewe'. (Suggested here is the concept of Loch Maree being at one time conceived of as an extension of Loch Ewe, possibly before the Columban missionary of the Celtic Church used one of the islands as his headquarters).

And beyond Kinlochewe, the sun outlined the winding gravel road like a silver thread, twisting its way up through Glen Docharty, competing with the glistening reflection of the river, Allt Dubhcharraidh as the latter tumbles down the

306 Only by Boat

long glen, past the ruins of the old Celtic chapel and monastic settlement, to feed into Loch Maree. This road was the gateway to the world outside for some ten miles further was Achnasheen, the railway watering stop for the steam engines, and the terminus where the mail and passenger bus from Aultbea and Gairloch met the train.

To the right and northwest, the long steep sloping hills edged the loch, past Ardlair, Slattadale, Kearnsary, Inveran, Tollie until the loch merged with the river, and through it with the ocean, past Poolewe and Loch Ewe.

The noise of the sheep now is muted as the car carries the visitors some distance along the lochside. The air is filled with the buzz and hum of insects, as the car comes to rest not far from the door of the cottage. Overhead, the monarch of the skies, the golden eagle hovers almost stationary above mighty Ben Slioch, the guardian of his Highland kingdom, effortlessly resting upon the air currents pushed upwards by the heat of the summer sun. How easily a glance upwards before entering the cottage provides the minister with the cue to the Scriptural graphic image, conveying the message of God's everlasting love, his omniscience and constant care of mankind, even for the little newborn child now to be baptised! Hear Moses, reflecting upon the blessing of those who are partakers in the Covenant of God's elective love.

> 'For the Lord's portion is his people; Jacob (Israel) is
> the lot of his inheritance.
> As an eagle stirreth up her nest, fluttereth over her
> young, spreading abroad her wings, taketh them,
> beareth them on her wings:
> So the Lord alone did lead him,
> and there was no strange god with him.'
>
> Deuteronomy 32:9,11

A tall Highlander, dressed in brown tweeds and 'plus fours' or knickerbockers, the uniform of the shepherd and gamekeeper, opens the car door and welcomes the minister. This courteous host could have been the laird, but for one significant difference. Few indeed of the latter could now speak the Gaelic tongue of the ancient hills, with which the minister was now addressed.

The party enters the cottage. The little boy now to be baptised, the second child of the family, was born just four weeks earlier in the humble cottage with only the competent unofficial midwife in attendance. Already having had the privilege of baptism, the proven obedience to the practice of the church, inwardly in heart and home, and publicly, when possible, in attendance at 'the means of grace'—the services of the sanctuary—the conditions incumbent upon the parents were taken as fulfilled.

Within, there is a goodly gathering, some twenty people, with little ones on knees, crowded together, women sitting and men standing. The father reminds the minister that his young wife is from the south and has not got the Gaelic, and English would therefore be appreciated.

A family Bible with red-edged pages, is set on the table for the minister's use. But the minister leaves this alone. He lays his own before him, a special English New Testament with unusually large print. Experience has taught him not to rely casually on Bibles big and small in homes or halls, where print is too small for his impaired sight. A short service of worship follows. There is no sense of haste. But the minister knows full well that most of those present had duties to fulfil, and had to get back to them. Nevertheless the Word is read and after prayer, a short exposition follows with relevant

exhortation to encourage all to 'seek the Lord while he may
to be found, and to call upon him while he is near.'[1]

But the minister stresses that symbolic initiation in any
form even of baptism, is not enough. Parents and children
must build on their faith. 'If any man will come after me, let
him deny himself, and take up his cross daily, and follow
me.'[2] The Word and Sacrament are wed together, and with
prayer and faith, the boy child is brought into the visible
church. The service of baptism takes place under the lee of
the mighty mountain of Slioch and not far distant from Isle
Maree with the historic ruins of St. Malrubha's chapel. What
more could a child need as signs of heaven's favour, the
mountain, pointing to God's protective love in a rather alien
world, and the Celtic chapel, linking the informal service
with the Celtic catholic church of history!

There is a postscript to this outing. When the Citroen
pulled in to the garage at the manse in Aultbea, some two
hours later, the evening had already set in. The minister's
eldest daughter Rachel found a parcel on the floor in the
inside back of the car—there was no built-in boot, or trunk
as it is called in north America. This must have been placed
inside the minister's car at some point when he was ferried
back to the main road. The parcel was damp and cool, it's
covering was brown sacking, tied with a bit of heavy-duty
fishing line. Other children crowded round the car in the
relative dark of the garage, all wanting to carry this parcel
into the house. Within moments, the parcel was laid on the
kitchen table. It was big. It was long. There was no mistaking
what it was. This was what the rich and privileged paid for as
the coveted goal of their fishing holiday on Loch Maree, and
at the same time the fare that the humble estate worker enjoyed

1. Isaiah 55:6   2. St. Luke 9:21

in his regular diet in its season. It was none other than a large brown trout (the exclusive secret wonder of Loch Maree), about twelve pounds in weight. Smiles creased every face and there were gasps of wonder as mother cut the line and unrolled the sacking from the contents. It was indeed a large fish. Newly caught, swelling in perfection, it lay there on its side, the prize of kings and queens. Soon, very soon it would grace the manse table, a banquet for the family themselves and also be listed on the menu for a visiting guest. How strange indeed, that the guest, who called on the following day should be General Martin, landlord of Huisbost, Glendale, where my father was born and brought up, in the Isle of Skye.

Chapter 25

Warrant Officers

The church at large, in its organizational system, is a backup for the congregations. Its existence and its expense is justified only as it furthers and facilitates the spiritual dynamic of team-work at the congregational level. The latter represents the dynamic life of the spiritual, as it inter-relates to the human situation. Like soldiers at the 'front', so parish ministers lived out their calling in congregations for the most part in obscurity and unnoticed in the larger picture of public life.

Naturally the teamwork principle meant that Mr. MacKinnon relied heavily upon those who worked at the 'front' with him. You could say that the 'missionary' was a kind of 'warrant officer', a senior non-commissioned officer, of the same 'genre' of the ruling elders or members of the Session.

The team of which the minister was the leading member had therefore an assistant preacher of the Word. He was the missionary or catechist to use the older usage. Indeed Aultbea or Locheweside as the north parish of Gairloch, was served in the previous century by a catechist until the Disruption. After that, with a settled minister in Aultbea, instead of living in Poolewe, the catechist was stationed there. There was a link between the catechist here and the evangelical stirring associated with Assynt and the assistantship there of Dr. Kennedy's father to the parish minister of Stoer, Mr. MacKenzie. There was a family of Urquharts near Ullapool, halfway between Aultbea and Stoer, several members of which became noted evangelical catechists. You will find Urquharts to this day, in the Lord's service chiefly in the eldership in this area from Gairloch to Ullapool, keeping alight the 'lamps of the sanctuary.' In many respects this ministry contributed in no small part to the foundation of steadfast conviction, and absence of extreme or extravagance of theological interpretation. The status of catechist inferred emphasis upon the teaching of the formal church doctrines as contained in the Westminster Catechisms, Shorter and Longer. The designation of missionary associated with a later and continuing age implied a difference of function. In this, conducting services and the preaching aspect of the Gospel was the primary duty.

Mr. MacKinnon thus came to a charge where the 'missionary' was highly regarded and where he filled a very necessary role as assistant to the minister. As a rule this was a man of natural and spiritual gifts who felt called, and was appointed through presbytery and the Home Mission Board of the Church in Edinburgh. Note, these missionaries were often ruling elders who showed the gift of preaching. But they were not ordained as missionaries, or preachers of the Word. If they were ordained it was to the eldership, and it was in the Scriptural category of ruling elder that they had identity but given a greater local standing. Also there was the fact that they were like the minister, set aside for the work of the church with requisite though often very inadequate remuneration. Many of these were ex-service men, or followed a trade before being called to their spiritual work. They made an interesting study as a special category, many of them showing marked traits that distinguished them as strong and occasionally eccentric individuals. On acceptance for the office, each was then appointed to a station under the supervision of the minister of the charge or the interim-moderator of the mission station.

Mr. MacKinnon had, as a rule, two missionaries as colleagues. One was assistant as mentioned, in the integrated charge, and lived in the mission house in Poolewe. The other was stationed in Little Lochbroom. During the long vacancies in Gairloch, he was also responsible for the mission stations at Kinlochewe and Alligin. Just think of the extensiveness of spiritual work and responsibility for a minister almost from his induction in Aultbea! Let it be said that the missionaries were without exception, a positive factor in Mr. MacKinnon's ministry. They fulfilled their role, deferring to ecclesiastical authority of the church and the place of the minister. This was symbolically observed in Aultbea and Gairloch in a specific and indisputable manner. The missionary on no occasion ascended the pulpit stairs to preach in the big church. He conducted the service of worship, from the smaller and more humble pulpit or precentor's box. This was standard procedure reflecting the respect given to the minister as the authorised ambassador from the court of the Divine King, set aside by the sacred 'laying on of hands,' exclusively linked to the ordination of the ministry by Scriptural warrant.

'Neglect not the gift that is in thee, which was given thee by prophecy, with the laying on of hands of the presbytery.'[1]

This is distinct from and on a higher level than the ordination of ruling elders whose ordination rests upon giving the right hand of fellowship by the minister.

'And when they had ordained them elders in every church, and had prayed with fasting, they commended them to *the Lord, on whom they believe.*'[2]

The linguistic distinction lies in the difference implied by the Greek, ordination to the ministry resting on the 'word,' phonetically read, *epithesis,* and in the ordination of the ruling elders, *chirotonew.*

To suggest that there was no difference appears as inaccurate reasoning. Both categories are indeed committed to preaching the Gospel. But the ministers of the Word teach and preach authoritatively within the broad framework of their contemporary age. Their proclamation can only be valid as it is asserted on an educated level. If not, the Gospel reasoning is crudely unconvincing. Thus the ministers have not only been called, but have committed themselves to the sacrificial process of being shaped and refined and being equipped by the Spirit, in the sanctioned process, intellectual and cultural, under the teaching ministry of the 'specialist' teachers in university and divinity college. It is not as if their role is given a divine aura, as petty gods. Rather their role as prepared vessels by education and grace qualifies them as 'facilitators' of religious and Christian influence.

This does not under-rate the role of the missionary. He was often a person of marked natural endowments as well as

1. 1 Timothy 4:14   2. Acts 14:23

of grace. Indeed that was the basis for his recognition and encouragement to fulfil his role in the church. Without exception, every one associated with Mr. MacKinnon had a transparent integrity. They were full-time servants in the church, sometimes with a family of children to care for, on a very limited income, yet rendered adequate by remuneration 'in kind' from the people about them. Only men who had the highest degree of commitment and altruism could stay the course, with no suggestion of discontent or agitation for 'more.'

Mr. Angus MacAulay was born on the island of Heisker in North Uist. His father and grandfather were catechists there. He came as missionary during the vacancy after Mr. MacNaughton left, at first living in the manse in Aultbea, and then transferring to Poolewe when my father came as minister. He maintained the long tradition from the previous century, when the Urquharts, father and son, of Lochbroom, set the standard, earning the respect and affection of the people. This was especially so during the vacancy after Mr. MacNaughton's ministry there. He and his wife were given special mention in an article in the Free Church Record, recording the ordination and induction to the charge of Aultbea and Poolewe, of the new minister on 17th July, 1924, and also in an article in the Inverness Courier at the time. We include here the pertinent comments made by Rev William MacKinnon, Gairloch.

> ...By far the larger portion (of the charge) is in Aultbea. The congregation kindly entertained the Presbytery and friends in the manse, under the kindly and efficient superintendence of Mrs. MacAulay the missionary's wife. Mr. MacAulay,

missionary there for some years, was ever diligent and industrious among the people, often working alone in the two large congregations. Mr. MacAulay is a sound theologian, and the people know his worth and they are most anxious to retain his service in the charge, to help the minister, for one man can never carry on the work of that charge alone...

Mr. MacAulay left in 1931. He always retained a special love for Inverasdale and Cove, and spoke of wanting to retire there. Though that was not to be, he kept up the links with the people. This was largely through the MacDonald family in Cove, of which one, Roderick, was a leading elder. He spoke at my father's induction, making a presentation to Mr. MacAulay. His brother Murdo had a fishing boat that used to call in at Uig, where the crew were sumptuously entertained by the missionary and his wife and their teenage daughter, Isabel. Subsequently on his deathbed, in Uig Skye, Mr. MacAulay spoke of Aultbea, and expressed the desire to visit there again before he died. His daughter Isabel, a retired teacher now resident in Glasgow has continued her affectionate relationship with childhood friends.

Mr. Donald MacIver was an elder in Aultbea as well as missionary in several places before his appointment at Poolewe. The image of missionary could not be encapsulated with honour to a greater degree than in the person of Donald Maciver. His physical presence was distinctive. Tall and manly, he had an air of grace and refinement. He was strikingly like the distinguished Yorkshire-born preacher, latterly of Westminister Chapel, London, Rev Dr. J. H. Jowett. Mr. Maciver stood out among his brethren. In dress he was immaculate, his hard collar faultlessly white, his necktie perfectly neat. His dark suit was beautifully cut and fitted his perfectly proportioned body, so that he could be taken for a rich diplomat or a national political leader. Leather gloves and umbrella were the natural complement of his clothes and the hard felt hat gave him the final touch as a man of distinction. There was a special reason for this. Most missionaries were qualified and followed a profession before they took up full-time duties for the church. Mr. MacIver was a skilled tailor.

Donald MacIver had something far more valuable than a good appearance. He had a special bearing, which made him an invaluable colleague of the minister. There is one last image of Mr. MacIver, shortly before the end of his earthly journey that cannot be forgotten. It illustrates the Christian fortitude and the calibre which marked him as a uniquely worthy and reliable colleague in the teamwork of the parish ministry. It was after the Allied invasion of France at the Second Front to hasten the end of the Second World War. On Saturday a telegram arrived at the mission home, that their beloved son Ian was killed 'in action'. It was not expected that the missionary would conduct the services on the Sabbath. But on Sabbath morning the grieving father was there in the church, declaring the 'unsearchable riches of Christ.'

It was not more than a year later that Donald MacIver, the missionary died in an Edinburgh hospital, one might say in his prime at the age of sixty-four. In a tribute to him and his work as missionary, my father wrote in the Free Church Record, at the time,

> 'In handling the word of God, he was
> deliberate. accurate, and impressive, and it was

noticed that his utterances were rapidly growing
unctious and weighty the nearer he drew to the
end of his beautiful and peaceful life.'

Allan Gunn who succeeded Mr. MacIver, was a
Lewisman from the fishing community of Ness. He had
previously been stationed in Alligin. There he was not averse
to crewing a local fishing boat when opportunity knocked,
during the herring fishing season. He always felt the better of
this. Physically Mr. Gunn was long and lanky, not unlike the
image of the cowboy on the ranches of North America. He
had very little flesh on his body. His face with its piercing
eyes was dominated by a large and expressive nose. He was
an anecdotal preacher, working his way with words to bring
his hearers to rapt attention using even eccentric expedients
related to his physical appearance, in order to gain his end.

His entrance leading to the precentor's box, before the
seated congregation at a service was slow and deliberate. After
some considerable time he would rise. He would survey the
congregation, his intense eyes moving over the congregation,
from left to right. You could almost hear his mind working,
checking all present and making an assessment of the
situation, like a military commander, weighing the odds
before making an assault. All this time, he had a hand raised,
stroking his nose with his thumb and his forefinger. Some
people felt he was counting the flock like a teacher to see
who was absent. Some were gratified that their presence was
thus appreciated, a kind of relief that their names would not
be marked absent, as teachers would do in the register in the
case of defaulters in the secular school.

As Allan Gunn proceeded into the sermon, his audience
were continually attracted to (or possibly distracted by) his

physical performance. For along with his not inconsiderable vocal gifts as a preacher, he exhibited unusual, to say the least, physical manifestations. Physically, his body was a cross between that of a born acrobat and contortionist, so that a service with Mr. Gunn the missionary was at times, at least to the eyes of children present, a match in entertainment for a performance of Houdini himself. An arm would coil round his head at the back so that his hand would appear on the other side of his head with his expressive fingers moving continuously. If you were not following the spiritual message, at least you were following the preacher's antics. A leg would appear round the side of the front of the precentor's box, the foot lifted up continually twisting and moving. More than once he alternated this acrobatic movement with the other leg, his hands pressed down on the pulpit stand. He then would raise himself, so that both legs would synchronise, curling round to the front, not unlike an illusion of levitation. One had to say that Allan Gunn was a striking preacher and children, at any rate, were very happy to attend church when he was preaching.

He was a natural friend whom children took to at once. He was equally entertaining, when out of the church, and was happy to give his time to the manse children, relaxing outside between services at the communion on a summer day. He was useful as a colleague in that he preached in English, which was increasingly being spoken with the advent of the Second World War and the impact of outsiders at the large naval base.

Mr. MacRae was a native of Soay, an island off the south of Skye. He laboured at the mission station of Little Lochbroom, some fifteen miles to the north of Aultbea, and on the other side of the great hill at Gruinard called the *Ca'dh Beag[1]*. It tended to look after itself, with only occasional services required of the minister, such as the annual communion and baptisms, and ecclesiastical meetings of Session, and Deacons' Court. Mr. MacRae was a gracious man of deep Christian character. He worked humbly looking after Little Lochbroom. He kept the 'garden' of the Lord, nourishing its people, tending the crops of the Lord's planting. The result was that when Mr. MacKinnon came to preach at the summer communion, taking the weekday services and a visiting minister taking the Sabbath services, this annual communion season could be called a reaping time, for the nurturing during the previous year. This was turned into a big occasion, since Aultbea church was closed for the Little Loch Broom communion.

One of the highlights was the journey back to Aultbea, by the bus and the few cars. The big hill of the Ca'dh Beag with its matchless view at Gruinard, had a gradient of one in four at its steepest and not less than one in seven for the rest. It was one way and gravel-covered, and truly formidable for motorists to ascend or descend. On several occasions motorists simply could not face the thought of starting up the hill because of the terror inspired by the sight of the twisting thread of gravel road, visible as it rose between the precipitous rocks and the sheer vertical dizzy drop to the river Gruinard and the sea below. Some car engines overheated and came to a stop, with a cloud of steam enveloping the vehicle, and pouring out from under the radiator cap on the front of the bonnet. Other drivers would begin ascending the hill, using second or third gear. As the car slowed down, they tried to change down gear, but in the hair-raising situation, the car lost momentum

1. Possible meaning- the little hill of big struggle

before the gear was engaged. Then it was panic to keep the car from rolling back to calamity. Another dread was the thought of meeting a sheep grazing on the grass in the middle of the hill or simply enjoying a siesta in the heat of the summer day. Any possibility of being brought to a stop was a frightening prospect. Early clutches were relatively primitive and synchromesh gear was rare and considered a luxury.

In this relative isolation, Mr. MacRae faithfully tended the pastoral flock committed to his trust.

Mr. Murray was a Lewis man, a big impressive-looking figure, also from Ness, where men were traditionally big physically, intellectually and some would say, spiritually. You could not forget Mr. Murray. He was very well dressed and had a walking stick, a really strong heavy one. There was a good reason. Mr. Murray was badly wounded at 'the front' in the Great War. One leg was considerably shorter than the other. He was, for several years, missionary at Little Lochbroom.

Alexander MacLean, an elder in Aultbea, was born on the other side of Lochewe, in Inverasdale. He was appointed to be missionary at Poolewe, in succession to Mr. Gunn. Mr. MacLean had preaching gifts, which potentially, had he the benefits of 'learning', would have enhanced his work. As it was, his transparent sincerity and '*durachdach*' fervent evocations were more than compensating virtues for anything he lacked. His prayers had a heavenly texture of one who loved the Lord. His uncomplicated thinking made people feel that he retained the joy of a child of God, without getting lost in a tangle of humanly originating unprofitable theological accretions. Gregor Forbes, his driver, related how he was personally blessed simply by the company of the missionary while driving Mr. MacLean to services on the Sabbath day, especially when Mr. MacLean was domiciled in his own home at Mellon Charles.

Malcolm Morrison, the last missionary colleague of my father we would mention, was another native of Ness in Lewis and a big man. He had a wide expressive face, and grace, natural and redemptive, gave him an air of magnanimity and benevolence. He was stationed in Kinlochewe over which for some considerable periods of years, my father exercised ministerial supervision, during Gairloch's long vacancies. Recollections of Mr. Morrison the missionary are vivid. One is of the communion in Kinlochewe. While the guest minister preached, Mr. Morrison was precentor. The precentor's presence was so overwhelming that it was difficult to listen to the minister preaching above him in the pulpit.

Mr. Morrison was a First World War veteran, like most men of his age. He was in his prime at the beginning of the Second World War, the time of which we speak. It was no surprise when he left to study at university and Divinity College for the ordained ministry. He gave sterling service in the Master's Vineyard, as minister in Partick Highland Free Church Glasgow until his work was done and he left the scene of this world, to enter the 'rest that remaineth to the people of God.'

You can see that Mr. MacKinnon was part of a team, a worthy team. He worked amicably with them all together, comprising the church's witness, making it the profound and primary influence which penetrated the community with the dynamic of heaven, in a quiet but continuous enduring manner upon old and young.

In all his ministry, he had no recorded crisis of human relations with his missionary colleagues. While no doubt these were all good men, sanctified by grace, it must be said that this record of harmonious teamwork in a wide and busy geographic sphere of service, was in a large measure due to the minister's personal qualities. He made things work. That was one of his great gifts. He had the qualities of the diplomat. He was like a driver who not only keeps the bus full of oil in the engine and gas in the tank, but was always alert to pour oil on the squeaky wheel or on any auxiliary part of the vehicle's moving parts that might undermine its performance. Likewise Mr. MacKinnon had a concerned awareness for the Cause as a watchful pastor. He constantly sought to keep things 'ship shape' and well. This meant maintaining a close and brotherly relationship with all members of his team 'at the front', especially his missionary colleagues.

Chapter 26

The N.C.O.s

The two brothers, **Murdo and John MacLean**, were spoken of individually as Murdo the elder and John the elder. They were inseparably linked together as a special unit of heaven's witnesses in the community of Aultbea. Their presence gave a texture of spiritual strength and richness of both humanity and divinity. In their support of the minister, they were not unlike Aaron and Hur who held up the arms of Moses in prayer.

As the two senior elders, they epitomised the dynamic essence of Aultbea as an ongoing role model for the Christian heritage in Scotland and in the many parts of the world where the Presbyterian system was emulated. Their lives were not lived on the national stage like those who were stars in the top echelons of the ecclesiastical hierarchy, of clerical and lay personnel. They were not actors in any sense of the word, whose performance would capture good coverage in ecclesiastical magazines like the Record or the Witness, or the secular daily newspapers. Murdo worked as a stone mason and road foreman, and John pursued his retail business; they lived out their lives uniquely, acknowledged by the members of their community as born leaders whose sanction was not just an ecclesiastical vote but the signification of the blessing of heaven.

John the elder

John was younger than Murdo. He was broad-shouldered, with a broad brow and a broad reddish beard. In appearance he bore a striking resemblance to Charles Darwin, the minister's son of Galapagos fame. One recollects him as always wearing a dark blue suit. When the minister spoke of him, it was with a clear sense of John the elder as a special support member of the Locheweside church team. His ordered mind was also valued in the office of congregational treasurer. Each year, at the annual congregational meetings, a very low key review following the weekly prayer meeting, John the elder would give the annual financial report. It was all in Gaelic, as the spoken language of every day in the community was likewise Gaelic, on work on the croft, relaxation at ceilidhs and also at political meetings. John the elder was always in the manse on the Sabbath day, along with two or more other elders, for their dinner.

He was the joy of the manse family. In the unanimous view of the minister's eight children, it was a sad day when John the elder was not there. John the elder had a lovable tolerance for the children. He needed this as he was besieged by them, little ones crawling at his feet, and older ones plaguing him for attention. His spiritual stature and his humanity did not clash. It must be said that there was a special reason for his attractiveness to the children. He always carried a bag of sweets or candies in one of the large pockets of his jacket. While his brother Murdo might favour the children with the plain white 'bachelor buttons', John had a variety of sweets that made his weekly visit to the manse an exciting and speculative occasion of pleasurable surprise. Boldly, the children gathered round him, and out came glassy mints, caramels, striped balls, brown toffee and black treacle sweets—a selection from the row of large sweetie jars, high up on the top shelf in the store back in Mellon Charles.

The image of the weekly scene on a Sabbath day in the Aultbea manse is classical as culturally definitive of an age that has long since passed away, before the fast-changing restless quest to replace it with something very different, but certainly not better.

Take a look with me at the scene in the dining room. The guests have had their dinner, sumptuously provided by my mother, at the white linen covered dining table. This was large so that twenty people could sit round it at special times like those on Friday and Sabbath of a Communion. After returning of thanks by one of the elders, chairs were turned round to face the fire. The minister stayed for a short while only. Then he excused himself. This was a home day, with a free afternoon. He redeemed it by having a well-earned siesta, with the advantage for all that he would be fresh and hopefully 'on form' for the evening service. Old and young felt they could only then relax. And indeed the elders frankly admitted that they did not want 'to light up' until the minister left the room. There was nothing to compare with this company in the view of the children.

The men loved to talk to the minister's wife. There is no doubt that my mother was quite plainly attractive, physically and spiritually. Spiritually she was on the same wavelength. Her life was totally diffused with Christ's love for his church.

Therefore to her, the fellowship of the worthies was a kind
of refreshing spiritual tonic for her, even as she had refreshed
them by her hospitality. It is also true to say that she was in
many ways the liaison between the minister and the elders,
the latter expressing any concerns, indicating any change in
the temperature of the congregation in any one segment which
the elder represented. And do not forget the children. It was
their unique privilege to share in this exclusive interaction
with the choice members of church and community.

However many might be in for dinner, John the elder sat
in the big Victorian high-backed leather easy chair, on the
left of the fire in the hearth. One could never forget one scene,
a 'still' from the archives of time. There was a sudden
commotion just after all were comfortably seated for the post-
dinner relaxation. There was a blazing fire in the hearth, small
flames, happily blue and mature, crowning the red burning
coals, that gave out a lovely warm heat. The draft regulator
was set nicely, for economy and efficiency. Without warning,
there was a distinct smell of carbon dioxide gas, a sickly smell,
always accompanying its nasty deadly cousin, the insidious
lethal smell-free, carbon monoxide.

The fire stopped drawing; it seemed to have lost its
draft. Something was in the chimney and obviously blocking
the passage of air, so necessary to enable the fire to burn
efficiently. All happened in a very short space of time. Soot,
black horrible soot, started to drop on the fire, pouring out in
bursts from the chimney and causing all to back away from
the fireside. Then a distinct scraping was heard and a noise
that was very familiar. The children recognised it at once. It
was the manse black cat. It was crying as if in great distress
so that all the children were upset. Then, out it came, tumbling

down from the chimney, skipping lightly over the top of the burning fuel, fortunately now dampened with soot. Recollection is that our dear cat was none the worse for its experience, barring a few singed whiskers and two sore forepaws. Mother loved animals and now she took responsibility for this 'member' of the manse family. While little ones crowded round her, she placed the cat in one of the big clothes washing sinks in the 'washhouse', next to the scullery. She had run an inch or two of cold water and added some baking soda. Now the cat stood with its paws in the cool healing waters. The effect was almost immediate. The distress cries lost their poignancy. And as the cat's head rubbed against our mother's ministering hands, the cries changed to 'purring', pure cat language for comfort and gratefulness. One of the girls, I think it was Rachel, the eldest suggested the cat was actually smiling. That may or may not be so. Rachel often led the others to imagine they were seeing things. The main thing was, the family cat was alright and would continue to fulfil its God-appointed function of pest control.

But we cannot linger. Back to the dining room. We speak of normal occasions from Sabbath to Sabbath, month after month, year after year. The usual routine was followed. This was the moment for action. Children, strong healthy wide-eyed children now circled John the elder, competing with one another with questions. And all the time waiting for the 'big moment'. John the elder had infinite patience. Soon after getting settled in the chair, he knew what was expected of him. At least six pairs of eyes were on him, holding him captive, watching eagerly for the 'moment,' He knew what he had to do. He knew what was expected of him. And let it be recorded for ever, that 'John the elder' never once let the

MacKinnon children down. His hand would find the sweets in the pocket and, holding the packet in his left hand, he picked out a sweet for each, always deferring to the preference of each.   This operation was repeated throughout the afternoon. I think there were several pounds of sweets in that paper bag as it could be seen bulging in the jacket of the elder's suit.

Unlike the situation in other places, all Aultbea elders smoked the pipe. John was given a gift from his son. This was a special pipe, in a leather case. Children watched every move. John took this pipe from the pocket—not the one with the sweets. He opened it deliberately and slowly, like a musician carefully taking out the violin from its case. He had a pouch with a blended mixture, and with a pungent strong smell from which he filled his pipe, slowly in a quiet orderly ritual which rarely ever varied. The tobacco in the palm of one hand was 'worked' with the pad of the other, like the pedestal grinding the grain in the quern. Then, as the children watched, John, holding the pipe with the yellow stem up between his thumb and his forefinger, cajoled the tobacco, bit by bit from the palm of his other hand,   pressing the tobacco into the bowl, with his finger until he was satisfied that it was full. The missionary, Mr. MacIver and another elder, Kenneth MacLean Mellon Udrigil also had pouches with a ready mix.   Others had a knife with which the Bogey Roll was prepared in the palm of their hand and then transferred to the pipe bowl, following the same deliberate ritual.   Meantime, conversation continued, with children looking to the expressive faces of the men as a question hung in the air, calling for an answer. The quiet process of the smoking convention was a brake on haste, and epitomised the practical wisdom of 'stopping to think before you speak.' And thus the afternoon passed, with sometimes the elder reaching out to pat a child's head, with a kindly word of acknowledgement.

John the elder was a shopkeeper. On a Wednesday the MacBrayne steamer called at the Aultbea pier with goods of all kinds from Glasgow to stock the local shops. Little children, walking home from Bualnaluib school, those getting home early, like little Angus and his classmate, Alda MacLean, three days younger in age, would meet both John and his brother Murdo bringing their stock back to the Mellon Charles shop some two miles away. There was the rumbling noise of cartwheels. The children moved to the roadside to give the approaching cavalcade a wide berth. Then they watched. There were two carts, one behind the other, coming along the road from the pier. The carts were loaded high with barrels of paraffin and salt. Here were big plywood boxes of tea, big bags of oatmeal and flour and bran, containers of methylated spirits and cardboard boxes of soap. There were items of hardware, brooms tied together in bundles, and washing boards, the most reliable washing machines that ran on plenty elbow-grease and never broke down.

When John's cart passed, his brother Murdo came opposite, with his cart similarly laden. Both were seated on the cart with the reins loosely held. It was as if the horses knew the Gaelic instructions of their masters. They knew the way home. They knew what was expected of them. They too were part of a team. Maybe they also knew that some of the bran on the carts was also for them as well as for resale. And one last observation; it seemed to the children that each horse was somehow like its master, John the elder's was a reddish brown,

flecked at its mattocks with grey. The one behind pulling
Murdo's cart, seemed very much older, its long thin head,
dignified and thoughtful, like its master, its black coat
matching his rough tweed coat with the high collar and
sweeping streamlined pocket-covers at the side, bulging with
the master's tobacco pouch.

What a picture to remember! Both men wore caps today,
not the hard felt hats of the Sabbath. Yet their appearance
was individual and distinctive. They sat erect, their beards
resting on their chests, pipes in mouth, now and then emitting
puffs of gentle smoke, which hardly left their persons, as the
horses ambled along on the gravel road at a leisurely pace.
The whole scene would make a modern movie, the carts
piled high with goods, rumbling over the road so that the
children could count the spokes of the big ironbound wheels.
And then there were the horses, each with that knowing look
as if they felt proud of being part of this special team, John
the elder and his brother Murdo. How matchless and unique,
even in their secular work, this pair, still retaining for the
passing children, the aura of spiritual identity as 'worthies'
that could not be simulated then nor in any age to come.
Remember these men were patriarchs, being both well over
eighty years old at the time, in the year 1938.

According to gifts so people serve, or should do so.
Therefore it was natural for John to be at the helm, both in
church matters and in his business. When necessary, John
conducted a service in the church. It was Murdo's role to
augment the spiritual offering of worship with the matchless
thoughts that like wings lifted hearers from the mundane to
the heavenly, in prayer. John was active in his business role,
by which he was known locally as *Ian an Ceannaiche*, or

John the shopkeeper. In the elder's role he was the people's representative, esteemed and recognised as a spiritual counsellor, and member of the ruling council of the local church, the Kirk Session. In this, he was John the elder.

Murdo the Elder

John the elder lived on one side of the Mellon Charles meeting house. His older brother, Murdo the elder, lived on the other side, in a croft house with a thatched roof and facing as most of the houses did, due east. Murdo in secular life was for some time a foreman, the overseer of gangs of workmen making or maintaining the arterial roads over a wide area of Wester Ross. Alick MacLennan, *Ali aig Coinneach* recounted an incident from Murdo's life as foreman of a work gang, labouring on the hill road through Glen Docharty.

A drover, Angus MacLeod from Achgarve was passing through with cattle, one of which could not go further, on the way from Aultbea to the market in Dingwall. Murdo the elder, according to the account told to me, took water from the stream and offered it to the animal. It refused. He then poured the water over the head of the animal and prayed as if it were a person. Within minutes, the beast struggled to its feet and never faltered until it arrived in Dingwall, long after midnight, along with the other animals.

The minister had in Murdo the elder a colleague whose mind he consulted almost like an oracle. His thinking was valued, and the answers he gave had an unusual and arresting effect, so that no one gainsayed. He was calm and scarcely every known known to be agitated.

To be fair, one must mention one occasion when Murdo the elder was slightly 'put out'. It happened like this. He was seated as usual in his favourite chair on the right of the fire in the manse. It was winter; the days were short; the fading light from the window   behind his high Victorian chair, left the patriarch in the shadows. He had just cut his Bogey-roll and refilled his long pipe. He was holding the pipe in his hand, with the index finger over the tobacco in the bowl. He was speaking to a question, carefully crafting every thought in chosen and deliberate words to which the other elders listened intently. Round the group of elders were children. They were also waiting for Murdo to light his pipe. The older girls, Rachel, Katie and Cathie liked to make paper tapers which they would ignite from the fire at the appropriate time and hand to the elder to light his pipe. On this occasion, one of them thought that Murdo was now ready. He had lifted his pipe towards his mouth. But his mind was still occupied with the topic under discussion. With just a hint of over eagerness, one does not like to use the word recklessness, a lighted taper was raised to the elder's face. The taper was not tightly folded. Now the small flame flared up. Everyone could see what was happening. One moment all was quiet and orderly in the darkened room. Next moment, a mini-conflagration burst out, literally in Murdo the elder's face as he leaned his patriarchal head on the back of the Victorian chair. It goes without saying that his long white beard was vulnerable. My sister did not pull the taper back immediately. The flame touched the beard; the elements of calamity were all in place. It was not the time for calm. Such was humanly impossible. And there were no exceptions. Murdo the elder, caught behind the flame raised both hands,   one to his vulnerable whiskers, the other to push away the over solicitous daughter of the manse. Within seconds the drama was over. The taper was thrown into the hearth, to burn itself out. Old

Murdo regained his decorum, his hand stroking his beard and feeling his moustache, checking that all was not lost, in a kind of damage control. Only then did he make an ambivalent comment upon children. With his head slowly moving from one side to the other, he expressed an opinion, that wariness was a necessary requirement or the young would cause excitement if not calamity. He was decisive. Never after this would a taper be used to help light the elders' pipes. The other elders had learned the lesson too. In their pockets they made sure that they had their box of matches, the only valid protection from the hazards of help from the ever obliging young.

Murdo the elder was a philosopher. But he was unencumbered by the considerations that entangle most of us in the web of compromise and thus empty our speech of true freedom. He was not qualified in his speech, if one might say, by any 'interest' except the two undisputed poles of altruism, namely his allegiance to his Redeemer and his love for people, especially those, young and old round about him in the immediate world of which he was a part. His physical presence represented an automatic unarticulated prescience on the part of those who knew him, that here was someone who had a likeness to the embodiment of God's grace in a composite of profound wisdom and universal understanding.

The well-known photograph of General Booth which reflects the love of God, and compassion for a broken humanity is almost an identical likeness of Murdo the elder. The white hair, the striking brow, the shaded depths of the eyes, the long aquiline nose, the kindness of the mouth, framed by the long white flowing beard were the same in both men. And in both the idea of supreme compassion, which rests in

God and springs from God, was personified.

Early in the Second World War, after the huge battleship HMS Nelson was crippled by a defensive mine, there were two air-raids on Lochewe. A flotilla of tugs and boom boats with their built-in bow cranes were tied alongside the massive battle ship, continually pumping to keep her afloat. She had been towed in close to the shelter of the high cliffs between the *Guallann Mhor,* Big Shoulder, at the inner end of the island and the *Rudha Thurnaig*, Turnaig Point. Travellers could look down from the road along the 'tops' between Aultbea and Poolewe and get an aerial view of the great battleship below. Can you imagine the thrill of growing boys seeing this historic battleship called after the greatest sailor in the world, Horatio Nelson, the immortal hero of Trafalgar, sitting there six hundred feet below! Also to complete the picture and the clues to the situation, a floating dock, the largest in the British Isles was already being towed north from the Clyde. In the event, it was found that the diving team did enough repairs to keep the ship afloat, and word was that when the dock arrived, it was found to be impossible to service the massive structure of the Nelson. Two nights in succession, the Germans did their best to 'get' the Nelson. But each time they were eventually forced to retreat when the fighter squadron from Stornoway some thirty miles away on the island of Lewis, took to the skies above Aultbea.

In the manse, three hundred yards from the pier, the children were shaken by the hour long episode, an action of alternating eerie droning hostile bombers and the continual detonating bursts of anti-aircraft guns. The sky was like a Christmas tree of tracer bullets, searchlights and exploding shells. How any plane could contemplate coming in again in consecutive sorties to attack, is hard to imagine. But this the Germans did, until the Stornoway Hurricanes came on the night scene. There was no mistaking their arrival. The hundred guns round Loch Ewe suddenly became silent, as the low flying Hurricanes, with their Rolls Royce Merlin engines screaming, filled the night air. The Germans knew it was 'no contest' and scuttled back across the North Sea to their base in captured Norway, before their fuel ran out. One remembers yet father going out and checking that all was well, the siren blaring out the All-Clear. And what then? Yes, a psalm of thanksgiving rising to heaven from the old manse, a mingling of adult and children's voices, crouching under the kitchen table, thanking God for his merciful deliverance.

Picture the scene on the following Sabbath day of which we speak, in the manse in Aultbea with the elders present. The day is far spent and the shadows of the evening draw nigh. The pipes have been given a rest from smoking. Mrs. MacKinnon gathers the cups which the children took from the elders after their afternoon 'cup of tea'. Soon they would leave the manse while it was still half an hour before the evening service began. There was no last minute rush with them. Especially with patriarchs, Murdo and John now in their late eighties, everything they did was deliberate and studied, reflecting the life of their souls being led by still waters, fed by the pastures of heaven, veritable 'trees of righteousness' nourished by the 'river of life'.

The conversation had been cut off or at least curtailed by the 'tea'. It was as if the whole company were waiting for an answer, an answer to the question previously under discussion, 'Will there be more bombing, and will there be loss of life

from the War in Aultbea yet?' The company could not disperse
without the last word, and that was still to be given. For Murdo
the elder had not yet given his answer.

The men rise to go. Mrs MacKinnon is thanked, in that
gracious manner reflecting a real appreciation for the
ongoing kindness of her hospitality. Murdo the elder has taken
his long pipe from little sister Ina, who had lifted it from the
hearth. It was now cool like the pipes of the others, an
essential, before putting the pipe in the pocket. The children
look to the elders with regret that they are leaving. But there
is also a cloud of uncertainty, an unrelieved anxiety for the
morrow. This fills the air as the room is somewhat darkened
by the foliage of the tall birch trees and the failing light. The
scene is set, a pervasive expectation is felt by all, adults and
children, that the 'last word' has yet to be spoken.

All are now standing. There is a pause as Murdo the elder
makes his way between the head of the big dining room table
and the window. His remarkable appearance is silhouetted
against the light. He reaches out his hand and lays it on the
head of Joan, the second youngest child. He turns round to
look towards his hostess. There are no contrived dramatic
postures. Yet the drama is there as much as any on the stage
of a Shakespearean play. He is involuntarily the central figure.
All eyes are riveted on his face and in a pregnant silence all
ears await his words. Now he spoke.

*'A Mhistris MacFhionghuin, ma 'se bhur toil e, iaram facal
a canntuin mar freagradh dh'an a cheist sin. Tha moran ann,
tha mi smaoineacheadh, 'sbi iad am fiosrachadh le bron, oir
cha tig olc agus cogadh'leath'fhein, agus fulang' moran
sluagh; gun teagamh bi bas agus sgrios am fad 'sam fagus.'*

(Mrs. MacKinnon, if you please, may I say a word in

answer to the question. There are many, I am thinking, who will be visited with sorrow, for war and evil do not come alone, but many people will suffer; without doubt, there will be death and destruction near and far away.)

His striking appearance was animated as though he were reading a message on the screen of his own mind, and seeking to communicate it to those in the room. He had a compelling authority, his patriarchal head moving slowly from side to side. He paused, his other hand came round from his side and with both he closed them round the head of the child before him. And then he went on,

'Ach tha mi 'g innseadh dhuibh, nach tig dochair 'sam bith do'n leanabh so agus ge be air bith a tha gabhail comhnuidh 'nan fhardach so, gus am bi deireadh air a'chogadh.' (But I say to you, that no harm will come to this little one, nor to any other who lives in this house until the war shall be over.)

Murdo the elder had spoken. There was a quiet assurance about him that had an immediate effect upon his hearers. Thereafter anxiety for immediate danger from the air-raids was more than countered by an assurance of safety. For the record, no more night raids were repeated.

So much for scenes in the manse. Come now with the minister as he makes a call at the home of Murdo the elder. The old Citroen, ten years old, certainly on its last tires if not its last legs, rounds the dangerous narrow bend past the meeting-house hill. This hill or Meall, the rocky eminence which gives this place the distinctive link with the Rising of the Jacobites, thus called 'the Hill of Charles', relates to the flight of 'Bonnie Prince Charlie' to the Isles and an episode of his hiding from the patrons of the Hanover dynasty, after the abortive rising and route of the Royalists at Culloden, some eighty miles away. Now the car stops. The house of Murdo the elder, his earthly lodging house nestles snugly in the hollow. The minister makes his way down the scarcely discernible footpath to the door, some hundred yards distant from the road.

The door is ajar, for the householder has been apprised of his visitor's arrival by the reliable signal of his faithful Collie dog, *Failte* (Welcome) barking defensively when the car had stopped on the road before the house. Greeting each other, the minister is then welcomed into the room on the right of the small lobby, past the two walking sticks, the rough homegrown hazel one with the natural grown crook, and the other, the varnished one with the steam bent handle, reserved for the prayer meeting and the Sabbath day.

The sun from the eastern-facing front shines through the window at an angle. The gable is dominated by a large whitewashed recess. This is the fireplace with a high mantle shelf and a wide aperture leading up to the funnel of the chimney. A chain, the *slabhruidh* with a large iron hook hangs down with an iron kettle, being heated gently by the peatfire on the hearth below.

To the left is a large curtained-off bed. On a small table is a large Bible. It is covered in soft leather, now cracked and worn. The edges of the pages are dog-eared and frayed though the Bible is shut. It bears the mark of much usage. You can hardly make out the writing on the rib, *Biobuill Naomh*, Holy Bible. Spectacles are open beside it, and a chair is drawn up at right angles to the table, as if someone was reading and then drew the chair round to kneel in prayer. A wooden clock hanging on the wall rhythmically measured its audible beat, as it ticked off the seconds on the time chart of its owner, as he lodged in this world in preparation for the world to come. The two men conferred for some time and then the minister took his leave, walking back to the car. The old elder stood in the doorway watching. What a picture to remember, a replay of history, a still from the film of time, of a man who had no double and could not be cloned nor copied in any authentic likeness.

One last picture of that incomparable colleague of Mr. MacKinnon, that sage of heavenly enlightenment and powerful cognitive discernment, stays forever. The minister with his younger son visits the old patriarch. He was now close to ninety years of age. Heaven was already waiting as it were with expectation for his arrival.

The smoke is rising from the chimney, but there is no response to the knock on the door. The minister goes round the back of the house. Murdo the elder had been kneeling at the well. Now he stands up. He comes towards the minister. They meet and greet each other. The old elder clasps a large glass jar with water from his well, a jar that is exactly identical to the big sweetie jars on the top shelf in his brother John the elder's shop. The picture is vividly clear, unfaded by time. The jar is not full. It is less than half full. There is scarcely enough for the basic needs of a person for the remainder of the day. How strange! Did this prince of prayer already know that soon, very soon, he would no more have need for these earthly waters?

A glance at the house gave a view of the roof at the back. It was exposed here to the prevailing wind and weather from the southwest, with its squalls and storms, its incessant showers of Atlantic rain and persistent gales. One could not help noticing other features. The thatch has not recently been renewed. There were patches of green and even some little primroses growing happily in this elevated location, as if they had escaped the nibbling sheep or the crushing imprint of a careless unfeeling human boot.

The minister took his leave. The image of Murdo the elder standing there with the sweetie jar held in his two hands, the cap on his head and the white beard flowing down over his chest, his watch chain hanging across his waistcoat dipping into the pocket, remains vividly in the memory.

Next day a hush lies over Mellon Charles and all of Aultbea. In the morning no smoke rises from the house of Murdo the elder. The sun has risen, shining with a peculiar intensity in an unusually cloudless sky. A poignant cry from the elder's faithful collie dog *Failte* is carried on the gentle breeze, so that neighbours on adjoining crofts, Murdo MacKenzie, Murdo MacLean, William MacLennan, read the signs. They converge at the closed door. The dog protests. It is in anguish. Its song is a wail, a cry, poignant even with the pathos of a human who mourns the loss of a loved one. The men speak consolingly. The latch is lifted; the dog springs forward, pushing the door inwards. The dog bounds into the room, its paws reach up to the bed. The wail is almost human, then subsides into a deep repressed cry. His master is gone. On a command, it lies down beside the bed.

The face of the patriarch was serene and noble in death as it was in life. He had departed quietly in the watches of the night. When Murdo the elder died, a lamp of the sanctuary was extinguished in the church of Aultbea, and though God would always have his witnesses, a minister could not have again such a helper—one whose sole life-purpose was to keep in touch with heaven and to communicate to others subconsciously in his person, in an unusual measure, the pervasive fragrance of His Master.

While there were many other colleagues, worthy elders, gifted, gracious good men, like Kenneth MacLean Mellon Udrigil, Murdo MacLennan Laide, Alexander Grant Bualnaluib, Donald MacIver Bualnaluib, Donald Munro Little Lochbroom, Alick Beaton Mellon Charles, Kenneth MacKenzie Mellon Charles, Murdo MacKenzie, Alick Cameron Tournaig, Alick MacLennan Poolewe, Angus Cameron Poolewe, Kenneth MacLean Poolewe, Alick Urquhart Naast, and in Cove and Inverasdale, Mr. MacPherson, Roderick Urquhart, Roderick MacDonald, Neil MacDonald. Nevertheless there was never the like of these two men the brothers Murdo and John MacLean, the elders. Born about the time of the Crimean War, they were alive during the ministry of all the Free Church ministers, beginning with James Noble, until their demise in the early nineteen-forties.

There is no doubt that the character of the extensive parish was strongly influenced by the powerful spiritual presence of these two brothers. While there was a total absence of egotistical assertion on their part, they symbolised the effective role of ruling eldership in the unique ecclesiastical situation in Aultbea when the unity and identity of the people with the reformed national church of history was challenged. Professor Dr. Alexander Renwick, himself a native of Wester Ross, and a descendant of a Covenanter, came to a Communion in Aultbea some years after the passing of both Murdo and John. In a letter of acknowledgment to the manse, he states that this visit to the communion in Aultbea was a unique experience. He spoke of the fellowship enjoyed that week and of the 'men' who supported Mr. MacKinnon in his ministry, the full latron of elders. He wrote that it seemed to him a page out of history, of the choicest days of the Scottish Church when the Sun of blessing shone upon its people with the benediction of heaven. How wonderful a testimony to Christian lives, that after their passing, the fragrant influence of these two elders, Murdo and John, still lingered over the vineyard where they worked for their master!

And the Lord God raised not again in Scotland, such mighty men, the spiritual representatives of the people, and colleagues of the minister, as **Murdo and John, the elders.**

Chapter 27

Room in the Inn

T he accelerated social change caused by the Second World War dramatically altered the ordered circumstances of ministers and their finances. Inflation shrank the purchasing power of those on fixed salaries. For the minister, inflation meant that his stipend was, in effect, equal to half or even a third of what it had been.

Realistically it is very hard for a minister to maintain a sense of his calling when he lacks the practical means to fulfil it. Humanly speaking, it is easy to become disillusioned, and to reflect that the set-up of the Church is not exactly Divinely authorised. MacKinnon Aultbea was at times troubled, just like other ministers about this. Even the informal help from kind and godly women, could not mask the inequity of the situation. How then did he retain a sense of his calling? The answer is found in the singularly profound conviction he held along with his peers, that the ministry was something apart and that it was the greatest honour for a person to be called to it, with all its frustrations. To the end of his life, his view of the 'Ministry of the Word' was undimmed, as the greatest profession on earth. He would quote Dr. Martyn Lloyd Jones, the distinguished London preacher when asked, 'How could a successful Harley Street surgeon sacrifice so much to become a minister of the Gospel?' He would then linger upon the surgeon-turned-preacher's reply, 'What sacrifice? What could I do for a Saviour who gave Himself a sacrifice for me?'

Yet the practical reality was there, a grim and growing discrepancy between income and expenditure for his work in the charge. My father was the first minister in Aultbea to own a car and use it for his work. Either through his own reluctance to raise the matter, or misconceptions about minister's remuneration—after all, ministers received salaries from Edinburgh—there is no recorded trace of motoring allowance or reimbursement for the extensive outlay incurred for his church work. The old pre-War perception persisted that the 'chariots of the Lord' still ran on the fuel of the spirit, and that the rubber tires on the new mode of transport were as cheap to replace as the iron shoes for the horse at the local 'smiddy'. It did not occur to the godly who held the key to the treasury of what was really now a comparatively affluent community, economically based upon national defense employment for all, that there are *spirits* and *spirits* and that even God meant the minister's car to fill up with the fossil kind that was pumped up from the earth.

It is known only to God what many ministers and their wives endured, shivering in big cold manses, always presenting an appearance of abundance, giving the best in hospitality to visitors at the manse, and themselves at times making do with gruel and staple foods like salt herring and potatoes. It has to be said that the manse children in Aultbea did not become aware of any stringency until retrospective realisation in later years. While 'want' might raise its ugly head in desperate situations for many ministers, for MacKinnon Aultbea the manse peat bank supplemented the cash purchase of coal. Not only so but the shores of Lochewe during wartime were strewn with driftwood of which a goodly portion was ferried in the family boat from the 'rocks' at the *Tigh-hallaigh* to fill the hearth on many a winter night with the warmth of a cheery blaze. There was always the financially cushioning effect of the produce from the glebe, a vital adjunct of the minister's stipend. With one to three cows, two or three dozen hens, ducks, and some sheep plus the harvest from the sea within a stone's throw of the manse door, inflationary high finance, domestic or societal, was masked by the immediacy of abundance 'in kind'. How could it be otherwise, as children drank fresh milk and pure cream, gathered the daily quota of eggs from the henhouse, and sat down to eat the best of ground fish and at times the scaly royal diet of prime salmon! But the strain was there, the chronic haunting nightmare of debt. Then the toll taken on the health of their parents was as unmistakable as it was irreversible. The fact is that the minister encouraged his wife to give to strangers and not to count the cost. She herself believed to an extreme, that every sacrifice had to be made in the interests of the Cause.

Just think of it, furnishing an eighteen room manse, raising a family of eight children, paying for a car and all its running expenses in a large parish like Locheweside, on a minister's now inadequate salary set in Edinburgh! And yet all seemed to go on smoothly, including a considerable list of further outlays, gratuitously incurred, without any financial recompense.

Before the War, while not affluent, ministers were certainly part of the comfortable 'establishment'. Like peers in the perceived social structure, this cosy permanence was blasted apart almost from the Declaration of War in 1939. There is no doubt that the Second World War was the cause of the crisis. Payment for the domestic help of two young women at Communion seasons, hospitality to delegates from missions and different church-related causes at home and abroad, like Bible Society and Mission to the Jews, and many more, orthodox and unorthodox, bit into the shrinking income of the manse.

Somehow the Free Church manse appeared to be taken for granted, a kind of God-ordained inn, always open and all for free. That seemed to sum up the situation. Here was a 'bed and breakfast' establishment and high tea and dinner as well for anyone with the remotest claim to a worthy cause. Here was the best of lodgings more than favourably comparable to that in the local hotel for the secular traveller, and just think of it, all this for free. Apart from the list of vague church society delegates, there was also a continual stream of other visitors. Hospitality was never rationed.

In a sense the manse children had a special social education. They were delighted to make a study of all visitors. There were politicians, ship's captains and ships' chaplains, Anglican padres, Presbyterian chaplains, from the Naval and army bases. These among an endless list of others of various social and professional standing were frequent guests, entertained in the drawing room with the adjournment to the dining room for a liberal feast of 'good things.'

The image keeps coming back of such occasions. I think of one where all are seated round the table for an evening meal. The army chaplain from the Poolewe army base is present. He is a Free Church minister, serving as war chaplain. There is a special interest in him, in that he is a son of one of my father's Divinity Hall teachers, Professor MacKay. The host minister sits at the head of the long table and his wife, serene and poised, sits at the other end. My happiest recollection of my mother was her beauty projected in her face, her soft natural skin, her lovely direct, arresting eyes that spoke of wistful inner joys of the soul, and her golden blonde hair curving attractively round her head. I recall how she engaged the batman/driver of the chaplain, in conversation. In later years I looked back and marvelled at the breadth and generosity of outlook mirrored in my mother's words. Though part of a very restricted Christian tradition, and brought up, without knowledge of modern employment, and its complicated social psychology, she made this person with very different affiliations, feel totally at home, as one of God's family of human beings in all its diversity and yet common unity. Her words linger with me yet, 'We hope and pray that the day will soon come when the world will see the fulfilling of the kingdom of God and his peace for all people.'

A long list of all kinds of people, including visitors from abroad, many from America and Canada, New Zealand and Australia, came in turn. That was in peacetime. Wartime was just as busy, but visitors were a different mix. It seemed that there was a compulsive urge to emulate18th century Dr. Johnson in making his famous tour of the Highlands, or Canadians who like to make a ritual trip across that vast country once in a lifetime from the Atlantic Ocean to the Pacific. The queue of visitors to the manse was endless, especially in summer, County Council colleagues, writer/ travellers, public school headmasters, church friends from England, Anglican ministers and divinity college professors, and many more. These comprised a hospitality list for a meal or afternoon tea or as overnight guests that justified the manse as the equivalent of a free hotel. But it was a guest house of welcome, a Christian welcome where visitors shared a blessing that made their contact with that Highland manse filled with its lively children, a memorable one.

Reciprocally, the effect upon the manse was also positive. The household was enriched by all this 'coming and going'. For the children of the manse, meeting all kinds of people in the social scale was an education in itself. But we must include a note on one category of visitors who possibly made a great impression upon the children, and at any rate provided them with a great deal of entertainment. These were the 'tramps.' We have to include a word about them for they were a special group of human beings who earned the ambiguous title of 'Gentlemen of the road.'

These came round to the back door. The children stared at them, wide-eyed, and the younger ones clung to their mother's clothes as these casualties of society presented their needs for basic human sustenance. Many of them were known to the manse. They were the regulars, making their annual itineraries until at last in turn they came no more, their hard comfortless life journey over, buried under layers of disappointment, and the 'challenging' visitations they were unable to cope with in this life. There just has to be a life beyond where there is some kind of contrasting rest for the many in this world whose life has never progressed beyond the bud of dreams, and where all the normal criteria spell out the death of hope—for that unending stream of 'lost men' showed in the window of their faces and especially their eyes, the full consciousness of their failure.

These 'gentlemen of the road' did not wish to come into

the house, but asked only for food. This was usually a bowl of piping hot potash, a composite nourishing soup of vegetables and meat. What they got on any one day was of course related to the manse menu. At times they received large pieces of bread with cheese and jam. A large chipped enamel mug or jug was handed in and filled with hot tea.Then generally there followed an overnight stay in the warm manse barn. All this was an accepted part of the social structure.

Many of these men showed traces of nobility of character. Their gaunt faces, and deepset eyes presented an unfathomable ocean of human experience, distorted and hard, the kind that brought suffering and bruising to the human spirit, so that they became dislodged from their place in conventional society. For them all, life had become too much to cope with. They became itinerant wanderers, throughout the land, dropping off each in turn, when weakness and weariness made that impossible. Some maintained a justifiable dignity. One would offer to sketch pictures, and the rough likeness of the children who would come forward was passed on from hand to hand, until at last the paper torn from a school jotter with the image drafted with the charcoal pencil became tattered and faded and then misplaced and forgotten. I've wondered since, if these had been preserved, they would have shown us an insight into the tramp's image of us, fat rosy-cheeked children sheltered in the nest of a big family home—such a contrast to the pieces of broken expectations now mirrored in the deep lined face with its worn-out looks of one whom life with its legitimate quota of human happiness has already passed by.

One thinks back to another. He would offer to mend metal pails and pans, riveting handles back or clenching them on bakelite tops or pan lids. Another would ask for knives and scissors to sharpen these as he waited out in the garage, while his lunch was prepared. There was a kind of honour in most by which they earned their 'bread'. It was common for them to eat their fill, but not to eat all. My mother allowed for this and she would always add plenty bread—large thick slices of sandwiches. Some of this would be put away in the tramp's knapsack for eating later in the day.

One regular tramp who came to the manse would lodge in an old ruined building, a disused farmhouse now obsolete since its fields were distributed to the crofters in Tighnafiline. The Aultbea children knew him because they had to pass this dark eerie building, Aird House, on the way home from school. Here in the semi-dark, with all kinds of imagined creepy things in the rafters high above, the tramp would make his lodging, sharing it with other wayfarers, of the natural world, bats and birds and rodents whose droppings made the floor of the large partitionless building into a carpet of indifferent texture and even colour. There was one compensating factor apart from the basic shelter from the elements. The lodger had a roaring fire of driftwood burning brightly in the hearth. Even as children, we liked to steal a bit of the warmth from this last but wonderful basic vestige of a domicile, now the only comfort for this traveller of the roads. Emboldened by numbers, for there was always a residual apprehension, the children would crowd round their scarecrow-like host in a circle, the leaders speaking to him and trying to elicit some response to all kinds of questions. At the root of it was the desire to establish some kind of relationship. This is a compulsive psychological necessity for all living creatures. We like to know where we are in relation to another. Life is a shared phenomenon on our planet, and in its many forms, the current of that sharing wants like an electrical current to flow from one to another. God surely meant that this be positive. Thus the children sought unselfconsciously to get through to this tramp. He was human and they wanted to get a response from his soul. They wanted to be reassured that he was really still alive, that behind the sad outward appearance, there was still the spark of life. And you know, it seemed that this meeting of tramp and children produced some results. Children did not judge as adults. Yes, they saw the tragedy. But in the face of their persistent questions and incorrigible continuous curiosity, his reserve was penetrated. Maybe also in the ring of innocent youthful faces, something of the once buoyant personality, even of the young boy, before the night of failure closed in on him, now stirred.

At any rate, prompted by the children he would lift a mouth organ to his dark half-shaven face. His fingers protruded from the cut-off mittens on his hands. Continually encouraged by the children, he would thus rise, into a crouching position. With mysterious skill, he would take his hands away from the instrument in his mouth. To the amazement of the children, the instrument continued to move swiftly from side to side, producing lovely popular melodies of human emotions, sad and happy, slow and fast that brought his young audience to a trance-like silence. But he was not finished. With a spoon in each hand, he now complemented his skilled playing with a drum-like tapping on both his knees, making them to vibrate rhythmically together, like the other music instruments of an orchestra. And when he would at last finish, he would get a great cheer of applause. I like to think of the head that then bowed in acknowledgment, like a performer on the stage, that in a little measure this scene of acceptance before little children, would nourish his inner being, when sadness and pessimism clouded his disposition. Maybe it was this, countering the obvious rejection of society multiplied for him, in a hundred places throughout the year, that kept the light of life alight for him and without which he like many who realize they are failures, might have capitulated to the darkness of oblivion. It is true that such visitors to the manse were at the bottom of the social ladder. They came to the back door. But somehow their continuing relationship with the church house added an undefinable value to the manse as a community institution. There was always room and food in the inn.

The lasting impression of one brought up in the Aultbea manse was one of 'plenty'. There seemed to be an abundance. Maybe it had something to do with the attitude of the parents. God would provide. And He did. This was true in the wider context of the church family, as illustrated by the following anecdote.

One evening, parents and children were sitting together round the fire in the sitting-room. It was approaching the end of the year, near Christmas. The Tilley pressure lamp hissed with its friendly familiar sound as it lighted up the sitting room with its mantle of white light. Ina and Cathie had just brought the mail from the Post Office. Mother opened the bundle of cards, and letters, separating those relating to the church from those relating to the family, the letters as a rule being differentiated by a typed address as opposed to being handwritten.

The family mail was read out aloud for all to hear. As a

kind of afterthought, the official mail was examined. There was one from Edinburgh. On it was the familiar sender's address, 'Free Church Offices, The Mound, Edinburgh.' Normally this would be an anticlimax. Mother opened the long envelope. She looked at the missive, perusing the formal typed writing. Dad was ensconced in his easy-chair, resigned as it were to an unrelieved acceptance of the usual financial strictures of his situation. A smile now crossed my mother's face. Then after a pause, she said, 'Dadda, hear this. It's from Edinburgh.'

Dad perked up, 'Yes! What is it? I hope it is good news.'

Now all were silent and waiting. Dad had come to life, sensing the dramatic, which was clearly personified in my mother's disposition and manner.

My mother paused, keeping everyone in suspense, and seeming to enjoy doing so. Anticipation increased.

'Come on, Mam, We're all waiting. What's in the letter? Read it out,' said Cathie. And so my mother read the letter aloud to her waiting audience.

'From Home Missions Board, Free Church Offices, The Mound, Edinburgh.

> Dear Mr. MacKinnon,
>
> At a recent end of the year meeting of the Home Missions Board, it was found that there was a small balance of income over expenditure. It was moved that this sum be forwarded to a needy minister of the Church. It was unanimously agreed by the Committee, that this be sent to the minister of Aultbea and Poolewe, to give some relief in bearing the burden of a large family and the commitments of a scattered charge in these wartime years. I therefore enclose the cheque and on behalf of the Committee, extend to you our warmest goodwill and

> prayers for God's blessing upon you and your family, in
> the work of the Church.

You should have seen the effect this letter had upon all, but especially upon my father. He was up in a moment from his easy-chair. Obviously overjoyed, he pulled his spouse up out of her chair, catching her in a loving embrace and twirling her round. It was the nearest thing the minister and his wife ever came to a 'dance' in the recollection of childhood memories before or after. All the children present were infused with the same spirit. The cheque, worth about one week's salary, was like a million dollars. There was something more in this gift than the monetary value it represented. This letter conveyed a signal, like that of a light from another ship to a lone mariner after weeks on the ocean, that he was not alone. The fact that the minister in Aultbea was not alone in this far-off Highland parish but had the support of the whole Church, was a token of encouragement that renewed his faith in human nature and strengthened his hand in the resolve with which he unstintingly pursued his calling.

At family worship that evening before retiring, there was a special note of gratitude in the voices of all as they sang from the Scottish Metrical Psalm 89, from verse 15,

> O greatly blessed the people are
> The joyful sound that know;
> In brightness of thy face, O Lord,
> They ever on shall go.

Chapter 28

The Communion

The climax of the Christian church year in Aultbea had arrived. That was the Sabbath day of the summer Communion season in June.

All roads lead to Aultbea and to its big church, centrally built in the middle of the community. Finlay, Alfred or Murdo Urquhart, the regular drivers are there with the mail-bus, and the passenger-bus full of parishioners from Laide and surrounding villages. Colin MacKenzie from Poolewe is there along with his brother Kenny *Ghard'ner*. Both have the big black Ford charabancs from the 1920's. These cars are spotlessly clean, with sidelights high on each side of the split windscreen and long trumpet like horns, making them the delight of children. Roddy *Botlan* is there from Inverasdale with the roomy broad low Austin Six. As it empties, one wonders how so many people could come out of one car.

I repeat, all roads lead to Aultbea. For heaven itself has smiled. Overhead is a cloudless sky, and the tranquil waters of the calm unruffled bay reflect the peace and reconciliation between man and his Maker, the sinner and his Saviour, celebrated in this incomparable enactment of corporate worship, this Sacrament and Memorial to God's active nature of ineffable love. Surely 'This is the day which the Lord hath made; we will rejoice and be glad in it.'[1]

Here is a day with a difference. Gairloch services are cancelled; every available bus and car bring people to Aultbea. Little Lochbroom is closed; likewise Kinlochewe, and Alligin. And everyone who can make their way to Aultbea, is there, some anticipating the Sabbath by lodging with friends for the duration of the Communion season.

This day is a rehearsal of the prophetic glory of the church. Here is a blend of expectation and obedience, where prophetic fulfillment is in part evidenced.   Here in part is fulfilled, and who can gainsay it, glorious, inspiring descriptions of the gathering of the redeemed from the centuries of time and all the corners of the world where men sit in sin's darkness. And the focus is Christ, the Fountain opened for sin and uncleanness, the fountain of life, as the phonetic rendering of Aultbea suggests. Hear Jesus in Scripture with that call of the elective power of God's Word, 'that will not return unto him void, but accomplish that which he please.'[2] 'And they shall come from the east, and from the west, and from the north and from the south, and shall sit down in the kingdom of God.'[3]

There is no doubt that for many of the devout, this is a foretaste of the everlasting Feast of heaven, where the redeemed are guests of the Eternal and are dressed in His righteousness to take the place prepared for them.

Today is an incomparable one for the minister. As usual Mr. MacKinnon was downstairs before the dawn. He had a penchant for preparation, for every duty laid upon him. This

1. Psalm 118:24   2. Isaiah 55:11   3. Luke 13:29

was a characteristic of his life in every sphere that demanded his energies and time. Possibly this came from the simple pragmatic preparation, learned when fishing since the days of his childhood. The wise fisherman, prepares for every uncertainty, by having an extra oar in the boat, by carrying a baler for emptying sea water shipped by a wave. He prepares his fishing lines beforehand and lays the *'lion beag '* or the *'lion mor,'* 'the 'small line' for haddock or 'the great line' for cod, carefully baiting them in the *cliabh*, the creel, and laying them out the day before. Only with this studied patient preparation, can there be expectation of a catch of fish. This was the practical lesson from his youth. Now he applied the same to the spiritual duties of his calling. No wonder there were great expectations this day of the Aultbea Communion. Therefore if you followed him in the early dawn, you would see him pass through the little wooden gate, and descend the steps down from the elevation of the manse to the door of the church hall and vestry. You would see him in the pulpit, preparing for the service, getting the big Bible ready, putting in markers in places at certain chapters, and making sure that there were psalm-books for the two assisting ministers, as well as one for himself. It would be all Gaelic in the church apart from the second Table which would be in English. In the hall the junior minister would conduct a service in English before adjourning along with that part of the congregation to join with the main gathering in the church for the communion. Then you would hear the minister in prayer, pleading with the Most High for a blessing, to make this day a glorious day for all with a special visit of His Presence.

It is his day, the Lord's day, his Master's day. It is his Feast day because it is the Feast of his Lord and he is the

Lord's servant, guiding his people, leading them in thought and heart in the ordered practice of the historic church to partake of the Sacrament and the privilege of the sanctuary so that it be not profaned.   Therefore a banner unseen but unmistakably real, sets this building of stone apart from any other, as the sacred House of God. 'Thou hast given a banner to them that fear thee.'[1]   On it is the word *Holiness*, without which no man shall see God. 'And holiness becometh Thy House, O Lord, for ever.'[2]

It was customary for an older minister to take the main services, like that of the "Question' day on Friday and the 'action' service of the Sabbath morning, and a younger minister to assist with the other services. Thus the younger ministers came at the time we speak of, men like MacDougall, Hope Street; MacLeod, Greenock; Aitken, Rogart; Lamont, Stoer. Later in the post-war years others would come to Aultbea.   Ross, Bettyhill; Martin, Carrbridge; Nicolson, Plockton; MacAulay, Back; Gollan, Shiskine; Fraser, Wick; Murray, Skerray; Morrison, Stoer; and his brother Morrison, Lochmaddy; MacFarlane, Kilmuir; Murray, Carloway; MacLeod, Portree. There must have been many more but these latter younger ones became known to the writer when their visit coincided with his vacations at home in the summer after 1945. You can understand that the list is not exhaustive. Five visiting ministers were asked to assist at communions each year by my father for his own charge.   As interim-moderator for Gairloch during fourteen years of vacancy he had to engage another six ministers from other parishes in the Gaelic speaking church of Highland people. Even the correspondence connected with this continual administrative work was not inconsiderable. Remember that there was no

1.Psalm 60:4   2. Psalm 93:5

telephone at that time.

Here we speak of the heights of Mr. MacKinnon's ministry, his first twenty years. In a sense, though parallel with the dark shadows of the Depression years and the grim destitution this brought to the urban south, as well as the strictures of War, this was the last bright flowering of an age. For better or worse it would be replaced. But in the spiritual sense, it had an unsurpassed glory for those who knew it, and that included young children, who were stamped forever with the vivid colours of its powerful spiritual, cultural and linguistic impressions.

And without question Aultbea represented the Highland church in the cultural, historical and linguistic uniqueness of that age, in a balanced, co-ordinated unity of a parish ministry, with only peripheral ecclesiastical defections or accretion, to qualify this. Thus at this climactic event of the Communion season, all else deferred to the ecclesiastical authority. Schools were closed on the Fast Day, as also shops. All work ceased and in effect Thursday was considered a Sabbath. On this 'day of humiliation and prayer', the day and the life of the whole community were brought to God, like vessels to be sanctified and filled with grace, so that there would be a sense, an overwhelming sense of corporate blessing through this penitential preparation of individual hearts.

The Communion Season lasted from Thursday until Monday. Thursday was the Fast Day, Friday, the 'Question' Day, Saturday was the Preparation Day, all leading up to the climax on Sabbath. This was the tradition in all the Presbyterian churches in the Highlands and it is still followed, with some variations, to this day.

No wonder then that on Sabbath morning, at every

junction and crossroads, people, walking, coming by car or bus, turned down the road from north, south, east and west, and made their way to Aultbea, with gladness and limitless expectation, for the great day of the feast had come.

Come with me to the Aultbea church on a Communion Sabbath morning. Look round and see the picture within this beautiful church. Close your eyes and yet see, as the curtains of time are drawn back. Now you hear the congregation break into singing, the incomparable singing of exquisite human praise led by the precentor. In the pulpit the host minister has his two colleagues. The 'action' sermon is now over. The worshippers from the English service have come into the sanctuary, some hundred or so, during the singing. The body of the church is full; the galleries at the back and sides are also well filled. The whole architectural symmetry of the house of God comes into its own as people dominate over the material. Yet there is a harmony in which the beautiful arches, rising gracefully above the supporting pillars of the galleries, complement the human gathering, and give all a picture of perfection. What a choice day this is! Seats are full of families. They are there from every hamlet in Locheweside, and from Little LochBroom right to Badluarach and Badtrailleach. The Gairloch minister, Rev. Hector MacRury, is there, having assisted with services on the Fast Day at Poolewe church. Friends from neighbouring congregations are there. MacDonald Ullapool would eventually come to Gairloch south. This Mr. MacDonald was a particularly gracious preacher, whom young people loved, in both Gaelic and English. He came from Uig in Lewis.

In the latron over the years just for a season, the mind can see a choice selection of spiritually-minded elders. Added to the Session of Aultbea are those from the 'other side', Poolewe, Cove and Inverasdale and also from Little Lochbroom. Then you have guests from Gairloch, like Finlayson, MacIver *Kowloon*, Laing, Campbell and MacRae, John MacPherson. All complement the numerous faces of men and women, and children in the body of the church, devout worshippers now identified with the believing people of God.

Now we follow the steps leading to the dispensing of the Sacrament. The senior minister who took the 'action' sermon will also dispense the first sitting, the Gaelic Table. What a noble list of gracious ministers fulfilled these duties! This day Rev. Donald Munro D.D. of Ferintosh, was meant to be here, but because of indisposition his place was taken by Dr. Munro's neighbour, Rev. Roderick Finlayson, a native of Lochcarron, and at this time minister in Urray.

Mr. Finlayson, though young, was a minister of intellectual stature and profound spiritual insights. He would yet give distinguished service to his Lord. On a more human note, he had made his mark in a small way as an amateur boxer, when serving in the Great War. In the Second World War he would hold a senior post of responsibility in the chaplaincy service of the military. Meantime he filled in for Dr. Munro at the Communion, carrying out the special duty of baptising the youngest of the six daughters of MacKinnon Aultbea. The little girl was given the name, Donalda Munro, a name of honour, indeed, being called after Dr. Munro.

But now the singing of Psalm 118, a communion hymn fills the church with solemn melody. Crowds in the galleries can be seen straining forward, caught up in singular attentiveness to the mystery being unfolded in the liturgy and symbolism before them. Not a few of these will one day

be constrained by compulsive grace and Christ's atoning love
to fill the ranks of the older generation as these leave earth's
scene for their eternal home.

The senior elders now come in from the hall, bearing the
bread and the wine. The white loaf is half cut into slices on
the napkin-covered silver tray. The art of cutting the
communion bread is a secret of the senior elders. It will be
passed on to successors. This is so designed, that the bread
will still be broken by the presiding minister in obedience to
Christ's command, right in the church before the people. The
manse children get a privileged close-up of all this. For the
manse seat is at the side of the pulpit, only a few feet from
the door. On their memories forever is stamped the indelible
picture of the bearded patriarchs, Murdo and John the elders,
as these overtly unique symbols of godliness and Christian
grace were known, now slowly and reverently bring in the
bread and the two communion cups and place them on a white
linen covered table.

The precentor stops. Mr. MacKinnon rises in the pulpit.
He addresses the people, *a' cur garadh timchioll air bord
an Tighearna,* (fencing) the Table. In some places the visiting
minister does this duty. But as a rule the host minister who
knows his people, claims this duty as his own to discharge.
The words are addressed to both onlooker and participant, an
edifying Scriptural instruction from Christ's command in St.
Luke:22, and St. Paul's letter in Ist Corinthians, chapter 11.
Here there is no harsh literalism, nor legal presumption that
might destroy the tender spiritual blooms of the young
tentative faith. There is instead an overt and incontrovertible
note of evangelical love. This is MacKinnon Aultbea's forte,
speaking of the heart and the motions of the soul. One has a

sense that he is standing at the open door of the Room of Mercy, as he speaks of the links that bind believers, not only as the saving work of grace to Christ in their spiritual experience, but also to the church, visible and invisible, through their witness in their generation. There is nothing added nor taken away from the clear simple mandate stated by both the Lord and the apostle. The Table is the Lord's. Those who love him, and in life do not contradict their profession of faith, are hereby invited to 'remember the Lord's death till he come.' The minister closes his words, words of encouragement and spiritual guidance in reading the relevant words or authoritative warrant in Ist Corinthians chapter 11 for administering the Sacrament, that encapsulate unequivocally, the characteristics of a professing communicant in Christ's church.

He now asks communicants to come forward to sit at the white linen-covered tables, ingeniously converted from the centre front pews. At the same time he calls upon the precentor to lead in singing some more verses of the communion psalm, 118. What an accompaniment to this act of solemn witness to the Christian Faith! The precentor chants out the line,

'*Cha-n fhaigh mi bas, ach maireann beo,*' 'I shall not die but live.' The congregation follow, the words sung to the Gaelic tune Coleshill accentuating the profound affirmation of salvation's triumph. Slowly men and women rise from their seats, walk down the aisles, and sit at the tables.

Time now is irrelevant. The beauty of holiness fills the House of God. Nothing can block out the prevailing sense of heavenly things. One and all in the sea of human faces, become captive to the glory of it all.

The precentor goes on, '*is innseam oibre Dhe* '. His voice lingers in the air, 'the works of God discover.' All repeat, in a continuous flowing wave of musical sound, that rises in positive projection of praise to the Throne of Heaven. The wavering grace notes emitted from hearts moved with human emotion and souls where the cup of salvation 'runneth over', linger in a blend of exquisite melody, charging the atmosphere with a powerful spiritual essence.

Christian experience is mirrored in the precentor's words as he chants,

'*Throm-smachdaich Dia mi ach gu bas.*' The Lord hath me chastised sore.'

Then the last line is chanted out and sung in unison,

'*Cha d'thug e thairis mi.*' 'But not to death given over.' With this is a note of overcoming, a testimony of continued victory, 'Hitherto the Lord hath helped me,' a reflection of a working daily faith that never takes God for granted.

Nearly all the seats are now taken. The elders are in their places having collected the communion tokens and are ready to serve the Tables. Mr. MacKinnon leans over the pulpit and taps the precentor on the shoulder, with the Psalm-book. He brings the singing to a stop. The minister again calls communicants to come forward, during the singing of the next verse.

The air is charged with spiritual resonance as the outward symbolism corresponds to inward spiritual experience. Indeed there is an overflow of grace itself. Many strangers to its power and many impressionable young people are themselves touched by the wonderful words of life that speak of salvation, free and full, and joy abundant.

Hear the verse, as the precentor sings out this last call,

this last invitation to come, resting upon the merits of the Saviour, to sit down at his Table with his people. This is a moment of great solemnity. How many hearts are moved; how many people pondered on the momentous consequences of 'holding back' or 'going forward'. Who can know these things? Only heaven is witness to the complex interaction of positive and negative thoughts that so often prevented simple obedience to witness on earth to the Saviour's redeeming love and atoning sacrifice. The precentor chants each line in turn,

> *O fosglaibh dhomh gu farsuinn reidh*
> *geatan an ionracais:*
> *Is racham orra-san a steach;*
> *Iehobhah molaidh mis.'*

English:
> O set ye open unto me
> the gates of righteousness;
> Then will I enter into them,
> and I the Lord will bless.

The ministers go down from the pulpit during the singing. The senior visiting preacher who took the 'action sermon' presides, standing at the end of the table with the communion elements before him on the little table. The last person to rise and take a place at the Gaelic Table is the minister's wife. As she has done so, her minister husband takes his place beside her. The usual liturgical order of dispensing the Sacrament is followed. What more can be said. Words can never adequately describe the motions of the spirit as the souls of believers feed upon the Body and Blood of their Lord.

Now the process is repeated, when the English Table will

be celebrated with the host minister presiding. The communicants rise during further singing and are replaced by more communicants. The Wine and Bread is renewed. The seats are now filled without any urging. This is the last Table. There are some who will not be here again for their earthly journey is coming to a close. Then there are several reasons for others. A few are guests from away. There are a few strangers who are sojourning locally and are professing Christians. The Table of the Lord is open to all who love the Lord. Thus an officer from the naval base or ratings from the ships are given to feel at home at this Highland Communion. There are others, from the south, English brides who came north to live in the Gaelic community with soldiers returning from the First World War. One thinks of the wife of the Laide elder, Morty Mor, (Big Murdo) Maclennan. The English Table served all who loved the Lord.

Then there were those who had another reason. They love the Lord, and they also have a special place in their hearts for their own minister. He has cared for them as their pastor; he has directed them to the 'green pastures ' where they have met the Good Shepherd; he has instructed them in the way that they should walk; he has comforted them in sorrow; he has showed them the love of Christ and the wisdom of God, in all the unfathomable fulness of both. Now as trees planted by a river they bear fruit. And it is their special joy to sit at the Table now as he dispenses the Sacrament.

In this situation, my father especially, brings the guests to the locus of heaven's stores and uses the graphic imagery of his poetic gifts to describe the blessings that belong to the 'people of God.' He stops and calls them to look through the window of time and gaze at the jewels that make Christ's crown more glorious than any other. And he speaks of the miracle for these eternal jewels of holy beauty and honour have been transformed like metamorphosed rocks, from the earthly frailty of human beings. This is one of his favourite themes. But above all the minister speaks of Christ Himself, and His Person. He leads his listeners to what is none other than the Gate of Heaven and the Door of the Mercy Seat. He brings the people to see that they worship a Crucified but also a Risen Lord. He enlarges on Christ's love; he dwells upon Christ's Sufferings; he illustrates the efficacy of the Atonement; he extols Christ as victor and intercessor. He closes, pointing out that all this belongs to the believer to make the heart rejoice here, as a child of God, and also as heir, to an inheritance with the saints in light in the hereafter.

Now the precentor leads with the singing of verses from Psalm 103 to the tune Kilmarnock. The house of the Lord is full of the vocal praise, the melody of a thousand voices, lifted up in the matchless cadences of the Gaelic language. The singing rises and falls in resonant alternating waves, perfectly synchronised together in a glorious unity, to the one Triune God, Father, Son and Spirit, Architect and Maker of the Universe, and Redeemer of Mankind. What a feast for a minister! Mr. MacKinnon's cup is full this day, yes, and overflowing. The heavy responsibilities of his office have been discharged. All has gone well. The Lord was present with his people. And now they adjourn until the evening.

In the evening the church is full to capacity. The manse children take it all in. They can look round, from their seats, facing the congregation. All round there is a sea of faces. Many though spiritually careless, though busy with the world, make a point of being there. The atmosphere is charged with drama--the drama of the possible. This night, may be recorded as 'the tale of the expected.' There is no limit to the expectations for God backs every cheque of faith that is drawn on the Bank of Heaven with its unsearchable Riches of Mercy and Grace, Forgiveness and Pardon from the spiritual mine of Calvary where the Son of God was crucified. The waves of possibility are not limited but may flow from heaven to knock down the pride of the most unlikely and bring him or her to know the saving power of a merciful and loving God.   There is no doubt, that this night, a soul here, another there, will be quickened, the seed sown over the years past, dormant in the cold heart of unbelief, will now germinate in the warmth of the Church's womb, and through the praying of many people who with the minister, make it their business to gather in the harvest for the Lord. The evening service has an evangelical theme. In this, the purpose will have clear definition. While that of the morning was to 'remember the Death of Christ in the Sacrament,' in the evening it would be to call the unconverted to come to Christ, to repent, to open their hearts to the overtures of heaven, to knock at the door of mercy, to call upon the Lord that the 'washing and regeneration of the spirit' may bring realisation to their lives, of the elective power of saving grace and divine love.

We speak now in general of the many communion occasions. The figures of noted evangelistic pleaders come back over the years of recollection. Norman Campbell Dingwall, a favourite and frequent visitor to the Aultbea communion, and also linked to my mother who was blessed by his preaching along with many others in the spiritual nursery of Stoer. His voice has a peculiar drawing power, as his big frame leans over the pulpit. How many heard that voice calling sinners to life, in the name of Christ, 'Awake thou that sleepest and arise from the dead, And Christ shall give thee light.'[1] Or as one person from Lochinver testified, Annie MacLeod, who was employed in the service of the Countess of Cromarty in the old mansion of the MacKenzies at Kildary, she could not forget Campbell Dingwall pleading with hearers at a Stoer communion to come to Christ- for this reason given by the Lord himself to Israel, '*seadh, le gradh siorruidh ghradhaich mi thu; uime sin tharruing mi thu le caoimhneas gradhach.*' 'Yea I have loved thee with an everlasting love: therefore with lovingkindness have I drawn thee.'[2] Annie rested all her hopes in this life and the life to come on this text fulfilled in Christ.

Then there is Mr. MacKinnon's classmate, MacIver Carloway. His is the face of a saint, one that mirrors a work of grace and a love for Christ, that makes people feel that Christ's love must indeed surpass all knowledge. Thus there is an effect before he begins preaching, as he intones his text with grace, that is unmistakably part of his own life. ' *Oir tha gradh Chriosd 'gar co-eigneachadh.*' 'For the love of Christ constraineth us...'[3] One thinks of quiet humble men like MacLeod Snizort, MacDonald Sleat, Ferguson Lochranza. These ministers and many more called people to repent and in the articulated presentation of the 'Good News', laid constraints on the conscience, of the spiritual challenge before one and all to respond to Christ's invitation,

'Come unto me, all ye that labour and are heavy laden, and I will give you rest. Take my yoke upon you, and learn of me; for I am meek and lowly in heart: and ye shall find rest for your souls. For my yoke is easy, and my burden is light.'[1]

It is impossible to forget the singing, led by able precentors.

1. Ephesians 5:14   2. Jeremiah 31:3   3. 2 Corinthians 5:14

This evening the guest precentors are Duncan Fraser, from GlenUrquhart, a contractor now residing in Poolewe. He is a trained singer, whose brother James Fraser succeeeded MacKenzie Plockton, and eventually became a professor; the other is known as Kenny *Ghobha*, originally from Inverasdale. He was a Gaelic Mod Medallist in his youth. He was touched by grace and since then, the secular songs however beautiful, were replaced in his repertoire by the immortal praise of God, especially the Psalms.

A hundred years could not suppress the memory of the praise lifted to heaven in the evening service of a Communion Sabbath in Aultbea. How could anyone forget Kenny Ghobh' leading the singing of Psalm 42 to the tune Stornoway! What incomparable waves of sublime feeling flow through one's whole being as the scene of that Sabbath evening fills the screen of the mind, unchanged, unfaded over the years from the shelves of memory! And with the visual imagery of the people of that day, no interval of time can suppress the glorious melody of praise, clothed in the excellence of precenting by a trained singer whose heart is at one with the words of his song. One hears him yet introducing the Psalm with the first two lines,

> *Mar thogras fiadh na sruthan uisge'*
> *ie buaradh ard gu geur,*

English:

> Like as the hart for water brooks
> In thirst doth pant and bray;

The congregation joins in, with the exquisite beauty of the tune Stornoway, as if it were custom made for the acoustics of the Aultbea church. Then there is the last singing before

---

1. Matthew 11:28-30

the benediction, that great doxology of the church, Psalm 72, verses 17-19, that attributes all power, blessing and dominion to the Eternal Son, whose name shall endure forever. The tune is Torwood.

1   Bidh 'ainm-san buan gu suthain sior,
    co-mhairean ris a ghrein;
    Is annsan beannaichear gach slogh;
    's beannaichear leo e fein.

2 Beannaicht' gu robh an Tighearn Dia,
    Dia Israeil a ghnath
    An ti a mhain ni miorbhuile
    le treis is neart a laimh.

3 Beannaicht'gu robh gu siorruidh buan
    ainm gloirmhor uasal fein;
    Lionadh a ghloir gach uile thir,
    Amen, agus Amen.

English:

1   His name forever shall endure;
    last like the sun it shall:
    Men shall be bless'd in him and bless'd
    all nations shall him call.

2   Now blessed be the Lord our God,
    the God of Israel,
    For he alone doth wondrous works,
    in glory that excel.

3   And blessed be his glorious name
    to all eternity:
    The whole earth let his glory fill.
    Amen, so let it be.

Sequel

The great day is over. On the Monday there is a kind of epilogue when the benediction is pronounced at the close of the service in the morning. The final service will be in the evening. Meantime there is the last dinner of hospitality in the manse.

After the meal in the dining room, the company gather in the drawing room for the last worship. Elders and guests come in, so that there are about twenty souls in all including the ministers, parents and children. There is a hush upon all. The room is charged with a sense of great solemnity. By tradition, John the elder leads the singing, from Psalm 84. The young children gaze into his face.They know him well since they could toddle through to the dining room on a Sunday to stand at his knee. They know his kindly ways and they do not forget the 'sweeties' which he always had in his pocket for them. They knew that his supply of sweeties could never run out because he had his shop in Mellon Charles full of sweeties in jars on the top shelf. The singing reaches a climax with the last verse.

> Sior-ghluasaidh iad mar sin gun sgios,
> a' dol o neart gu neart:
> An Sion nochdar iad fadheoidh
> an lathair Dhe nam feart.

English:

> So they from strength unwearied go
> still forward unto strength,
>
> Until in Sion they appear
> before the Lord at length.

My father closes the worship with a prayer. The Thanksgiving service follows in the evening, bringing the great communion season in Aultbea to a close. On Tuesday morning the guests in the manse take their leave. As one and all leave, a silence obtains in the manse. Another communion has come and gone. The children wish that it would have continued. But nothing in this life continues for ever.

After one of these communions, Mr. MacKinnon pondered on the joy and blessedness of the fellowship of colleagues and all the people in the gatherings since the previous Wednesday when the ministers had arrived. In himself he felt the pain of parting and missed the collective sharing of heaven's benediction in the services of the sanctuary round the Word and Sacrament. It was natural for him to put these thoughts in verse. He penned this hymn, which some fifty years later is sung in homes and at informal gatherings of fellowship in the Island of Lewis, at least in one community, namely Lochs. This was not found in past copies of the Free Church Record. Rev Donald MacDonald, minister in Bernera, sent it to the Gaelic editor Rev Duncan MacLeod, Helmsdale, who had it published in the January issue of the Free Church Record in the Gaelic portion, 1995. We give it here with a translation.

Deireadh an Orduigh

Seisd: Eiribh rachamaid a so
        Eiribh rachamaid a so
        Eiribh rachamaid a so
        Oir chan eil fois gu fuireach ann.

1   Sfheudar dhomhsa 'ndiugh bhi triall
     's m'aghaidh do an ard an iar
     Mi dealachadh ri pobuill De
     's gur cianal tha mi faireachdainn.

2   De math dhomhsa dhol a dh'inns'
mar tha faireachainn mo chridh'
Do'n mhuinntir nach tuig mi
gu diblidh ni iad fanoid orm.

3   Chan eil fois ann fon a ghrein
ach an fhois a th' ann an Criosd
So an fhois air nach tig crioch
gu siorruidh anns na flaitheanas.

4   Is iongantach an Soisgeul fein
bheatha th'ann do phobuill De
Ni E'nt-ordugh dhaibh na neamh
gus am feum iad bhi dealachadh.

5   Na biodh campar oirbh no gruaim
Mu bhi dealachadh Di-Luain
Thig an latha 'san teid sinn suas
's bidh 'n t-ordugh buan 's cha dealaich sinn.

6   Ma tha canan ann do ghradh
air an talamh anns gach ait'
Cia mar bhios e gu 'h-ard
'san aite tha cur thairis leis?

7   Sud am far am bheil an ceol
chan eil iomradh ann air bron
Miltean miltean ann is coir
a ' seinn air gloir Immanuel.

8   Gu bheil biodh ac' air a bheinn
bhios ri deanamh daoine tinn
Mil is bainn' aca ga roinn
Air oighreachan nam flaitheanas.

9   Sud far 'm bi an comann cruinn
air an glanadh o gach foill

Anns an trusgan fear na bainns'
A ' seinn le Haleluia.

10   Rachadh dhachaidh do gach ait
air ur beannachadh o'n ard
Cuimhnichibh aig caithir-grais
  Na cairdean a bha maille ruibh.

English: **The End of the Communion**

Chorus: Let us rise and leave this place
    Let us rise and leave this place
    Let us rise and leave this place
    For here there is no lasting rest.

1   This day I have to take my leave
My face again to westward turn.
Away from those that love the Lord
A parting that I always mourn.

2   What profit is it to tell abroad
the deep emotion of my heart,
To those who cannot understand;
They mock me as a man apart.

3   There is no rest beneath the sun
but that repose that's found in Christ.
This is the rest that endless lasts
eternally in heaven's bliss.

4   How wonderful the Gospel is,
the life it gives thy people dear.
It makes the ordinance like heaven
until at last they part from here.

5   Be not vexed and be not sad
that on Monday we must sever.

The day will come we'll rise on high
Communion there will last for ever.

6   If there is language in your love
upon on the earth where e'er you live
Think how it must be on high
Where He'll eternal blessings give.

7   There you have the music true
without a note of pain to tell.
Thousands, thousands, many more
Sing glory of Immanuel.

8   There is food upon the Mount
Making people long for more.
Milk and honey to divide
Among his heirs, in heaven's store.

9   His people will be gathered there
Washed from all deceit and sin,
In the bridegroom's garments clad,
Halleluiahs loud they sing.

10   Disperse to homes with blessings rich.
Wheree'er you are, be of good cheer.
Remember at the Throne of Grace
All friends you met that gathered here.

Chapter 29

Anecdotes of Colleagues

Aultbea belonged to the presbytery of Lochcarron which comprised the congregations in Wester Ross from Kintail and Glenelg in the south to Ullapool and Coigeach to the north. The natural meeting-place was Achnasheen, which was reached from the west and from the east, in part by the regular train on the Kyle of Lochalsh/ Inverness route. Mr. MacKinnon along with ministers and elders from Gairloch and Aultbea area travelled to the presbytery by road.

Rev Robert Park was minister in Coigeach for a short time, prior to his induction as minister in the historic congregation of Strontian. Assisting him at a communion in Strontian in 1962, I was curiously intrigued with the wealth of stories he could relate, some of them from his time in the Presbytery of Lochcarron.

Mr. Park recalled once sailing in the Minch on Rev. Donald Ferguson's ex-fishing smack as it battled against a strong southwesterly to reach Tarbert in Harris. He had been having a nap in the foc'sle, the sleeping quarters in the bow, when the wind had got up. Mr. Ferguson, the skipper, anticipating the gale, battened down the fore-hatch from the deck above. The gale brought large seas aboard, as the hardy Zulu cut its way homeward through the seas against the headwind. For two hours Robert Park was locked below in this the most uncomfortable part of the boat, with the bow rising and plunging like a bucking horse as it met the waves. Thrown about by the motion, his situation was doubly uncomfortable as water spewed in fine streams from the deck above, giving him an experience of intermittent short sharp showers of salt water rain. The experience made a lasting impression on him. He told how he shouted until he was hoarse to no avail. So that he had no rest of body or mind, nor had he any idea what was going on outside except the awful sensations of his predicament, until at last the relative calm of a weather shore brought shelter and relief. The fact is that St. Kilda born Rev Donald Ferguson was afflicted with severe deafness, and did not have his hearing aid in commission en route. In the wheelhouse of his boat with the Kelvin 26/30 petrol/paraffin engine faithfully but loudly pounding away, he could not possibly hear his crew, Robert Park, in the foc'sle, where he envisaged him sleeping down below in perfect peace.

Rev Donald Ferguson, the minister/sailor was a close friend of my father's. Born on St. Kilda, he was minister in Lochranza on the island of Arran for many years. Every year he recommissioned his converted fishing boat, and would take young people from Glasgow on a holiday cruise. Many of them never forgot these trips on the minister's boat. And the minister did not forget his calling. Each young person was given a pamphlet with the story of God's redeeming love in Christ Jesus. He lived to be over a hundred years of age.

Robert Park spoke of the way things were done in the presbytery of Lochcarron. 'Get things done' was the motto, as expeditiously as possible and with the minimum of paperwork. He told how little time was wasted at meetings, in part due to the strictures of time dictated by the limited period the trains from east and west stopped at Achnasheen. There were presbytery meetings at other locations, inductions and congregational visitations. But statutory meetings were held as a rule at Achnasheen, where routine matters only were on the agenda. These meetings were short and sweet. (Achnasheen was the location where the constitutionalists met in 1900, as a remnant holding up the standard of the Church of Scotland-Free when the majority of ministers were cajoled into giving up their historic ecclesiastical principles in favour of a do-it-yourself Voluntaryism.)

You could say that the presbytery, which has so often bogged down ministers and elders in a whole time-wasting day, was kept in perspective, and in the case of the presbytery of Lochcarron, barring some special circumstance, was reduced to what can only be called a 'whistle-stop' meeting, with the privilege of a good social dinner for its members.

This was Mr. Park's first presbytery meeting after coming to Coigeach, which was then a ministerial charge. He had set off in the early morning by car to Ullapool. From there he took the Mail bus over the *Diridh* road or the Destitution road, to the railway station at Garve. From Garve he caught the daily west-bound train from Inverness and arrived at Achnasheen in roughly the same condition as the train itself— very thirsty. To explain, Achnasheen, was like an oasis in an African desert. Situated in the middle of something very similar it was rightly named as 'the place of storms.' But it had a special value. It was the 'watering stop' for the trains on the lifeline to the north west and the Hebrides, the

Inverness/Kyle of Lochalsh Railway line. As a rule each day both east and westbound trains crossed here. The leaving hour of the train from Kyle depended upon the arrival time of the McBrayne steamer plying across the Minch from Kyle to Stornoway. One train had to wait at Achnasheen for the other as there was only a single railway line. The result was that ministers and elders could come from both directions and a presbytery meeting could be held, utilizing the period the trains were in at the station. My father with the Gairloch/ Aultbea members had the advantage of enjoying a good dinner in the Achnasheen hotel before the trains pulled in with the other members of presbytery. It is also true that at times business was despatched at what might be called a working dinner, especially when my father's friend and neighbour Ronald Fraser took his old car up the glen from Lochcarron, using the trip to do some visiting of parishioners living in the glen, especially in the Achnashellach area.

The presbytery of Lochcarron was flexible. Members were not slaves to the Standing Orders which were considered as expedients to get things done and were suspended should they impede decisions of common sense. One thinks of the sheer stupidity where in the 1980's the Canadian Parliament in Ottawa had the bells ringing for a week, calling striking members to return for a quorum. The slave to expediency cannot distinguish between its rules and the greater law of principle, which they are formulated to implement.

On this occasion, Mr. Park, the novice minister from Coigeach, arrived at the station just as the Inverness-bound train, having topped up its boiler with water, was about to leave. That was his last chance to get back home that day. He told how terribly thirsty he was and hungry too. He was greeted by the members of presbytery, right there on the platform. Half of the members had already climbed aboard the west-bound train from which he disembarked. The others were standing there on the platform, with business obviously now over. Just think of it, this new young minister, arriving after a five hour journey at his first meeting of presbytery. And all the seasoned 'old hands' happily coming to a conclusion of church business, without letting circumstances in the least way bring any fretting or harassment. All he could remember was the pronouncement by the moderator, of the closing benedictory prayer. Then his brethren counselled him to run for it as fast as he could or he would lose his train back to Garve and be stranded. He had to run and cross the pedestrian overhead bridge without any more ado. The guard's whistle blew and he just managed to climb aboard the train before it picked up speed and left the station. The experience had left him with mixed emotions. While he had to admire the speed with which the Lochcarron Presbytery expedited business, he regarded that long day as a marathon. It was a weary Rev Robert Park that turned off the ignition of his little Austin late that night at the Coigeach manse.

It was thus that the experience of Mr. Park in his description of his first meeting of the Presbytery of Lochcarron reflected the 'get things done' policy with minimum drag from unnecessary baggage. Following this principle in its many-sided aspects, Mr. MacKinnon pursued his calling. This is not to say that Highland ministers did not take time to relax and mix the social element with that of church work. Many presbytery meetings were protracted, especially when members were able to take their cars as roads were tarmacadamized and thus were much easier on the vehicles. Also the development of hard-wearing tires made punctures, which were a real 'trial' for Highland ministers in the early days of my father's ministry, if not things of the past, at least few and far between. Sometimes two spare wheels were carried to obviate the possibility of being stuck even on a short journey in an isolated area.

There was a wise sharing of the social and business. Thus hotel staff were always ready with a first class dinner for presbytery or a good afternoon tea. Brethren despatched their business and enjoyed sharing anecdotes in the comfortable surroundings of the hotel lounge. My father loved such meetings with his brethren. A company of ministers who are also friends is a treat to listen to in conversation when they are relaxed. The stories they exchange in the peer atmosphere after their church meetings are full of humour and enjoyment. This is a veritable recharging of their batteries, providing a fresh addition of humour in the form of a stockpile of anecdotes in the coming days for congregational purposes at speaking occasions such as wedding receptions. MacKinnon Aultbea liked to have a pocketful of stories and was ever a keen collector of fresh material. Furthermore, quite apart from diversionary entertainment, he found in practice that using humour was an effective expedient for defusing a crisis so often arising from misunderstandings, in the course of ordinary congregational meetings. The social aspect of presbytery life was a continuing source of keeping fresh, a necessary requirement for every public speaker as well as the clergy.

The liaison with other ministers, and the consequent familiarity with other congregations maintained a sense of corporate historic witness. Thus even the commemorative stones of past spiritual heroes were dear to him. Assisting for the first time at the Communion in Lochcarron, he stopped on the way out of the township to look at the graves in the old historic churchyard. As he looked on the grave of Maighstir Lachlann, the mighty minister of the past, and on those of the other noted servants of the Lord, he put his thoughts into verse. Here is the poem he composed.

Sgir Lochcarroin

1

O! Sgir Lochcarroin nam frithibh's nam beannaibh
Cha n-e brioghmhorachd t-fhearainn dh-fhag maireann do   chliu
Cha n-e treunadas d-fhearaibh ann am batalaibh neimheil
Dh'fhag reusonan d-onoir cho ionmholt is ur,
Ach gras Mhaighstir Lachlainn mar fhaidh 's marAbstol,
'S cha bhasaich d'eachdraidh gus am paisgear na duil.

2

Tha aireamh de' d' mhacaibh ro laidir 'san t soisgeul
A sasuchadh ocrach le focal na reit,
'Se urnuighean Lachlainn 's uir bhi 'nad achlais
Dh' fhag druchd air do bhailtean 'sa choisinn dhuit e.
'S ro chubhraidh am boltrach tha ag ungadh do lochan
'Se tighinn o'n lagan 'sna choidil an treun.

3

Na cairdean a chluinneas na roinn so a leanas
A rinn mi an cabhaig 's mi airtnealach sgith
Air dhomh bhi air m' aineol am baile Lochcarroin
A seirm na naigheachd do'n anam bheir sith,
Tuigeadh iad uile gu'm bheil mi am shuidhe
Aig duslach a 'churaidh gun duine ach mi fhin.

4

Tha te a bha ainmeil thalad fo tholomon
'Sni a h-iomradh aig deireadh mo dhan,
Ceit mhor a bhean ionmhuinn b'fhad i fo iomagan,
Chluinneadh na tulaich i tuireadh gach la;
Ach fhuaradh i dhachaidh is fuasgladh o'masladh
'Sa peacaidhean sgreataidh gu'n do mhaith Fear a graidh.

5

'Se iocshlaint Iehobhah a ghlan i o' neoghloin
O! innleachd ro ghlormhoir 's tu dochas nan al,
O! dheas laimh na morachd mo thaic is mo chomhnadh
Troimh an teich romham Iordan 's pog mi am bas;
O! tarruing le d' chordaibh m'anam an comhnadh
Mach o'n otraich gu solas do ghrais.

Translation:

Parish of Lochcarron

1

O, Lochcarron of the deer-forests and the mountains
It is not the beauty of your land that perpetuates your fame
It is not the prowess of your menfolk in the grim battles of war
that justifies your honour as pure and ever new,
But the grace of Reverend Lachlan as a prophet and apostle;
thus your history will last until all mankind is no more.

2

The number of your heroes is large in the Gospel,
Satisfying the hungry with the Word of Peace,
The prayers of Rev Lachlan, his dust in the hollow
have left dew on your walls, and earned you the praise
It's fragrant the perfume that lingers over your waters
And rises from the low ground where sleep all your braves.

3

Friends reading the verses that now are to follow
Composed when I was tired and drowsy,
Finding myself in Lochcarron with which I was unacquainted,
Preaching the news that brings peace to the soul,
They'll understand that now I am sitting
at the dust of the hero alone with myself.

4

Another's at rest over there 'neath the hillock,
With praise of her I will end my song,
Great Kate, beloved woman, distressed in spirit so long
The hills were witness to her cries and her tears
But she won in her homecoming relief from reproach,
For her Saviour forgave all her mortifying sins.

5

It's the balm of Jehovah that cleansed her uncleanness'
O invention so glorious, the hope of your offspring,
O Right Hand of Majesty, my support and my help
That flees the Jordan before me, in which I shall kiss death.
Let the cords of your grace, my soul draw forever,
From the mire of despair to the hope of your love.

****

Many stories are told of ministers, and their eccentricities, especially the bachelors. One, Rev Walter MacQuarrie, minister at Knockbain in Easter Ross, was crossing the Kessock Ferry to Inverness from the Black Isle. The ferry was not large. Passengers were standing on the deck near Mr MacQuarrie, a formidable figure, tall and imposing in his black clerical dress and distinctive non-Roman white clerical bow tie. MacQuarrie was a rightwing conservative by any standards as well as being a bachelor. One of his parishioners found himself standing next to the minister. He had been careless about church attendance and now was quite nervous, finding himself right beside his spiritual boss and a very straight-speaking one at that. He was very solicitous in his enquiries for the minister's health as they shook hands. Then he got excited as the minister's eyes searched his face. He had a black-out of memory recall and for the moment forgot that the minister was a bachelor. The result was that he nervously added without thinking, 'And how is Mrs MacQuarrie?' To which MacQuarrie, answered crisply, 'I never heard her complaining.'

Another minister whose parish was in Sutherland was one day working in the manse garden, when the duchess came up the drive in her big shiny black chauffeur-driven limousine. He greeted her with conventional politeness. Then, suddenly becoming conscious of his rough garden clothes, he added, 'If I had known you were coming I would have put off my trousers.' Happily the lady did not misconstrue his intentions, and he often told the story against himself.

The manse family were close students of the behaviour of others, parishioners and visitors who came to the manse, but especially those ministers who stayed for almost a week at a time when assisting at communions. One minister MacGowan used to rise early and dressed in a full-size striped bathing suit with the trouser part right down beyond the knees. At daybreak, he would run down from the manse, over the road and plunge into the sea for a healthy swim. This was considered rather eccentric behaviour for a minister. The manse boys would look out of their bedroom window, trying to distinguish MacGowan the minister in his spectacular striped swimsuit, from the mackerel fish or the royal salmon as they did their acrobatic exercises, a regular sight that broke the calm waters of the summer morning.

However gifted and zealous a minister of the Word may be, he is still only one person, admittedly a key one, as a member of a team. Mr MacKinnon was always aware of this. From the beginning he saw himself as a humble servant of the Lord, given the exalted privileges of his calling, yet as it were, only one player on the field of service for Christ's winning team, against the many rival teams who compete for victory and the crown of Christ's kingdom. But not only so, he did not lose sight of the fact that there were a thousand other teams in every cell of the church's structure, similar or dissimilar to that of his own in its sphere of service. Always there was this concept of being part of a team, on the congregational level, on the denominational level and in the greater enterprise of the church in its catholic mission in the contemporary age. This sense of being part of a team permeated conversation with his family as it touched on many different aspects of shared life. This covered a lot of ground touching every kind of subject, during the long evenings especially in the winter, gathered round the sitting room fire. There, the process of transfer of the common heritage was passed on from parents with clear and strong convictions, to the family of boys and girls who never let up, quizzing their parents, and extracting from them all of value from past experience. The social and religious structure of society was suited to this. Even the economy by which oil lamps discouraged the use of different rooms brought everyone together in the family room, to share the white light of the tilley lamp. This cosy situation lent itself to the welding together of family ties, and the confirmation of identity as a family, the MacKinnon family, as members of the community church, as part of the national church, Church of Scotland— Free, and as part of the catholic church of Christ on earth with all its baggage in history and all its real estate in heaven.

Mr. MacKinnon never forgot his student days at University and in the Divinity Hall in Edinburgh. He would speak at length of his professors for whom he always held a special regard: Principal McCulloch, Drs. Bannatyne,Cameron MacLean, Moore, MacKay. The prayers these teachers lifted to heaven, short and eclectic in language at the beginning of each class, were a model for students and made a lasting impression upon my father. It has to be said that more than thirty years later, students found the same spirituality epitomized in the pre-class prayers of their professors, in the Free Church College.

Ties to fellow students preparing for the ministry remained unbroken over the years. It was one of the joys of the ecclesiastical tradition that he could bring these friends repeatedly as guest preachers at the many communions that were held annually. Colleagues were referred to as if their parish, like his own was their second name. Among his special friends found at communions in Aultbea, were MacIver Carloway, MacLeod Back, MacLeod Snizort, MacDonald Sleat, MacDonald Strathpeffer, afterwards of Duke Street, MacKinnon Portree, Matheson Stoer, afterwards of Glen Urquhart, Finlayson Tolsta, Ferguson Lochranza, Shaw Leith, Fraser Kiltarlity, MacKinnon Rothesay, Fraser LochCarron. Most of the Gaelic speaking ministers were at one time or another at communions in Aultbea or taken to one of those in Gairloch during its lengthy vacancies and also to Little Lochbroom, Kinlochewe and Alligin. Among them were Dr.

Munro Ferintosh, (Angus)MacKay Kingussie, Cameron Resolis, Campbell Dingwall, MacRae Plockton, MacLeod Dornoch, Sutherland Duke Street, Finlayson Urray, Campbell Garrabost, MacRae Stornoway, Morrison Ness, MacRae Kinloch, Campbell Greenock, Collins St. Columba, MacKenzie Leverborough, Morrison Duirinish. But the Gaelic was not a dividing line of friendship. Mr. MacKinnon always had a place in his heart for other college friends, especially like himself linked to one charge for the greater part of their ministry. Among them were the two faithful brothers, Alex Fraser Dunbarton and Donald Fraser Aberfeldy. In later years there were younger men including sons-in law, Donald Ross Bettyhill and later of Delny, and Alistair Gollan of Shiskine, Burghead and latterly of Lochcarron. One also recalls young ministers like Lamont Stoer and Ferintosh, and MacDougall Hope Street, MacDonald Ardesier, MacDonald Glenshiel, Murray Skerray, among many others, during the post Second World War period of Mr. MacKinnon's ministry.

You can see that there was a continual exchange of pulpits going on, ministers coming to Aultbea manse, staying for nearly a week. At the same time there was the reciprocal call to assist at communions elsewhere. Being a bi-lingual preacher, my father was called as guest preacher in the large Gaelic-speaking congregations in the north and west Highlands and Glasgow city Gaelic congregations. The Aultbea minister waited for the mail every Fall, and was delighted when letters came with invitations to several communions. over the coming year. Host ministers booked early in advance to get their preachers. He sometimes had to make choices as dates clashed. He could not hide his sheer delight at the prospect of going to the big Glasgow congregations, also those in Skye and Lewis. His natural pleasure in preaching in other large congregations, was matched by an equal enjoyment of the fellowship of his peers, a real and sweet joy that ministers everywhere share with like-minded members of their incomparable calling.

The bonds generated by spiritual affinities either with our childhood friends or through the fellowship of service later on in life, are sometimes very strong. It is true, that these may be reduced to sentiment, but even then in their natural interaction of spirit, there is a species of virtue that we just cannot dismiss. MacKinnon Aultbea had this to a marked degree. The ties between him and the flock over which he ministered, were generically the same that bound him on the denominational level to the team of his day, the Free Church. For him it was the church of the parish, justifiably so as ninety per cent of Aultbea were Free Church. Also the Free Church justified its continued identity throughout the 20th century, on the Chalmer's principle that it aimed at maintaining the Reformed concept of national establishment even though this be in a minority relationship to the rest of the Church in Scotland, a hard position for many ministers to maintain, with the seemingly intractable positions, rather dogmatically taken on both sides. But then the Scots are known to be almost as prone to division as their English brethren south of the border. The point we would emphasize is that many able men gave their loyalty to the ecclesiastical position, leaving any change or reunion with the other sections of the church in Scotland, as only a visionary pipe dream, almost an eschatological adjunct to the creed. Nevertheless, spiritual affinities from youth to age generated a loyalty that had a certain virtue. This resulted in a nearness to the people that acted like an adhesive, binding the church together in a sense of a common destiny. This might be construed as negative with its overtones of linguistic exclusivism, more imagined than real in the case of the Gaelic speaking people. In any case, the personnel of the Free Church struggled to maintain a clearly defined witness of the national heritage of the Church. There is no doubt that Mr. MacKinnon was sustained by this teamwork spirit, a concomitant of working together for the whole church. He associated also with ministers of the United Free Church and the old Parish. Perhaps the Gaelic was the special link of friendship. At any rate, he saw himself as a member of a team and valued the inter-church fellowship of colleagues near and far.

His love for special minister friends and professors whom he esteemed, was very evident when one of these was called to glory. When Professor MacLean, who had been at his induction, passed away in 1943, my father returned home from the General Assembly the following year in Edinburgh, a visibly changed man. The change was taken note of by the family in the manse. 'What's wrong Dad?' one of his children asked of him; 'why are you so sad?' He explained that for him, he had come to a watershed in his thinking. All of the professors who had taught him in the Divinity College had passed on. He put it this way, 'I haven't the same heart for another Assembly.' When word came that MacIver Carloway had passed away, the Aultbea minister became even more visibly affected. He became very quiet for several days. He had lodged with MacIver during College days. They were close friends always. Like himself, MacIver was beloved by his people with that special tie found where the ministry is long, even life-long, so that generations are born to know their minister in all the varied stages from birth to maturity. It was natural for him to put in verse his thoughts of grief and loss for a brother minister whose earthly journey was now over.

Marbhrann
Do'n Urr Iain MacIomhair, Carlobhagh

1
Tha iomadh neach an Carlobhagh
's na laithean so fo leoin,
Ri caoidh an teachdair aluinn ud
A chairich iad fo'n fhoid.
Tha iondrainn ort 'san fhion-lios
Bho'n chriochnaich thu do shaothair,
Oir samhail Iain MhicIomhair
Cha robh lionmhor am measg dhaoin'.

2
Is iomadh focal beannaichte
Chuir do theachdaireachd an ceill
Tha cuimhn' orr' anns na flaitheanas
Ann an lathair ainglean De.
Bha peacaich 'deanamh aithreachais
Fo bhuaidh do theagaisg fein,
Bha mor thoilinntinn agadsa
Bhi 'g altrum as na treud.

3
Bheathaich thu gu fallainn iad
Leis an mhil o'n charaig chruaidh,
'S thug thu smior na cruithneachd dhoibh,
'N uair 'thionaileadh an sluagh;
Gu abhainn lan de sholasan
'S tu threoiricheadh an treud,

'S cha'n iongnadh iad bhi leointe
Is bronach 'na do dheigh.

4

Bu theachaire ro dhileas thu,
Bha firinneach gu bas;
Bu bhuachaill maith nan caorach thu,
Air raointean glan a ghnath;
Is uchd cho truasail caomh agad,
A ghuileaneadh na h-uain,
Is cridhe blath an aodhair
Lan caomhalachd do'n t-sluagh.

5

O! b' iongantach leinn an t-eolas
Ann an raointean gloir is grais,
Oir rinn E fein do threoireachadh
Go mullach Pisgadh ard;
Air tir Chanain gu'm b'eolach thu
Mar neach bha comhnuidh shuas,
Is dh'fhag sud blasd' do chomhradh dhuinn,
Le soluimteachd 's buaidh.

6

'N uair sgaoileadh tu na bagaidean
'Thug thu air ais o'n tir,
'S a mholadh thu na beannachdan
'S nach bi' gu brath ann dith,
Bhiodh muinntir anns an eisdeachd
Air an geurachadh le cail,
A' misneachadh a cheile
Gu bhi treubhach anns a bhlar.

7

O bhlais thu fein 'na d'anam air
Gur maith 'sgur milis Dia;
'S e sud a rinn do tharruing

Bho na faileasan tha shios,
Is mheasadh tu na amaideas
Gach aighear tha 'san t-saoghal;
'Sann dh iarradh tusa sonas
Ann an comunn Fear do ghaoil.

8

'S e gloir Uain a thaladh thu
Gu tir an aigh tha shuas
Gu faiceadh tu' na lanachd E,
A' dealradh ort gun ghruaim,
Gun pheacadh 'ga do sharuchadh,
Gun fasalachd no cruas,
Ri mealtuinn gnuis do   Shlanuighear
Ri snamh'na chomunn buan.

Translation:

Eulogy to Rev John MacIver, Carloway

1

There are many souls in Carloway,
These days who are grieved in heart
Mourning for a pastor
They have laid to rest beneath the sod.
There's anguish in the Vineyard
Since now your work is done
For the like of John MacIver,
There are few indeed 'mongst men.

2

It's many the blessed words
Your ministry proclaimed,
In the presence of the angels,
The record there remains.
Through your preaching
Sinners sought forgiveness

Goodwill was in abundance
As you nourished all your flock.

3

You gave them without measure
With the honey from the rock;
You gathered in the people
With the finest of the Wheat;
To the river of consolations,
You guided all the flock,
It's no wonder they are heartbroken
And grieving at your loss.

4

For faithful pastor you were truly
And steadfast ev'n to death;
A good shepherd of the sheep
On the pastures of the Word.
In your arms, so kind, compassionate,
You were bearing up the lambs,
With the warm heart of the keeper,
All the flock you kept with love.

5

O! Wonderful the knowledge
The pages speak of glory and of grace,
For He himself has led you
To see views from Pisgah's crowning height.
Of Canaan's land you knew full well
As one who oft was there,
That gave your speech to us a a solemn sweetness,
In the victory you won.

6

When you spread out all the clusters
You brought back from the land
When you magnified the blessings
That will never be undone,
The people in your hearing,
Their longings you enlarged

Strengthening one another
In their conflicts to be strong.

7

Since in your soul you tasted
The sweetness of the Lord;
This brought you from the shadows
And the sin of life that's low.
And you thought of them as foolishness,
The pleasures of the world;
You sought the heavenly happiness
The communion of your Love.

8

You were drawn to joys of heaven
By the glory of the Lamb
To see his greatness and his fulness
Shining on you without frown,
Without sin and shame harrassing,
Nor tribulation's thongs,
Your Saviour's face beholding
Embraced in His eternal love.

———————

Chapter 30

The Family Man

Mr. MacKinnon's public ministry was nourished by a very happy family life. His wife was a vital complement in fulfilling the mandate of his great calling. Theirs was a shared approach, where both were subservient to their Master and their Lord. There is a distinct advantage when a couple are on the same wavelength. You can see this in other spheres of life. A couple who are both immersed in the world of music have this unity and harmony. The secret is that they both are committed to something greater than their own selves. Thus the corollary is that egotistical compulsion defers continually to that which is greater and which is shared by both. Think what is the great over-riding purpose of a minister's calling, namely proclaiming the Word through which fellow human beings come to possess the 'unsearchable Riches of Christ.'[1]

There was no happier image of a family man than MacKinnon Aultbea surrounded by his family of boys and girls. His children coveted his presence and vied for his attention, always waiting for his return when he was absent. How can one express their longings as they looked out on a winter's night their eyes scanning the darkness of the mountain

1. Ephesians 3:8

road as it skirted the clifftops from Poolewe to Aultbea, all looking for the lights of the manse car. How each one would guess, as car headlights shone in the darkness at the different corners, That's Dad, that's Dad.' At last it would be Dad and the car would come up the driveway and come to a standstill in the garage. Then it was a competition to be first to greet him and arms were raised to receive his fatherly embrace. For he loved every one of them. He never burdened them with his concerns and cares. Rather he condescended to their level. Thus he would use his gifts to make poems about Santa Claus—he himself would fill the role at the party at Christmas in the manse. An explanation of his absence at some moment in the party was always the same:, ''Dad had to go to the barn, while Santa was making his visit.' Any other questions that might arise in a child's mind as a sequence in the chain of logic was 'out of order.' Also the manse puppy would challenge him to compose some verse reflecting its antics at worship and its exasperating conduct of irreverence, mildly abhorred by Mrs MacKinnon. A part verse comes to mind, 'He barks and plays when daddy prays, and makes my mother angry.' Needless to say the children regarded the doggy tricks like pulling the slippers off father's feet when he was praying on his knees at family worship, as a God-given harmless but very entertaining diversion.

Somehow in spite of a very busy life, MacKinnon Aultbea would make time to take the family on holiday. His children would never forget those holidays in the 1930's with the big square Citroen. Sometimes the bell-tent was borrowed from Mr Murchison the schoolmaster, who also had a large brood. Some years the Citroen itself was used as a travelling home. There was the snag that every night at bed-time, the seats had to be removed so that all could sleep in some semblence of order and questionable comfort inside on the floor. No allowance was made for the irritating obtrusions of metal slides for the seats that precluded any prolonged repose for little ones. As for Dad, nothing seemed ever to trouble him and certainly nothing could keep him from his sleep and healthy snoring, an ever fresh subject of amazement for wakeful children in the watches of a starry night.

A holiday trip to Aberdeen stays in the memory. My father was a man of the moment. As he motored on with his family crowded in his big Citroen and the large wicker hamper strapped on the carrier at the back, he would shout out of the window at a likely passer-by, 'Aberdeen road? Aberdeen road?' demanding confirmation or redirection. He would never dream of stopping. In fact stopping and starting off again in those early days of motoring was a performance in itself, what with chancy clutches, and non- synchromesh gears. Then there were the trips to Glasgow and Edinburgh as well as Aberdeen. These were educational trips for the children. Who could forget the majesty of King's College, Aberdeen, one of Scotland's oldest seats of learning! Or how could one over-emphasize the effect of the urban beauty of Princes Street on the impressionable mind of a Highland boy or girl, and the towering graded refinement of the Scott Monument, with the dark shadowy silhouette of Edinburgh Castle framed in the afternoon sunlight. But more, over to the West coast nothing could match the fascination of a boy with the chain driven steam mechanism of the Erskine Ferry plying its journey back and fore over the mighty river Clyde.

And then there was the visit to the Glasgow Museum where the perceived ancestors of human life itself could be seen in fabricated reconstruction, life size, instead of the pen drawings from the pages of the manse Encyclopedia. There are other images that remain imprinted upon the memory, even after sixty years, such as the vast fleet of steam- powered drifters and trawlers in Aberdeen and Peterhead where we camped. One remembers walking along the dockside on a Sunday near Dee Street where my father took us to worship at the Free Church.

Afterwards in the sunlight there were the endless rows of fishing boats in for the weekend, tied up at the quay—no Scottish fishing-boat ever fished on the Sabbath day. What fascination to see the long smokestacks of their triple-expansion steam engines and the dark-brown tanned mizzen sails lowered and made fast, with gaff to boom, the sure hallmark of the fishing boat that waits in the night hours, for fish to come on the lines, or surface fish to come into the nets. There was a large fleet of them, with long funnels, masts and rigging, like a huge field of telegraph poles and wires, making a complex pattern against the skyline. Here were the large fleets of herring drifters that, in season waited through the predawn for the golden bounty of nature's harvest of the sea, the 'silver darlings', the life-blood of the economy in the north-east of Scotland in particular. On another trip the venue was Glasgow, Scotland's greatest commercial city on the West coast.   Here, was the continual rumbling of the Clydesdale horses as they pulled the four-wheel wagons, scores of them, up and down the cobbled streets, beside the parallel passenger-carrying tram-cars, on Jamaica Street and Union Street, carrying loads of all kinds of merchandise from huge containers of fresh vegetables to wooden casks of beer and Scottish malt whisky. A little Highland boy felt a stranger until he saw something very familiar. It was a lorry with the oval, rugby-ball shaped side windows, exactly like the old road lorry that the County workmen used to maintain the gravel roads in Aultbea. It was of course an Albion, the Scottish built hardy vehicle that just would never wear out. When it was retired in Aultbea from active service, like so many products of that time, it was as good as ever. Yet there were over two hundred and fifty thousand miles on the speedometer, in a day when a small saloon car needed a reconditioned engine after thirty thousand miles. But the Albion was Scottish built to last. The new consumer cars on the market followed the new principle of manufacturing ethics, a guarantee of new replacement orders, namely built-in obsolescence. Surely this was an education for the manse children.

One summer before the Second World War, Mr. MacKinnon camped at Pitlochry, in Perthshire, and surely one of the most beautiful towns of inland Scotland north of the Tay. At Pitlochry, small planes used a stretch of the land beside the camping site for landing and taking off. Short flights were being offered on a canvas wing-covered aeroplane. Alas, fairness to all six of the family then born and present precluded any one individual from getting airborne. And the cost for all to do so would frankly be too much for the minister's pocket. But the memory will never fade with them, of that time long ago in a bygone age. In the mind's eye the scene of the aeroplane is still fresh and graphically clear, sixty years later. What a performance compared with developed procedures. The pilot clothed in his leather jacket, high leather gaiters and leather helmet, helping up his two passengers. Then he climbed in himself. His ground partner cranked the big wooden varnished propeller, pulling it round in short

Karate-like motions with his hand.

The cylinders fire, the engine stops, then back-fires, the propeller whizzing back in a deadly reverse shuddering motion. The pilot adjusts the fuel/air mixture and the prop is cranked again. The engine bursts into life and runs ever so sweetly. Every one clears away. The ground partner waves a flag; the pilot revs up his motor so that you cannot see the blades. Everyone now wave to the passengers. The latter can be seen with a strange expression on their faces in the open cockpit. Their faces have a rather sallow look as if their stomachs are giving them some trouble. Their appearance has a vague mixture of expectation and also apprehension as the small plane pulls over the grass and wobbles its way for a distance before it lifts into the air, all the time the engine emmitting a deafening roar.

Another vivid recollection persists, of motoring along a country road in Aberdeen-shire. It was towards evening. We needed milk for eight of us which meant at least a gallon. The MacKinnon children were brought up on gallons of milk and cream, crowdie, *slaman* and fresh butter. We came to a standstill at a big farm. It was the right kind as a large herd of beautiful dairy cattle were being led into the byre. Two of the older girls went off from the car with the empty pail. The dairy was close to the roadside where the car was stopped. The girls came back to say that if they waited a short while until the milking started they would get their milk. When they came back the second time, the big enamel pail was full, full of warm creamy milk, straight from the cow's udder. One remembers the cost of that delectable pail of milk, which reminded us of our dear cows and the pails of milk they always gave us at home in Aultbea. The cost was one silver sixpence.

Yes, Mr MacKinnon was a great Dad. Scenes at bed-time or in the car on these camping holidays are unforgettable. There, everyone cosily wrapped up, we would commit ourselves to our Maker and thank him for the day that was ended. Thus if you were listening, you would hear the family singing together the immortal hymn bequeathed to the Christian church by the Hebrews. All the voices joined in to the tune Kilmarnock or Martyrdom or Evan, the Scottish Metrical Version of Psalm 23.

> The Lord's my shepherd, I'll not want.
> He makes me down to lie
> In pastures green: he leadeth me
> the quiet waters by.
>
> My soul he doth restore again;
> and me to walk doth make
> Within the paths of righteousness,
> even for his own name's sake.

We always sang at least two verses. And we also sang from other psalms like 121, 103, 46, 1, 63. There was no need of a light to worship with such praise. For all were used to singing them at home at family worship and in church, both in Gaelic and in English. Then Dad would repeat some Scripture phrases and close in a short prayer. That was not the cue to sleep, no way. This was the beginning of the show. Now came all the questions from the young, questions about every subject from the fertile imagination of children. And all were fired at Dad. Mam who was only with us sometimes would let him have the 'floor.' Dad, relaxed and with an incomparable and believing receptive audience, was not slow to respond with answers. But more, he regaled the children with stories of his life. He seemed to have an inexhaustible store of stories, some of other people, sometimes of quaint ministers, who were well known and liked, but who were definitely eccentric. But it is from his own life that he told stories that kept his children in trance-like attentiveness. Thus he would revisit his childhood island of Skye and bring to life boyhood experiences that thrilled the children with delight. Then again he would speak of Canada and loved to tell of adventures, his own and those of others from that virgin continent of benevolence and opportunity.

The fact is that MacKinnon Aultbea had a great humanity. And ultimately isn't humanity the best portrait of divinity. He merged into the conventional life, clothed in the trappings of his profession. But the man behind the ecclesiastical mask which the children more than anyone else saw, was a real man, with a capacity to live life to the full without the painful literalism of any religious regimentation. For example while camping at Peterhead the day was hot and the children were feeling quite uncomfortable. Along came an icecream vendor with a little cart. Here was a test case. It was the Sabbath day. The idea of buying anything on the Sabbath was a sin, if the Fourth Commandment was interpreted literally. But here were seven thirsty children. All eyes looked to him. Dad made his decision. 'Rachel, here's the money. Get an icecream for everyone and get one for me as well.'

'Hurrah, Hurrah, What a Dad!' the children thought, and was that ice cream delicious! At home on another occasion, the tide was driven by a strong southwesterly wind so that it kept coming up higher on a Sabbath evening, threatening to wreck the manse boat. As a rule no one went out for recreation, fishing or otherwise on the Sabbath day. But Dad had no compunction in giving permission to pull the boat up higher, right across the mainroad through the manse gate to safety.

The children of the Aultbea manse recognised in their Dad a 'freed spirit'. He was freed by Christ, the Truth who makes us truly free. Yes, the children saw that their Dad was not the slave of narrow-mindedness. He saw distinctions between principles which are absolutes, as binding and of God, and on the other hand, rules which are relative; they are to be recognised as derivative, and are to be adopted for their utility by the exercise of intelligence and down-to-earth common sense. The latter lie in the area of interpretation and are closely related to expediency, namely secondary laws to achieve primary ends. But they are not an end in themslves. How many well-intentioned people get entangled in this ecclesiastical web, and religion for them is a prison of repression, rather than a door to freedom. Remember my father was a poet as well as a preacher. The poet can no more be contained in spirit than the eagle that soared over Tollie Rock above Loch Maree. But we all need not be poets in order to be free. We are set free by Christ. But in my father's case there was that double disposition of enlightenment, that of the poet and the believer. Thus he whose soul was set free by His Redeemer came out of the open prison cage of human enslavement and his spirit soared to the heights of human joy, leading others, where they were willing to share in his vision. His children 'saw' this. He was Christ's slave, and at the same time Christ's freeman. They saw that his whole life was one of freedom. Freedom and service are partners. We are set free to serve; we serve to demonstrate that we are free.

If mother was *'never bate'* (that is, never beaten by circumstances), our father earned the title of *'never late.'* He was never known to be late for a service or appointment, through slackness or thoughtlessness. He practiced punctuality almost to the extreme. You ask, 'How could he do this when it was common for the car to have a puncture when the minister was travelling even on the Sabbath day between Aultbea and Poolewe, especially before the gravel roads were paved?' The answer is that he built in this as a possibility, and allowed an extra twenty minutes for one puncture. Thus all journeys were begun early. Dad was adamant in coercing everyone to get up and get ready. All were resigned to this inexorable pressure and acquiesced. One occasion comes vividly to mind. He was driving his son to catch the early train which passed through Achnasheen about seven o'clock from Kyle on its way south to Inverness. He arrived on that frosty morning at five-thirty am. The long wait for someone to stir at the station or hotel is a painful memory that never went away. Father was not a patient man and left at once to get back to Aultbea, for he had duties to attend to.

Habitually he rose in the morning between five and six a.m. The early morning was his time. After his personal devotions, he supervised the domestic scene. This was the only time of respite for his busy wife. Memories for the children come back easily and vividly of these times long ago. A call from Dad to get up could not be ignored for long. First call was a raised voice, politely announcing Waking-time. Second call was different. Dad had his methods. He took a coal shovel and an iron poker to give a gong effect. The sound was not really quality music but travelled up through the bedroom doors right to the third storey. Children tried to block out the sound with the clothes, pulling the bedcovers over their ears. But it was no use. All would eagerly shout, as Dad named each one, vying with one another trying to put conviction into their voices: 'I'm coming. Yes, I'm up.' Sometimes when Dad took them at their word and stopped the fearful clatter, they would curl up again under the warm clothes to extract some more precious rest before the final 'must.' How sweet these minutes were! But what a price had to be paid. Dad knew the score. The third call was irresistible and had immediate and positive results. Dad would come to the stairway in the hall, and as he started climbing the stair, he banged the awful shovel/poker alarm so that it grew louder and louder. The noise was so inexorably intolerant that everyone jumped out of bed and even came out onto the landing, protesting vehemently. The end was achieved. Soon all were down in the kitchen for breakfast.

There on dark winter mornings, the kerosone lamp shone with its cosy yellow light, and each in turn was welcomed by Dad, with a fatherly kiss. Dad's kiss was so different to Mam's. Dad had not yet shaved and his face had a spiky growth not very different from the skin of a dogfish or a carpenter's sandpaper. Dad's word was law when it came to requirements. A large spoonful of straight cod-liver oil, or of the special Elgin white Cod-Liver Oil Cream, was the order of the day. Then a plate of porridge, the real stuff, and Dad of all people in this world, knew how to make it. The spoon must stand in it by itself. That was the 'litmus test.' This was real food. And apart from a piece of bread and cheese, would be the only physical fuel to sustain the children until they came home from school, some nine hours later.

You could tell when Dad was not at home. Then Mam filled in. She got up and made the porridge. This was quite different to that made by Dad. It was softer, better cooked. There were few if any lumps in it. It reflected the gentler touch, the more patient operation of the feminine species. It has to be said that our father inculcated a belief in oatmeal as the very 'staff of life.' He himself, like many Highlanders saw the porridge as a compromise, a concession to the tame domesticated life which processes and refines the basics until sometimes the 'good' is taken out of them. For him the cereal was Brose, uncompromising Highland brose, the dynamic instant food that helped to make the Scottish soldier the incomparable soldier of history. Brose made with water, cold or hot is the primal sustenance that can give energy as nothing else. Those who have crossed oceans—I think of Peter Tangvald among other ocean-going 'loners'—have proved this, that is Scots oatmeal food as brose or porridge. But then Tangvald was a cousin to the Northern Scot, sharing as a Dane the Norse heritage with the Celt.

These glimpses of family life are here briefly included, only to illustrate the 'super Dad' MacKinnon Aultbea was for his big family. To see his face smiling and welcoming, when children came down for breakfast before going to school, was a treat indeed. The preacher, the pastor, the poet was also the paternal guardian of his own loving family, and was loved with a great love in turn by them all.

Chapter 31

The Measure of a Man

I f man is the measure of all things, according to the Greek proverb, it is fair to ask what is the measure of man himself? At what point is a 'still' to be taken to capture a working image of him that becomes the yardstick we use to measure? At what point is the reading of measurement to be taken, in the sequence of development from birth to death? For the Christian, the point of measurement is that which he becomes. Faith means an extension beyond philosophy, for what a man becomes is not apparent in time. Christ gives eternal life, which contrasts with the biological but does not contradict it nor cancel its course from birth to death. For my father, the biological clock was now bringing him to the evening of his day. That is not to dismiss these years of human decline as negative. There is a glory in the evening whether it be of our common astronomical day or that of our earthly pilgrimage. Who has not enjoyed going out on an evening walk or rowing out in the calm of the tranquil waters of the bay, pulling in a few dozen mackerel!

Was it not in the evening when the day was far spent that

our Risen Lord revealed himself in one of the most glorious spiritual experiences for two of the disciples on the road to Emmaus! [1] There is no doubt that this post-War phase of my father's ministry had a character of its own that related not only to the changes, social, economic and spiritual round about, but to the decline of his strength. To the end he acted as if this were the same. But that did not cancel the inevitable for him nor for anyone else. There was a sweet harmony as both he and my mother, with the family for the most part away from home, enjoyed a period of closeness and mutual happiness 'on their own'. Like the proverbial *Derby and Joan,* they were more together. Mr. MacKinnon was accompanied by his wife on visits throughout the congregation. They were often to be found strolling in the garden and enjoying the beauty of that incomparable setting of flowers and ferns, with the ever present birds all chirping as they darted round the apple and plum trees: and there were the insects, with their continual buzz, with the butterflies parading their spectacular colours to project on all the miracle wonder of the Creator's genius.

Physically my father was short of stature, but with a compact dynamic strength. He spoke of his stature as a virtue. As he put, he did not have so far to bow when he knelt to pray. He spoke of great men and was kept from any negative thinking by history where men like St Paul, the first century builder of the Christian church, Napoleon, the aspirant to ruling a united Europe and Lloyd George, the Welshman politician who was to Wales what Churchill was to England, were all short men. He liked to quote Lloyd George who said that in Wales, a man was measured from the point of his chin to the crown of his head.

1 St. Luke 24:13

For better or worse, physical strength was considered an estimable virtue in the Scottish Highlands. Thus you have caber tossing, wrestling, hammer throwing which are linked to the Highland Games now commonly celebrated every summer all over North America in states with large Scottish ethnic populations like Ohio, Montana, Arizona, the Carolinas and indeed where ever you go as well as in Canada from Nova Scotia to British Columbia. The whole image of the Highland cultural and spiritual identity, the four elements of strength, cultural, linguistic, spiritual and physical comprise one composite image of memory. It is quite an experience to see many from other ethnic backgrounds, throwing the hammer, playing the Scottish pipes, and more than anything else to hear a young man read the Scriptures of the Gaelic Bible, converse with a degree of competence, and read a letter from his pen in the ancient Celtic tongue, now for the most part scrapped and discarded in much of Highland Scotland. And is he of Scottish blood? Not a drop of it in his veins. His name is Jonathan Kibler, a young man of promise who if he is spared will keep the light of the Gaelic language shining brightly in the Third Millenium. The fact is that the study of the Gaelic Bible not only is a means of keeping the language alive but it has a greater value. For the devotional use of the Gaelic Bible sanctifies the life in the process of learning from it.

We stress here that physical strength was considered as a high priority in the Highland concept of what a minister should be. Maybe this reflects a shallow judgment. Nevertheless that is not necessarily so. Aultbea had several men who were noted for their physical strength. Feats of strength were performed in the course of everyday life. When the automobile came into vogue, one man who had a car and a mechanical bent, was told by Alick Forbes the garage man that the main crankcase 'big ends' needed attention as there was a loud 'knock' in the engine. The man in question took the engine out of the car at his home, and walked to the garage, carrying the engine on his shoulder. A companion walked casually along the road with him, engaged in conversation with him. No one thought that this was unusual. Men were used to carrying ploughs and cartwheels to the smiddy in Ormscaig to have them repaired. When the modern autocar came on the scene, it did not occur to them at first to do anything differently. By tradition, going back to the 18th century and the days of Rev. Aeneas Sage and *Maighstir Lachlan*, redoubtable big ministers of Lochcarron, who subdued the wild men of that area, ministers were expected to give as good a performance in some physical feat of skill or strength as much as in the pulpit. Even the reputation of strength was enough to earn respect. Thus you have Rev John MacRae of Lochalsh, *Macrath mor,* the big MacRae, a redoubtable figure of strength.

Aultbea was the perfect place for Rev Angus MacKinnon. A weak man physically would be out of place at that time. Remember that much of the work connected with the cultivation of the land and indeed building and moving of burdens was done using physical strength. We think it sufficient to speak of only one strong man. He lived not far from the manse and we knew him personally, seeing him on a daily basis, as a neighbour, crewing his big black, tarred boat while he set his salmon net, or giving him a full day's work right round the clock taking in the hay and the corn oats at harvest time.

Murdo Aird was not an unusually big man. He was, however, extremely well-built. When I think of him, Rocky Marciano the stocky American World Heavyweight champion, who turned lesser men like Britain's poor Don Cockell into blubber, and demolished many others with his scything body punches, comes at once to mind. Rocky had a moderate physic but developed unusual strength through his work in the meat market of New York. Murdo Aird was like that boxer, Rocky Marciano, a powerful physical machine who had seemingly invincible body strength, especially around the torso and the legs.

When the tide was out, it meant that Murdo sometimes had to pull his big heavy boat to launch it in order to get out to his salmon net between his house and the pier. Murdo Aird did this on his own so that the big heavy tarred Highland *sgoth* could be floated off the shore to get out to the net. The boat had thole-pins and thwarts for six men to row, with a very broad beam when the lug sail was not in use. In other words the boat was designed to be handled by two to four men at sea and at least four, when moved on land. Furthermore, the boat had the usual reverse curve that gave an inside hollow keel. In this, the bilges, there were several hunderweights of stones for ballast. Murdo removed this only when retarring the boat, never more than an annual event.

When making a cart load on the croft, stretching behind his house from the roadside to Tighnafiline up on the hill, or from the more distant field at the Culchointich, Murdo Aird had a special heavy steel fork made by the *gobha*, the blacksmith at Ormiscaig. This was skilfully tempered and had an ash-handle, three times thicker than the usual and more similar to a fence post. The reasoning behind this being,

that while another man might take three or four forkfuls to
lift a hay-stook up to the boy 'making the load', as a rule
Murdo dug his special fork into the stook and lifted it up in
one action. One would have to say that working with Murdo
Aird required a special skill on the part of the lad on the top,
'making the load.' Just think of a whole stook of hay coming
up to you and having to place it correctly, the whole stook at
one time instead of the usual way in which the hay was spread
out evenly. The idea was to be able to place it in one quarter,
using four stooks for the basic shape of one level of the load
so that they inter-locked. Needless to say, the load was higher
and more compacted and heavy than the normal, like
everything else Murdo Aird did. In fact in spite of this, the
load was also tighter and less likely to fall apart through the
compression of the complete stooks. *Making a load* was
always an art; making it with Murdo Aird was something
more. If not done properly, the load might shift when the big
ironbound wheels which gave the cart a dangerously high
centre of gravity, like a top-heavy boat that is liable to capsize,
rocked the cart as the horse pulled it over the rough and
often boggy ground to get to the road. Everything about
Murdo's work was big. A local carpenter, Alick MacKenzie
of Bualnaluib, known as the *Spider* (his son Angus, also a
carpenter, was known as the *Fly*) because of his work at one
time on the steeples of Glasgow churches, made a new cart
for Murdo Aird. The previous one prematurely gave way.
The new one was made of hardwood and the trams or shafts
were at least double ordinary specification. It was almost
impossible for an ordinary man to lift up the heavy trams,
far less move the cart alone. On a working day on the croft,
the cart could be seen with an enormous load tightly tied

down with ropes. Murdo Aird shared with other crofters, the
broken-up Aird farm, tenanted by Mr. Muir when my father
first came to Aultbea in the mid nineteen-twenties. This was
in addition to his own family croft. This was accessed through
the hill outside the perimeter of the croft-land. One working
day, taking an enormous load of hay back to his barn, the cart
wheel on one side sank into the soft peaty ground. The cart
heeled over, threatening to capsize. All the Gaelic
encouragement would not avail and the big faithful horse at
last looked as if its legs would give way. It was then Murdo
Aird came into his own. He bowed down beside the horse,
still cajoling the animal to continue, while he himself appeared
beside it, with his arm locked onto the shaft as if he was part
of an equine working pair. The cart kept going, the wheel
lifting out of the rut and on to firmer ground. Murdo Aird
with a short dynamic effort had done what seemed impossible.
I remember him yet, saying afterwards between gasps of
breath, to the horse, '*Shin thu bhalaich, shin thu bhalaich;
rinn thu gle mhath.* 'That's it boy, that's it boy; you did very
well.' I think the horse had a look of perplexity on his very
intelligent face, as if he were thinking to himself, *Why is he
thanking me, I would have collapsed and the cart would have
overturned, if Murdo Aird himself had not saved the day!* Then
it was a walking pace through the gate of the common land
from Culchointich, along the village road through
Tighnafiline, and then down the county-maintained road to
Aultbea village by the seaside. The journey ended and the
load was brought home to the barn at the crossroads leading
to the pier. This was the West-end in contrast and in friendly
rivalry to the east-end with its shops and hotels. At mid-day
there was dinner for the workers, Murdo and his young

assistant hay-load maker. Then the horse, again the biggest in Aultbea, soaked with sweat, was given a rest, unhooked from the cart and allowed to go back up the field to graze and rest for the dinner hour. It is hard to forget Murdo Aird's horse. He was strong and big, and infinitely patient. *Ali Shim's* horse was fat and shiny and had to be continually given a crack on the rump with the rope. If not he would simply take a rest, pulling the plough or the cart to a stop. One felt that he was a bit spoilt, getting too much tender loving care from Ali Shim' and especially Mrs MacKenzie in Tighnafiline.

One recalls giving a day's work on the croft taking in the hay, after Ali Shim' had died. His widow was scolding the horse, ordering him to stop eating from a bag of oats in the barn, while we were harnessing him up. He took a long time to obey her and when he did, the look he gave his mistress was a lazy tolerant one in which you felt he was saying to himself, 'Alright, but I know you won't do any harm to me, becaus*e you just like me as one of the family.'* The impression was that he felt that he would like early retirement so that he could lie down and roll in the field or just 'sleep in', snoozing away in the comfortable warm quarters of the stable with the full barn of hay and plenty oats just for himself.

Next door was Allan MacLeay's horse. Allan was other worldly and often just went through the motions, doing the minimum on the croft. His horse seemed to sense this and did the same. It paired with *Ali Shim's* horse. *Ali Shim* had always to keep cracking the whip at both of them, but never very vigorously, to keep them going at the plough. Then there was *Alla Domh'll Allan's* horse, next door to Murdo Aird's. She was a mare. The two were paired for ploughing. Watching them, you felt that Murdo Aird's horse always took the strain of pulling the plough as if he was making allowance for his much smaller feminine partner. There is no recollection of Murdo Aird needing to use the whip.

There was something noble about Murdo Aird's horse. One time while a young rider was on it, bareback, the horse grew a bit impatient and broke into a trot. Now any one who knows horses at all also knows that you need stirrups to achieve the required rhythm to ride when the horse is trotting. If you are an inexperienced youngster riding bareback there is certainly a problem. The young boy of nine became disorientated, slipped off the round sweating body of the horse and found himself hanging under the horse's neck, still holding onto the horse's mane as the gravel road rushed past below. The horse had the wisdom of a human. He came to a standstill and gently lowered his head, so that his young friend could get his act together and gather his wits. Do you wonder that the young boy never forgot this experience and would remember Murdo Aird's big kindly horse until he would leave the stage of this mortal life!

Dinner provided by Annie, Murdo's wife, was a large roast of beef, which was soon demolished by the working team. Usually a horse is taken to the cart, a logical arrangement when you think of it. But not so for Murdo Aird. After dinner he would take the horse's place between the shafts and heavy as it was, he pulled it through the deep ruts of the road leading to the croft at a higher elevation. It was quite something to see this, a man turning the usual process on its back, 'bringing the cart to the horse.'

During and immediately after the Second World War, liberty ships took loads of miscellaneous packing boxes and

scrap wood of crates, back from naval ships and piled them
on the pier. Murdo Aird habitually took loads of this firewood
back home, on his big heavy cart. Again, Murdo Aird did not
believe in wasting time for this operation. Instead of the bother
of getting hold of the horse and harnessing it to pull the cart,
he simply picked up the cart and pulled it along the road
through the naval base to the pier. As he passed back again
with the cart piled high with wood, most of the boxes broken
up on the pier by Murdo when he was loading, sailors and
WRENS stood still in amazement at the sight of a human
being actually taking the place of a horse.

Other stories cannot be verified at first-hand but were
currently accepted as true, about another strong man who lived
in Isle Ewe. Here is just one of them we add in the passing, as
told by *Aonghas an Eilein*, Angus the island. This relates to
the time before horses were used. All work was done manually,
including the ploughing using the *cas chrom*. Seaweed was
habitually taken up in creels from the shore as fertilizer for
the croftland. On this specific occasion, a specially large
creel, made for this man, was full on the shore. Another man
helped him raise the creel onto his back. The helper's woollen
jersey caught in the wickerwork creel, so that he was himself
lifted up along with the creel. Only when the strong man
reached the croft and laid his burden down, did he notice that
he also had carried his helper who was nearly choked to death
in the experience, and unable to make a sound of protest. He
did suggest that he thought that the creel was inordinately
heavy, or as he put it, that he himself was not feeling as
strong as he should be.

This is not to extol physical strength unduly, but to
emphasise that it was a factor and a significant one in the

thinking of the people. It was inevitable that even subconsciously people applied this measure to a man, whatever his calling. This was a simple fact of life. It was not a handicap were it found in a minister and indeed could be a real asset.

One day when father was in his prime, he asked his younger son to sit behind the steering wheel of the car. Father was out front cranking the engine several times, as was the custom to free the engine. Then the 'assistant' would switch on the ignition, and the next crank would bring the engine to life. Most earlier cars with the weak six volt ignition system required this procedure when the engine was cold in the morning. Sadly the said assistant let Dad down badly on this occasion. Starting the car had reached the second stage. Somehow, and he could never explain it, he had pushed the car into gear. At the same time he switched on the ignition. Father bent down to crank the car vigorously in the final starting procedure. Without any delay, the engine fired and at the same time as it burst into life, the car also shot forward, pushing Dad before it. My father backed away but could not escape. The car with its steel bumper hit him in the legs and with such force that the wall of the garage behind cracked. Then the engine 'stalled'. It is not known if father even mentioned this experience to anyone else except his spouse. His face turned white as searing pain stabbed at his system. His young son was frozen with fear, passively unable to move. He knew he had done wrong and failed miserably. He waited for Dad to speak. Father came round and looked at him and said gently, 'Angus, you shouldn't have done that.'

It has been mentioned earlier that MacKinnon Aultbea had unusual leg muscles. They protruded out from the front, much

as the calf muscles did at the back. On this occasion he
returned to the manse. Mother looked at the dark double
indentation like two bands across both legs, corresponding to
the grooved shape of the steel bumper of the car. The powerful
legs had taken the shock and somehow the legs did not break.
Again after being soothed with vaseline, and a cup of tea, the
minister went out, the car was started and off he drove on a
pastoral duty.

Regrettably the shore in front of the manse was not a steep
slope. Therefore the tide exposed a long shore when it was
low. The consequence was that the boat often had to be pulled
up over the stony shore above the tide mark. If not it meant
anchoring the boat with a stern anchor, so that she would stay
afloat. But if there was any kind of sea running in the exposed
bay especially, pushed by winds from the south and east, the
boat could be damaged by continually striking the bottom
until the sea came in past her. And also there was the likelihood
that the stern anchor would drag, causing a chronic and very
unsatisfactory situation. The young folks favoured this and
for another very good reason, the boat though not large was
very heavy, of seasoned salt-water soaked larch, and they had
no mind for the arduous task of pulling it up the shore. But
not so for Dad. In order to pull the boat efficiently, it required
two people, one on each side so that the boat remained on an
even keel and thus was not damaged in her clinker planking.
Dad would take one side gripping it very near the bow, his
son the other. For a few yards all was well, then the son
would stumble, and his contribution to the pulling would
cease. But the boat continued on its way. MacKinnon Aultbea
simply walked with the boat beside him until he reached
above the tideline. Recollections just will not go away of

literally catching up on him and the boat, near the road in front of the manse gate. There is no question, there was a bit of a mischievous smile upon Dad's face as he feigned surprise at the obvious disparity in strength between himself and his growing son. There was a special reason for haste in doing this chore. The minister made a point of never being seen in public, unless he was dressed in his clerical clothes. Thus if there was the possibility of any parishioner coming along the road at the time of disembarking, he would do anything to avoid meeting them in his casual old clothes used for the boat.

We inferred that even exhibiting feats of unusual strength was not divorced from humour. And humour was often to be found in the different aspects of everyday life including the happy chores connected with the sea and boats. On one occasion, coming ashore on a calm day, after setting the net, and therefore later in the day, a man was passing along the road. The tide was in at the time so that Dad as usual delayed coming ashore until the man had passed. There was the added reason that the good citizen had obviously been visiting the hotel and had some strong refreshment before he left to return home, which disposed him to sing a song as he went along the road back to his home. After he had passed, the boat was pulled in a moment and secured, Dad leaving the work to his son, hurried off as usual to get inside the manse gate and up to the house. When the son came into the kitchen it was obvious that Dad had told Mam about the man who had passed along the road and who we could hear singing a Gaelic song in the calm of the evening. And there was a broad smile on Dad's face as he repeated some lines of the song. The song the man was singing went like this,

'Chur mo leannan cul rium,
'S te ur cha dean i stath dhomh.'

English:

My love has turned her back on me
And another will not do any good.

The fact was that the man's good wife found her partner's busy life rather heavy going. It is also true that she came from the south and was thus not fully climatized, one might say, to the ways of the Gaelic community of Aultbea. Therefore every so often she felt she had to get away from it all for a break, a not unreasonable desire. But she always came back. Possibly it would obviate a lot of marital tension and even marriage breakdowns, if partners did go off for a season. This is just mentioned to illustrate that a minister's life was full of potential humour and MacKinnon Aultbea could share with his wife the funny side of a situation just as others about him did in the community. Humour is never far from the serious, and the funny side of life has its own virtue.

My father loved to go out to the net to take in the fish, if in Providence they were caught in its mesh. Could there be any happier diversion for a busy minister, than to row out on a summer morning to the *Tigh H-allaidh* where the trammel all-purpose net was set not far from the shore. While a son or daughter held the oars, back-watering or rowing ahead as required, MacKinnon Aultbea simulated his spiritual calling as a 'fisher of men,' as he stood there in the stern. Now he is pulling in the laden net, hand over hand, extricating the individuals who were unfortunate to be caught and who would

find their way on to the manse or some other table. One
occasion stays indelibly in the memory. As the net comes
over the transom, a big writhing green conger eel reaches the
hand of my father. Most people would distance themselves
from this violent creature which potentially could snap off
the human hand with its powerful jaws. Now you can see the
wicked look in its eyes. The young crew calls, 'Dad, look at
the conger. Watch it, Dad'.   But Dad answers,

   'It's alright, its alright. I see a lovely cod.' The fact is that
he was not even looking at the vicious creature at his hand.
His eyes were peering over the stern with delighted expectation
of the big *bodach ruadh* (codfish) waiting its turn to be
brought inboard.   But what of that three foot long conger,
that threatened the peace of the small boat and had to be dealt
with, without more delay? While my father held the net in
one hand, with the other, his fingers closed in round the
conger's head, like the jaws of a joiner's clamp.   For two
more minutes, the sea viper writhed and twisted, trying to
free himself, but to no avail. The big mouth now stayed open
in a wicked and grotesque concession to the power of the
minister's grip. He was lifeless and still. With the one hand
my father had strangled the creature. It would be cured and
hung up in the manse barn, to be eaten by my father as a
personal delicacy throughout the coming year.

   What an incomparable relaxation for a busy ministerial life,
and what a hand to shake for the privileged members of his
congregation! It has to be said that MacKinnon Aultbea's
handshake was potentially like a steel vice.   Not a few, and
these were men, testified that it was nothing less. It could be
so warm and gentle to some. But he had the capacity, the
secret weapon if you like, to use it for pastoral purposes to

signal concern for dilatoriness or remissness in attending
church. No one can be sure if he did use it occasionally for
this purpose. But then no one can be sure that he didn't. It is
certainly true that he could 'bring any man to his knees' with
the power of his handshake, as well as with the power of his
preaching. It is a real error to connote Christian meekness
with weakness, just as it is mistaken to connote virtue with
physical strength. MacKinnon Aultbea was well aware of
this. He was not hard on people, nor had he the propensity to
trangress the border of the individual's autonomy and freedom.
But he did grieve inwardly and showed disappointment when
those he had hopes for were not in church. He had a particular
desire for the conversion, the turn-around of lives that were
being wasted. They were on his list for work in the Master's
Vineyard and he was ever looking for their response to the
overtures of Heaven's mercy and the dynamic thrust of the
Spirit's power. For his own part, he had a stoical sense of
duty. It really did not occur to him to make any indisposition
an excuse or a reason for not fulfilling every duty and
obligation. This was illustrated in his own life. His strength
was more than physical. It was that of resolve never to give
up; never to fail in doing his duty, as long as it was humanly
possible to do so.

There is no doubt that he had an unusually strong
constitution. He brushed off normal health threats as irritants.
He had some kind of physiological armour-plated immunity
which preserved him from the normal afflictions like colds
or influenza and other 'spoilers' that suddenly force us to
cancel appointments and withdraw from commitments. But
there was something in his will that made him resolute in
doing what he had to. He was very human like everyone

else. Often he knew exhaustion with the perpetual demands upon his time and energies. But he never complained. There was an element of what one might call a humble heroism in his make-up that made him present to others an air of health, well-being and strength. He was a minister, a servant, called to attend to others with their ills and spiritual sores and pains. This was communicated to his parishioners.

It is true all ministers have access to great spiritual resources so that they can give out, like emptying a well, knowing that the well will still be full at the end of the day. But this was personal, related to Mr. MacKinnon's presence as a man. He communicated strength, both spiritually and psychologically. This was noticeable on his pastoral visits, when at least one of his children often accompanied him for the ride. His touch on the shoulder of the bereaved, his unchanging appearance, dressed in the symbolic uniform of his calling comforted mourners even before he spoke. Then he drew out the special balm of heaven designed for broken hearts, conveying the incomparable treatment described by the prophet as 'the oil of joy for mourning and the garment of praise for the spirit of heaviness.'[1]

No pen can adequately record the currents of communication between a 'real' minister and his people. As he preaches on the Sabbath and goes in and out among his people, homes are touched with the heavenly. For the fragrance of the Master which fell like dew on the face of the pastor in the secret place of prayer before the break of day or even in the night watches, still lingers like perfume, in the duties of the day. This is what ministers are born for. And it is really tragic that many congregations side-track the minister from his primary and glorious work to waste his energies in secondary duties,

1. Isaiah 61:3

which could easily be carried out by other people. There is no substitute for a 'real minister', one who has been baptised and anointed in that special hallowed experience where he is commissioned to do the Master's bidding, in proclaiming the Word of Life and leading people to the place of Mercy and to the river that makes glad the 'city of God.' Communities are robbed when 'ministers' are relegated to the background in the order of social necessity. Communities with the thousands of families and needy individuals become starved and vulnerable to the corroding negativism of sin and the arrows of deliberate enmity and exploitation, when they cease to have the visible structural protection of the Most High as represented by his ministers. Is that not what ministers are, powerful protective representatives of heaven's love? Are they not guides to lead people to find the Saviour and his redeeming peace? Are they not bearers of good news, of free pardon, of lasting joy, of journeying mercies, and protective care? Communities need, above all else, individuals, in this the highest calling on earth, God's representatives, ambassadors of the King of kings, under-shepherds of Christ, the Great shepherd of his church, to care for His sheep, keepers of God's vineyard, that there might be much fruit for the Master, watchmen on the walls of Sion, on faithful duty to guard the church and fulfil their commission in its defence against its professed enemies of secularism and evil.

Mr. MacKinnon was worthy of these designations, as were many of his faithful peers. Regard for him was transparent on the part of his people. In war-time he was like a rock to them in all the real and imagined fears which threatened Aultbea along with the rest of the world. There was a powerful sense that where he was present, somehow all would be well.

You must have felt this about some other people, in secular life. How much more powerful and substantive this must be when the person carries the authority of heaven itself and the human vessel whose *raison d'etre* is his singular calling! That is no vain sentiment. And let us be quite clear, it is an earned regard. In Aultbea and wherever that characterises relationship of pastor to his people, the community is enriched and the secular somehow sanctified by the spiritual, like the reciprocal humbling in response to Jonah's preaching to the people of Ninevah.

Mr. MacKinnon unquestionably represented the basic commitment which made the minister of the Gospel a vital part of the Christian community.

Central to everything he participated in was winning souls for Christ and bringing people to realise that their baptism was not just an empty superstitious act. Rather, that their baptism into the church introduced them to the covenant principles of living and loving as God's people in this world. Logically it followed that they, baptised as the children of Promise like Israel of old, should appropriate these blessings when they came of age to think for themselves, and to live in anticipation of the Gospel hope within them of everlasting joy.

428

Chapter 32

Coming into the straight

S t. Paul spoke of the Christian life journey as a race. However long or short, even as a marathon, at last the athlete comes to the finish. He comes into the stadium, after all the grueling hours of effort and endurance. Now he appears for the last stage, the final round of the track. All the past endeavour, the pain and preparation, the resolution and running, is now kaleidoscoped into this last finale. He has come into the straight. He is now coming into the finishing line. He will break the tape. He will savour sweet victory.

The Christian race has one very marked feature. It is a handicap race. We all have a handicap of one kind or another and yet we all can be winners. And there is this, the final list of winners may be in a different order. Remember Jesus' words, 'There are last which shall be first, and there are first which shall be last.'[1] It's necessary not to allow the metaphor of the spiritual to become so important that it is perceived in its literalism as the message it is designed to illustrate. Thus the words of St. Paul and those of our Lord are complementary both in their intent and in their content. And even the wisdom

1. St. Luke 13:30

literature of the Old Testament is not contradicted. The race is not to the swift, nor the battle to the strong ...'[1]

MacKinnon Aultbea was now approaching seventy. He had passed over the top of the hill, a climb for most of the way with little respite. But then his journey was full of single-minded purpose. This meant endurance, sacrifice, service, risk, misunderstanding, putting one self on the line, implied by the calling of the ministry. This last segment of the course was in a sense downhill, the descent from the mountain. He had crossed the obstacles, he had gained victory after victory through the years; he had fought many battles for his Master's redemptive campaign. It's true, he was not on the honours list in the world even of the church. He was just an ordinary parish minister, one of the anonymous many who fulfilled their commission. I recall one time broaching the subject of recording his life in a book. A faint smile was the only response. Why worry, when you think of the glorious commendation that is given in heaven, when those who served the Lord in faithfulness on earth 'receive the crown of life' that fadeth not away. Physically and spiritually, it was like 'coming in to the finish.' It still involved striving, but the 'end of salvation' the goal, the prize of the high calling of the Christian life was closer to fulfilment. And this was forever, and no mortal eye could see nor ear hear, what God has prepared for them that love him.

With declining strength, he soldiered on, in a changed environment and in effect a different day. There were no regrets that he had followed the Jew from Highland Galilee who was the Saviour of the world. He had been born into a harsh childhood environment with little or no concession to the complex appetite for the full life that is taken as the norm for

1. Ecclesiastes 9:11

the most humble in the egalitarian day of the technologically developed age. It surely must be a record that he was never known to be ill. His children have no recollection of any occasion in which he was indisposed. If he was not well at any time, he did not show it or seek a remedy, other than 'fruit salts' or 'baking soda.' For over thirty years he had not been absent from the pulpit, through ill-health. Neither did he fall victim like others in the home and community to the recurring epidemics of influenza or even the common cold, notoriously frequent then and still a significant disruptive irritant, irrespective of palliative or prescription, and no respecter of persons. But that did not mean that he was immune to all germs, allergies and the more serious threats to human health. In an age when physicians gave little or no pre-emptive advice and, with the hindsight of the research knowledge of half a century later, it is clear that there were large gaps in medical knowledge. Mr. MacKinnon fell victim to insidious hypertension. Healthy and constitutionally very strong all his days, slowly but inexorably, his arteries were hardening. Now it became more and more difficult to fulfil the exacting physical demands, and the even greater demands on his mental resources that were part of his spiritual responsibilities linked to the extensive charge of Locheweside. He had to give up his public service as county counsellor, a role which he took over when he first came to Aultbea, in succession to MacKinnon Gairloch before him. He visibly slowed down in other ways. He had less interest in ecclesiastical involvement away from Aultbea. Journeys to assist at other communions became less frequent. And when he did return from these, especially the big ones in Lewis, he was spent and exhausted. Hypertension is a slow but steady killer. Yet at that time it was not given much, if any, attention. Neither were the pre-emptive conditions to mitigate it, in selective dieting, heeded by the public, even if these were known by the health specialists. Ideally, MacKinnon Aultbea should have moved to a small undemanding parish with its reduced responsibilities. But he didn't. He would stay in Aultbea for all his ministry. The links with it were not easily undone.

He was not unique in this. But it was a fashion that was on the way out. He knew only too well that in the changing new age, it was possible for a minister to stay in a parish too long and in effect be an anachronism, holding the spiritual work back, rather than being the catalyst of dynamic progression. He knew, too, that a big charge could not continue to thrive with a minister who was 'over the hill.' He had served in the 'heat of battle' of his day, sparing nothing of his life strength in giving out. He had no intention of coasting along at the expense of the Cause. The Cause of Christ in this world has no place for passengers especially at the front, where ground is lost or won, the ground of human hearts for the Lord of glory.

The trouble with hypertension or common high blood - pressure is that the victim is unaware of what is happening to him. The more the trouble affects him, the more he tries to achieve in his work. Thus my father soldiered on, with his motoring and his ministry, like everyone else in this finite world having also to bow to the inevitable. Take one example of a warning in Providence, from which he and those with him barely escaped with their lives.

He was driving along a two-way road near Inverness when his presence of mind became impaired without his realising

it. Bit by bit on a straight stretch of road, the car moved over
to the wrong side, just gradually. The road fortunately was
clear at the time of oncoming traffic. Suddenly there was a
violent impact and the sound of breaking glass. The side of
the car had struck a telegraph pole at the road side. It was a
curious collision. Cars at that time had the hinges of their
doors projecting sometimes three or even four inches from
the side of the car. Further the doors opened forward. The
upper projecting hinge had caught the telegraph pole. It could
be that just before this, mother advised my father to straighten
the car up. Possibly he suddenly gained full awareness and
pulled the steering-wheel decisively round. The effect with
the little Ford which had cross springs and not much of shock-
absorbers by today's standards, would mean the car would
swerve, its body leaning sideways. causing the collision. At
any rate the car slewed round and nearly turned over. Daughter
Katie was in the back seat. Providentially her large leather
case was in an upright position on the seat between her and
the window. It says much for my father that he brought the
car under control. It is difficult to accept the immediate sequel.
Mother and daughter were 'up to high doh.' They rightly felt
that there had been a near calamity. But my dear father
dismissed the incident as trivial. He did not even stop the car.
Later when the marks of violent impact were clearly evident
especially the broken window, and the bent door hinge, it
could be seen that in spite of himself he had been clearly
shaken. The invincible strong man that never gave in to
weakness, that shrugged off common aches and pains, that
was never once out of the pulpit for a common cold, now
knew he had reached a turning-point, a decisive one that he
could not ignore. From then on he gave in to his daughter

Katie's offer to drive the car to services and to fulfill other
duties. Within the space of six months, two consecutive
strokes brought the imperative signal to announce his
retirement. The man who would not give up at last had to
throw in the towel. He could not come out for another round.
For him, still patently healthy, his dark hair belying his true
condition, he hadn't really given himself a fighting chance to
recover. He would not take even one day from his preaching
duties after his first stroke. The writer was home in Aultbea
on vacation when that happened.

It was the Sabbath night after an exacting day of preaching.
He had been in his element. In Inverasdale, the hall was full
with people and filled also with a glorious sense of God's
Presence. The minister was empowered by the liberty of the
Spirit, lifting up Christ before the people, graphically
describing Divine Love and the healing that comes to the
human heart from the sufferings of the Saviour. His text was
a feast, a banquet for the soul, especially for those who
hungered and thirsted for righteousness, Christ's, because
they were tired of their own and realised that no one is justified
in the sight of God except by the righteousness of Christ which
we have by faith. It was this that my father distributed among
the congregation, a veritable banquet for the soul. He had
introduced Isaiah 53, along with the New Testament encounter
of Philip the evangelist with the Cabinet minister from the
government of Ethiopia, who wondered to whom that chapter
of prophecy referred[1]. It was as if he stalled on the text in
verse 4 and 5. He could not leave it. Listeners were hungry
for more. The people in Inverasadale were at a feast and time
meant nothing. They drew virtue itself out of the minister.
The service was two hours before it closed. I can hear him

1. Acts 8:27

yet reading out the text, he himself savouring the import as his own soul fed on the riches of heaven. There was an abundance, as he pointed out. Yes, enough and to spare for all who would accept the invitation to the feast. And many did that night.

> 4. Gu deimhin ar n-anmhuinneachd ghuilan e, agus ar doilgheasan dh-iomchair e; ach shaoil sinne gu robh e air a bhualadh, air a smachachadh le Dia, agus air a chlaoidh.
> 5. Ach lotadh e air son ar-peacaidh-ne, bhruthadh e air son ar n-aingidheachdan: leagadh airson smachachadh ar sith, agus le a chreuchdaibh-san shlanuicheadh sinne.

English:

> 4. Surely he hath borne our griefs, and carried our sorrows: yet we did esteem him stricken, smitten of God, and afflicted.
> 5. But he was wounded for our transgressions, he was bruised for our iniquities: the chastisement of our peace was upon him; and with his stripes we are healed.

My father looked upon life here as a wonderful opportunity for the seed of the eternal Word to be sown, take root, be nurtured, and come to fulfillment. Time represents the synthesis of this. It may be short or it may be long for each of us. The essential point is that there be movement, a progression, where the land of our uncultivated barren spiritual being is cleared, like a Canadian forest. That is achieved through the ordered activity of the Christian community of which the Church is a dynamic and central influence, in all the expediency of a good unified parish organisation. Within this context, the Word or the eternal seed is sown and the sequence of seasons follow one another until fruition. Then old or young, we live here producing fruits fit for the Master's use, in a broken and needy world.

Then there is the corollary, the inevitable consequence of a life lived in and for Christ. When God comes for us to take us out of the dimension of time, we ourselves are gathered in like a harvest; our lives are presented 'faultless before the presence of His glory'.[1] Thus my father preached. This was his theme that night in Inverasdale meeting-house. And all of such glorious blessings came from Calvary and the Finished Work of Christ, of whom Isaiah prophesied.

Words cannot express such profound spiritual motions of souls doing business with heaven nor can any 'minutes' of such a meeting convey the glory and the grace of such services, when a minister reaches the heights of preaching, albeit in a plain humble meeting-house on the shores of Lochewe in the northwest Highlands of Scotland. But of course the human vessel, the servant of God whose glorious work it was to break the Bread of Life, was spent. The people of Inverasdale dined well that sabbath night in the old meeting-house. There was an abundance of spiritual food, for the soul, for the heart even for the body. Why, the Gospel is the healing therapy for the whole man! 'A feast of fat things, a feast of wine on the lees, of fat things full of marrow, of wines on the lees, well refined.'[2]

There was enough and to spare, given out from the open doors of heaven as MacKinnon Aultbea held nothing back in the preaching of the unsearchable riches of Christ, that evening

1.Jude, v 24   2. Isaiah 25:6

with the lamps of the sanctuary burning brightly in the old meeting-house. One can see the scene yet. At last the minister must stop. His hand is raised. And you hear the words, *'Gairmidh sinn air ainm an Tighearna.'* 'Let us call upon the name of the Lord (in prayer).' Then he gives out the closing psalm of that sweet time of worship, just two verses as the time has passed, followed by the benediction.

My father was ever conscious of the need to redeem the time. Time was an expedient for the synthesis of man's potential, and God's mercy. Nature spoke to him as a metaphor of the spiritual and as a record of the seasons of the soul's experience from its conception as the elective will of heaven, its awakening and development in human consciousness to its final maturity in the unseen beyond.

Here is a poem composed by him illustrating this. It has to be said that whatever translation is made into another language, none can match the flowing nuances of the original Gaelic tongue.

An t-Earrach agus am Foghar

1.

'Se maduinn Earraich neoineanach
'n uair bhios am por 'san fhonn
'S am fochann maoth ag comhdachadh
gach sgod a rinn an crann

2.

A'ghrian ag aiseag deo dha
's ag ol dheth braon na h-oidhch',
An samhla tha mi meorachadh
na'm b'eol dhomh chur an cainnt.

3.

Is samhla sud air diadhachd
's air diomhaireachd nan gras,

'S air siol na rioghachd shiorruidh
am pobull Chriosd a fas.

4.

Thig air tus am fianuis e
's thig sin an dias fo bhlath,
'S le druchd is grian an Tighearna
cha chrion a freumh gu brath.

5.

Air leum gu'm faic mi Fogharadh
am tionalaidh nan sguab
Bith dlothan air an cruinneachadh
o achannan an fhuachd.

6.

Is cuid a chuir gu muladach
le subhachas a' buain,
'S an Tighearna ri cur urram orr'
's toirt uile dhoibh an duais.

7.

Ach dhomhs' is ceisd 's gearan e
mo bheatha bhi cho blian,
Nach faic mi innt' an toradh ud
's nach lorgaich mi an siol.

8.

Ach tha mo shuil gu muinghineach
ri trocair mhor an Triath
Gu'm fiosraich esan m'fhasalachd
le ghrasan saoibhir sior.

English:

Spring and Autumn

1.

Surprising morn of Spring,
when seed in earth is found.
The tender leaves now cover
where the plough has turned the ground.

2

The sun renews the life-strength,
and drinks the dew of night
These reflections fill my thoughts
And now in words I write.

3.

This is like a picture
of God's most gracious deeds
as on the seeds of holiness
Christ's own people feed

4

At first you see its presence
as it brings the ear to life,
the dew and sun of heaven,
so that the corn will never die.

5.

For me to see the Autumn,
the time of gathering straw,
the sheaves are stooked together
from the cold ground of the field.

6.

Those that were sown with weeping
with joy shall now be reaped,
The Lord above rewarding them,
and honouring their worth.

7.

When I my own life now review,
it seems so poor and bare,
A harvest great I cannot see,
and even seed itself is rare.

8.

But my eye looks up with confidence
to the Mercy of the Lord,
that he provides fulfilment,
in rich and sweet accord.

———————————

After the service that night, MacKinnon Aultbea went home. He had given all. He had held nothing back. He had not rationed his resources. With his kind of preaching, the preacher is captive to the message. Many times he had preached in faithfulness, knowing the cold days of spiritual frost, the cloudy days when heaven's sun did not get through, to warm the soul at least overtly in the service. But that night in Inverasdale, there was in a great measure, what every preacher coveted, a powerful sense of the Presence of the Lord. In this, the preacher had 'liberty.' He rejoiced in his role, the honour of bringing the glad tidings. In this, the message had a dynamic immediacy.

But there was a price to be paid. That night, back in the Aultbea manse sometime after midnight, mother called out in alarm. Dad was on the floor at the bedside, unconscious. Lifted back into the bed, he lay there. At last he came round. Dr Hunter next door came over in his dressing-gown. Before the doctor could say anything, my father asked how he, the physician himself, was keeping. It was no use. He would not accept that anything unusual had happened. He had no recollection of his 'bad turn'. He was up for breakfast within hours at the usual time and back in the pulpit on the following Sabbath. But the bell would not stop tolling. Within months he had the second stroke. Then the writing was on the wall. Even he, with all his strength, now was visibly weakened and in effect was incapacitated. MacKinnon Aultbea had to face facts. His work was done. He had been obedient to the heavenly vision; he had answered the call; he had redeemed the time; he had contributed his life to his generation, as a messenger of the "Good News," and as comforter of God's people. He had faithfully ploughed the field, he had sowed the seed, he had nurtured the plants. Sometimes he had rejoiced in seeing fruits for His Master. Now like the runner in the relay race, he had to hand the baton to another. And in the obedience of running the race set before him, he himself would be gathered in, would be claimed as a trophy of heaven's grace.

Physically that meant a great disruption. He and his family would have to move out of the manse and with no place else to live in, he would have to leave Aultbea and seek residence elsewhere for the limited time that was obviously left to him.

My father retired, initially staying for a short period with his daughter Katie, married to Skye-born Rev Donald Ross minister at Delny, Kilmuir Easter. Then the old soldier of the Lord, along with his spouse, spent a short but happy year in a newly built County Council cottage at Kildary. He never preached again. On one visit to the Raigmore hospital to see mother who had an operation, he was told of a member of his old parish being in another ward. He stopped at the bedside. What a meeting! He was calm and out-giving in that dynamic therapeutic manner that a human being who is God's messenger is uniquely qualified to express. The old parishioner seemed infused with great joy and after her old pastor's prayer, could not speak with emotion, as they parted. But then the ties that bind the people of the Lord who subscribe to the Covenant of Grace, trusting in the Finished Work of Calvary, these ties are enduring and though there is a physical parting, they have both a shared heritage of the Christian faith, the one faith, and an inheritance before them, too glorious for words to describe or citizens only of the seen world to understand.

Latterly Dad became invalided. Mother nursed him as she had cared for him all their married life. The strong man became helpless as a child. There was no detectable weakness in any part of his body. Even his heart was pronounced as in perfect condition. Only this, the blood could not get through the arteries. Nothing could be done. That was the verdict of the specialist who came to see him as he lay in weakness in the room in Kildary.

Chapter 33

Departure

W
hat a glorious day it is when God calls one of his faithful servants home! Remember how Simeon, when he had seen the holy child Jesus, said; 'Lord, now lettest thou thy servant depart in peace, according to thy word: for mine eyes have seen thy salvation.'[1]

And for MacKinnon Aultbea, the Scottish Highland minister, the hour of departure was at hand. Looking outwardly more or less as he always did, with his head covered in a mat of black hair, his soul was ready for the last call. He had done all he could for his Master. He would be taken up into that heavenly abode, *an dachaidh bhuan*, the eternal home, 'the house of many mansions' which the Lord has prepared for them that love him. There is something special about the ambassadors of Christ, the messengers commissioned to proclaim the Gospel of Peace as they reach the hour of departure. Their death is a landmark in history, the history of the church's pilgrimage. For their lives are not lived unto themselves, and the message they proclaimed has gone out into the world, Sabbath after Sabbath over the years. It is

1. St. Luke 2:29-30

their burden to sow, and to water, but it is in the sovereign and elective will of God himself to give the increase.[1] And where there is faithfulness in proclaiming the Word of Life, then there is the triumphant assertion by God himself that it will be accompanied by good success.

We read through the prophet of the uniqueness of the Master Creator's thoughts, and the dynamic influence of His sanctified Word, as distinct from the most profound thinking of his creatures. This was one of my father's favourite themes and even as he lay on his deathbed, memories of his days in the pulpit came back to members of the family, like the background accompaniment of a drama, and these memories linger yet over the years, as sanctified thoughts that characterize all the King's messengers who are faithful to their commission.

Images of him in the pulpit again came before the mind, his compelling presence, not as a monarch but as a messenger, not as a personality projecting its own egotism, but as a preacher, one who like John the Baptist, was an introducer. For to the end of his life he was stamped by a deep humility, reflecting his conviction that Christ his Master was incomparably unique, the latchet of whose shoe, he was unworthy to unloose.[2] I see him still, and hear him, his voice rising and falling in the undulating waves of the Gaelic language, and also in English, with the matchless phrases that spoke of the eternal verities that are food and drink for the human soul.

> Iarraibh an Tighearna, am feadh a tha e r'a fhaotainn; gairmibh air, am feadh tha e am fagus.
> Treigeadh ant-aingidh a shlighe, agus an duine eucorach a smuaintean; agus pilleadh e ris an Tighearna, agus nochaidh e trocair dha; agus ri ar Dia-ne, oir bheir e

1. I Corinthians 3:6   2. Mark 1:3

maitheanas gu pailt.

Oir cha'n iad mo smuainte-sa bhur smuainte-se, ni mo is iad bhur slighean-se, mo shlighean-se, deir an Tighearna.

Oir mar tha na neamhan ard seach an talamh, mar sin tha mo shlighean-sa, ard seach bhur slighean-se, agus mo smuainte-sa seach bhur smuainte-se.

Oir mar a thig an t-uisge a nuas, agus an sneachd o neamh, agus nach pill e an sin, ach gun uisgich e an talamh, agus gun toir e air fas torradh a thabhairt uaith, a chum gun tabhair e siol dhasan a chuireas, agus aran dhasan a dh'itheas;

Is amhuil a bhios m'fhacal-sa a theid a mach as mo bheul: cha phill e a m'ionnsuidh gun tairbhe; ach comhlionaidh e an ni as aill leam, agus bheir e gu buil an ni mu'n do chuir mi mach e.

English:

Seek ye the Lord, while he may be found, call ye upon him while he is near.

Let the wicked forsake his way and the unrighteous man his thoughts: and let him return unto the Lord, and he will have mercy upon him; and to our God, for he will abundantly pardon.

For my thoughts are not your thoughts, neither are your ways my ways, saith the Lord.

For as the heavens are higher than the earth, so are my ways higher than your ways, and my thoughts than your thoughts.

For as the rain cometh down, and the snow from heaven, and returneth not thither, but watereth the earth, and maketh it bring forth and bud, that it may give seed to the sower, and bread to the eater:

So shall my word be that goeth forth out of my mouth: it shall not return unto me void, but it shall accomplish that which I please, and it shall prosper in the thing whereto I sent it.[1]

1. Isaiah 55:6-11

But now the night is over. The dawn of another Sabbath is breaking on earth. The last call has come as the family are gathered round the bedside. What a fitting day for a faithful soldier of Christ to go to glory! Are not the chariots of heaven at the gate and the angels of the Lord now already there to take his soul from the earth, so that he be parted from the finite and brought into the celestial city!

There is no need for consciousness itself. All people eventually sink below it. The minister of the Gospel, the herald of hope, the giver of good news, was now passive. Is not the reality as well as the spirit expressed in the negro spiritual, now true as it is under every clime on earth and wherever a believer is at the opened gate to glory!

Swing low, sweet chariot,
Coming for to carry me home.

All the storms of life are past, all the strivings, all the anxieties; all the needs, physical and otherwise are now irrelevant. They don't matter. Why? Yes, because Christ is now 'all in all.'[1] There is no rim where sky and sea meet, no horizon, for he is now taken by the great pilot into the harbour of eternal joy. Of course his place was ready. Did not his Lord say to his disciples, 'I go to prepare a place for you!'[2] He would be forever the guest with the redeemed, the guest of Christ who reigns over all, for the Father hath given the Son 'the heathen for his inheritance and the uttermost parts of the earth for his possession.'[3]

Long before this when he was converted in Vancouver, he composed the poem, 'The Prodigal Son', describing his conversion. Now the last verse is about to be completely realised, like a boat being launched at 'high water.'

1. Colossians 3:20   2. St.John 14:2   3. Psalm 2:8

Dh'iarr e culaidh dhomh a mach, bu taitnich' bha 'na bhuth,
Is rinn e maiseach mi gun dail, le fainne 's brogan ur.
Is fhuair mi sath de'n fheoil a b-fhearr, de'm bheil am faileadh cur,
S'bidh mi gu brath le aoidhean graidh ag ardachadh a chliu.

English:

He ordered out a coat, most pleasing in the store,
He dressed me up without delay, with ring on hand and shoes on feet.
And I was filled with best of fare, the richest flavours known.
And I'll forever sing his praise with all the guests of love.

And through Christ and his Finished Work of atoning sacrifice, all anger even of God and recalcitrance of man give way to reconciliation, as the morning light dispels the darkness of the night. Thus as Christ's efficacy permeates receptive mankind, the church, born in the womb of the elective will of heaven, takes form. And those within it are born of heaven, are citizens of God's kingdom, and heirs of glory. What could any one want more than this, to be with Christ forever! All relationships, even that between husband and wife, parents and children, are now terminated at death. The contract of the Redemptive Covenant by which we are sealed by the indwelling Spirit, to Christ the Son, the personification of the Father's love is perpetual, for ever and forever, life that shall never end.

The orb of the morning sun was stamped on the window curtain of the bedroom at Kildary; the sunbeams could not be kept out by the cloth. No more could the walls of the seen world keep out the glory of the eternal, nor the rays of the Sun of Righteousness which bring to humanity the dimension of everlasting completeness and healing of all that was spiritually broken. Now the soul of MacKinnon Aultbea, the Highland minister who served the Lord in his church, distributing the unsearchable riches from the 'company store,' the heavenly company store, left its earthly tent to bear forever the image of the heavenly.

The little boy who climbed into the minister's gig, and received the prophetic blessing of the aged minister, the growing lad who dived off the rocks at Galtrigil, now lay still.

The youth who left the shores of Scotland to join the thousands of exiles to hew out a living in the virgin land of Canada; the young soldier who witnessed on his knees among others in an army barrack room in the Great War, was now at peace.

The man whom Jesus found, and who found Jesus, had run the race, had finished the course, and was now claimed for a seat in heaven among the redeemed; the man who served his Master on the stage of life in all the varied obligations of his high calling, who said on one occasion to his younger son, while at a Communion Fast day in Little Loch Broom, 'What I do for Christ is nothing, as I think of what Christ has done for me,' was now at rest.

It was easy for the mind to think of the angels taking him to heaven. Furthermore it was difficult, yes impossible, to deny the belief that the humble boy from Glendale, *Aonghas Ian Bhig,* who became the winsome preacher, the beloved pastor, the Celt with the bardic gift, but above all the 'child of God' and the 'servant of God', was already at rest. It was reasonable to assume the corollary to his departure from the earth, namely that he was now united to Christ, that he was already joined to the great company of the Redeemed.

There is authoritative foundation for this belief, given unequivocally in the canon of Scripture and in the Westminster Confession of Faith, with all the shades of theological emphasis. It answers the perennial question that faces all living, and expresses the reassuring certainty with which believers can contemplate departure, with anticipation rather than apprehension.

In Gaelic, the answer is :

> Tha anama nam creidmeach ri -am am bais air an deanamh iomlan ann an naomhachd, agus air ball a' dol gu gloir; agus tha an cuirp, air dhoibh bhi sior-cheangailte ri Criosd, a gabhail fois'n an uaighibh gu ruig an aiserigh.

English:

> The souls of believers are at their death made perfect in holiness, and do immediately pass into glory, and their bodies being still united to Christ, do rest in their graves till the resurrection.[1]

There was a man taken from the quarry of a hard and cruel world, whom grace transformed from being an anonymous servant of self, to become a servant of God, whose testimony was that God found him, and by his magnetic love, redeemed him, gave him a commission in his Master's service and made him an heir of glory.

And even as Christ, the stone of stumbling, the rock of offence is made the chief cornerstone, so his servant was cut and shaped by God's Hand in his providence, was smoothed by grace, and polished like a precious stone to show the varied colours of its spiritual metamorphosis.

In that short but greatest synopsis describing subscription to the Christian faith, as a life which demonstrates the all-

1. Catechism #37

prevailing principle of love, we read,

> Oir tha sinn a faicinn 's an am so gu dorcha tre ghloine; ach an sin chi sinn aghaidh ri h- aghaidh: 's an am so is aithne dhomh ann an tomhas; ach an sin aithnichidh mi eadhon mar tha aithne orm.

English:

> For now we see through a glass darkly; but then face to face: now I know in part; but then shall I know even as also I am known. [1]

Then the dimension of time and the finite that we live in here on earth is eclipsed by that which is greater than time, namely the dimension of the eternal. The eternal does not succeed time. It already exists beyond the perception of the finite, as it were beyond the horizon. Already the concert of praise has begun and goes on, recruited each day of time from the ranks of men and women who have been faithful to the principle of generic divinity, that composite of law and love in regenerated humanity. To be part of this is man's true destiny.

Then we can reflect the glory of our Redeemer for ever and ever like the stars in the night sky that are irradiated with light. There is a sequence to it all in the evolution of history. As we look to another millennium since God sent His Son in human form, we cannot know the year nor the hour when there will be a glorious mass metamorphosis in which Christ the Son will come again in the clouds. We do believe from reading the Scriptures that it will coincide in some way with the mass conversion to Christ of the Hebrew people. What an incentive to close in with Christ and his saving invitation while the door of mercy is still open! For one thing is certain

1. I Corinthians 13:12

for everyone of us, the day of grace will be succeeded by the day of judgment. But for those who are the purchased possession, the stones that were found in the quarry of a lost and sinful humanity, they are now made perfect. They are sanctified, the saving judicial standing before their God is corroborated in the sanctifying of their lives by the indwelling Spirit. They are now, 'finished' stones to be set in the crown of the King. Then the galaxy of the new heaven and the wonder of the New Jerusalem, the transformed world will be unveiled.

That was the vision that this Highland minister, Rev. Angus MacKinnon Aultbea projected and illustrated as preacher, pastor and poet. He preached 'Christ..the power of God and the wisdom of God'[1] , and sometimes, just sometimes, he captured a vision, glorious glimpses of the 'King in his beauty, and the land that is a very far off.'[2] But he was ever setting forth the beauty of Christ. What follows as the corollary of a life of faithfulness, no mortal eye nor ear can see now nor hear, but will do so in the hereafter, where mortality gives place to immortality.

Who cares if the individual cannot then be identified among the multitudes of the redeemed in the spiritual Milky Way of that transformed world. But each one is known to God, and as each one walked in his light on earth, he shall reign, shining forever. Though MacKinnon Aultbea lived life here on earth to the full, identifying with immediate loved ones and all humanity with the generic love that flowed from his communion with God, nevertheless, this hour of the great change marked the satisfying of supreme desire. For him as for all who tasted that the Lord was gracious, who were given to drink from the fountain of life this was the hour not of dissolution, but of completeness. Now the earthly is

1.I Corinthians 1:24   2. Isaiah 33:17

transformed into the heavenly, the corruptible into the incorruptible. The shadows of life flee away before the presence of the celestial light from Christ the Solar centre of the redeemed world, or the world of the redeemed.

Now is fulfilled for him and for all believers like him, the graphic description by the 'Apostle of the North' Dr. MacDonald of Ferintosh, in his hymn, so loved by my father, 'The Christian on the other side of the Jordan.' We quote one verse.

> Ach fhuair mi nis na dh'iarradh leam;
> Is m' uile mhiann gu brath!
> Le naomhachd rinneadh sgiamhach mi,
> An coslas Chriosd gu slan:
> Le soills' na gloir, shar-lionadh mi,
> 'S mi dluth do Dhia, gun sgail.
> Is caithear leam an t-siorruidheachd,
> A' snamh gu sior, 'na ghradh.

Translation:

> For now I've found what I desired,
> All longings met forever.
> Through holiness I now am pure,
> In likeness to the Lord, my Brother.
> With glorious light I'll follow on,
> No shadows, close to God.
> And all eternity I'll spend,
> To bathe forever in His love.

How true. For our life then will be an animated reflection of the glory of our Lord. And of a minister of the Gospel, the 'craftsman' who was skilled in the tools of his trade, using the Word of God, more than any other, it surely is true that as he was faithful unto death, he shall receive a crown of life.[1]

Sentiment cannot gloss over Scripture as we contemplate the earthly scene of our human habitat. There is a continual war of good against evil, of the Church against the negative drawing power of the world, of the forces of righteousness against the subtle enemies of Christ and his kingdom.[2] We are not prophets. But God has given prophecy. All is not clear in the manner in which the future will unfold, but the content of the prophets' message leaves all who read and take heed without excuse.

Listen to one of God's beloved prophets, who followed the call of God since he was a young man. This is linked unquestionably with the visions of John in the Book of Revelation. The import is apocalyptic. As I write I am empowered to add that the third millennium since the first visitation of Christ as a child cannot be excluded from the time interval of the second visitation, the Second Coming of the Son. Prophecy is unambivalent;

> .... and there shall be a time of trouble, such as never was since there was a nation even to that same time: and at that time thy people shall be delivered, every one that shall be found written in this book.
> And many of them that sleep in the dust of the earth shall awake, some to everlasting life, and some to shame and everlasting contempt.
> And they that be wise shall shine as the brightness of the firmament; and they that turn many to righteousness as the stars for ever and ever.[3]

The gravestone marks the corporeal resting-place of Rev. Angus MacKinnon in the Aultbea cemetery at Mellon Charles. Identified in life as MacKinnon Aultbea among his

1. Revelation 2:10   2. I John 5:1-13   3. Daniel 12:1-4

colleagues, he is the only minister who is buried in the cemetery, and the only one whose whole ministry is identified with the parish of Locheweside or North Gairloch. Appropriately the stone stands among those that mark the graves of his beloved people. The centuries of time will eventually see their dissolution, like the gravestones that lie broken and forgotten in the burial places of history. But what does it matter! For the faithful servant of his Lord is given an immortal crown, and his name is recorded on the Master Computer of exclusive Omni-Science, in the very heart of God.

Human memory will fail, languages will cease to be used like the Gaelic tongue used in this Scottish Highland parish; new generations already rise up, succeeding one another to merge into the millenniums of time.

But all that, as aspiration and realization, is like the hour glass of a day, or the digital timepiece bought and discarded, from the mechanical world of a soulless technological society. In contrast those whose portion is with the people of God, endure forever, sharing with them the Christian destiny of the spiritual Israel, who are described in the incomparable last words of Moses, God's great servant.

> 'Is sona thu, O Israel; co tha cosmhuil ruit, O shluagh air a shaoradh leis an Tighearna.'

English:

> 'Happy art thou, O Israel: who is like unto thee, O people saved by the Lord.' [1]

The epitaph on the gravestone, composed by Rev Roderick A. Finlayson who by then held the Chair of Systematic Theology in the Free Church College, and who had baptised

---

1. Deuteronomy 33:29

Donalda, the youngest of the eight children of the MacKinnon family, reads like this, with the name of his life partner added at later date.

Erected by his attached congregation
to the Memory of
THE REVEREND ANGUS MACKINNON
born in the parish of Duirinish, Skye, 1885,
Died at Kildary, 22nd December, 1957.
Minister of the Free Church congregation
of Aultbea and Poolewe from 1924 -1955.
A man of tender feeling, deep Christian experience,
and rich poetic gifts, he was a
winsome preacher of the evangel, a devoted
pastor, and a loving husband and father.

*"Bith iad leamsa, tha Tighearna nan sluagh
ag radh, anns an latha sin an dean mi suas
mo sheudan.:* Malachi III:17.

Also his beloved wife and our loving mother
CATHERINE MATHESON
Born in Stoer 19th February, 1900
Died 25th December, 1982

On hearing of the passing of MacKinnon Aultbea shortly before printing, Professor Finlayson, editor of the Free Church Record, wrote in his last editorial, January, 1958.

The late Rev. Angus MacKinnon

...The death of Mr. MacKinnon will be mourned throughout the Highland area, where his preaching was so highly appreciated, and particularly by the congregation of Aultbea and Poolewe, to whom the whole of his ministry, exceeding thirty years was devoted.

Mr. MacKinnon was a vigorous and original preacher, a master of pure idiomatic Gaelic, and a man deeply

grounded in the doctrines of grace... Coming of stock
who seemed to have the poetry of the Western Isles in
their very blood-stream, Mr. MacKinnon was himself a
bard of no mean order, and the deep exercises of his own
soul were often revealed in verses that combined felicity
of expression with spirituality of conception. Poems from
his pen began to appear in the Monthly Record at the
time when he was on active service during the 1914-18
war and were kindly received by Gaelic-speaking readers.
A collection of these might form a fitting memorial to
their gracious composer...

Here is a formal tribute written by his colleague and friend,
Rev Ronald Lamont Fraser, fellow presbyter and minister of
Lochcarron. It appeared in contemporary newspapers and the
Free Church Record.

REV. ANGUS MACKINNON

A tribute by Rev. R.L. Fraser

The ranks of the ministry have been weakened by the
passing to his rest on 22nd December, 1957, of Rev. Angus
MacKinnon, Senior minister of the Free Church
Congregation of Aultbea and Poolewe.

Mr. MacKinnon was born and brought up in Glendale,
Skye, and in a home respected for piety and for parental
upbringing. On his mother's side he was related to the
late saintly Rev. Norman Macleod who was minister of
Portree, Skye, prior to the Union of 1900. There was a
marked resemblance between the two men.

In his youth he emigrated to Canada, and in the city of
Vancouver, experienced the saving change which led him
to devote his life to the Ministry of the Gospel. On his
return to the home country, he served with the Armed
Forces during the First World War. He studied for the

Ministry of the Church and on completion of his studies was license to preach the Gospel, by the Presbytery of Edinburgh. In July 1924, he accepted a unanimous call from the Congregation of Aultbea and Poolewe in the Presbytery of Lochcarron, where he laboured for the long period of 31 years, until his retiral from the active ministry through ill-health.

In the beginning of his ministry, he was supported by a loyal band of worthy elders and praying people whose place was filled in succession throughout the years by others like-minded. He had many seals to his faithful ministry amongst them which resulted in a strong attachment on the part of minister and congregation. to each other.

During the Second World War he served as Presbyterian Chaplain to the Forces stationed at the naval base in Aultbea. He spoke of this service as an experience which was of untold benefit to his ministerial life. For over 20 years, he represented the district as a member of the Ross-shire County Council where he made his influence felt in matters pertaining both to the secular and spiritual life of the people.

As a preacher Mr. MacKinnon had unusual poetic gifts and talents which he consecrated to the service of his Master. His facile use of the Gaelic language, in which he excelled, his art of graphic and illustrative description, his forceful and winning voice, rivetted the attention of his hearers and gave urgency to the Evangel which it was his delight to proclaim. At Communion seasons in many congregations of our Church, his presence was warmly welcomed by young and old.

Possessing a strong physique, he unsparingly gave of his time and service to minister to the needs of the flock within the bounds of an extensive parish. He was never absent from the pulpit through ill-health.

His peaceable and affectionate disposition won for him an abiding place in the hearts of the brethren who were privileged to enjoy his friendship, while in his walk, he was circumspect, seeking to adorn the doctrine of his Saviour, Jesus Christ. As a Christian, he was humble, ever remembering that he owed all to the Sovereign Grace of God, who had called him to be an ambassador for Christ.

Mr. MacKinnon was blessed with a worthy partner who proved an ideal helpmate during a happy married life. The hospitality which they both so generously afforded in the manse, especially at communion seasons, will be remembered by many. To his family, three daughters of which married ministers, he was a devoted and loving father.

In his prolonged illness, while often passing through deep waters, he was sustained by the Word and Presence of his glorious Redeemer. On a Sabbath morning he was called to his eternal rest to hear the voice of welcome, "Well done, good and faithful servant" and to share in the beatific Vision of the Heavenly Jerusalem.

At his home in Kildary, where he was nursed so faithfully and tenderly by his wife, a funeral service was conducted by a number of ministers representing the neighbouring presbyteries. At Aultbea where his remains were interred awaiting a glorious resurrection, a large congregation gathered in the church, to show their respect and esteem for a pastor beloved. Thereafter, his remains were interred in the Mellon Charles cemetery, fittingly, according to his own wishes, among his adopted people and the parish of his spiritual labours.

A Minister's Wish--A Poetic Legacy to the Church

The following poem was composed when he knew he was coming near the end of his earthly pilgrimage. Though a minister, he knew the reproach of Christ his master, in the assaults of the prince of darkness, his own vulnerability to doubt, and the normal negative experiences shared by all in a life lived by faith. The poem touches the realism of human conflict between the forces of good and those that seek continually to snuff out the Light of the World. But the poem brings assurance of victory for the 'afflicted and poor people, who put their trust in the Name of the Lord.'

Durachd Teachaire Chriosd

1.

Tha sgeul agam ri h-aithris,
'S cha 'n 'eil fada agam ri luaidh.
'S dhaindeoin buaireadh Shatain
'S dhaindeoin taire sluaigh,
B'e sud mo mhiann is m'iarrtas
Is dh'iarrainn e gach uair
Gu 'n tugadh Dia 'n fhabhar dhomh
Gach trath bhi air a luaidh.

2.

Na leigeadh Dia gu sgithichinn
An tim bhi deanamh sgeul
Air prisealachd nan geallaidhean
Mar bharantas do 'n treud.
Is eifeachd shiorruidh bhuadhach
Fuil an Uain choisinn e,
Is eadarghuidhe a ' Bhuachaille
Thug buaidh 'na uile dhreuchd.

3.

O moladh, moladh siorruidh dhuit
Gu robh E iosal truagh.
'S air dha bhi dioladh m'fhiachan-sa
Gu 'n riaraich E an uaigh,
"S gu 'n sgar E uaipe 'n t-ughdarras
Bha aig' bho thus air sluagh
'S fa dheoidh gu 'n d' eirich m' Aiseirigh
Le caithream a bhios buan.

4.

"Leag mise 's chuir mi cuideachadh
Air Curaidh treun nam buadh."
'S tha E nis air ardachadh
Mar Shlanuighear a shluaigh.
'S ged a bhruth a namhaid
A shail le iomairt chruaidh
Rinn Esan briseadh mairean
Air a chlaigeann greannach cruaidh.

5.

Is Maisich', O is Maisich' Thu
Na clann mo shluaigh gu leir.
Is milse leam do bhriathran
Na fion bho mhil nan geug.
Tha boltrach chubhraidh oirdhearc
Lionadh seomair m' anam fein,
'N uair dhearcainn troimh na sgothan
Air do ghloir aig deas laimh Dhe.

6.

Na m'fheoil-sa cha 'n eil fallaineachd
'S aig m' anam cha 'n eil sith.
'S dh' aindeoin boidean 's aideachadh
Tha 'n anshocair 'n am chridh,
'S mo naimhdean guinneach ardanach

Cha tarr mi 'n cuir fo chis.
Gu cogadh tha iad togarrach
An sith 'n trath labhras mi.

7.

'Se dh-fhag 's an am so cianail mi
'S mi riaraicht air gach doigh
An seann duine a bhi miannachadh
'Se 'g iarradh gu bhi mor.
Tha sgealb 's an fheoil 'g am sharuchadh
Gach la le iomadh deoir.
Och! Och! is duine truagh mi
Co dh' fhuasglas air mo leon?

8.

Ach ged is treun an seann duine
'S ged dh'fhag e mall mo cheum
Is ged is lionmhor teanntachdan
An so an gleann nan deur,
Thig an t-am 's an caochlaidhear
Gach aon g' aite fein,
'S bithidh mise troimh an t-siorruidheachd
A mealltuinn iomhaigh Dhe.

9.

Bha cairdean agam uair-eiginn
'Nuair bha mi 'n cruas na daors',
Ach 's fhad' bho rinn iad m'fhuathachadh,
Is suarach mi 'n an suil.
Ach Caraid caomh nan truaghan
Tha E suairc rium 's gach cuis,
'S cha treig E ri mo bheo mi
'S aig sruth Iordain bithidh mi saor.

10

Ach falbhadh iad no fuireadh iad
Is Tusa Fear mo Ghraidh.

'S ann ort a bhios mo smuaintean
'N uair is cruaidh a bhios am blar.
Mo dhaingneach treun 's gach cruadal Thu
Mo bhuaidh Thu anns gach cas,
'S a' Carraig air an d'fhuaradh mi,
Cha ghluaisear I gu brath.

11.

A' Chlach a dhuilt na clachairean
Clach-chinn na h-oisne I,
O anam, feuch nach suidhich thu
Air bunait eil' ach I.
Air eagal 'n uair a dhearbhar thu
Am meidhean feirg an Uain,
Gu 'm faigh thu duais nan cealgairean
An dorchadas bith-bhuan.

12.

Mo bhraithrean caomh na sgithichibh
'S bithibh dileas anns gach am.
Ged tha sibh fulang mi-cheartan
Is mi-run air gach laimh.
'N uair chruinnicheas E na diobairich
As na tirean bhos 's thall,
Bithidh gach diblidh bochd a chuidich leis
An culaidh bean na bainns'.

Translation

A Minister's Wish

1

I have a story to relate
And short the time to tell
In spite of Satan's wiles
And much contempt as well.
This my conviction and desire
I'll seek this all my days,

That God his favour give to me,
And I forever give Him praise.

2

If God permit, I'll never tire
Redeeming time to spread the Word
The valued promises of Truth,
The warrant of a people's God.
The eternal atoning victory
By the shed blood of the Lamb,
The pleading of their Shepherd
Who in all things won.

3

Eternal praise be given to thee!
That as the meek and lowly One
He was paying all my debts
And taking from my grave the sting.
The one who stripped himself of power
He had before recorded time
And then in resurrection rose
In triumph of Thy will divine.

4

Let me now enlarge on Him
Virtuous champion of strength
For now that He is risen
As Saviour of His people
And though the enemy bruised his heel
With many a subtle ploy,
He gained a lasting victory,
Crushing his hard and wicked head.

5

O Thou who art the Fairest
Of all the sons of men
Your words to me are sweeter far

Than wine or sap from any tree
Your perfume fragrant beautiful
Fills the chamber of my soul
When glimpses through the clouds I see
Your glory set at God's right hand.

6

There is no health within my frame
And for my soul no peace
In spite of vows and all confessions
Within my heart there's grief
The powerful foes that fight within
I cannot these subdue
They seek a conflict to augment
Although I speak to them in peace.

7

This has left me now distraught
Though full in many ways
When self asserts its craving pride
To seek some earthly fame.
A thorn within my flesh I have
It grieves me every day,
O wretched man, I truly am!
Who'll take this hurt away?

8

But though the old man stalwart is
And surely slowed my step,
In troubles that have met my course
Through this, the vale of tears,
The time of change that comes to all
Each one to his own place,
I shall throughout eternity enjoy
The image pure of heavenly grace.

9

I once had friends long time now gone
In days of bondage tried,
It's long since they have turned on me
I'm now indifferent in their eyes.
But the kind Friend of all the poor
Is constant at all times
In life He'll not forsake me,
And at Jordan's bank I will be free.

10

Let them come and let them go
Thou art all my heart's desire
On thee alone will be my thoughts
When I face the enemy's fire
My fortress in the face of strife
My triumph in every strait,
The Rock I reached for refuge
Remains unmoved for ever.

11

The stone rejected by the builders
Now is made the Cornerstone,
O Soul take heed you never trust
In anyone but Him.
For fear that, when you're tested
By the balance of God's Truth,
That you receive the wage of guile,
For darkness justly follows sin.

12

My kindly brethren, do not tire,
Be diligent each day,
Though you injustice suffer much
And injury in many a way.
When Christ the outcasts gathers in,
From countries near and far,
All the meek he saved are dressed
In garments of His wedding guests.

Epilogue

Across the glens and over the heatherclad hills that give the Scottish Highlands a singular grandeur that appeals to visitors from every corner of the earth, and in every settlement across the seas where the Scottish Church has transplanted its hardy spiritual roots, with its unique culture, language and music, the graves of the church's ministers who carried the Fiery Cross of Christ's challenge, signify hallowed and sacred records of the same. May generations look beyond the city capitols, and visit the country churchyards, and pause before the memorial stones. There they will see the field officers in the Forces of the King of kings, who in their generation led the companies of faithful witnesses and fought a 'good fight' in the Master's service. Of such, was MacKinnon Aultbea.

There is almost a mystical link between the spiritual and the sea. Both were woven into the texture of MacKinnon Aultbea's life. Therefore the ocean, with all its changing moods of storm and calm, little boats, schooners and tall ships, represents the very metaphor of life and the journey we all take across its waters. We close this record of a Highland Minister therefore with those thoughts encapsulated in the words of Dr. MacDonald, the Apostle of the North, words which MacKinnon Aultbea was so fond of quoting. They speak of completeness, of triumph, of fulfillment, of anticipation of meeting Creator and Redeemer.

1.

Sud thairis air gach buireadh mi,
gach cunnairt cuain 's gaoith,

Gach laigs', is cionnt is truailidheachd,
Gach pian, is gruaim is caoidh.

2.

Is sud a steach do'n luchairt mi,
'S am faic mi gnuis an Righ;
''Sna chomunn iomlain, urail-san,
Gu seinn mi 'chliu a chaoidh.

Translation:

1.

Then I leave behind temptation,
Danger too, of wind and sea,
Weakness, guilt and all corruption;
Mourning, gloom and pain shall flee:

2.

Then I'll be within the palace,
Where my eyes shall see His face,
And in fellowship unbroken
I shall sing the praise of Grace.

———————————————

Appendix

The First Published Complete Gaelic Bible.

Two hundred copies of this were distributed for Scottish Gaelic speakers in 1686. The main editition edited by Robert Kirk , in Roman type published in 1690 has been called the Bedel Bible. This seems a contradiction as William Bedel died nearly fifty years earlier. There is a reasonable explanation.

This distinguished scholar and preacher was born in Essex on Christmas Day 1571. At Cambridge, he studied in the newly-founded Puritan Emmanuel College in 1884, graduating MA in 1592. The express aim of the College was to train candidates for the ministry. His first duty as Fellow was instructing students in the fundamentals of the Faith. He was in other words a catechist, a term adopted later in the Presbyterian Church in Highland Scotland as was the name 'precentor' as leader of praise. Bedel was an outstanding scholar, with special aptitude for languages which he used to become an authority in the Old Testament-related Syriac, Arabic and Hebrew. He became rector of St. Mary's at Bury St. Edmunds, Suffolk. Here he attracted large crowds as a powerful preacher, and gained the attention of church leaders among whom was Archbishop Usher who persuaded him to cross to Ireland to become provost of Trinity College, Dublin, in 1627.

An interesting point is the fact that he passed a rule, *De Mora Sociorum,* for students, a copy of the Code of Emmanuel, Cambridge. By it, 'Irish students by birth... should cultivate their native language, in order that they might become better qualified to labour among their people.'

Possibly linked to his stay as chaplain to the ambassador of Venice, he sought common ground between Catholic and Protestant. For this he was attacked from both sides by extremists, on the Protestant side, by Dr. John Hoyle, who was out for his blood. His stay at Trinity was short. But in that short time he gave to Gaeldom a golden gift of the first translation of the whole of the Old Testament. The translation was made from the original by this master linguist who supervised the Gaelic scholars. The result is a highly erudite and clear Old Testament, easily readable as Scottish Gaelic with a strong flavour of Irish. In the absence of standardized spelling, there is a simplicity in that used which is essentially phonetic and therefore more intelligible to the ordinary reader.

Bedel having been involved in stormy controversy at Trinity was consecrated bishop of the united bishoprics of Kilmore (Co. Cavan) and
Ardmagh(Co. Longford), both immensely rich, in 1629.

This man was a fearless reformer. The Anglican Church was corrupt in its
government as was its Roman predecessor. After all, Henry VIII to some
extent merely nationalized the Roman Church to gain its lucrative income for the monarchy.

For example Bedel was outraged by the extortion practised by the church
against the ordinary people. This is illustrated in a letter he wrote to Archbishop Laud of Canterbury on Ist April, 1630.

'Extortion by ecclesiastical courts is practised against poor Catholics ...'
which he says, ' In very truth, my Lord, I cannot excuse, and seek to
reform.'

He also incurred the ire of his peers in opposing the common practice of
'Pluralities' by which a favoured person lay or clerical could hold several
church offices as an absentee, and draw the combined income for himself.

In 1690, this translation of the Old Testament along with that of the New
Testament by William O'Donnell, 'faithfully translated from the original
Greek' and edited by Robert Kirke was the first Gaelic Bible for gen-
eral distribution in the Highlands of Scotland. Just as St. Columba brought
the Gospel a thousand years earlier to Gaelic Scotland, now the written
Word was given to the people of the Highlands in their own tongue. This
Bible was used especially in homes throughout the Catholic areas of the
West Higlands and Islands long before the Presbyterian people were given
this glorious gift for their spiritual sustenance. Moreover in the evictions
of the tens of thousands of people from the Highlands of Scotland and
Ireland, the same Bible accompanied many families to the New World.
(The Story of the Translation of the Scriptures into Scottish Gaelic by
Donald MacKinnon)

*See John Carswell's Gaelic translation of Knox's Book of Common
Order. Also 1996 Revised edition by Roderick MacLeod.

** Note also Motion introduced in Tron Church Conference,1886. 'To
remove all obstacles to the reunion of Scottish Presbyterianism...With a
view to reunion among all who hold by the principles of the Reformed
Church of Scotland.'   — *Reliquae Celticae*, Dr.Alexander Cameron

Bibliography

The Days of the Fathers in Ross-shire.   John Kennedy
The History of the Scottish Highlands and Islands.   W. C. MacKenzie
Annals of the Disruption.   Thomas Brown
The Trial and Triumph of Faith.   Samuel Rutherford
Documents of the Christian Church.   Henry Bettenson
From Iona to Dunblane. W.C. Somerville
Records of Grace in Sutherland.   D. Munro, edited by K. MacRae
A Celtic Miscellany. Kenneth Jackson
Life of Alexander Whyte. G.F. Barbour
Transactions of the Gaelic Society of Inverness.Vo.1, 2.
Disruption Worthies of the Highlands. Alexander Duff
Religious Life in Ross. James Noble
Steadfast in the Faith. William Macleod
Ministers and Men of the Far North. Alexander Auld
Whose Faith Follow. G.N.M. Collins
The Story of the Scottish Church. A.M. Renwick
The Apostle of the North. John Macleod
Cascheum nam Bard.   Lachlann MacKinnon
Rosg Gaidhlig   William Watson
Strath and the Isle of Skye. D. Lamont
Memoirs of Clan Fingon. D.D. MacKinnon
Sar Obair nam Bard Gaelach   John MacKenzie
Life and Hymns of Peter Grant   H. MacDougall
Gairloch and Guide to Loch Maree. J.H. Dickson
History of Skye. Alexander Nicholson
Walking Tour of Wester Ross. Seton Gordon
A Hundred Years in the Highlands. Osgood MacKenzie,Bt.
Caraid nan Gaidheal.   Norman Macleod.
A Well-Watered Garden.   Laurie Stanley
Memorabilia Domestica. Donald Sage ed. by his son D. Fraser Sage
The Celts. Nora Chadwick
The Highland Clearances. John Prebble
Church and State in Scotland. 1560-1843   Thomas Brown.
The Spiritual Songs of Dugald Buchanan . Donald MacLean
The Cruise of the Betsy   Hugh Miller

Inshore Craft of Britain Vol. 1 Edgar J. Marsh
Gaelic Hymns   John MacDonald

Sources of Research:
National Library of Scotland, Edinburgh
Free Church of Scotland Library, Edinburgh
Beaton Institute, U.C.C.B. Sydney, Nova Scotia

Original Material:
My father's letters, diaries, notebooks,
sermon notes and manuscripts of poems
Ecclesiastical correspondence and Call to Aultbea.